palgrave advances in the crusades

Palgrave Advances

Titles include:

Patrick Finney (*editor*)
INTERNATIONAL HISTORY

Jonathan Harris (*editor*)
BYZANTINE HISTORY

Marnie Hughes-Warrington (*editor*)
WORLD HISTORIES

Helen J. Nicholson (*editor*)
THE CRUSADES

Jonathan Woolfson (*editor*)
RENAISSANCE HISTORIOGRAPHY

Forthcoming:

Jonathan Barry (*editor*)
WITCHCRAFT STUDIES

Katherine O'Donnell (*editor*)
IRISH HISTORY

Richard Whatmore (*editor*)
INTELLECTUAL HISTORY

Also by Helen J. Nicholson

MEDIEVAL WARFARE: THEORY AND PRACTICE OF WAR IN EUROPE, 300–1500

THE KNIGHTS HOSPITALLER

THE KNIGHTS TEMPLAR: A NEW HISTORY

LOVE, WAR AND THE GRAIL: TEMPLARS, HOSPITALLERS AND
TEUTONIC KNIGHTS IN MEDIEVAL EPIC AND ROMANCE

THE MILITARY ORDERS, VOLUME 2 (*editor*)

CHRONICLE OF THE THIRD CRUSADE: A TRANSLATION OF THE
ITINERARIUM PERGERINORUM ET GESTA REGIS RICARDI

TEMPLARS, HOSPITALLERS AND TEUTONIC KNIGHTS:
IMAGES OF THE MILITARY ORDERS, 1128–1291

Palgrave Advances
Series Standing Order ISBN 1–4039–3512–2 (Hardback) 1–4039–3513–0 (Paperback)
(*outside North America only*)

You can receive future titles in this series as they are published by placing a standing order.
Please contact your bookseller or, in the case of difficulty, write to us at the address below
with your name and address, the title of the series and the ISBN quoted above.

Customer Services Department, Macmillan Distribution Ltd, Houndmills, Basingstoke,
Hampshire RG21 6XS, England

palgrave advances
in the crusades

edited by
helen j. nicholson

First published 2005 by
PALGRAVE MACMILLAN
Houndmills, Basingstoke, Hampshire RG21 6XS and
175 Fifth Avenue, New York, N.Y. 10010
Companies and representatives throughout the world

PALGRAVE MACMILLAN is the global academic imprint of the
Palgrave Macmillan division of St Martin's Press LLC and of
Palgrave Macmillan Ltd.
Macmillan® is a registered trademark in the United States,
United Kingdom and other countries. Palgrave is a registered
trademark in the European Union and other countries.

ISBN-10   1–4039–1236–X hardback
ISBN-13   978–1–4039–1236–7 hardback
ISBN-10   1–4039–1237–8 paperback
ISBN-13   978–1–4039–1237–4 paperback

This book is printed on paper suitable for recycling and
made from fully managed and sustained forest sources.

A catalogue record for this book is available
from the British Library.

Library of Congress Cataloging-in-Publication Data
is available

10 9 8 7 6 5 4 3 2 1
14 13 12 11 10 09 08 07 06 05

Printed and bound in Great Britain by
Antony Rowe Ltd, Chippenham and Eastbourne

contents

list of maps and plates

maps

plates

preface

This volume is intended as an introductory guide to how certain concerns and approaches have been applied to the study of the crusades. It is not a history of the crusades but, rather, an analysis of how different aspects of crusading studies have developed and where they are now. Each chapter offers an interpretative and historiographical study and concentrates on issues such as methodology and source analysis, rather than giving an account of events. Contributors have not concentrated solely on the crusade in the Holy Land, but also consider the crusading movement in other crusading fields as appropriate.

This guide is aimed both at postgraduates and at academics within the discipline, to provide an overview and context for their research. It is hoped that it will also be useful to scholars outside the discipline who encounter crusading language, for example, in the context of other research, or who wish to view a cross-section of the research being done in the area.

The contributors include older scholars with a well-established reputation within and outside the field of crusading studies, and younger scholars whose work has already made an impact within the field. As editor I am delighted to have been able to include contributions from scholars working in the US, Greece, France and Germany as well as the UK. Their various approaches to the debates they discuss present readers who are approaching the subject for the first time with an overview of the wide spectrum of views held by leading scholars in this field. The views they put forward here are their own and do not necessarily represent the views of the editor.

My thanks are due to my colleague Professor Peter Edbury and to Palgrave's anonymous readers for their very constructive and helpful comments, criticism and suggestions. I am also grateful to John Morgan of the School of History and Archaeology, Cardiff University, who took some of the photographs, to Nigel Nicholson for producing the maps and the index, and to the copyright owners of the plates in Chapter 4 who gave permission for the reproduction of the images in this book. All translations in this book, unless otherwise credited in the notes, are by the authors. The chapters by Sven Ekdahl, Jean Flori and Jean Richard were translated into English by the editor.

Helen Nicholson

chronology of the crusades, 1095–1798

1053	Pope Leo IX's forces are defeated by the Normans at the Battle of Civitate.
1064	Barbastro (Spain) is captured by a combined Christian force.
1070s	The Hospital of St John is founded at Jerusalem to care for poor sick pilgrims. Later it takes on military responsibilities.
1071	The Byzantine army under Emperor Romanos IV Diogenes is defeated by the Seljuk Turks at Manzikert.
1074	Pope Gregory VII plans a military expedition to assist the Byzantine emperor against the Seljuk Turks.
1084	The Seljuk Turks capture the Byzantine city of Antioch in Syria.
1085	Toledo (Spain) is captured by King Alfonso VI of Castile.
1086	Alfonso VI of Castile is defeated by the radical Muslim Almoravids at Sagrajas/Zallaqa.
1087	A Christian naval force attacks and plunders al-Mahdiyyah (North Africa).
1095	The First Crusade is preached by Pope Urban II at the Council of Clermont.
1099	The First Crusade captures Jerusalem. The Latin (western European) kingdom of Jerusalem is founded.
1100–01	An expedition to the East is defeated by the Turks.
1119	Battle of the 'Field of Blood': Prince Roger of Antioch is defeated by Il-ghazi ibn Artuk of Mardin.
1120	The military religious order of the Temple is founded in Jerusalem.
1122–24	A Venetian naval expedition goes to the Holy Land: Tyre is captured.

1129	A crusader expedition sets out to attack Damascus but is unsuccessful.
1144	Zengi, ruler of Mosul and Aleppo, captures Edessa.
1146	Death of Zengi.
1147	Lisbon is captured by Alfonso I of Portugal and crusading forces.
1147–49	The Second Crusade. The crusaders besiege Damascus, but fail to capture it. Military expeditions are also launched in Spain against the Muslims and in the Baltic area against the Wends.
1153	The forces of King Baldwin III of Jerusalem capture Ascalon.
1154	Nūr al-Dīn (Zengi's son) captures Damascus. In Spain, the radical Muslim Almohads of Morocco win control of Granada.
1163–69	King Amaury (Amalric) of Jerusalem campaigns against Egypt.
1169	Saladin becomes vizier of Egypt.
1172	In Spain, the Almohad caliph takes control of Seville.
1174	Death of Nūr al-Dīn. Saladin seizes Damascus.
1187	Saladin captures Jerusalem.
1189–92	The Third Crusade. Aim: to recover Jerusalem. It fails, but recovers some territory for the Latin Christians.
1193	Death of Saladin.
1197–98	The German crusade recovers some territory for the Latin Christians and converts the Teutonic Hospital at Acre into a military religious Order, known as the Hospital of St Mary of the Teutons ('the Teutonic Order').
1202–04	The Fourth Crusade. Aim: to assist Christians in Holy Land. It captures Constantinople.
1209–26	The Albigensian Crusades.
1212	The Children's Crusade. It breaks up before it leaves Europe.
1212	In Spain: the battle of Las Navas de Tolosa. The Almohads are defeated by a combined Christian force.
1217–21	The Fifth Crusade. Aim: to conquer Egypt. It is initially successful, but the crusaders are cut off when the Muslims open the sluice gates of the Nile.
1228–29	Crusade of the Emperor Frederick II. He recovers Jerusalem for the kingdom of Jerusalem by a treaty with al-Kāmil, the Ayyūbid sultan of Egypt.
1229	King James I of Aragon captures the Balearic Islands.
1230s	The Teutonic Order begins military operations in Prussia.
1233	James I of Aragon invades the kingdom of Valencia.

1237   The Teutonic Order takes over the Order of Swordbrothers in Livonia.

1238   James I of Aragon captures the city of Valencia.

1239–40   Crusade of Theobald, count of Champagne and king of Navarre, to Acre. Theobald negotiates a peace treaty with al-Ṣāliḥ Ismā'īl, Ayyūbid ruler of Damascus.

1240–41   Crusade of Earl Richard of Cornwall, to Acre. Richard recovers territory for the kingdom of Jerusalem by negotiation with al-Ṣāliḥ Ayyūb, sultan of Cairo.

1242   The Livonian branch of the Teutonic Order is defeated at Lake Chud (Peipus) by a Russian force led by Prince Alexander Nevsky.

1244   The crusaders finally lose Jerusalem.

1248–54   First crusade of King Louis IX of France: to Egypt. The crusade captures the port of Damietta, but is defeated at al-Manṣūra in February 1250. Louis then goes to Acre.

1250   A Mamluk coup in Egypt overthrows the Ayyūbids.

1251   First 'Shepherds' Crusade': a religious movement that set out to help King Louis.

1258   The Mongols capture Baghdad.

1260   Battle of 'Ain Jālūt (Ayn Jalut). The Mamluks of Egypt defeat the Mongols. In the same year, Baibars becomes sultan of Egypt.

1261   Michael Palaeologos recaptures Constantinople and becomes emperor.

1263–71   Sultan Baibars campaigns in Syria and Palestine.

1270   King Louis IX's second crusade besieges Tunis, but achieves nothing.

1274   The Second Church Council of Lyons discusses plans for recovering the Holy Land. No decision is reached.

1277   Death of Baibars.

1291   Acre is captured by al-Ashraf Khalīl, sultan of Egypt. The remaining 'Latin' (western European) territories in the Holy Land fall to the Muslims soon afterwards.

1306   The Hospital of St John of Jerusalem begins the conquest of the Greek Orthodox Christian island of Rhodes.

1309   The Teutonic Order moves its headquarters to Marienburg in Prussia. The Hospital of St John moves its headquarters to Rhodes.

1312   Pope Clement V dissolves the Order of the Temple.

1320   The second 'Shepherds' Crusade'.

1332–34	The first naval crusading league is set up, to fight Muslims at sea. Over the following years a series of such leagues are founded for this purpose.
1365	Peter I of Cyprus's crusade captures Alexandria, but withdraws soon afterwards.
1375	Cilician Armenia is conquered by the Mamluks.
1386	Queen Jadwiga of Poland marries Jagiełło of Lithuania. Lithuania accepts Christianity.
1389	Battle of Kosovo Polje: the Ottoman Turks claim victory.
1390	A French expedition sets out to capture al-Mahdiyyah (North Africa). The siege ends with a peace treaty and the French withdraw peacefully.
1396	Battle of Nicopolis: the western European crusaders are defeated by the Ottoman Turks under Bayezid I.
1402	'Tamerlane' (Timur the Lame) captures Symrna (now Izmir).
1410	The Teutonic Order is defeated by a combined Catholic Christian Lithuanian-Polish force at Tannenberg/Grunwald.
1420–31	Crusades against the heretic Hussites; fail.
1444	The crusade of Varna: fails to defeat the Ottoman Turks.
1453	Constantinople is conquered by the Ottoman Turks under Mehmed II.
1480	The Hospitallers successfully defend Rhodes against the Ottoman Turks. The Ottomans capture Otranto in Italy, but lose it the following year.
1492	The Muslim city of Granada falls to the forces of Isabella and Ferdinand of Castile-Aragon.
1497	The Spanish capture Melilla in North Africa.
1516–17	The Ottoman sultan Selim I defeats the Mamluks and conquers Egypt.
1518	Martin Luther's *Explanations of the Ninety-Five Theses* state that Ottoman attacks on Europe are God's punishment for Christians' sins and so the Church authorities should not resist them with arms, only with prayer.
1522–23	Rhodes falls to the Ottoman Turks, commanded by Süleyman the Magnificent.
1529	The first Ottoman siege of Vienna. The Ottomans are repulsed.
1530	The Hospital of St John moves to Malta.
1565	The Hospital of St John defends Malta against the forces of Süleyman the Magnificent.

1571	Cyprus is conquered by the Ottoman Turks. Battle of Lepanto: a victory for the Catholic Christian Holy League against the Ottoman Turks, but Cyprus is not recaptured.
1645–69	The Ottoman siege of Crete: Crete falls to the Ottomans.
1683	The second Ottoman siege of Vienna: the Ottomans are repulsed.
1684–97	The formation and operations of the Holy (Crusade) League.
1798	The Hospital of St John on Malta surrenders to Napoleon.

chronology of main secondary texts

1611	J. Bongars, *Gesta Dei per Francos*
1639	T. Fuller, *The Historie of the Holy Warre*
1675	P. L. Maimbourg, *Histoire des Croisades pour la déliverance de la Terre Sainte*
1751	Voltaire, *Histoire des croisades*
1776–88	E. Gibbon, *The History of the Decline and Fall of the Roman Empire*
1784	J.-B. Mailly, *L'Esprit des croisades*
1807–32	F. Wilken, *Geschichte der Kreuzzüge*
1811	first volume of first edition of J.-F. Michaud, *Histoire des croisades*
1827–29	J. Voigt, *Geschichte Preußens von den ältesten Zeiten bis zum Untergang der Herrschaft des Deutschen Ordens*
1841–1906	*Recueil des historiens des croisades*
1906	D. C. Munro, 'The Speech of Pope Urban II at Clermont, 1095'
1935	C. Erdmann, *Die Entstehung des Kreuzzugsgedankens*
1945	P. Rousset, *Les origines et les caractères de la première croisade*
1951	S. Runciman, *A History of the Crusades*
1953	G. Constable, 'The Second Crusade as Seen by Contemporaries'
1955–89	K. M. Setton (editor), *A History of the Crusades*
1956	R. C. Smail, *Crusading Warfare, 1097–1193*
1957	F. Gabrieli, *Storici arabi delle crociate*
1965	H. E. Mayer, *Geschichte der Kreuzzüge*
1968	E. Sivan, *L'Islam et la Croisade: Idéologie et propagande dans la reaction musulmane aux Croisades*
1969	J. Brundage, *Medieval Canon Law and the Crusader*

notes on contributors

Nora Berend is Lecturer at the University of Cambridge and a Fellow of St Catharine's College Cambridge. Her research specialism is medieval Hungary as a frontier state in the medieval period. She has published several articles, and her book *At the Gate of Christendom. Jews, Muslims and 'Pagans' in Medieval Hungary, c.1000–c.1300* was published in 2001. She has also edited with David Abulafia a collection of essays: *Medieval Frontiers: Concepts and Practices* (2002).

Sven Ekdahl is Research Professor of Medieval History at the Polish-Scandinavian Research Institute, Copenhagen. He has published extensively on the history of the Teutonic Order in Prussia, including *Die 'Banderia Prutenorum' des Jan Długosz –eine Quelle zur Schlacht bei Tannenberg 1410. Untersuchungen zu Aufbau, Entstehung und Quellenwert der Handschrift* (1976), *Die Schlacht bei Tannenberg 1410: Quellenkritische Untersuchungen* (1982) and *Das Soldbuch des Deutschen Ordens 1410/1411* (1988).

Jean Flori is a specialist in aristocratic mentalities (chivalry) and ideologies of war (holy war and crusade). He has devoted a dozen books and around a hundred articles in numerous international historical and literary journals to these themes, including most recently: *Pierre l'ermite et la première croisade* (1999), *La guerre sainte* (2001); *Guerre sainte-jihad-croisade* (2002); *Aliénor d'Aquitaine, la reine insoumise* (2004). He was Director of Research at the CNRS, at the Institut Universitaire de la Recherche scientifique de Rabat (Morocco), and then at the Centre d'Études Supérieures de Civilisation Médiévale de Poitiers (CESCM). He retired in 2001.

John France is Professor in History at the University of Wales, Swansea. His research specialisms include medieval warfare and the crusades, and his publications include *Victory in the East: A Military History of the First Crusade* (1994) and *Western Warfare in the Age of the Crusades 1000–1300* (1999), as well as numerous articles. He has also edited the works of the monastic writer Ralph Glaber (1989).

Maria Georgopoulou is Director of the Gennadeios Library at the American School of Classical Studies at Athens and has taught History of Art at Yale University. Her work explores issues of artistic production and ethnic identity and she is particularly interested in cross-cultural and colonial situations in the area of the Eastern Mediterranean. Her recent book *Venice's Mediterranean Colonies: Architecture and Urbanism* (2001) examined the architecture and urbanism of Venetian Crete in the context of Venetian colonialism in the later Middle Ages. She is currently completing a project on thirteenth-century Mediterranean art focusing on the production and trade of portable objects within their social context.

Deborah Gerish is Assistant Professor in History at Emporia State University. Her PhD dissertation explored the creation of royal identity in the Latin Kingdom of Jerusalem between 1099 and 1187. She has published a number of articles from her research, and is currently writing a book on the twelfth-century kings and queens of Jerusalem, and working with Niall Christie in comparing Christian and Muslim understandings of holy war.

Margaret Jubb is Senior Lecturer in French at the University of Aberdeen, Scotland. Her main research interest is the representation of the crusades in medieval and early modern western literature. She completed her Cambridge PhD thesis, a critical edition of the *Estoires d'Outremer et de la naissance Salehadin*, under the supervision of the late M. Ruth Morgan. It was published in 1990 and was followed by a broader study, *The Legend of Saladin in Western Literature and Historiography* (2000).

James Muldoon, Emeritus Professor of History, Rutgers University, USA, is now an Invited Research Scholar at the John Carter Brown Library at Brown University. He is author of many books, including *Popes, Lawyers, and Infidels: The Church and the non-Christian World, 1250–1550* (1979), *The Americas in the Spanish World Order* (1994), and *Canon Law, the Expansion of Europe, and World Order* (1998), a collection of his articles.

Alan V. Murray is Lecturer in Medieval Studies and Editor of the *International Medieval Bibliography* at the University of Leeds, England.

He researches on the crusades, German history and literature in the Central Middle Ages, and prosopography. He is author of *The Crusader Kingdom of Jerusalem: A Dynastic History, 1099–1125* (2000), has published numerous articles, and is editor of *Crusade and Conversion on the Baltic Frontier, 1150–1500* (2001), and of *The Crusades: An Encyclopedia* (ABC-CLIO, forthcoming).

Helen J. Nicholson is Reader in History at Cardiff University, Wales. She is a specialist on the history of the military religious orders, and also researches and publishes on the history of the crusades. Her recent books include *The Knights Hospitaller* (2001), *Medieval Warfare* (2003), and *The Crusades* (Greenwood Guides, 2004) and she is associate editor of the journal *Crusades*.

Jean Richard is member of the Academie des Inscriptions et Belles Lettres and Emeritus Professor of the University of Dijon, and is a distinguished scholar of both the history of the crusades and the duchy of Burgundy, with over 200 publications. His first publication was *Le comté de Tripoli sous la dynastie toulousaine (1102–1187)* (1945) which was republished in 1999. His books include *Le royaume latin de Jérusalem* (1953: English translation by Janet Shirley published 1979); *Saint Louis* (1983, English abridgement 1992); and a general study of the crusades, *Histoire des croisades* (1996; English translation by Jean Birrell, 1999).

Eleni Sakellariou is Lecturer in European Medieval History in the Department of History and Archaeology, University of Ioannina, Greece. She has published on the demographic and economic history of southern Italy in the late Middle Ages, and on the history of Latin Greece after the Fourth Crusade. She is currently preparing a book on 'The Kingdom of Naples between Aragon and Spain. Demographic growth and economic change at the end of the Middle Ages', under contract with Brill Academic Publishers.

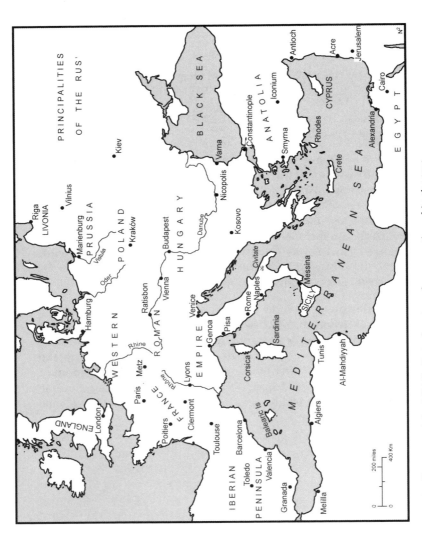

Map 1. Europe and the Middle East, showing places mentioned in the text.

introduction: definition and scope

helen j. nicholson[1]

The crusades were a startling and spectacular phenomenon which exerted a powerful influence on European development over a period of many centuries. Crusading was a many-faceted experience and much recent writing has been devoted to explaining how the remarkable notion of salvation by slaughter arose and to understanding the mentalities which gave rise to it. Out of this has arisen an exciting debate about the nature of crusading, between the 'pluralists', chiefly British and American, who argue that the crusade was essentially an arm of papal policy and others, mainly continental European, who argue for an organic connection between Jerusalem and the movement. This may currently be the dominant theme in writing about the crusades, but it is most certainly not the only one.

Study of the crusades has expanded rapidly in the last 50 years, not only in the number of scholars involved but also in the broadening of the discipline itself. The field now encompasses not only the study of military expeditions from western Europe to the Middle East between 1095 and 1291, but also expeditions with similar religious rationale to the Iberian Peninsula and the Baltic area and against heretics and other groups within Catholic Europe throughout the Middle Ages and into the early modern period. Modern scholars have demonstrated that 'crusader ideology' continued to be employed at least until 1798, when the military religious order of the Hospital of St John lost its headquarters on the island of Malta, and was also employed during the First World War, the Spanish Civil War and the Second World War – and is still employed at the present day. Scholars working in the area of crusading studies conduct research not only into military tactics and battles but also into areas such as recruitment and motivation, the states set up by the crusaders in the Middle East and the Baltic area, the use of crusading ideology by political leaders in the West, canon law, material culture, and the military religious orders that were set up to work alongside crusaders although their members were not themselves crusaders in a strict sense.

The crusades can be contextualized within a discourse of holy war which had its roots in the Old Testament and derived more immediately from the European Christians' defensive wars against Muslim invasions of Sicily, southern France and Spain in the eighth and ninth centuries that advanced as far northwards as Poitiers in 732. The crusades may also be contextualized within a discourse of Christian unity, whereby all Christians bear a responsibility for all other Christians, in this case the Christians of the former territories of the Christian Byzantine Empire lost in the seventh century to Muslim invaders in the Middle East and North Africa. In that the First Crusade of 1095–99 was a response to a Byzantine emperor's appeal for military forces from the western Europeans, it followed a tradition of Byzantine imperial employment of western mercenaries; the immediate context was that of the Seljuk victories over Byzantine forces in Asia Minor, especially the battle of Manzikert in 1071, and the capture of Antioch in Syria in 1084. These Byzantine Christian defeats contrasted with the situation in western Europe, where Christian commanders had been winning territory from Muslim rulers in the Iberian peninsula and Sicily, while in 1087 a Christian naval force from Italy attacked and plundered al-Mahdiyyah on the north African coast. The crusading expeditions to recover former Christian-ruled territory in the Middle East were made possible by the recent economic upturn in the West, which also underlay a drive for religious reform and renewal that found expression in the reformed papacy of the second half of the eleventh century. It was one of the reforming popes, Urban II, who actually initiated the First Crusade.

The crusades were symptomatic of the rapid changes taking place within Europe, which would lead to that region's transformation from a relatively underdeveloped and backward area of human civilization, at a time when China was the leading world power while Baghdad, Cairo and the kingdoms of India were powerful political and cultural centres, into becoming from the sixteenth century onwards a major influence in the world. The crusades did not themselves bring about this change, for the crusades to the Middle East did not succeed in establishing permanent settlements, while crusades against the Ottoman incursions in south-eastern Europe from the fourteenth century onwards were strikingly unsuccessful. However, the crusades formed part of a period of European expansion and development, and some of the administrative developments produced in response to crusading requirements, such as methods of levying taxation to pay for crusades, would have a long-term impact on systems of government within Europe.

This volume is a collection of essays setting out the current state of scholarship on certain aspects of the study of the crusades, and drawing attention to certain problems that concern scholars or that may form the focus for future research. Yet before considering how scholars have advanced our knowledge of the crusades, it is necessary to ask what the crusades were, where they took place, and when they began and ended – if, indeed, they have ended.

The *Oxford English Dictionary* defines a crusade as: 'a military expedition undertaken by the Christians of Europe in the 11th, 12th, and 13th centuries to recover the Holy Land from the Muslims', and, by extension: 'any war instigated and blessed by the Church for alleged religious ends, a "holy war"; applied especially to expeditions undertaken under papal sanction against infidels or heretics'. These are the fundamental characteristics of the crusades under consideration in the present volume: they were a type of holy war undertaken by Christians in the Middle Ages. The word 'crusade' is derived from the cross that those who took the vow to join one of these expeditions sewed on to their garments. The earliest recorded use of the term 'to be signed with the cross' dates from 1097, less than two years after Pope Urban II preached a sermon at the Church Council of Clermont that launched the expedition now known as the First Crusade. The terms 'to be signed by the cross' or 'to take the cross' – *se croisier* in medieval French, and *crux suscepit*, *crux accepit* or *crucizo* in medieval Latin – appear in writings about the crusades composed during the twelfth century.[2] From these terms the words 'crusade' and 'crusader' later developed. According to the *Oxford English Dictionary*, the earliest use of the word 'crusade' in English was in 1577, but according to the French *Robert* Dictionary the equivalent French word *croisade* had appeared in France more than a hundred years earlier.[3]

Until the fifteenth century, the military expeditions that historians now call crusades were usually called 'pilgrimages', even though, unlike traditional pilgrimages, fighting would be involved. Clearly expeditions to Jerusalem were pilgrimages of a sort in that the city is holy to Christians, as it contains the Holy Sepulchre, the site where Christ reputedly rose from the dead on the first Easter morning, and has been a place of Christian pilgrimage from the early centuries of Christianity. However, not only military expeditions to Jerusalem were called 'pilgrimages', but any war anywhere against an enemy of Christendom. Such expeditions were also called *passagia* or passages, meaning voyages or journeys, and *negotium Christi*, Christ's business. When in the late fourteenth century the English poet Chaucer was describing the character of the Knight in his *Canterbury Tales*, he depicted him fighting 'in heathen places' 'when we took Alexandria', 'in Prussia, in Lithuania … and in Russia … in Granada … and in North Africa, raiding Benamarin, in Anatolia … when Ayas and Attalia fell'. These were all actual expeditions which had carried the spiritual privileges of a crusade and which historians now describe as crusades, yet Chaucer never used crusade terminology in talking of them; the nearest he came to doing so was to describe the Knight as 'jousting for our faith at Tramissene'.[4]

Although from a modern point of view, the crusades may appear as aggressive wars (as is demonstrated, for example, in modern historiography of the crusades in the Baltic States, Poland and Russia) (see Chapter 8), in the Middle Ages they were always depicted by Latin Christians as defensive wars against an evil aggressor. That aggressor might change – it could be the threat of the Cathar heresy in southern France, or a king in Sicily who did not acknowledge the pope in Rome – but the same imagery was used. By 1450 the main external threat had become the Ottoman Turks in Anatolia and the Balkans, who captured the Greek Orthodox city of Constantinople in 1453 and were only barely repulsed from Belgrade in 1456. Scholars have noted that the same rhetoric was used against Ottomans as against earlier enemies, with reference back to the crusades of earlier centuries.[5]

Alongside this rhetoric there remained an awareness, as there had been since the earliest commentators on the crusades, that the Muslim opponent was a noble warrior and worthy adversary, who shared many important qualities with western warriors, despite the difference in religious belief. This contradictory image of the Muslim enemy is considered below by Margaret Jubb (Chapter 10).

In 1518 Martin Luther declared that the Ottomans who were attacking Christendom were acting as God's agents, inflicting God's punishment for Christian sins, and that the authorities of the Church should not resist them with weapons. In 1529 in his 'On War against the Turk' he amended his position to state that secular princes rather than the Church authorities should defend Christian people in battle.[6] This meant a complete break with the crusading past, when the Church had prompted and organized expeditions against those designated as enemies of Christendom. Although some Protestant writers later in the sixteenth century did continue to use the old crusading language, the days when all western Christendom united in the crusade were over.[7]

Some aspects of medieval crusading continued after the Protestant Reformation. The military religious Order of St John of Jerusalem (the

Hospitallers), which had migrated to Rhodes and then to Malta, continued to wage war against Muslim pirates in the Mediterranean until it was evicted from Malta by Napoleon in 1798.[8] Crusading language was still used in wars against the Ottoman Turks.[9] Some scholars would argue that crusade imagery and concepts were important in the voyages of exploration and conquest of the New World in the sixteenth century.[10] In Spain the *cruzada*, a tax that was originally raised to finance the war against the Muslims, collected by the Spanish monarchs by the authority of the pope, continued albeit in amended form into the twentieth century and was not finally abolished until 1915.[11] Crusade imagery was utilized in depictions of wars in the twentieth century, particularly the First World War,[12] and more recently in connection with the Gulf Wars.[13]

Although crusades had always been the focus of historical writing and analysis, after the crusades ceased to be current events and became 'fully in the past', historians' approach to them changed.[14] Early works written from the new point of view included Jacques Bongars's collection of primary sources on the crusades, *Gesta Dei per Francos* (1611), which is considered by Jean Richard (Chapter 9), and Thomas Fuller's *Historie of the Holy Warre* (1639).[15] Although Fuller attempted to present a balanced account, giving both reasons in favour and reasons against holy war, as a Protestant minister it is hardly surprising that he was hostile towards the concept of crusading. The threat from the Ottoman Empire was real, but he was confident that it would fall eventually, through the work of God rather than men.[16]

Sven Ekdahl (Chapter 8) and Jean Richard consider below the impact of the Enlightenment on the historiography of the crusades.[17] Like the writers they describe, the English historian Edward Gibbon considered that the crusaders were inspired by fanaticism, and the results of the crusades included the inquisition, the friars, indulgences and 'the final progress of idolatry'. On the other hand, in his judgement the crusades undermined 'the Gothic edifice', bankrupting or wiping out the feudal nobility, and so brought about the freedom of serfs and of peasants' lands and businesses because the nobles had to sell them to raise the money to go on crusade.[18] It was also in the period of the Enlightenment that the first western European scholarly study of Islamic history and the Muslim sources for the crusades began.[19]

Ekdahl and Richard note that historiography of the crusades changed again in the early nineteenth century, in what Constable has termed 'the third period of crusading historiography', when national feeling and the romantic movement led writers to depict the crusades more favourably, although their depictions often lacked critical analysis.[20] The growth of the modern 'scientific' approach to the crusades and to history in general was reflected in the publication of works that adopted a critical approach to the primary sources, as well as collections of primary source texts (mostly narrative, but also some documentary sources) in France, Germany and England (see Chapter 9).[21]

The wider availability of sources facilitated the composition of general histories of the crusades (see Chapters 5 and 9). Earlier general surveys tended to concentrate on political and military events. It was not until after the Second World War that the six-volume *History of the Crusades*, produced by scholars of the United States and edited by Kenneth M. Setton, offered detailed studies of crusader art, architecture, economics and other aspects of social and cultural history of 'the crusader states', so-called by modern historians because they were initially established by crusading expeditions.

In modern times, and particularly since the Second World War, scholarship of the crusades has been influenced by various developments in the field of medieval history as a whole. The history of the crusades forms part of the history of the expansion of Latin Christendom in the Middle Ages, and as such plays an integral role in Robert Bartlett's magisterial work on 'the making of Europe' where he defines the crusades as 'the best example of a papally-orchestrated war of conquest'.[22] Related to this subject are the historical debates over the importance of the frontier and of colonalization or colonialism during the Middle Ages; the question of how the crusades have been studied within these contexts is considered in the present volume by Nora Berend (Chapter 7) and Sven Ekdahl (Chapter 8). The crusades have also attracted scholarly attention in the context of the persecution of heresy and political dissenters during the Middle Ages, a point noted below by James Muldoon (Chapter 2).[23] The study of crusading warfare has developed within the context of the expansion of research into medieval warfare, as John France (Chapter 3) explains. Modern scholars ask not only what happened on a crusade but how crusades were organized and financed. As study of military logistics has expanded, this has been reflected in research on the crusades;[24] regrettably it has not been possible to include a chapter on logistics in this volume. A number of studies on the organization of crusades have been published in recent years, and it has become clear that the need to finance crusades stimulated the development of systems of administration to assess and collect taxation. However, it is arguable that only rulers with a well-developed system of administration could take part in crusading.[25] Historians have also asked how the crusades were justified and how far the Church developed canon law in response to this need, as James Muldoon (Chapter 2) considers.

The Annales school of thought, which developed in France in the 1940s, developed a new approach to history through a broad sweep of evidence including geography, economic history, demography and sociology. Following this lead, modern scholars of the Middle Ages use a wide variety of approaches to their subject, exploiting different forms of evidence. In this volume Maria Georgopoulou (Chapter 4) surveys how material culture and art have been used to expand our knowledge of the culture of the 'crusader states' of the Middle East, while Alan V. Murray (Chapter 5) shows how prosopography has widened knowledge of those who took part in crusades. Postmodernism, with its claim that the history we write cannot be an epistemology – a means of gaining knowledge – but only a literary genre,[26] has had some impact in crusading studies in encouraging new approaches to the literary sources. Scholars ask why and how these works were written and how historians may use them, as John France considers here (Chapter 3), while Deborah Gerish (Chapter 6) explores how far crusade historians have adopted a gendered approach to the literary sources and offers suggestions for further work.

Perhaps the most significant development for crusading studies, however, has been the debate over the definition of 'crusade'. As no absolute definition of 'crusade' in the past can be assumed, which definition should historians adopt for their research?

In 2001 Giles Constable divided the current scholarly views on the definition of crusading into four basic positions: (1) traditionalists, 'who ask where a crusade was going' and 'hold that a true crusade must be directed towards the east'; (2) pluralists, who 'ask how a crusade was initiated and organized'; (3) those who look for 'a spiritual or psychological definition that emphasizes the inner spirit and motives of the crusaders and their leaders' and regard crusading as a popular movement rather than institution-led; and (4) the 'generalists, who broadly identify the crusades with holy war and the justification of fighting in defense of the faith', emphasizing the importance of the concept of the just war.[27]

The underlying cause of these differences is the fluidity in medieval definitions of the crusade. When contemporaries had no single word to describe what historians now call a crusade, how can modern historians expect to define it? The great French scholar Paul Rousset defined a crusade as follows: 'La croisade est une guerre bénéficiant de privileges ecclésiastiques et enterprise pour le recouvrement des lieux saints' ('A crusade is both a war that profits from ecclesiastical privileges and an enterprise for the recovery of the holy places').[28] Many modern scholars agree with him that a crusade must by definition aim at the ultimate recovery of the Christian holy places. In 1978, in his review of the first edition of Jonathan Riley-Smith's *What Were the Crusades?*, Hans Eberhard Mayer wrote:

> As far as I can judge, we agree on the characteristics of a crusade except for one, indeed vital, point: While I contended that, within the framework of the other criteria, proper crusades were only those directed to conquer Jerusalem or to defend Christian rule there, Riley-Smith insists that the broader concept of the canonists should be retained and that we are dealing with crusades whenever the church equated or, at least, associated an indulgence for a holy war with that promised to the Holy Land crusaders, the common denominator being that the church was seen as a political entity to be defended with the same means on all fronts.[29]

Yet even if the Church regarded expeditions to different locations as being of equal merit, did those who took part in them do so? Jean Flori (Chapter 1) argues that motivations for crusading differed substantially between crusading fields, and that those for crusaders to Jerusalem cannot be equated with those for crusaders against heretics, where crusaders fought an internal enemy, or those to the Iberian Peninsula or the Baltic, where land settlement was a more important motivation for crusaders than it was in the Holy Land.

Jonathan Riley-Smith is the best-known scholar of the present day adhering to the 'pluralist' definition of the crusades and his contribution to the scholarship of the crusades has been immense, both through his own research and through that of leading scholars who began their academic careers as his research students. In his *What Were the Crusades?* he defined a crusade as being a military expedition where the pope initiated an appeal to potential participants to take a special vow in a public ceremony of 'taking the cross'; the pope granted participants various privileges including the 'crusade indulgence'; and the war conformed to the principles underlying or limiting the bearing of arms by Christians, so that it had to be justifiable war and a holy war, with a just cause and legitimate authority. There would be organized preaching, crusade taxes would be levied and papal control over the expedition would be ensured through the presence of a papal legate.[30] This definition is now very widely followed, but not all scholars adhere to it. It excludes expeditions that were not authorized by the papacy, such as the so-called 'Children's Crusade' of 1212.[31]

Constable noted scholars such as Alphandéry (on whom see also Flori, Chapter 1) as advocates of the 'spiritual or psychological definition' of crusading. While admitting that he himself had been 'counted among the pluralists', Constable added: 'but I am reluctant to exclude the "popular" crusades or to deny that at least a spiritual orientation toward Jerusalem was an essential aspect of crusading'.[32] He cited Ernst-Dieter Hehl as speaking for the 'generalists': 'he argued that a crusade was a war fought at the order of and with the authority of God'.[33] As this 'generalist' definition barely sets a crusade apart from any other form of holy war, the difficulty is to define what distinguished the expedition preached by Pope Urban II in 1095 from earlier holy wars against external threats to Christendom.[34] Yet the debate over definition has been productive in that scholars are winning a deeper understanding of the complexity of medieval Christian approaches to warfare.

Modern scholars have responded to accusations that crusades were a manifestation of imperialism or colonialism by considering the impact that the crusades had on the 'enemy' cultures. Eleni Sakellariou (Chapter 11) explores Byzantine Greek reactions to the crusaders. It is interesting that modern Greek historians have had little to say about the crusaders. While scholars in the Iberian Peninsula and the Baltic have been especially interested in relations between the crusaders and the 'target' peoples (see Chapters 7 and 8), recent publications by Carole Hillenbrand and others have demonstrated that until the late nineteenth century, Islamic historians had little interest in the crusade, so that modern Islamic condemnation of medieval crusading is arguably more a result of modern political problems in the Middle East than a reflection of past historical realities.[35]

The studies here have been grouped into general areas of approach. The first three chapters deal with different aspects of the practicalities of crusading: why warriors were drawn to join the First Crusade, how the Church approached the problem of the legal basis of crusading, and how the crusades to the Holy Land were fought. The following six chapters explore different forms of evidence that historians have used, and different routes by which historians have approached the available evidence. The final three chapters examine how the crusades have been depicted. Although the scope of modern crusading studies is so enormous that it has not been possible to include studies of every aspect of the subject, it is hoped that the list of suggested further reading will enable readers to access wider scholarship in the field.

notes

1. I would like to thank contributors to this book for their contributions to this introduction.
2. C. Tyerman, *The Invention of the Crusades* (Basingstoke, 1998), p. 21, citing *Epistulae et chartae ad historiam primi belli sacri spectantes: Die Kreuzzugsbriefe aus den Jahren 1088–1100*, ed. H. Hagenmeyer (Innsbruck, 1901), p. 142; C. Du Fresne Du Cange, *Glossarium mediae et infimae latinitatis* (Paris, 1840–50), vol. 2, p. 680 ('crux assumere'); *Le Robert Dictionnaire de la langue française*, 2nd edn, vol. 3 (Paris, 1992), pp. 64–5.
3. *Le Robert Dictionnaire*, vol. 3, p. 64.
4. Geoffrey Chaucer, *The Canterbury Tales*, General Prologue, lines 48–67, in *The Riverside Chaucer*, 3rd edn, ed. L. D. Benson (Oxford, 1987); M. Keen, 'Chaucer's Knight, the English Aristocracy and the Crusade', in *English Court Culture in the Later Middle Ages*, ed. V. J. Scattergood and J. W. Sherborne (London, 1983), pp. 45–61; N. Housley, *The Later Crusades, 1274–1580: From Lyons to Alcazar* (Oxford, 1992), pp. 281, 342.
5. G. Constable, 'The Historiography of the Crusades', in *The Crusades from the Perspective of Byzantium and the Muslim World*, ed. A. E. Laiou and R. P. Mottahedeh (Washington, DC, 2001), pp. 1–22, at p. 6; Housley, *Later Crusades*, pp. 84, 99–100, 385, 388, 420.
6. Martin Luther, 'Explanations of the Ninety-Five Theses' (1518), in *Luther's Works*, ed. H. T. Lehmann, vol. 31: *Career of the Reformer*, ed. H. J. Grimm (Philadelphia, 1957), pp. 27–33, 91–2; 'On War Against the Turk' (1529), in *Luther's Works*, vols 44–47, *The Christian in Society*, ed. J. Atkinson: vol. 46, ed. R. C. Schultz (Philadelphia, 1967), p. 186.
7. Constable, 'Historiography of the Crusades', pp. 6–7; M. J. Heath, *Crusading Commonplaces: La Noue, Lucinge, and Rhetoric Against the Turks* (Geneva, 1986); F. L. Baumer, 'England, the Turk, and the Common Corps of Christendom', *American Historical Review*, 50 (1944–5), 26–48.
8. J. Riley-Smith, *The Crusades: A Short History* (London, 1990), pp. 251–4.
9. E. Bóka, 'Crusader Tradition in the Seventeenth-Century European Political Thought', *Südost-Forschungen*, 53 (1994), 39–59.
10. F. Fernández-Armesto, *Before Columbus: Exploration and Colonisation from the Mediterranean to the Atlantic, 1229–1492* (Basingstoke, 1987), pp. 212–17; Housley, *Later Crusades*, pp. 308–12; P. Moffitt Watts, 'Prophecy and Discovery: On the Spiritual Origins of Christopher Columbus's "Enterprise of the Indies"', *American Historical Review*, 90 (1985), 73–102; and see James Muldoon (Chapter 2, this volume).
11. Housley, *Later Crusades*, pp. 314–15.
12. E. Siberry, 'Images of the Crusades in the Nineteenth and Twentieth Centuries', in *The Oxford Illustrated History of the Crusades*, ed. J. Riley-Smith (Oxford, 1995), pp. 365–85.
13. D. Gutwein and S. Menache, 'Just War, Crusade and *Jihad*: Conflicting Propaganda Strategies During the Gulf Crisis (1990–1991)', *Revue Belge de Philologie et d'Histoire*, 80 (2002), 385–400.
14. Constable, 'Historiography of the Crusades', p. 7; Tyerman, *Invention of the Crusades*, p. 109.
15. See Constable, 'Historiography of the Crusades', p. 7.

16. Thomas Fuller, *The Historie of the Holy Warre* (Cambridge, 1639), especially pp. 282–6.
17. See also Tyerman, *Invention of the Crusades*, pp. 109–14.
18. Edward Gibbon, *The Decline and Fall of the Roman Empire*, 7 vols (London, 1904–06), vol. 6, ch. 61, pp. 444–6.
19. R. Irwin, 'Orientalism and the Early Development of Crusader Studies', in *The Experience of Crusading*, vol. 2, *Defining the Crusader Kingdom*, ed. P. Edbury and J. Phillips (Cambridge, 2003), pp. 214–30.
20. See also Constable, 'Historiography of the Crusades', pp. 8–10; Tyerman, *Invention of the Crusades*, pp. 114–18.
21. See also Constable, 'Historiography of the Crusades', pp. 9, 11; Tyerman, *Invention of the Crusades*, pp. 119–20.
22. R. Bartlett, *The Making of Europe: Conquest, Colonization and Cultural Change, 950–1350* (Oxford, 1993), p. 20.
23. See also R. I. Moore, *The Formation of a Persecuting Society: Power and Deviance in Western Europe, 950–1250* (Oxford, 1987).
24. See J. H. Pryor, *Commerce, Shipping and Naval Warfare in the Medieval Mediterranean* (London, 1987); J. H. Pryor, *Geography, Technology and War: Studies in the Maritime History of the Mediterranean, 649–1571* (Cambridge, 1988); J. H. Pryor, '"Water, water, everywhere, Nor any drop to drink." Water Supplies for the Fleets on the First Crusade', in *Dei Gesta per Francos: Études sur les croisades dédiées à Jean Richard – Crusade Studies in Honour of Jean Richard*, ed. M. Balard, B. Z. Kedar and J. Riley-Smith (Aldershot, 2001), pp. 21–8; M. Barber, 'Supplying the Crusader States: The Role of the Templars', in *The Horns of Hattin*, ed. B. Z. Kedar (Jerusalem, 1992), pp. 314–26; reprinted in M. Barber, *Crusaders and Heretics, 12th–14th Centuries* (Aldershot, 1995), no. XII.
25. W. C. Jordan, *Louis IX and the Challenge of the Crusade: A Study in Rulership* (Princeton, 1979); G. Constable, 'Financing the Crusades in the Twelfth Century', in *Outremer: Studies in the Crusading Kingdom of Jerusalem Presented to Joshua Prawer*, ed. B. Z. Kedar, H. E. Mayer and J. Riley-Smith (Jerusalem, 1982), pp. 64–88; S. Lloyd, 'The Crusading Movement, 1096–1274', in *Oxford Illustrated History of the Crusades*, ed. Riley-Smith, pp. 34–65.
26. This definition is based on K. Jenkins, 'Postmodernism', in *An Encyclopedia of Historians and Historical Writing*, ed. K. Boyd (London and Chicago, 1999), p. 952.
27. Constable, 'Historiography of the Crusades', pp. 12–15.
28. Quoted by J. Flori, 'Paul Rousset, historien de la croisade et pionnier de l'histoire des mentalités', *Medievalismo: Boletin de la Sociedad Española de Estudios Medievales*, 9 (1999), 179–90, here 181.
29. H. E. Mayer, review of J. Riley-Smith, *What Were the Crusades?* in *Speculum*, 53 (1978), 841–2, here 841.
30. J. Riley-Smith, *What Were the Crusades?* (Basingstoke, 1977). See also J. Riley-Smith, 'History, the Crusades and the Latin East (1095–1204): A Personal View', in *Crusaders and Muslims in the Twelfth-Century Syria*, ed. M. Shatzmiller (Leiden, 1993), pp. 1–17.
31. M. Barber, 'The Crusade of the Shepherds in 1251', in his *Crusaders and Heretics, Twelfth to Fourteenth Centuries*, no. IX; G. Dickson, 'The Advent of the Pastores', *Revue Belge de Philologie et d'Histoire*, 66 (1988), 249–67; G. Dickson, 'La genèse de la croisade des enfants (1212)', *Bibliothèque de l'école des chartes*,

153 (1995), 53–102; G. Dickson, 'Stephen of Cloyes, Philip Augustus, and the Children's Crusade of 1212', in *Journeys Toward God: Pilgrimage and Crusade*, ed. B. N. Sargent-Baur (Kalamazoo, 1992), pp. 83–105.

32.　Constable, *Historiography of the Crusades*, p. 13.

33.　Ibid., pp. 13–14.

34.　For some of the debates see John Gilchrist, 'The Erdmann Thesis and the Canon Law, 1083–1141', in *Crusade and Settlement*, ed. P. W. Edbury (Cardiff, 1985), pp. 37–45; J. Gilchrist, 'The Papacy and War against the "Saracens", 795–1216', *International History Review*, 10 (1988), 174–97; Tyerman, *Invention of the Crusades*, pp. 8–29.

35.　C. Hillenbrand, *The Crusades: Islamic Perspectives* (Edinburgh, 1999), pp. 589–616; J. Riley-Smith, 'Islam and the Crusades in History and Imagination, 1 November 1898–11 September 2001', *Crusades*, 2 (2003), 151–67.

part I
aspects of the practice of crusading

1
ideology and motivations
in the first crusade

jean flori

introduction

The ideology of crusade did not suddenly appear with Pope Urban II's appeal at Clermont in November 1095. Scholars now acknowledge that it resulted from a slow evolution that, in the course of one millennium, led the Church from its original pacifism preached by Jesus of Nazareth to the concept of holy war that blossomed before the end of the eleventh century. Pope Urban II, however, added to this ideology a new sacral dimension which derived from the distinctive objectives of the crusade, the liberation of Jerusalem and the holy places. This new dimension explains its immense success. It transformed the former 'ordinary' holy war into a 'most holy' war, the crusade, whose ideology would dominate the western mind for several centuries, reactivate the *jihād* in the Muslim Near East and, in its turn, arouse other ideologies against it, which would lead on the one hand to the Protestant Reformation and on the other to the birth of secular thought.

the ideology of holy war before the crusade

Historians of the First Crusade agree that Pope Urban II, born from a knightly family and a former monk of Cluny, knew the knightly mentality extremely well. He knew how to utilize in the interests of the Church the knights' aspirations for salvation and their desire to see the dignity of their profession as warriors given recognition.[1] Even before his pontificate, the popes of the Gregorian reform had begun to give widescale ideological value to knights. From the end of the tenth century and throughout the

15

eleventh century, the institutions of peace (the 'Peace and Truce of God') had vilified and excommunicated warriors who took up weapons against the interests of the churches, but also praised and blessed those who, in contrast, were committed to ensuring their protection. Thus, some historians have argued that the Peace of God prepared minds for the crusade.[2] As recent scholarship has traced, during the eleventh century liturgies were developed for the formal presentation of weapons to the advocates and defenders of churches, along with numerous blessings for weapons and those who received them, thus giving value to the work of these knights who agreed to place their sword at the service of the Church.[3]

It has long been recognized that this was especially true for defenders of the papacy.[4] In 1053 Pope Leo IX, in order to protect the papal domains from the Normans of Sicily, recruited many warriors in Germany by offering them spiritual rewards. They were crushed at the Battle of Civitate (1053), but the pope affirmed that through their death in this conflict they had acquired the crown of martyrdom in Paradise.[5] A few years later, in order to effect papal plans for reform (in particular, to free the Church from the influence of lay princes), Popes Alexander II and Gregory VII also recruited warriors, conceding to them the *vexillum sancti Petri* (St Peter's banner), thus giving moral value to their combat. One such was the knight Erlembaud, who fought with weapons for the papacy against the partisans of the clergy of Milan, who were resistant to the Gregorian reform. In his letters, Gregory VII calls these knights 'soldiers of Christ' (*milites Christi*), the very phrase that, 20 years later, would designate the First Crusaders. The pope also affirmed that Erlembaud was carrying on 'God's war', and his death won him the crown of martyrdom. Many miracles took place at his tomb and, a little before calling the crusade, Pope Urban II had him beatified.

Many scholars have underlined that in the West in the eleventh century, popular religious belief began to concede that it was possible to win Paradise through dying with one's weapons in hand, if one was carrying on the 'good fight' for the Church and Christendom.[6] Gregory VII often reproached his *militae sancti Petri*, his army of St Peter, for being less ardent in the service of their patron saint, gatekeeper of Paradise – in spite of the eternal rewards which their service could win them through the remission of their sins – than were the knights of the world who served their temporal lord in return for cheap perishable goods.[7]

Although the course and extent of this development is debated, scholars generally agree that by the end of the eleventh century, combat carried out by warriors who engaged in the churches' service, and even more so in the papal cause, had achieved a high level of ideological value as sacred warfare.[8] However, in spite of this, warriors were still seen as sinners because of their profession – following the ancient belief in the defiling effect of bloodshed – and they had to do penance for it. They achieved their salvation through warfare, but not yet by warfare.[9]

The conversion of warfare was taken a step further when Urban II issued the call to crusade at Clermont. Rather than the military expedition making way for penance, it took the place of penance – as affirmed by canon 9 of the Council.

Most historians consider that this advance in the process of 'making war sacred' derived from the special features of the expedition.[10] It did not simply protect churches, even the Church of Rome, but would recover from the infidel the Holy Sepulchre – the primary holy site of Christendom, far more significant than Rome and Santiago de Compostella. The warriors of the crusade were no longer fighting simply for St Peter; they transformed themselves into the soldiers of Christ, entrusted – as were formerly the Hebrews of the Bible – with re-conquering the promised land marked by the tomb of Abraham, the father of believers. For them it was also marked by the (empty) tomb of Christ, the son of God, who was crucified in Jerusalem but who must return one day to Jerusalem in glory, to fight with the help of the faithful his last combat against Antichrist and his followers.[11]

The ideology of crusade thus went far beyond the ideology of holy war from which it stemmed. It is necessary to remember this when tackling the question of the crusaders' motivations and, to a large degree, the definition of the crusade – a question which (as was shown in the introduction to this volume) is still controversial today.

problems of methodology

Why did crusaders, from 1095 onwards, respond to repeated appeals from the popes? Before examining this question, it is advisable to distinguish various factors that, while not confused by historians with the crusaders' motivations, are none the less too often associated with them: a misleading approximation.

First, we should not confuse the crusaders' motivations with the goals (or objectives) of the crusade. From 1095 onwards, many factors drove the popes to preach the crusades. The call to crusade at Clermont can be situated within the framework of the movement to 'liberate the Church' initiated by the reforming popes of the second half of the eleventh century. The papacy, hitherto hindered in its expansion, wished to emancipate the Church from temporal powers and, placing itself at the head of the knights – the rising power in the West – go to deliver the Holy Sepulchre, and to work for the union of the Christian Churches by aiding the Christian empire of the East. Gregory VII had already stated as much in 1074.[12] The crusade can also be located in the movement of Christian reconquest, of *dilatatio christianitatis*, which started with the Spanish *reconquista* and continued in Sicily and in the Mediterranean islands before extending into the Near East.[13] Scholars disagree over the significance of these factors in the papal decision to call the crusade, but in any case the crusaders who answered the call were largely unaware of papal diplomatic or political intentions. Their motivations were different, and the popes knew it. This was why, in their calls to crusade, the popes stressed not the political factors which were perhaps the original cause of their intervention, but (in line with their understanding of the mentality of the laity whom they were addressing) the motives which could encourage the laity to answer their call.

We do not know, alas, the exact terms employed to preach the First Crusade.[14] The chroniclers, in their own ways and strongly influenced by their own clerical tradition, reconstructed Urban II's speech, which aroused the crowd's enthusiasm and the ardent response of the warriors who took the cross with the cry of 'God wills it!' The historical accuracy of their testimony is today widely debated, and the pope's success with his lay audience was probably far less a result of what he actually said than of his delivery, which was nearer – if not in its topics, at least in its expression – to the concerns and mentalities of the warriors whom he wanted to rouse.[15] We have even less information about the content of the sermons of the 'inspired' popular preachers who, like Peter the Hermit, had such an unheard-of success with the crowd that they recruited more than a third of all the first crusaders.[16] It would be wrong to neglect the impact of these popular preachers who drove so many towards Christ's tomb. It is likely that the motivations driving them were similar to those of the other lay crusaders, including the 'feudal' armies, in particular the 'lesser knights' who constituted the major part of the crusade contingents. These motivations may be discerned with a considerable degree of certainty through their aspirations, their hopes and their behaviour during the crusade.[17]

Papal letters relating to the crusades are of great interest for historians of crusade ideology, but they primarily express ecclesiastical perceptions of the enterprise and its theological justification, rather than the crusaders' motivations for taking part. The charters issued by the crusaders as they departed on crusade seem at first sight more appropriate vehicles for transmitting the crusaders' true motivations, and Giles Constable and others have recently studied them from this viewpoint.[18] It is inadvisable, however, to place undue trust in the formulations of these charters, which were written by monks and generally aimed at comparing the crusaders to earlier ordinary pilgrims. In all these sources, the historian must be conscious of the effect of the distorting lens of ecclesiastical ideology.

Finally, it is necessary to remember that the crusade concept evolved. Very early indeed, from the time of Urban II and Paschal II for Spain (against the Moors), and again of Eugenius III for Spain (against the Moors) or for the Baltic areas (against the Wends), the popes endeavoured to transform the crusade into an institution which would serve the Church or, more precisely, the Holy See.[19] This conversion of the crusade into a tool of the papacy involved the transformation of the major features of the crusade (the designation of the crusaders as soldiers of Christ, the commutation of penance) that in the original crusade had been the direct result of its objective and its primary destination (that is, the liberation of the eastern Churches and the recovery of Jerusalem), into normative and constitutive characteristics of the crusade whatever its destination might be. It is clear that crusade ideology, and the motivations of those who took part in the First Crusade and expeditions whose purpose was the liberation and protection of the Holy Land, would differ in some respects from those who took part in expeditions to other regions. I would argue that other expeditions were actually holy wars that profited from the privileges of crusade in consequence of this institutionalizing of the crusade.

the crusaders' motivations

In the modern world, some have come to believe that the crusade was a screen hiding more worldly objectives: a thirst for lands and wealth, a desire for colonial expansion, a search for earthly glory, and so on. Research by historians of the crusades, particularly since the Second World War, has showed that religious factors were in fact dominant. Yet still it is advisable to distinguish carefully between the various aspects of this 'idealistic' dimension.

spiritual motivations

pilgrimage and remission of sins

Pro remissione peccatorum ... This expression appears as a leitmotiv in the majority of ecclesiastical documents, not only in connection with the crusade, but also pilgrimage, donations, legacies, penances or more generally any work considered as pious and intended to please God and the Church by satisfying divine justice. The phrase was applied to many warlike undertakings even before 1095, and Pope Urban II included it in his letter to the Flemish: 'At a council held in Clermont, we solemnly ordered them, for the remission of all their sins, to take part in this expedition.'[20] Here it is a phrase too vague to conclude anything more from it than this: the crusaders, by engaging in this enterprise, received the assurance that their action was meritorious and could contribute towards counterbalancing the faults that they had committed.

Canon 9 of the Council of Clermont is more precise: 'If anyone, prompted by piety alone and not to earn honour or money, will set out on the road to Jerusalem in order to liberate God's Church, that journey will suffice for all penance.'[21] This canon thus establishes that the expedition to Jerusalem replaces all the other penances prescribed to expiate their previously-confessed sins. This appears natural, insofar as Urban II had preached an expedition whose goal was Jerusalem and whose objective was the liberation of the holy places.

The form of words used at Clermont seems to indicate that this was a simple commutation of penance, the crusade-pilgrimage replacing any other hardship that would previously have been prescribed by the religious authorities for the repenting sinner. May we, then, speak from this moment of a 'plenary' indulgence? Yes, no doubt, if this term is understood to mean that participation in the expedition was considered to be sufficient, because of the cost and danger, 'to replace' any other penance that might be required. But here what was being remitted were the penances imposed by the Church, which had to be suffered in this world to obtain full remission of confessed sins; historians agree that this was not the plenary indulgence in the later meaning of the term, namely the remission of the sufferings that the sinner would have to undergo in the other world, in a 'purgatory' that, at this date, was still a vague concept even in the minds of theologians.[22] With the passage of time, the crusade to Jerusalem (and other sacralized wars that the papacy would assimilate to the crusade by allotting them precisely these same indulgences) would come to be regarded as a means of escaping, through this plenary indulgence, from whole or part of the suffering to be undergone *post mortem*. As the theology of indulgence did not develop until after Clermont, Urban II's declaration cannot be interpreted in the latter sense. On the other hand, it is not impossible that the knights, the laity and even some of the ecclesiastics had misunderstood his meaning and believed that their participation in the crusade-pilgrimage at least contributed towards facilitating their entry into Paradise.

Were these first crusaders all 'penitents'? The question is important in determining crusaders' motivations. Admittedly, all were sinners in the eyes of the Church (and probably their own), requiring confession and penitence. But of what kind and on which level? The pilgrimage to Jerusalem, armed or not, was prescribed for the most odious and most serious sins, homicides or sacrileges, and it is hardly likely that all those who answered the cries of 'God wills it' with enthusiasm were inspired by this spirit of penitence and regarded their participation in the expedition as a penitential action. Jonathan Riley-Smith and Marcus Bull have emphasized this penitential dimension (which is certain for at least some of the crusaders), citing the crusaders' own declarations in the charters written at the time of their departure.[23] The vocabulary of these charters does indeed often express a real compunction and a consciousness of sin: the crusader's departure is stated to be accomplished 'in remission of my sins', 'for the salvation of my soul', and so on. However, the monks who wrote the charters made three unwarranted assumptions: first, they compared these crusaders to the earlier pilgrims and penitents; second, they likened to pious donations the sales, renunciations and mortgages that the crusaders had made to raise money; and third, they often allotted to these duly-recorded concessions (as much as to the expedition itself) the merit of having been made 'for the remission of their sins' or 'for the salvation of their soul'. The emphasis laid on the sins of the givers and their desire for penitence seems to me to derive far more, at least in certain cases, from the monastic formulation of these documents that traditionally preceded the departure for Jerusalem, than from any real motivation of penitence driving the knights to set out on crusade. The need for money and support of all kinds would have led some crusaders to allow themselves to be depicted as repenting and penitent. In addition, the charters confer meritorious and redemptive value on the *donation* that underlay the written charter as much as on the *expedition* that was the *raison d'être* for the charter through the financial needs that it caused, although the expedition itself could have been prompted by very diverse motives.

The penitential aspect set out in the charters could certainly have been the root cause of many knights' departures. The expedition's destination allowed it to be compared to a pilgrimage, and they were certainly described as pilgrims, penitents going to Jerusalem for the remission of their sins. But this was not necessarily the knights' sole motivation. They probably, as has been recently argued, perceived themselves as combatants of the faith, *militia Christi*, putting their courage and their sword at the service of their Lord, through love, certainly, but also expecting from him spiritual rewards in return for their service, as would knights of the world serving their temporal lord with their arms.[24] They could have been drawn into going to fight the Muslims in the East for many different reasons, as indicated in documents that, although of ecclesiastical origin, are less permeated with the monastic doctrine that it was impossible to be saved outside a monastery except as a monk or penitent.

merits of the holy war: spiritual rewards for the soldiers of God

By 1095, knights had already become aware of the importance of their profession. They were no longer completely convinced of the need to become a monk in order to reach eternal salvation, and they aspired to gain heaven while remaining in their profession. Repeated appeals to them from the churches and the popes to provide armed protection against their enemies led, as we have seen, to the sacralization of certain wars and the ideological valorization of these warriors. During the twelfth century, it would lead to the formation of chivalric ideology, in which protection of the churches formed only one aspect. In 1095, as historians of knighthood have shown, this chivalric ideology was not yet formed.[25] It was thus not in its name that knights took the cross; quite the contrary.[26] But Urban II, like Gregory VII before him, recognized the dignity of the warriors' profession when it was put at the service of the good cause: that of the Church, the pope, and more still of Christ. There was no longer any question of penitence, but of positive value. Even a monk like Guibert de Nogent saw in the crusade not only a legitimate war, but a holy war aroused by God, able to lead a man to salvation as a knight, without needing to take the monastic habit.[27]

the crown of martyrdom?

Such a holy war deserved reward. Did Urban II promise the crown of martyrdom to those who perished during the expedition? Opinions are divided.[28] The principal arguments against this point are twofold: at this time Urban II could not affirm this dogmatically because the doctrines of martyrdom were not yet well established; moreover, the crusaders themselves asked for prayers for their dead companions. These arguments are not conclusive, for the doctrines of indulgence, of the crusading vow and of the protection of crusaders' property were themselves also badly defined. In addition, it is of little importance whether Urban II was or was not 'officially authorized' to make such a promise; the significant point is whether the crusaders themselves believed that he had done so. We have little reason to doubt that they did believe this, because the chroniclers and crusaders themselves in their letters refer to such a belief. It was by no means opposed to their requests for prayers for the departed, as such prayers would be in reference only to the sovereign decision of God in their case.[29]

Was the prospect of dying as a martyr a motivation? Today, in secular materialized societies, it may appear a weak attraction. It was regarded differently in a medieval society where religion, like familiarity with death, was omnipresent and people lived divided between the fear of hell and the hope of eternal life. The warriors in particular knew the dangers of their profession, which did not prevent them from sometimes practising it with pleasure. The preaching of the crusade as a most holy war did not only give value to their profession, it granted them the hope of obtaining, through the exercise of their trade in Christ's service, the eternal happiness that had originally only been available to the persecuted confessors of the first centuries, then to the saints – generally drawn from the ranks of the high clergy – and then monks. The attraction of this prospect should not be overlooked; in fact, it is comparable with that which the 'martyrs' of the Islamic *jihād* profess today.

socio-religious motivations

There were also other motivations that, while less doctrinal, were no less religious in nature and were perhaps in the eyes of the masses more persuasive than those previously considered.

religious solidarity

In his sermon at Clermont, as Riley-Smith and others have underlined, Urban II touched on several topics taken from the Gospels: Jesus gave his life on the cross to save his own people; in return, he asks today that they take his cross to free his tomb and to deliver his faithful people from oppression; there is no greater love than to give up one's life for one's brothers: however, our Christian brothers of the East are persecuted by the Muslims, the holy places are profaned, the churches defiled; to give help is a duty of brotherly love, to serve Christ is a duty of the faithful, and so on. Historians judge that these reasons, even if the pope was quoting them directly from the Gospels (which is far from being certain because they were clearly given a warlike dimension), were most probably understood by the knights from a different point of view, nearer to clan-solidarity and revenge than the love for one's neighbour that Jesus preached.[30] In any case, the various forms of this speech reconstructed by the witnesses show clearly that it appealed to the values that most deeply concerned the knights of this feudal society: the sense of community based on a single religion (Paul Rousset in particular has established that the concept of 'Christendom' was born and developed in the eleventh century),[31] the identity-reflex reaction against an adversary of 'alien' religion. The modern racist or xenophobic reflex is not far away from that which designated Muslims as an 'abominable and perverse race', likened to the pagans of Antiquity and demonized by their 'impious' religion and behaviour, which was described as shameful, cruel and perverse.

As historians such as Norman Daniel and John V. Tolan have underlined, the demonization of the adversary, traditional in all war propaganda, was already perceptible in the writings of, for instance, Gregory VII.[32] This theme of the 'abominable' Saracen was very popular with the knights, stimulating their enthusiasm and raising the profile of their military action, as is shown by the omnipresence of the theme in the epics and in medieval romance.[33] This sort of argument was extremely effective in motivating the deeply emotional medieval crowds.[34] It still is nowadays.

In 1095, the actual situation of the Christians in the East did not require military intervention. But the pope's alarmist description had great impact on his listeners, more especially because he skilfully combined it with the still more stimulating theme of the harassments and persecutions that the Turks had inflicted on pilgrims. The pilgrimage to Jerusalem, which was growing in popularity at that time, constituted one of the major dimensions of a new spirituality. It played a considerable role in redemption and, in the eyes of the laity, it constituted a true 'way of salvation'.[35] The idea, although false or exaggerated, that this way of salvation was in some way blocked or cut off by the invasions of the Seljuk Turks was unbearable to them. A possible additional factor was concern that this Muslim invasion would advance towards the West, following the defeats of the Byzantine Christian army at Manzikert in 1071 and of the Spanish forces at Zallaqa in 1086. The political situation in the East and in the West had certainly considerably improved since then, but the Muslim threat in these two areas was very far from dissipated. Epic poetry, particularly the *Chanson de Roland* and the Guillaume d'Orange cycle, preserves traces of the burning memories left by the Muslim occupation in Europe, especially in southern France, where Urban II met particularly great success during his preaching.

eschatological dimensions

The crusade must be analysed within the historical-religious perspective of its contemporaries: that God directs the course of History and leads it towards its goal, the New Jerusalem, which will descend from Heaven at the end of time, after the final victory in the Holy Land of Christ and his faithful people against Antichrist and his supporters. It is God who, because of his people's sins, has chastised the Church through the invasions and domination of the Arabs, just as under the Old Law he formerly punished the Jewish people through the domination of the Assyrians and the Babylonians. But these chastisements were to educate them. If his people repented again and became faithful, God would put an end to the punishment, restore his people and give them the victory.

Now this time of restoration has come, proclaimed Urban II in his letters. As Paul Alphandéry and others suggested, it is therefore not impossible that he conferred an eschatological dimension on the planned expedition. According to Guibert de Nogent, the pope indeed suggested to the knights that their victory in the Holy Land was to some extent necessary for the accomplishment of God's prophetically announced plan.[36] Guibert was the only person to mention this topic in the pope's preaching. However, it is unlikely that he introduced it himself because at the time he was writing nothing had happened to support it. It is more logical to believe that the other chroniclers omitted this dimension from the papal sermon, since the capture of Jerusalem had not given rise to any tangible manifestation of Antichrist linked to the approaching end of the world.

This belief was no less popular at the time that the crusade expeditions were in preparation. The eschatological dimension can be found alongside more material and down-to-earth incentives, in the letter of Emperor Alexius to Count Robert of Flanders; false or not (this is disputed), this letter can be classified among the *excitatoria*, propaganda documents intended to mobilize crusaders.[37] The impact of this belief was therefore far from being negligible. As shown by historians such as Robert Chazan, Flori and Riley-Smith, such eschatological perspectives also lay at the origin of the anti-Jewish pogroms in the Rhineland. Emich von Flonheim, aroused by the 'inspired' preachers of the crusade from the entourage of Peter the Hermit, in fact claimed to be the 'emperor of the Last Days' who, according to prophecies then popular, would go to Jerusalem after having 'converted' the Jews (voluntarily or by force). There he would reign for some years before giving up his sceptre and crown to the returned Christ on the Mount of Olives.[38]

Alphandéry undoubtedly exaggerated the importance of this eschatological expectation, seeing in it the primary motivation of the common crusaders, and for too long historians over-reacted against him. Nowadays the reality of this eschatological dimension is generally acknowledged and it is being studied more closely.[39] The innumerable celestial 'signs' and the 'marvels' mentioned by chronicles were certainly not all proofs of eschatological expectations, but reflected a climate favourable to the expression of such hopes, which is also found in the 'popular' crusades of the children or the shepherds. Such eschatological expectations were present not only during the First Crusade, but in almost all major expeditions to the Holy Land.

to convert the infidel?

The conversion of Muslims (who were classed as 'pagans'), was hardly mentioned in the propaganda for the First Crusade. It was a question only of fighting, repulsing, overcoming and possibly of massacring the infidel, not of converting them. The chroniclers, however, noted some cases of Muslim conversion, which have recently been studied by, among others, Jean Flori and Svetlana Luchitskaja.[40] In the majority of cases, these were 'pragmatic' conversions in response to specific needs. The conversion of infidels cannot therefore be upheld as even a minor motivation for the First Crusade, except from a perspective of rallying 'pagans' to the 'true religion' in the face of the obvious superiority of the 'true God' who gives victory to the Christians in a sort of ordeal or 'judgement of God'.

Most scholars now agree that the situation was different in later crusades,[41] but the hope of converting the infidel was a motivation for preachers aspiring to martyrdom rather than for the knights who, as we have seen, could hope for the crown of martyrdom through fighting with the sword.

On the other hand, the 'conversion' of heretics was a real motivation for crusading and was presented as such by ecclesiastics who preached such crusades. Indeed, although canonical legislation prohibited the use of force to convert 'pagans', it authorized the use of constraint to destroy heresy. It is thus very likely that such motivations drove some knights to destroy the Albigensian Cathar heretics in southern France following Pope Innocent III's call to crusade. It is still more probable that these 'religious' motivations were supplemented by material considerations, since heretics' lands could legally be confiscated and their goods plundered.[42] As for crusade expeditions in the Baltic area, they were to a certain extent 'missionary wars', but also and above all an aspect of the German *Drang nach Osten*, the 'push to the East', a colonization movement into the region.[43] This point underlines the great differences, even on the level of motivations, that distinguished the crusades to the Holy Land from other sacralized expeditions which were preached as crusades by the papacy.

socio-economic motivations

glory in the eyes of god and men

Is this to say that the crusaders to the Holy Land, and especially those of the first expedition, prototype of the crusade, were free from all material motivation? It is probable that such motives existed and that Urban II was conscious of them, as the Council of Clermont and some of the pope's letters stress that the expedition would only take the place of penance for those who undertook it 'out of piety alone, not to earn honour or money'. Can we believe that all the penitents completely expelled from their heart all trace of such motives? And, especially, can we believe that all the crusaders considered themselves to be penitents? It has been argued above that the majority of the knights had other motives, which were based above all on their warlike profession and their new dignity acquired by the exercise of this profession in holy war.

Let us recall that in the *chansons de geste*, which have been regarded by many scholars as the best expression of the chivalric ideology in formation,[44] the act of combat itself is constantly glorified. The crusaders regarded plundering and the spoils taken from the enemy as fully compatible with their mission, and chroniclers exalted the military glory of their leaders whose exploits they narrated 'for love of God'. On this basis, the Council of Clermont's restriction can have applied only to those crusaders who set out as penitents, following an ecclesiastical judgement on them, and hence affected only a minority.

The fame acquired by crusaders was clear from the beginning. Bohemond (who later became prince of Antioch), met with great success when he came to France in 1106 to seek funds and warriors. He even managed to marry Constance, the daughter of King Philip I of France. The reputation won by successful crusaders was equalled only by the shame and opprobrium experienced by those who, after having taken the vow to set out, stayed at home, gave up during the course of the journey, or ran away.[45] Historians have generally agreed that the search for personal glory must have been important for most knights of the First Crusade, otherwise Urban II would not have alluded to it.[46] It seems particularly glaring in certain cases, such as that of the prince-troubadour Duke William IX of Aquitaine.[47]

Yet it is difficult to evaluate how far crusaders of 'common blood' shared this motivation. It was probably a minor factor during the First Crusade, when the concept of knighthood was still in the process of formation and the chivalric ethic was not yet established.[48] However, this dimension became more pronounced during the twelfth century.

Many documents bear witness to it, both the arguments used by crusade preachers and motives expressed by poets. Around 1188, Conon de Béthune affirmed that one must go to Syria to 'perform knighthood', so as not to fail one's Saviour and to win Paradise and also to acquire 'both praise and approval and the love of one's beloved'.[49] Thus the theme of glory is mingled with the theme of vengeance, while the service for a Lady's love is combined with the service of God, although these were in fact competing motives. The search for fame became dominant in later crusades, such as the crusades in Prussia (*Reise*) from the 1330s onwards, where despite the crusade privileges and indulgences, the desire for glory and a taste for hunting, luxury and ostentation were flaunted, under the influence of an aristocratic and chivalric ideology conveyed by Arthurian romances.[50]

It was probably this increasing level of aristocratic pride and ostentatious wealth, combined with the failure of the enterprises led by powerful nobles, that prompted the formation of the 'popular' crusades, the Children's Crusade and the Shepherds' Crusades. The 'pluralist' historians of the crusades tend to see these movements as marginal, standing outside a concept of crusading that is defined by the decisions and definitions issued by the popes; but arguably in many ways, and particularly in their objectives (to recapture the holy places and the city of Jerusalem), these expeditions perpetuated the original spirit of the crusades.

Were crusaders drawn to the East by the hope of material gain? Some sources suggest that they were, by underlining the poverty and need in the lands of the West and the misery of its inhabitants, glorifying in contrast the wealth of the sumptuous East. Certain chroniclers placed this sort of speech among the arguments used by Urban II at Clermont. We can hardly exclude this possibility that this was a motive for crusaders. Some recent historians have gone further and suggested that the crusade could have constituted a kind of economic 'outlet' for certain aristocratic families, in particular for younger knights, deprived of land by the system of inheritance then established in the West, which marginalized them.[51] This hypothesis has been strongly and convincingly countered by Jonathan Riley-Smith.[52] In the field of macro-politics, or even of the macro-economy, it is evident that the crusade resulted from a demographic expansion in the West and the development of its social structures, and even today we see a revival in the old theories explaining the crusade in terms of economic theory.[53] Another question much discussed nowadays is whether the crusade can be linked to 'colonization'. This debate, originally launched by Joshua Prawer, does not concern us directly here because the crusaders' motivations in the First Crusade were not affected by the concept of colonization. At most they were linked to 'reconquest', which is very different.[54]

The crusade was undoubtedly an outlet for warriors, an ideology that met their aspirations in many fields. But it cannot be deduced from this that aristocratic families were 'helped' by sending one of their members on crusade. Riley-Smith underlined what the crusaders' charters reveal by their very existence: the cost of taking the cross was enormous and in order to cover the expense families seriously impoverished themselves by selling land or goods, and became heavily involved in debt through loans or mortgages. In addition, the majority of crusaders were by no means disinherited junior members of their family. Those who were men without inheritances – such as Bohemond – were from very wealthy and influential families and had already enjoyed a considerable military reputation in the West.

As for the hope of gain, Riley-Smith estimates that as the majority of crusaders could hope to win little or nothing, this could not have constituted a motivation for setting out. The majority of crusaders, he adds, had made provision to return to their homes and did not intend to settle in the East. As for the survivors, they returned alive but generally poorer than at their departure, except in holy relics. Here his hypothesis appears less convincing. Even those who acquired rich domains in the East, such as Raymond of Toulouse or Godfrey de Bouillon (who in fact were already provided for in the West) could nevertheless have made provisions for these lands if they had returned home. In addition, the first crusaders would clearly not have known before their departure that they would return poorer. Even if the hope of gaining wealth seems 'mathematically weak' to us, it may nevertheless have been an incentive; all the players were aware of the possibility. Lastly, the hope of spoils in the East, which was believed to be rich and sumptuous, with the attraction of Byzantium, the lure of exoticism and a taste for adventure, could constitute a temptation to set out. The material dimension should not, therefore, be excluded from the first crusaders' personal motivations. It was most probably only a minor dimension, but the pope nevertheless envisaged and condemned it for penitents.

vassalic and family solidarity

Did the crusaders always make their own decision to set out? There are many examples of individuals – such as William Marshal acting on behalf of his late lord Henry the Young King – who set out for Jerusalem to fulfil the vow of a master, a lord, a relative or a friend.[55] We should also not exclude the possibility that the crusading crowd included (especially among the humble and the servants) people whose personal motivations stood outside the categories considered so far. As John France has argued, these could have joined the crusade out of fidelity to a lord, friendship for a comrade, or simple dependence.[56]

conclusion: 'psychological' motivations

All the factors mentioned above could have played a great role in the crusaders' decision to set out. These are, if we dare to use the phrase, the 'rational' motivations. There were others, perhaps of paramount importance, which could have caused a crusader to take the vow under the influence of emotion, whose great importance in the 'romantic mentality' has been underlined. Numerous historians have remarked on Urban II's talent for oratory and the success of his preaching, due to his knowledge of knightly mentality.[57] I have for my own part emphasized the extraordinary charisma of Peter the Hermit and the 'inspired' preachers of his genre, charisma evoked by Guibert de Nogent and revealed through the success of his preaching.[58] Yet the success of these preachers, including the pope, rested far less on the value of their arguments and the reasoning that they invoked, than on their ability to 'stir the hearts' of their listeners.[59] Their success depended on their ability to create a climate of moral and religious pressure through an appeal to the emotions. The cry 'God wills it' was an excellent translation of the emotional response to this appeal to their instincts. So with the signs and marvels; whether they were real, exaggerated or imaginary, they none the less reflected the climate of exaltation aroused by the preaching of the crusade, the desire to 'deal with' a long-feared, demonized enemy. It is necessary to add to the equation the extraordinary level of emotion and the powerful images evoked by the themes of Jerusalem, Christ's inheritance, the place of Christ's preaching, death and resurrection and his return in glory before the end of time. Jerusalem, a place that the 'infidel' had dominated for several centuries and that Christ, it was believed, now demanded that they liberate and purify, thus making them participants in the realization of his divine plan in the history of the world. Their victory would be a prelude to Christ's final victory.

notes

1. A. Becker, *Papst Urban II (1988–1099)*, 2 vols (Stuttgart, 1964), vol. 1, pp. 24–78; J. Riley-Smith, *The First Crusade and the Idea of Crusading* (London, 1993), p. 12.

2. J. Flori, 'L'Eglise et la guerre sainte: de la paix de Dieu à la croisade', *Annales: Économies, Sociétés, Civilisations*, 47 (1992), 88–99; H. E. J. Cowdrey, 'From

the Peace of God to the First Crusade', in *La primera cruzada novecientos años después: el concilio de Clermont y los orígenes del movimiento cruzado*, ed. L. García-Guijarro Ramos (Castello d'Impressio, 1997), pp. 51–61; J. Flori, 'De la paix de Dieu à la croisade? Un réexamen', *Crusades*, 2 (2003), 1–23. The most famous statement of the case is by C. Erdmann, *Die Entstehung des Kreuzzugsgedankens* (Stuttgart, 1935), translated by M. W. Baldwin and W. Goffart as *The Origin of the Idea of Crusade* (Princeton, 1977), pp. 59–67, 75–7. For a contrary view, see M. Bull, *Knightly Piety and the Lay Response to the First Crusades: The Limousin and Gascony, c. 970–c. 1130* (Oxford, 1993), pp. 20–69.

3. J. Flori, 'Chevalerie et liturgie. Remise des armes et vocabulaire "chevaleresque" dans les sources liturgiques du IXe au XIVe siècle', *Le Moyen Age*, 84 (1979), 409–42; J. Flori, 'Les origines de l'adoubement chevaleresque: Étude des remises d'armes et du vocabulaire qui les exprime dans les sources historiques latines jusqu'au debut du XIII siècle', *Traditio*, 35 (1979), 209–72; M. Keen, *Chivalry* (New Haven and London, 1984), pp. 64–77.

4. Erdmann, *Origin of the Idea of Crusade*, pp. 148–81; E. Delaruelle, 'Essai sur la formation de l'idée de croisade', *Bulletin de littérature ecclésiastique*, 42 (1941), 24–45 and 86–103; 45 (1944), 13–46 and 73–90; 54 (1953), 226–39; 55 (1954), 50–63; repr. in E. Delaruelle, *L'idée de croisade* (Turin, 1980), especially p. 46ff.; *A History of the Crusades*, ed. K. M. Setton, vol. 1: *The First Hundred Years*, ed. M. W. Baldwin (Philadephia, 1955), pp. 222–5; I. S. Robinson, 'Gregory VII and the Soldiers of Christ', *History*, 58 (1973), 169–72; J. Gilchrist, 'The Papacy and War against the "Saracens"', *International History Review*, 10 (1988), 174–97; H. E. J. Cowdrey, 'Pope Gregory VII and the Bearing of Arms', *Montjoie: Studies in Crusade History in Honour of Hans Eberhard Mayer*, ed. B. Z. Kedar, J. Riley-Smith and R. Hiestand (Aldershot, 1997), pp. 21–35.

5. *Patrologiae cursus completes, series Latina*, ed. J. P. Migne, 217 vols and 4 vols of indices (Paris, 1834–64), vol. 143, cols 500 and 527, vol. 165, cols 1117–18.

6. Erdmann, *Origin of the Idea of Crusade*; Delaruelle, 'Essai sur la formation'; P. Rousset, *Histoire d'une idéologie. La croisade* (Lausanne, 1983), pp. 25–40; C. Violante, 'La pataria e la militia Dei nelle fonti e nella realtà', in *'Militia Christi' e Crociata nei secoli XI–XIII: Atti della undecima Settimana internazionale di studio, Mendola, 28 agosto – 1 settembre 1989* (Milan, 1992), pp. 103–27; H. E. J. Cowdrey, 'The Genesis of the Crusades: The Springs of Western Ideas of Holy War', in *The Holy War*, ed. T. P. Murphy (Columbus, 1976), pp. 9–32; J. Flori, *La guerre sainte. La formation de l'idée de croisade dans l'Occident chrétien* (Paris, 2001), especially pp. 101–88.

7. Gregory VII, 'Registrum', ed. E. Caspar, Monumenta Germaniae Historica Epistolae selectae, vol. 2 (Berlin, 1967), II.49, pp. 188–90, and IX.21, p. 602; *The Register of Pope Gregory VII, 1073–1085: An English Translation*, trans. H. E. J. Cowdrey (Oxford, 2002), pp. 139–40, 420–1.

8. On this evolution, see Flori, *La guerre sainte*. Older discussions include Erdmann, *Origin of the Idea of Crusade*; Gilchrist, 'Papacy and War'; J. Riley-Smith, *The First Crusaders, 1095–1131* (Cambridge, 1997), pp. 40–52; C. Tyerman, *The Invention of the Crusades* (Basingstoke, 1998), pp. 8–13.

9. Distinction underlined by H. E. J. Cowdrey, 'Christianity and the Morality of Warfare during the First Century of Crusading', in *The Experience of Crusading*,

vol. 1: *Western Approaches*, ed. M. Bull and N. Housley (Cambridge, 2003), pp. 175–92.

10. P. Rousset, *Les origines et les caractères de la première croisade* (Neuchâtel, 1945), especially p. 27 ff., p. 134ff.; H. E. Mayer, *The Crusades*, trans. J. Gillingham, 2nd edn (Oxford, 1988), esp. pp. 27–37; H. E. J. Cowdrey, 'Pope Urban II's Preaching of the First Crusade', *History*, 55 (1970), 177–88 (repr. in H. E. J. Cowdrey, *Popes, Monks and Crusaders* (London, 1984), no. XVI); J. Flori, *Pierre l'ermite et la première croisade* (Paris, 1999), pp. 108–51; Flori, *La guerre sainte*, p. 316ff.

11. The role of Jerusalem as a goal for the crusade from the beginning has been debated by historians, but is now generally accepted: *The First Hundred Years*, ed. Baldwin, p. 244 and n. 51; Cowdrey, 'Pope Urban II's Preaching'; Mayer, *The Crusades*, pp. 9–11; Riley-Smith, *First Crusade and Idea of Crusading*, pp. 20–5. See also M. Bull, 'Views of Muslims and of Jerusalem in Miracle Stories, *c.* 1000–*c.* 1200: Reflections on the Study of First Crusaders' Motivations', in *The Experience of Crusading*, vol. 1, ed. Bull and Housley, pp. 13–35.

12. Gregory VII, 'Registrum', II.31, pp. 165–8; *Register of Pope Gregory VII*, trans. Cowdrey, pp. 122–4. Erdmann, *Origin of the Idea of Crusade*, saw the reform papacy as crucial to the development of the crusade ideology; Gilchrist, 'Papacy and War', argued for a continuity in papal attitudes towards warfare from the ninth century onwards; see also *The First Hundred Years*, ed. Baldwin, p. 224.

13. The extent of influence is debated. Bull, *Knightly Piety*, pp. 70–114, argues that events of Spain were 'of minimal relevance' for the First Crusade at the level of lay piety, but Riley-Smith argued that 'Urban regarded the new crusade to the East as part of a wider movement of Christian liberation and did not distinguish it from the Spanish Reconquest': *First Crusade and the Idea of Crusading*, p. 20. Baldwin also relates the two movements: *The First Hundred Years*, ed. Baldwin, pp. 231–3.

14. For an attempt to reconstruct Urban's Clermont sermon, see D. C. Munro, 'The Speech of Pope Urban II at Clermont, 1095', *American Historical Review*, 11 (1906), 231–42.

15. P. J. Cole, *The Preaching of the Crusades to the Holy Land, 1095–1270* (Cambridge, Mass., 1991), pp. 5, 9–33; P. J. Cole, '"O God, the Heathen have come into your Inheritance" (Ps. 78.1). The Theme of Religious Pollution in Crusade Documents, 1095–1188', in *Crusaders and Muslims in Twelfth-Century Syria*, ed. M. Shatzmiller (Leiden, 1993), pp. 84–111.

16. On the total numbers on the First Crusade, see J. Flori, *Croisade et chevalerie, XIe-XIIe siècles* (Paris and Brussels, 1998), pp. 319–43; J. France, *Victory in the East: A Military History of the First Crusade* (Cambridge, 1994), pp. 122–42; J. Riley-Smith, 'Casualities and the Number of Knights on the First Crusade', *Crusades*, 1 (2002), 13–27.

17. P. Alphandéry and A. Dupont, *La chrétienté et l'idée de croisade* (Paris, 1954, repr. 1995); Riley-Smith, *First Crusade and Idea of Crusading*, pp. 90–119; and more recently Flori, *Pierre l'ermite*, pp. 179–99.

18. G. Constable, 'Medieval Charters as a Source for the History of the Crusades', in *Crusade and Settlement*, ed. P. W. Edbury (Cardiff, 1985), pp. 73–89, and the numerous works of J. Riley Smith, especially 'The State of Mind of Crusaders to the East, 1095–1300', in *The Oxford Illustrated History of the Crusades*, ed. J.

Riley-Smith (London, 1995), pp. 66–90, and *The First Crusaders, 1095–1131* (Cambridge, 1997).

19. See, for instance, Tyerman, *Invention of the Crusades*, pp. 16, 30–5.

20. Urban II, 'Letter to all the faithful in Flanders', in *Epistulae et chartae ad historiam primi belli sacri spectantes: Die Kreuzzugsbriefe aus den Jahren 1088–1100*, ed. H. Hagenmeyer (Innsbruck, 1901), pp. 136–7.

21. Text in R. Somerville, *The Councils of Urban II*, vol. 1: *Decreta Claramontensia* (Amsterdam, 1972), pp. 71–81.

22. See N. Paulus, *Geschichte des Ablasses im Mittelalter vom Ursprunge bis zur Mitte des 14. Jahrhunderts* (Paderborn, 1922); Mayer, *The Crusades*, pp. 23–33, 293–5 n. 15; and more recently J. Richard, 'L'indulgence de croisade et le pèlerinage en Terre sainte', in *Il concilio di Piacenza e le crociate*, (Piacenza, 1996), pp. 213–23. On the formation of the concept of purgatory, see J. Le Goff, *La naissance du purgatoire* (Paris, 1981), translated by Arthur Goldhammer as *The Birth of Purgatory* (Chicago, 1986), but compare to B. P. McGuire, 'Purgatory, the Communion of the Saints, and Medieval Change', *Viator*, 20 (1989), 61–84.

23. See especially M. Bull, 'The Roots of Lay Enthusiasm for the First Crusade', *History*, 78 (1993), 353–72; M. Bull, 'Origins', in *Oxford Illustrated History of the Crusades*, ed. Riley-Smith, pp. 13–33; J. Riley-Smith, *The First Crusaders, 1095–1131* (Cambridge, 1997); J. Riley-Smith, 'The Idea of Crusading in the Charters of Early Crusaders, 1095–1102', in *Le Concile de Clermont de 1095 et l'appel à la Croisade (Actes du Colloque Universitaire International de Clermont-Ferrand (23–25 juin 1095)* (Rome, 1997), pp. 155–66. For Jerusalem as a pilgrimage destination prescribed for serious sins see J. Sumption, *Pilgrimage: An Image of Medieval Religion* (London, 1975), pp. 98–103.

24. On this point see also J. Flori, 'Jérusalem terrestre, céleste et spirituelle: trois facteurs de sacralisation de la première croisade', in *Segundas Jornadas Internacionales sobre la Primera Cruzada (Huesca, 7–11 set. 1999)*, ed. L. García-Guijarro Ramos (forthcoming); Keen, *Chivalry*, pp. 51–63.

25. On this point, see J. Flori, *L'essor de la chevalerie, 11ème-12ème s.* (Geneva, 1986), pp. 268–303; Keen, *Chivalry*, pp. 44–63; C. B. Bouchard, *Strong of Body, Brave and Noble. Chivalry and Society in Medieval France* (Ithaca, NY, 1998), pp. 75–102; J. Flori, *Chevaliers et chevalerie au Moyen Âge* (Paris, 1998), pp. 203–34.

26. On this opposition see J. Flori, 'Croisade et chevalerie; convergence idéologique ou rupture?', in *Femmes, Mariages, Lignages (XIIème–XIIIème siècles), Mélanges offerts à Georges Duby* (Brussels, 1992), pp. 157–76; Bernard of Clairvaux, *In Praise of the New Knighthood: A Treatise on the Knights Templar and the Holy Places of Jerusalem*, trans. C. Greenia (Kalamazo, Mich, 2000), ch. 2, p. 38.

27. Guibert de Nogent, *Gesta Dei gesta per Francos*, ed. R. B. C. Huygens, Corpus Christianorum Continuatio Medievalis 127A (Turnhout, 1996), Bk 1 part 1, pp. 86–8.

28. Jonathan Riley-Smith denies it, Jean Flori affirms it, H. E. J. Cowdrey and Colin Morris are undecided: J. Riley-Smith, 'Death on the First Crusade', in *The End of Strife*, ed. D. Loades (Edinburgh, 1984), pp. 14–31; H. E. J. Cowdrey, 'Martyrdom and the First Crusade', in *Crusade and Settlement*, ed. Edbury, pp. 47–56; C. Morris, 'Martyrs on the Field of Battle before and during the First Crusade', in *Martyrs and Martyrologies*, ed. D. Wood, *Studies in Church*

History, 30 (1993), pp. 93–104; J. Flori, 'Mort et martyre des guerriers vers 1100; l'exemple de la première croisade', *Cahiers de Civilisation Médiévale*, 34 (1991), 121–39; J. Flori, 'Les héros changés en saints ... et les saints en héros. Sacralisation et béatification du guerrier dans l'épopée et les chroniques de la première croisade', *PRIS-MA: bulletin de liaison de l'Equipe de recherche sur la littérature d'imagination du moyen âge*, 30 (1999), 255–72.

29. On this point, see Flori, *Pierre l'ermite*, p. 216ff.; Riley-Smith, *First Crusade and the Idea of Crusading*, pp. 114–19; *The First Hundred Years*, ed. Baldwin, p. 248.

30. See the numerous works of J. Riley-Smith, including 'An Approach to Crusading Ethics', *Reading Medieval Studies*, 6 (1980), 3–19, and 'Crusading as an Act of Love', *History*, 65 (1980), 177–92.

31. P. Rousset, 'La notion de chrétienté aux XIème et XIIème siècles', *Le Moyen Age*, 4th series, 69 (1963), 191–203; Rousset, *Histoire d'une idéologie*, pp. 31–3.

32. N. Daniel, *Heroes and Saracens: An interpretation of the Chansons de geste* (Edinburgh, 1984); J. V. Tolan, *Saracens: Islam in the Medieval European Imagination* (New York, 2002).

33. M. Bennett, 'First Crusaders' Images of Muslims: The Influence of Vernacular Poetry?', *Forum for Modern Language Studies*, 22 (1986), 101–22; M. A. Jubb, 'Enemies in Holy War, but Brothers in Charity: The Crusaders' View of their Saracen Opponents', in *Aspects de l'épopée romane: mentalités, idéologies, intertexualitiés*, ed. Hans van Dijk and Willem Noomen (Groningen, 1995), pp. 251–9; Tolan, *Saracens*.

34. P. Rousset, 'Recherches sur l'émotivité à l'époque romane', *Cahiers de Civilisation Médiévale*, 2 (1959), 65–7; Munro, 'Speech of Pope Urban II', 238, 242; Cole, '"O God, the Heathen have come into your Inheritance"'.

35. D. R. French, 'Journeys to the Center of the Earth: Medieval and Renaissance Pilgrimages to Mount Cavalry', in *Journeys Toward God: Pilgrimage and Crusade*, ed. B. N. Sargent-Baur (Kalamazoo, 1992), pp. 45–67; B. Hamilton, 'The Impact of Crusader Jerusalem on Western Christendom', *Catholic Historical Review*, 80 (1994), 695–713.

36. Guibert de Nogent, Bk 2, part 4, pp. 113–14.

37. *Die Kreuzzugsbriefe*, ed. Hagenmeyer, pp. 129–36; for a summary of the debates over this letter see *The First Hundred Years*, ed. Baldwin, p. 228 and n. 14.

38. J. Riley-Smith, 'The First Crusade and the Persecution of the Jews', *Persecution and Toleration*, ed. W. J. Sheils, *Studies in Church History*, 21 (1984), pp. 51–72; R. Chazan, *European Jewry and the First Crusade* (London, 1987); J. Flori, 'Une ou plusieurs "première croisade"? Le message d'Urbain II et les plus anciens pogroms d'occident', *Revue Historique*, 285 (1991) 3–27; Munro, 'Speech of Pope Urban', 240–2; N. Cohn, *The Pursuit of the Millennium: Revolutionary Millenarians and Mystical Anarchists of the Middle Ages* (London, 1957; new edn, 1993), pp. 63–73. For the legend of the Last Emperor see M. Reeves, *The Influence of Prophecy in the Later Middle Ages: A Study in Joachimism* (Oxford, 1969), pp. 299–302.

39. A. Vauchez 'Les composantes eschatologiques de l'idée de croisade', in *Le Concile de Clermont de 1095 et l'appel à la Croisade*, pp. 233–43; Flori, *Pierre l'ermite*, pp. 175ff. and 271ff.; for an earlier appraisal of Alphandéry's theory, see E. O. Blake, 'The Formation of the Crusade Idea', *Journal of Ecclesiastical History*, 21 (1970), 19–20.

40. J. Flori, 'La croix, la crosse et l'épée. La conversion des infidèles dans *La Chanson de Roland* et les chroniques de croisade', in *'Plaist vos oïr bone cançon vallant?' Mélanges de Langue et de Littérature Médiévales offerts à François Suard*, vol. 1 (Lille, 1999), pp. 261–72; J. Flori, 'Première croisade et conversion des "païens"', in *Migrations et diasporas méditerranéennes (Xe-XVIe s.)*, ed. M. Balard and A. Ducellier (Paris, 2002), pp. 449–57; S. Luchitskaja, 'L'idée de conversion dans les chroniques de la première croisade', *Cahiers de Civilisation Médiévale*, 45 (2002), 39–53.

41. See on these points E. Siberry, 'Missionaries and Crusaders, 1095–1274, Opponents or Allies?' in *The Church and War*, ed. W. J. Sheils, *Studies in Church History*, 20 (1983), pp. 103–10; B. Z. Kedar, *Crusade and Mission: European Approaches towards the Muslims* (Princeton, 1984); and, more recently, L.-A. Hunt, '*Excommunicata generatione*: Christian Imagery of Mission and Conversion of the Muslim Other Between the First Crusade and the Early Fourteenth Century', *Al-Masāq: Studia arabo-islamica mediterranea*, 8 (1995), 79–153.

42. W. L. Wakefield, *Heresy, Crusade and Inquisition in Southern France, 1100–1250* (London, 1974), pp. 93–4; M. Barber, *The Cathars: Dualist Heretics in Languedoc in the High Middle Ages* (Harlow, 2000), pp. 112–13, 120–3; M. Lambert, *The Cathars* (Oxford, 1998), pp. 97–106.

43. *Crusade and Conversion on the Baltic Frontier, 1150–1500*, ed. A. V. Murray (Aldershot, 2001). See Chapter 8 in this volume, by Sven Ekdahl.

44. See for example Keen, *Chivalry*, pp. 51–2, 103–7.

45. J. A. Brundage, 'An Errant Crusader: Stephen of Blois', *Traditio*, 16 (1960), 380–95; compare to P. Rousset, 'Etienne de Blois, fuyard, croisé, martyr', *Geneva*, 9 (1963), 163–95.

46. See for example Riley-Smith, *The First Crusade and the Idea of Crusading*, pp. 29, 41.

47. The best study of this unusual character remains that by J. C. Payen, *Le prince d'Aquitaine. Essai sur Guillaume IX et son oeuvre érotique* (Paris, 1980).

48. See on this Flori, *L'essor de la chevalerie*; Keen, *Chivalry*, pp. 18–43.

49. *Les chansons de Conon de Béthune*, ed. A. Wallensköld (Paris, 1921), pp. 6–7.

50. Keen, *Chivalry*, pp. 171–4.

51. See for instance Mayer, *The Crusades*, pp. 21–3; for further discussion of this problem see R. Bartlett, *The Making of Europe: Conquest, Colonization and Cultural Change, 950–1350* (Harmondsworth, 1994), pp. 24–59.

52. See especially J. Riley-Smith, 'The Motives of the Earliest Crusaders and the Settlement of Latin Palestine, 1095–1188', *English Historical Review*, 98 (1983), 721–36; J. Riley-Smith, 'Early Crusaders to the East and the Costs of Crusading, 1095–1130', in *Cross-cultural Convergences in the Crusader Period (Essays presented to Aryeh Graboïs on his sixty-fifth birthday)*, ed. M. Goodich, S. Menache and S. Schein (New York, 1995), pp. 237–57; J. Riley-Smith, 'The State of Mind of Crusaders to the East, 1095–1300', in *Oxford Illustrated History of the Crusades*, ed. J. Riley-Smith, pp. 66–90.

53. G. M. Anderson et al., 'An Economic Interpretation of the Medieval Crusades', *Journal of European Economic History*, 21 (1992), 339–63.

54. J. Prawer, *The Latin Kingdom of Jerusalem: European Colonialism in the Middle Ages* (New York, 1972); J. Prawer, 'The Roots of Medieval Colonialism', in *The Meeting of Two Worlds: Cultural Exchanges Between East and West during the*

Period of the Crusades, ed. V. P. Goos and C. V. Bornstein (Kalamazoo, 1986), pp. 23–38; discussion in J. Richard, 'La croisade; l'évolution des conceptions et des stratégies', in *From Clermont to Jerusalem: The Crusades and Crusader Societies 1095–1500*, ed. A. V. Murray (Turnhout, 1998), pp. 3–25; *Le partage du monde: échanges et colonisation dans la Méditerranée médiévale*, ed. M. Balard and A. Ducellier (Paris, 1998).

55. *History of William Marshal*, ed. A. J. Holden, trans. S. Gregory, notes by D. Crouch (London, 2002–), lines 6891–906, 7239–302.

56. On this type of motivation see J. France, 'Patronage and the Appeal of the First Crusade', in *The First Crusade, Origin and Impact*, ed. J. Phillips (Manchester, 1997), pp. 5–20.

57. For example, Riley-Smith, *First Crusade and Idea of Crusading*, p. 12; Mayer, *The Crusades*, pp. 8–9.

58. Flori, *Pierre l'ermite*, pp. 66–89, 244–9, 467–82.

59. Rousset, 'Recherches sur l'émotivité à l'époque romane', 65; Cole, *Preaching of the Crusades*, pp. 14–15, 19, 23, 33–6.

2
crusading and canon law

james muldoon

At first glance war and law seem to be an unlikely pairing. After all, war suggests the breakdown of lawful order so that the end of war suggests the restoration of law and order. Since there appears to be little likelihood that violence will disappear from human society, however, if violence cannot be eliminated, bringing it under some control is the next best solution. The law of war, a web of laws, customs and practices designed to identify the legitimate bases for going to war and to regulate the exercise of armed force in the course of a war, gradually developed.

Shakespeare illustrated the medieval approach to controlling war and violence in his *Henry V*. The play opens with a discussion of the legal basis for the English king's claim to the French throne and the principles of the law of succession. The two clerics who discuss the problem eventually conclude that the Salic Law on which the Valois monarchs based their succession to the throne of France in 1328 was not in fact applicable. This law rejected any claim to the French throne by a candidate whose claim came through the female line, the basis for the English monarch's claim to the French throne. The English clerics concluded, however, that the Salic Law did not in fact govern succession to the French throne so that the present king was a usurper, not the rightful monarch, and therefore Henry V's attempt to seize the French throne was a legitimate war.

The course of the war in France as Shakespeare presented it illustrated some of the rules of war. Seeking to insure that he was seen pursuing his legitimate claim to rule and was not simply seeking to enrich himself at the expense of the French, Henry V forbade looting and ordered the hanging of several soldiers guilty of it in defiance of his order. On the other hand, after the French killed the unarmed camp servants in violation of the rules of war, Henry ordered the killing of those Frenchmen whom

37

the English had captured, a violation of the laws of war justified by the actions of the French. In ordering this act, the English stressed that the French had violated an important principle of the law of war and deserved punishment.[1] The role of law in warfare was not, however, restricted to the causes of war and violations of the rules of war. The end of a war can also generate legal issues. What will be the status of those defeated in a war? Is it legitimate to kill, exile or enslave the defeated? Can the victors seize the private property of individual members of a defeated society? Then there are such practical issues such as how long must a presumed widow wait to remarry if her husband does not return from war but his death is not absolutely certain?

Given the number of issues that war and efforts to control violence can generate, it should come as no surprise that the canon law, the law of the medieval Christian Church, dealt with them. As Stanley Chodorow has pointed out, the first volume of the universal canon law, Gratian's *Decretum* (1140), was an attempt 'to develop a Christian theory of the structure of society and ... his work is one of the most significant works of political theory written in the mid-twelfth century'.[2] Given Gratian's goals, it is obvious that he would have to deal with violence and war if he was to develop a complete theory of Christian society. That being the case, we should not be surprised to learn that the crusade, the most famous kind of medieval war, existed within a specific canon law framework that distinguished it from other kinds of war. While any medieval war involving ecclesiastical interests is usually labelled a crusade, strictly speaking only those wars that fitted certain specific criteria were true crusades in the legal sense.

At the same time, it is important to recognize that the *Decretum* and the other fundamental canon law text, the *Decretales* (1234), have no entry for 'crusade' or 'crusader'. Legal materials dealing with the crusade exist only as individual texts scattered throughout the basic canonistic source collections and the commentaries on those works. James Brundage has noted that the canonists never came 'to grips in a systematic way with clarifying his [the crusader's] role in medieval society' and, as far as is known, no canonist ever wrote a treatise on the crusade.[3] In effect, it has been modern scholars such as Brundage and Michel Villey who have brought these scattered legal sources together and organized the material into the kind of treatises that medieval canonists might have written but did not.[4]

As the crusades were fully developed at the point at which Gratian was compiling the *Decretum*, at the point at which universities were beginning, the lack of intellectual interest in crusades is especially puzzling. In the sixteenth century, the discovery and conquest of the New World, a situation that had much in common with the crusades, generated a vast literature about the legitimacy of the conquest, the rights of the indigenous population and other legal issues, issues that had arisen earlier in conjunction with the crusades. This literature appears related to the fact that at the time, the Spanish universities were experiencing a great revival of interest in scholastic philosophy, and the encounter with the New World presented a series of new and important moral issues that attracted scholarly attention. One wonders why the crusades did not have the same effect on Gratian and those who followed him.

To understand the way in which the canon lawyers approached issues that affected crusaders and crusades, it is necessary to understand the structure of that law. Canons or laws of the Church, that is the numerous regulations that popes, bishops and Church councils had issued, had existed since the earliest days of the Church. Over time, various churchmen had produced a number of collections of such canons for the use of ecclesiastical officials in particular regions. Around 1140, Gratian, apparently a monk in Bologna, published a volume, the *Decretum*, designed to organize the texts on which the law of the Church was based into a coherent whole for the use of Church administrators and lawyers everywhere.[5] In doing this, Gratian made a fundamental contribution to the process of ecclesiastical centralization that was crucial to the ecclesiastical reform movement, the Investiture Controversy, of the eleventh and twelfth centuries, a movement that reached its peak at the Fourth Lateran Council in 1215. He provided the basis for a legal system, a legal infrastructure so to speak, encompassing the entire Church with the pope as the supreme judge of Christian society.

While much of the reform movement concerned matters of internal Church administration such as liturgical and ritual practices, the most famous aspect of the movement concerned the relation between ecclesiastical and secular rulers. In an age when the kingdoms of Europe were only beginning to emerge, when Church officials possessed a great deal of authority in the secular sphere, and when the line between Church and State was only coming into existence, it was logical for ecclesiastical and secular officials to clash over the extent of their respective jurisdictions. Indeed, as the legal historian J. N. Figgis famously observed: 'In the Middle Ages the Church was not a State, it was the State: the State or rather the civil authority ... was merely the police department of the Church.'[6] While this observation rather exaggerates the power of the Church, it also explains why the canonists were concerned with the issues of war and violence. Ecclesiastical leaders would expect to play a significant role when secular rulers planned to wage war.

The publication of the *Decretum* and the establishment of schools of canon law were significant factors in the development of the Church's institutional structure and in the formation of the lawyers who would administer it. The reform movement of the eleventh and twelfth centuries, the Investiture Controversy, saw the creation of an autonomous Church whose leadership sought to be free of secular interference in its operation. Every diocese was to have its court for hearing cases, and the papal court was the ultimate court of appeal. The pope was *iudex omnium*, the judge of all Christians, and one of his most important routine activities was to sit as a judge. Decisions of the papal court, decretals, became the basis for new law. Within a few years after the appearance of the *Decretum* several small collections of important decisions appeared for the convenience of teachers and practitioners. Pope Innocent III (1198–1216) even sent a collection of his own decretals to the law school at Bologna and instructed the teachers to regard these decisions as the basis of the current law. A second volume of canon law, the *Decretales*, published in 1234 at the command of Pope Gregory IX (1227–1241), brought together all or part of more than 2000 decretals that various popes had issued. Subsequently, canonists produced several more small collections of decretals that were included in the *Corpus Iuris Canonici*, the complete collection of canon law materials published in the sixteenth century. Soon after the *Decretum* and the *Decretales* appeared a body of commentary on the texts that had been collected emerged. Initially, these commentaries consisted of brief marginal or interlinear notes explaining obscure words and phrases and providing references to related texts. Eventually they grew longer, approaching the level of treatises on specific topics, although, as we have seen, not on the crusade.[7]

Because the crusade was not an explicit topic in the volumes of canon law, the lawyers discussed crusades and crusading from several angles, some of which might seem strange to us. In the first place, the crusade was related to the discussion of the just war in the *Decretum*, an issue of great significance in the eleventh and twelfth centuries. Less obviously, the crusade was discussed in connection with pilgrimages and, above all, in connection with the legal obligations associated with the taking of vows, specifically the vow that crusaders took. Subsequently, the initial success of the crusades and the European occupation of parts of the Near East that followed generated a number of problems that led to the issuance of papal judicial decisions on specific matters such as the validity of the marriages of non-Christians. These decisions in turn generated more legal commentaries. Finally, the crusades raised some broader issues of a political nature as, for example, the right of the Muslims to possess land in the face of European Christian expansion into the Near East and the rights of non-Christians generally, issues that foreshadowed the debate about the rights of the native peoples of the Americas in the sixteenth century and beyond.

War presented Christian intellectuals with a difficult problem, the place of violence and of warriors within Christian society. For the first thousand years of the Christian Church, Christian thinkers had accepted war as a necessary but unfortunate aspect of life, an aspect not to be encouraged. They were not, however, pacifists. Those who killed in battle were not condemned outright but were required to do penance for their actions even if done in self-defence. On the other hand, soldiers who exchanged the military life for the clerical or monastic life, especially those martyred for their action, were Christian heroes. Only clerics were explicitly forbidden to bear arms.

Gratian included key elements of the traditional opinions about war and soldiers in Causa XXIII of the *Decretum* which opened with a brief statement concerning the situation facing some Christians who were being threatened by heretics. Was it proper for orthodox bishops to employ force to protect their flocks from the violence perpetrated by the heretics? Gratian then broke down the problem into eight separate questions. The primary proposition concerned whether or not the bearing of arms was lawful in order to defend the faithful? Another question of special interest to subsequent crusaders concerned the possessions of the heretics. Could the faithful seize their possessions in the process of defending themselves? To a very great extent, Gratian drew upon the writings of St Augustine (d. 431) for statements on these issues. As Frederick Russell has noted, 'The die for the medieval just war was cast by St Augustine, who combined Roman and Judaeo-Christian elements in a mode of thought that was to influence opinion throughout the Middle Ages and beyond.' 'The influence of St Augustine suffused the entire Causa', according to Russell.[8]

Gratian is important in the development of the concept of the crusade, because he set the terms of all subsequent debate about the place of violence and those who engage in it within Christian society. Gratian's position was that force could be legitimately used to defend the Christian community, but that the clergy could not bear arms. Arms were restricted to laymen who would employ force under the direction of their spiritual leaders. Furthermore, Gratian did not see war in a positive light. It was to be engaged in only in self-defence, only when forced upon Christians by their enemies.

By the beginning of the eleventh century, however, ecclesiastical opinions about war and warriors began to change, and the traditional negative judgements about war were being challenged, but why this occurred is not clear. In the 1930s, Carl Erdmann pointed out that some scholars argued that the Muslim concept of *jihād*, a war for religious reasons, had influenced Christian thinking on war but that this theory never received widespread support.[9] Others have suggested that the crusade was rooted in the tradition of the just war and the holy war. The theory of the just war stressed the natural right of a society to defend itself against attack, while the notion of the holy war encompassed the use of force and violence in serving the goals of the Church, such as defending the Church against its enemies. The crusade, however, differed from these kinds of war in a very significant way. Those who engaged in just or holy wars were accomplishing a legitimate end but they had to do penance for their actions. The crusader, however, was not only engaged in a legitimate task, his task was a virtuous one for which he was granted an indulgence for the temporal punishment due for his sins, thus guaranteeing him eternal salvation.

We can trace the changed attitude of Christians to war and warriors to the efforts to control violence in Christian Europe associated with two movements that began at the end of the tenth century, the Peace of God and the Truce of God. These popular movements reflected the efforts of the inhabitants of various regions led by their bishops to reduce the violence endemic in a society headed by a warrior aristocracy. Unable to outlaw war, they sought to limit the times that armed violence could be legitimately employed and to identify persons who could never be the objects of legitimate violence. This meant that Christians should not fight during important liturgical seasons such as Advent and Lent and must avoid killing innocent civilians such as women, children, clerics and the poor. While this approach to peacemaking may amuse modern observers, it was a pragmatic response to conditions in the eleventh and twelfth centuries. If war could not be eliminated, it could at least be limited in time and its consequences restricted to those who voluntarily engaged in it.[10]

The difficulty lay in turning the violent proclivities of the European military aristocracy to a morally acceptable use. That is, if the warrior nobles of Europe wished to engage in combat, they should be provided with legitimate opportunities. As one modern observer has observed, the answer to the dilemma was to create peace within Europe by exporting the violent to the frontier with the Muslim world in the Near East.[11] The Muslims who had conquered and occupied large parts of the Byzantine Empire, especially the Holy Land, provided a suitable outlet for European aggression. A war against the advancing Muslims was a just war of defence. It was also a holy war in that such a campaign would protect Christians and Christendom from conquest.

In order to make war with the distant Muslims an especially attractive proposition, however, the very act of going on crusade had to be invested with moral value, a value signified by the grant of an indulgence to those who would go. Being a warrior had to be understood in positive terms, that is being a warrior was to become not simply a necessary but morally ambiguous act but rather a morally positive one, a means of winning eternal salvation.

The notion that arms could be employed to further ecclesiastical ends was of course not new in the eleventh and twelfth centuries. Ecclesiastical and secular officials had used the language of the holy war, the war for the interests of the Church, for some centuries in order to justify their wars. To a great extent, such wars actually tended to express the interests of secular rulers who called upon ecclesiastics to bless their wars. The Church reform movement, however, as it led to the development of a Church institutionally distinct from secular power, asserted the superiority of the spiritual authority over secular power, and placed the pope at the apex of a hierarchically-constructed Church created a new role for the pope. In the course of becoming masters of the institutional Church structure, these popes began to claim a more active role in the direction of Christian society, a role that included a voice in the making of war. Pope Gregory VII (1073–85), perhaps the most determined papal reformer and the most aggressive supporter of an expanded papal role in public affairs, played a leading role in bringing war under direct ecclesiastical control and granting the warrior a positive moral status. Responding to the call of Emperor Alexius Comnenus (1081–1118) for assistance after the destruction of the Byzantine army at the battle of Manzikert in 1071, Gregory even announced his intention to lead an army to assist in the defence of the Byzantine Empire against the advancing Turks, although in fact he never did lead such a crusade because of the problems that he faced within Europe. The role of leader of a Christian army that Gregory VII asserted was, however, a forerunner of what was to become a fundamental aspect of the crusade, papal leadership. That is, a pope would call for a crusade, provide an indulgence for those who responded to the call, and, as in the First Crusade, arrange for a papal legate to lead the crusaders.

All of these elements came together when Pope Urban II (1088–99), after Gregory VII one of the most aggressive Church reformers, called for a crusade at Clermont in 1095. Urban's call emphasized that the campaign he was announcing contained elements of both the just war and the holy war traditions. The crusade was a legitimate war of defence, because the advancing Muslims threatened the security of the Christian world. Urban described the Turks as 'an accursed race, a race utterly alienated from God ... [that] has invaded' Christendom and a race that 'has depopulated them [Christian lands] by sword, pillage, and fire ... .' Furthermore, the pope argued, Christians living under Muslim rule in the East were suffering under Muslim rule and should be freed. In saying this, he was apparently unaware that eastern Christians had generally come to a peaceful accommodation with their Muslim masters and did not require the help of their European brethren. In addition, Urban argued that Jerusalem, the scene of Christ's passion and death should be liberated from the hands of the infidel and returned to the faithful.[12]

The crusade was, however, more than a just or a holy war, it was a means of insuring one's salvation by dying in battle and being freed of the temporal punishment here on earth or in purgatory due to one's sins. Urban exhorted his hearers to 'undertake this journey for the remission of your sins, with the assurance of the imperishable glory of the kingdom of heaven'.[13] This line and similar phrases elsewhere have generated a great deal of scholarly controversy. The language suggests a plenary indulgence, but the theology of the indulgence had not yet been worked out in detail. Regardless of what Urban intended, the language was understood to mean that participation in the crusade 'wiped away the blot of sin altogether and that the crusader was automatically restored to a state of spiritual innocence'.[14] There was no suggestion here that the crusader would have to do penance for having killed someone in battle, as was the case earlier even in a just war or a holy war. The act of killing in the crusade was now not only morally acceptable, it provided a guarantee of eternal salvation as well. Finally, Urban assigned a papal legate, Bishop Ademar of Puy, to lead the crusading army. As Fulcher of Chartres enthusiastically asserted: Ademar 'acting as vicar-apostolic, ruled the whole army of God wisely and thoughtfully, and spurred them to complete their undertaking vigorously'.[15] Warfare and warriors could not receive any higher accolade.

Some have suggested that by giving violence a morally legitimate function, the theorists of the crusade in effect justified in moral terms the military function that was the central justification for the status of the medieval aristocracy. Rather than giving up the military vocation and entering a monastery in order to atone for his sins and thereby win salvation, the knight could now achieve salvation by exercising his warrior skills in a crusade. The subsequent creation of orders of monk-knights such as the Knights Templar and the Teutonic Knights completed the transformation of the warrior from a necessary evil to a specialized kind of cleric.

Urban II's call for a crusade clearly provided the basic elements for a general theory of the crusade: a just cause, the defence of Christendom, a plenary indulgence for one's sins, and papal leadership. One might have expected the lawyers to bring the various elements into a coherent statement of the nature and characteristics of the crusade, yet this did not occur. Instead, the canonists discussed the crusade within two existing canonistic categories, the pilgrimage and the vow.

The pilgrimage, the journey to visit a holy site, was a longstanding Christian devotional practice, stretching back to the fourth century when Christians would travel to Palestine to see the sites associated with the life of Christ. Even after the Muslim conquest of the Near East in the seventh century, Christians could generally travel safely to Palestine. Pilgrims were even a significant part of the Near Eastern economy, as they required places to stay and places to eat, animals to ride and guides to take them around, so that it was advantageous to the local economy to encourage pilgrims to come and prudent to insure their safety.

During the eleventh and twelfth centuries, the pilgrimage acquired another aspect, a journey to a holy site for the purpose of expiating one's sins. By travelling to a designated site, the sinner would be freed from the temporal punishment that his sins had earned. A crusade was also a pilgrimage but of a special kind, one in which the participants bore arms that they planned to use in defence of Christendom, quite specifically to restore Jerusalem to Christian control. Fulcher of Chartres made this point when he summed up the theme of his chronicle thus: '... I carefully arranged the deeds, most distinguished in the Lord, of the armies of the Franks who, by God's ordination, made a pilgrimage to Jerusalem ... .'[16] The unsuspecting reader might conclude that the chronicle would describe the activities of a number of pious Christians who had travelled peacefully to Jerusalem simply to pray at the sacred sites and insure their salvation. The pious language, however, masked a bloody campaign that ended with the capture of Jerusalem and the beheading of 10,000 people in the confines of Solomon's Temple where the slaughter caused the feet of the crusaders to be 'stained up to the ankles with the blood of the slain'.[17] For doing this, the crusaders earned a plenary indulgence, forgiveness of all the temporal punishment that each had earned by his sins, benefiting from Urban II's promise that all who go to the Holy Land with a right intention 'can substitute the journey for all penance for sin'.[18]

In addition to the guarantee of salvation, the pilgrim, and therefore the crusader, was also provided with some material support and was the beneficiary of a number of legal protections.[19] For some centuries, ecclesiastical law had required religious houses to feed and house pilgrims, a valuable provision inasmuch as many who set out for the Holy Land required material support. Monasteries and other Christian institutions were expected to feed and house pilgrims as they passed on their way to their destination. Designed as it was for those travelling as individuals or in small groups, such a requirement must have been an enormous burden on monasteries on the roads leading to the Holy Land when a horde of crusaders appeared at the door. In addition, the crusaders benefited from another privilege accorded pilgrims. Pilgrims, like all peaceful travellers, were deemed to have the right to travel anywhere without interference from secular authorities. They had to be admitted and allowed to pass through any Christian land. Here again, a privilege created to protect small numbers of ordinary travellers took on a different complexion when claimed by a large body of armed travellers burdened with a number of unarmed servants, camp followers, and so on, marching through the countryside foraging for food.

Finally, in theory at least, a crusader possessed a bundle of specific rights that placed 'their wives and children, their property and possessions' under the protection of the Church. Until crusaders returned home, 'no lawsuit shall be instituted hereafter in regard to any property of which they were in peaceful possession when they took the cross'.[20] In addition, crusaders received exemptions 'from tolls and immunity from taxes ... from arrest or seizure ... and later pilgrims enjoyed the right to appoint an attorney to safeguard their interests during their absence ... '.[21] While these privileges were no doubt not always honoured in practice, they do reflect the medieval Church's concern for the welfare of the pious traveller and could provide an inducement for a man to travel to the Holy Land to fight the enemies of the Church and, at the same time, protect his property from suits.

The other basis for canonistic analysis of the status of the crusader was the canon law of the vow, like the pilgrimage, long a part of the Christian life. For centuries, Christians had signified the special nature of religious undertakings by making a vow, a formal promise to undertake some course of action. A vow was not simply a private matter between an individual and God, it was a public undertaking, made under ecclesiastical auspices and in the presence of witnesses.

The crusader's vow, signified by taking the cross, that is by putting a cross on one's clothing to demonstrate his commitment to go on crusade, publicly linked the crusader to the Church and provided both privileges and responsibilities. Above all, having made the vow, the individual had to fulfil it unless legitimately excused by ecclesiastical authority. The crusader who failed to fulfil his obligation endangered his eternal salvation and laid himself open to legal sanctions in this life as well. By encouraging the taking of the crusader's vow, the Church was able 'to convert the momentary zeal of would-be crusaders into a permanent obligation which could be enforced, if need be, by legal compulsion'.[22] This was also a recognition that while crusading could have once relied on the enthusiasm of potential crusaders to staff an army, experience had shown that enthusiasm was not enough. Only enthusiasm backed by compulsion if necessary would make a crusade possible in the long run. As the canon lawyers discovered, justifying the crusade was not the only legal issue that arose from the crusade. There also emerged a number of cases involving the status of those who participated in a crusade or who were directly affected by a crusade.

Many of these issues, like so many other legal matters that appeared in the course of the great reform movement, were resolved in a series of decretals that Innocent III issued in the course of his pontificate, a reflection of the fact that his reign saw the consolidation of the reforming policies that had been developing since the eleventh century. The Fourth Lateran Council (1215) that he summoned incorporated the principal reforms generated by the reform movement into a body of law and completed the formation of the institutional structure of the Church.

One of the most important issues that concerned the canonists and that Innocent settled was the crusader's vow, especially the situation of someone who vowed to go on crusade and then was unable to go. From the beginning of the crusades there had always been those who, swept up in the enthusiasm generated by crusade preachers, vowed to go on crusade but who subsequently became aware that there were circumstances that would prevent them from actually going. Some were too old to be of use in crusading warfare while others were too young or in poor health. Furthermore, there were those who vowed to go but whose presence would be a burden to the crusaders, especially the pious non-combatants who vowed to accompany the actual crusaders but who could not serve as soldiers. Innocent III issued decretals to deal with such issues. Given his role in developing the centralized papal monarchy, it should be no surprise that he determined that individuals could be released from their vows, something that some canonists had denied, but that only the pope could determine whether or not an individual should be released. Inasmuch as the crusade required military service, commuting the vows of those unfit to provide such service made a great deal of sense, as did restricting inclusion in the crusading armies to those who were suitable for combat. Innocent III also declared that the responsibilities the crusader vowed to fulfil were inheritable. The heirs of a man who died before fulfilling a crusading vow were responsible for fulfilling or commuting it.

The crusade vow also raised legal issues that affected the development of the theology and law of Christian marriage. For example, could a married man vow to go on crusade without first securing the consent of his wife? Urban II had suggested that the crusader should not be 'hindered by love of children, parents, and wives', implying that such attachments should not hold a man back from going to Jerusalem.[23] This was a complicated issue, however, because canon law gave a wife important rights including conjugal rights. If a husband went off on crusade, was he depriving his wife of her rights? Was a crusade vow superior to a marriage vow? In general, the canonists sided with the wife, requiring a husband to obtain his wife's consent before going on crusade. Innocent III, however, declared in a decretal decision that a man could lawfully go without spousal permission, but subsequent canonists appear, as James Brundage pointed out, 'uncomfortable' with this decision and were 'chary' in their comments on the decretal.[24]

A second legal issue that arose from the crusade and involved marital issues concerned the remarriage of a crusader's presumed widow. Specifically, how long would a crusader have to be missing and presumed dead before his widow could remarry? Furthermore, if a man presumed dead suddenly reappeared, would the wife who had remarried now have to return to him? Here again, a serious problem was rendered even more complicated by the Church's marriage law, this time its absolute rejection of divorce. In this case, the second marriage was invalid because of the existence of the first husband. Given the confusing nature of combat, the fog of war, it was not always possible, however, to determine an individual's fate. If killed, his body might be summarily dumped into a mass grave without any attempt at identification. If captured, he might be held for ransom, but he might also be held as a prisoner or enslaved. In such cases, a wife might never know her husband's fate. The canonists wrestled with this issue in a variety of ways, some arguing that if there was no evidence of a husband's survival after a given number of years (the number varied), a woman could legitimately remarry. On the other hand, some canonists argued that a woman could not legitimately remarry until there was definite proof of her husband's death. Here again, several realities collided. Given the importance of marriage alliances, the remarriage of a presumed widow could be of great importance to a family's status and well-being. Furthermore, the fact that the Church judged sex outside of marriage as sinful, demanding absolute certitude about a man's death could impose a life of celibacy on his wife. The Church's position that a valid marriage could be ended only by death thus worked against any easy solution to the problems that a widow or a presumed widow faced.

Issues of marriage law also arose as a consequence of the crusaders conquering and ruling lands with large Muslim populations. Responding to missionary efforts, some Muslims became Christians. A polygamous Muslim male convert posed a difficult problem for the lawyers, however, because he posed the question of which of his wives was his legitimate wife according to canon law. His conversion also presented the social and economic question of what would happen to the surplus wives of the convert if the Church insisted that the convert become monogamous. A similar problem would, of course, exist if one or more of the wives of a Muslim man wished to become Christian. One solution might have been to tolerate the existing plural marriages for the lifetime of the converts but not allow subsequent polygamous relationships. Some argued that as the ancient Hebrew patriarchs had been polygamous, so the converts at the initial stages of their Christian life could be allowed to retain their plural wives. There was also the problem of the legitimacy of the offspring of polygamous marriages. Innocent made the interesting judgement that in some cases while the marriages of infidel converts were invalid, the children of such marriage should be considered as legitimate 'for reasons of public utility', although he did not explain this argument in any further detail, leaving later commentators in something of a quandary.[25]

The goal of converting the slave-holding peoples of the Near East to Latin Christianity posed another problem of great economic concern for the canon lawyers, the question of whether the reception of baptism would automatically free a slave. The issue was not a new one. St Paul after all had counselled Christian slaves to be subject to their masters. Gradually there developed the custom that Christians would not enslave other Christians. Thus, Christian prisoners of war had to be ransomed, not sold into slavery, admittedly a belief not always followed in practice. But what of an enslaved non-believer? Would a Christian master have to manumit a slave who chose to receive baptism? The papal response was that baptizing a slave did not free him, although manumission was encouraged. It was believed that some slave owners discouraged missionary efforts among their slaves, fearing that there would be pressures to free the converts.

There was one more topic of economic interest in canon law linked to the crusade, the question of trade with the Muslims. Was trade with the Muslims allowable? This was an important issue and a complicated one because several interests were involved. In the first place, there were the Christian Italian merchants who were engaged in such trade and had been for centuries. Canon law forbade trade in materials of war with the Muslims as enemies of Christendom but did not otherwise forbid trade with them. One reason for limiting the ban on trade with Muslims to war materials was the fact that many canonists had argued that all mankind was free to travel in peace everywhere. While this argument supported the Christian claim to possess the right to send missionaries everywhere, the canonists also applied it to merchants as well. Indeed, the refusal to allow peaceful missionaries or merchants into a society could justify the entry of Christian troops to protect the missionaries and merchants as they asserted their right. Consequently, in peacetime, trade with Muslims – and with other non-Christians – was permissible.

Innocent III not only resolved a number of the legal issues that the crusades had generated, he also widened the scope of the crusading movement itself. Until his pontificate, the crusade in the narrow legal sense had been proclaimed only to support campaigns against the Muslims in the Near East, that is against specific enemies of Christendom. In 1207, however, Innocent granted an indulgence to those who would wage war against the Albigensian heretics of southern France. Using a striking surgical image, Innocent noted that 'since wounds that do not respond to the healing of poultices must be lanced with a blade', peaceful means of reconciling the heretics having failed, the secular power in the person of the King of France should move against this nest of heretics and surgically remove them from the body of the Church. Those who engaged in this pious endeavour would be taken 'under the protection of Blessed Peter and ourselves' while in this service. Furthermore, the crusaders would receive rewards in this world and in the next because 'we wish all the goods of these heretics to be confiscated and made public property' and we 'grant the remission of sins' to the crusaders as well.[26]

The grant of crusading privileges to those engaged in wars against those whom the papacy saw as the enemies of Christendom both within and without became common in succeeding years. As James Brundage has pointed out:

> Under the technical guise of crusades, we find wars of aggression against the European rivals of the papacy, against the Hohenstaufen in southern Italy and Sicily, against rebellious barons in England and rebellious peasants in Germany, against heretics in Provence, pagans in Livonia, Moors in Spain, and domestic enemies in the Papal States ... .[27]

The crusade became a fundamental instrument of what R. I. Moore termed a 'persecuting society'.[28] It also became an important source of funds for the papacy in its search for revenues in the later Middle Ages. The funds generated by request to commute crusading vows were put to a number of uses other than their nominal purpose, the defence of Christendom.[29]

To a great extent, the decretals of Innocent III that concerned aspects of the crusade continued to determine the legal issues that arose, although the gradual decline of the crusading movement and the end of the crusader kingdoms with the fall of Acre in 1291 made the narrow legal issues less significant. The notion of crusade, both in a broad popular sense and also in the narrower legal meaning of the term remained of some interest to the canonists. Indeed, even as the crusaders were losing their last footholds in the Near East, the question of the legitimacy of the crusades emerged within the canonistic tradition. As we have seen, the canonists had not discussed the crusade in general terms, focusing instead on specific issues relating to crusading but not questioning the right of the Church to authorize these wars. In the mid-thirteenth century, however, one canonist did raise the issue of the crusades in fundamental terms. Sinibaldo Fieschi, better known as Pope Innocent IV (1243–54), perhaps the most brilliant canonist ever to serve as pope, compiled a commentary on the *Decretales* that included a discussion of the legitimacy of the crusades, specifically whether or not Christians actually possessed the right to seize the lands of the Muslims. The importance of this commentary lay not only in what it said about the legitimacy of the medieval crusades but in its later role in the debate about the legitimacy of the Spanish conquest of the Americas, sometimes seen as a crusade, and the subsequent development of international law.

Innocent IV raised the issue of the legitimacy of the crusades in a commentary on a decretal of Innocent III that concerned commuting the crusading vows of those who were unable or unfit to fulfil their vows.

In his commentary, Innocent IV accepted his predecessor's reasoning about the necessity of commuting some vows and provided only a brief discussion of the matter. Instead, Innocent IV focused his discussion of the vow on the fundamental issue of the right of Christians to invade and occupy the lands of the Muslims at all and the right of the pope to grant indulgences for those who went on crusade. Placing the crusade within the tradition of the just war, he observed that as the Muslims had seized the lands now held by the crusaders from their Christian inhabitants, presumably meaning the Byzantine Empire, the crusaders were only regaining possession of Christian lands lost in an unjust war of aggression. Furthermore, inasmuch as the Holy Land was the place where Christ lived and died, it held a special meaning for Christians and should not be in the hands of unbelievers. Innocent IV also employed several other arguments to justify Christian re-conquest and occupation of the Holy Land, but these generally adhered to the path that the canonists had been taking for a century.

What set Innocent IV's commentary on the vow apart was his broadening the discussion of the crusade to consider whether or not Christians had the right to seize all lands occupied by the Muslims anywhere, not just the formerly Christian lands in the Near East. His answer was that they did not, because Muslims, like all men everywhere, possessed a natural right to possess their lands and to govern themselves in peace. In the course of this discussion, Innocent IV traced the origins of mankind from its earliest days through the establishment of government and the creation of private property, stressing the natural basis for government and property. Thus, Christians had no right to seize lands that the Muslims had acquired legitimately, so there could be no crusade, no papally authorized armed pilgrimage to seize such lands.

Innocent IV did not stop his discussion of the rights of non-Christians at this point, a point that would have placed a clear limit on the pope's right to intervene in the affairs of non-Christian societies within and outside of Europe in order to punish evildoers and to protect innocent populations. He went on to observe that within Europe popes acting as the ultimate judges of what was true Judaism had ordered the burning of the Talmud because it contained teachings contrary to the Mosaic Law as these popes understood it. Moving from non-believers within Christian society to infidels beyond the bounds of Christendom, Innocent IV, having defended the right of infidels to their lands on the basis of natural law, thus protecting them from invasion, then argued that infidels were also bound to adhere to the terms of the natural law, because that law was accessible to all rational human beings. If a non-Christian ruler was acting in violation of the natural law, the pope could order a Christian ruler to punish or even to remove him if he refused to reform. Innocent IV did not, however, discuss in detail the specific violations of the natural law that would justify such intervention, although he did suggest that the worship of many gods instead of one God might justify intervention, a rule that, if followed, would authorize the Christian occupation of just about every known society.

Taken as a whole, Innocent IV's commentary on the vow moved from a discussion of the legitimacy of the crusade to a sketch of a Christian world order in which all mankind would be comprehended within one of three legal communities, Christian, Jewish and infidel, with the pope as the ultimate judge of each community. Given the model of the crusade, under the circumstances that Innocent IV outlined, the pope could authorize Christian rulers to enforce the terms of the natural law on infidel rulers who refused to adhere to them.[30]

Innocent IV's views about the legitimacy of the crusade and his conception of a Christian world order did not go unchallenged. His own student, Henry of Segusio (d. 1270), better known as Hostiensis, an important and widely cited canonist in his own right, directly challenged his master's views. Hostiensis asserted that with the coming of Christ, only Christians possessed the right to property and government. That being the case, Christians could in theory legitimately lay claim to the entire world, not just seek the return of Christian lands lost to the Muslims, although Hostiensis prudently rejected such a conclusion.

From the thirteenth to the sixteenth centuries, when canonists, philosophers and theologians discussed war between Christians and non-Christians, they did so in the terms that Innocent IV and Hostiensis had established. The opinion of Innocent IV prevailed, however, because Hostiensis's opinion that infidels had no right to property and government was seen as a revival of the ancient Donatist heresy. The Donatists, and later heretics such as John Wyclif (d. 1384) and John Hus (d. 1415), had argued that since the birth of Christ, legitimate possession of property and self-government rested on being in the state of grace so that only Christians could possess them. Critics of Hostiensis's position always pointed out this association with heretics in discussions about these rights.

Even after the end of the crusader kingdoms in the Holy Land, the nature of relations between Christendom and the non-Christian societies that bordered it continued to attract the attention of canonists. At the Council of Constance (1414–18), for example, representatives of the King of Poland and the Teutonic Knights battled for control of Lithuania in the language of Innocent IV and Hostiensis. Paulus Vladimiri, representing the king, denied the Knights' claim that the Lithuanians, being infidels, had no right to their lands so that their conquest by the Knights was a legitimate exercise of force. Vladimiri argued that the King of Poland did have legitimate possession of Lithuania, because his ancestors had acquired it according to the terms that Innocent IV had established.[31] This legal language also provided the framework for the great debate about the legitimacy of the conquest of the Americas that rocked the Spanish intellectual world in the sixteenth century.

Two points are worthy of special mention at this point. In the first place, it is clear that by the thirteenth century, the canonists had no hesitation about the legitimacy of war. Those who killed in the course of a properly authorized campaign were no longer required to confess their action and do penance. Indeed, the very act of soldiering and killing could entitle a man to a plenary indulgence that would guarantee his admission into heaven. At the same time, it is also worth noting that there was always some opposition to the crusade and there were critics who condemned the practice of calling crusades. This did not always mean that force should never be employed in Christian relations with non-Christian peoples, but missionary efforts should proceed in a peaceful manner whenever possible.

The loss of Acre in 1291 did not mean the end of calls for crusades to regain possession of the Holy Land. Popes continued to call for crusades to regain possession of Jerusalem, although the calls generally went unanswered. The fall of Constantinople in 1453 gave an added impetus to such calls, but even then there was no significant response. Pope Pius II (1458–64) not only called for a new crusade, he died on the way to lead it, an action that recalls Gregory VII's proposal to lead a crusade in person.

As Norman Housley pointed out, however, the 'key elements of crusading, vow, cross, and indulgence, remained features of European religious and public life' on into the sixteenth century, but they were not employed to liberate Jerusalem.[32] Following the lead of Innocent III, popes granted indulgences to those who fought in the internal European religious wars of the fifteenth and sixteenth centuries, beginning with the Hussite Wars in eastern Europe.[33] As he points out, some of the religious wars were, in Catholic terms, holy wars, wars in defence of the Church and the faithful but without an indulgence for those who fought. Others were, however, crusades in the narrow legal sense.

The most extensive application of the body of law that arose from the crusades came on a new frontier as the Portuguese and Spanish pushed out into the Atlantic in the fifteenth century. A series of papal bulls, over a hundred issued in the fifteenth century alone, asserted the right of these Christian nations to seize the islands and even the people of the Atlantic, the Canaries, the Azores, and so on, as well as land on the coast of Africa and, eventually, to occupy the Americas. Central to all of these bulls is the assumption that war will be necessary in order to achieve the goal of preaching the Gospel to the newly encountered peoples.

The series of papal bulls that Pope Alexander VI (1492–1503) issued to authorize the Spanish to occupy the Americas echoed the language of the crusade as well. The fundamental bull, *Inter caetera* (1493), opened with a forceful assertion of the responsibility of the respective rulers to ensure 'that barbarous nations be overthrown and brought to the faith itself'.[34] Alexander VI showed no reluctance to employ force not only in the defence of the Church but in its expansion as well. The pope saw in these new campaigns a continuation of the Spanish wars against the Muslims that had recently ended with the surrender of Granada to Ferdinand and Isabella. Indeed, as is well known, Columbus having an 'obsession with Jerusalem', saw the wealth of the New World as providing the economic basis for one last crusade that would liberate Jerusalem at last.[35] From Columbus's perspective, the way to Jerusalem was now by way of the New World.

In the long run, the placing of war and violence within a canonistic legal framework marked a significant moment in the history of Christianity. For the first time war and violence became positive goods, a means of salvation, when engaged in under specific legal circumstances. Perhaps it also signalled recognition that war and violence could not be eliminated from Christian society so the Church should find some way of legitimizing and directing the energies of the violent. Combat against the enemies of the faith under the direction of the pope, rewarded by lands in this world and salvation in the next, was one solution to violence within Christian Europe. By asserting the right to authorize and to lead crusades, popes and the canon lawyers reinforced the pope's position at the very apex of the hierarchical medieval political order. The crusade was a dramatic example of the papal conception of a Christian world order. In the course of the crusades, secular rulers at all levels, even the Holy Roman Emperor and the kings of Europe, served the pope, providing the strong material arm required to implement papal spiritual judgements. The law of the crusade could also justify an expansionist Christendom. If the pope was the judge of all mankind as Innocent IV argued and could condemn those who violated the natural law, then world rule was at least theoretically possible. In a curious way, the medieval canonists' conception of the crusade provided one of the intellectual bases for subsequent notions of a legally-based world order.

notes

1. On the laws of war generally, see M. H. Keen, *The Laws of War in the Later Middle Ages* (London, 1965).
2. S. Chodorow, *Christian Political Theory and Church Politics in the Mid-Twelfth Century: The Ecclesiology of Gratian's Decretum* (Berkeley, 1972), p. 7.
3. J. A. Brundage, *Medieval Canon Law and the Crusader* [henceforth cited as *Canon Law and the Crusader*] (Madison, 1969), pp. 189–90.
4. In addition to *Canon Law and the Crusader*, see also Brundage's *The Crusade, Holy War and Canon Law* (Aldershot, 1991) which reprints many of his articles on the topic. The other work is M. Villey, *La Croisade: essai sur la formation d'une théorie juridique* (Paris, 1942).
5. The origins of the *Decretum* are quite obscure: see J. A. Brundage, *Medieval Canon Law* (London, 1995) for a brief survey of the history and structure of the canon law. More recently A. Winroth in *The Making of Gratian's Decretum* (Cambridge, 2000) has challenged almost all of what has been believed about Gratian and the *Decretum*.
6. J. N. Figgis, *Political Thought From Gerson to Grotius 1414–1625* (New York, 1960), p. 5.
7. Brundage, *Medieval Canon Law*, pp. 54–6, 180–1.
8. F. H. Russell, *The Just War in the Middle Ages* (Cambridge, 1975), pp. 16, 56.
9. C. Erdmann, *Die Entstehung des Kreuzzugsgedankens* (Stuttgart, 1935), translated as *The Origin of the Idea of the Crusade*, trans. M. W. Baldwin and W. Goffart (Princeton, 1977), pp. 31–2.
10. On these peace movements, see *The Peace of God: Social Violence and Religious Response in France around the Year 1000*, ed. T. Head and R. Landes (Ithaca, NY, 1992).
11. T. Mastnak, *Crusading Peace: Christendom, the Muslim World, and Western Political Order* (Berkeley, 2002), pp. 43–4.
12. *The First Crusade: The Chronicle of Fulcher of Chartres and Other Source Material*, ed. E. Peters, 2nd edn (Philadelphia, 1998), p. 27.
13. Ibid., p. 28.
14. Brundage, *Canon Law and the Crusader*, p. 151.
15. *The First Crusade*, ed. Peters, p. 54.
16. Ibid., p. 48.
17. Ibid., p. 91.
18. Ibid., p. 37.
19. Brundage, *Canon Law and the Crusader*, pp. 11–15.
20. *The First Crusade*, ed. Peters, p. 239.
21. Brundage, *Canon Law and the Crusader*, p.15.
22. J. A. Brundage, 'The Votive Obligations of Crusaders: The Development of a Canonistic Doctrine', *Traditio*, 24 (1968), 77–118 at 77.
23. *The First Crusade*, ed. Peters, p. 27.
24. J. A. Brundage, 'The Crusader's Wife: a Canonistic Quandary', *Studia Gratiana*, 12 (1967), 427–41 at 435.
25. J. Muldoon, 'Missionaries and the Marriages of Infidels: The Case of the Mongol Mission', *The Jurist*, 35 (1975), 125–41 at 129.
26. *The Crusades: Idea and Reality, 1095–1274*, ed. L. and J. Riley-Smith (London, 1981), p. 80.

27. Brundage, *Canon Law and the Crusader*, p. 136.
28. R. I. Moore, *The Formation of a Persecuting Society: Power and Deviance in Western Europe, 950–1250* (Oxford, 1987).
29. Brundage, *Canon Law and the Crusader*, pp. 136–7.
30. J. Muldoon, *Popes, Lawyers, and Infidels: The Church and the Non-Christian World 1250–1550* (Philadelphia, 1979), pp. 5–15.
31. F. H. Russell, 'Paulus Vladimiri's Attack on the Just War: A Case Study in Legal Polemics', in *Authority and Power: Studies on Medieval Law and Government*, ed. B. Tierney and P. Linehan (Cambridge, 1980), pp. 237–54.
32. N. Housley, *Religious Warfare in Europe, 1400–1536* (Oxford, 2002), p. 12.
33. Ibid., p. 58.
34. F. Gardiner Davenport, *European Treaties bearing on the History of the United States and its Dependencies to 1648* (Washington, DC, 1917), p. 61.
35. F. Fernández-Armesto, *Columbus* (Oxford, 1991), p. 109.

3
crusading warfare
john france

In recent years much attention has been devoted to the military history of the crusades. This recent research, however, has highlighted the problems posed by the source material, problems that earlier researchers were often unaware of or simply overlooked. Contemporary chronicles record war, but explain very little about it. This means that a great volume of sources, western and Oriental, has to be examined and consideration has to be given to record evidence, letters, artefacts, inscriptions and archaeological remains. The volume of material is the greater because crusading was always very diverse and involved theatres of operation in northern and eastern Europe as well as the Eastern Mediterranean. Part of the fascination of the crusades in the Eastern Mediterranean is the contrasting styles of war which clashed in the Middle East. Given the diversity of the subject, students approaching crusading warfare should familiarize themselves not only with the historiography but also with the serious problems which face researchers in this area, and hence this chapter offers a multifaceted approach. In the first section there is a survey of recent work on crusading warfare. The second section discusses the problems posed by the source material. In the third section an effort is made to explain why styles of war were so very different. The concluding section seeks to analyse the military problems of the crusades, as military campaigns in distant and strange lands and those of the Europeans who settled in the Holy Land.

recent writing on crusading warfare

In recent years medieval warfare has become a very popular field of study and a number of general works give some coverage of crusading warfare and set it in its European context, notably those of France,

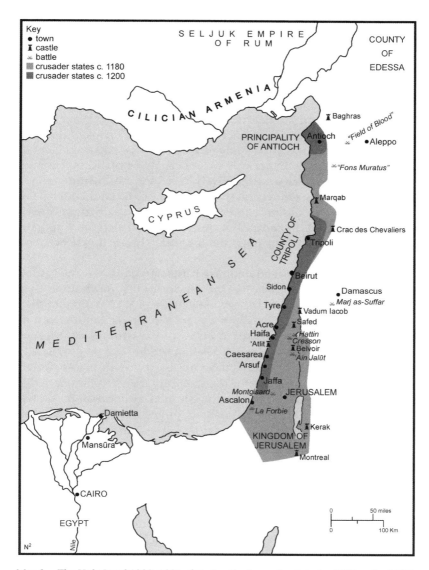

Map 2. The Holy Land 1098–1291, showing the 'crusader states' c. 1180 and c. 1200.

Nicholson and Verbruggen.[1] The best introduction to crusading warfare is by Smail, now extended to 1291 by Marshall, and there is a useful summary by Edbury. Crusading in the later Middle Ages, once neglected, has recently excited much interest and there is an excellent study of its warfare by Housley.[2]

Some studies of individual crusades have a military focus, notably those by Asbridge and France for the First Crusade. Queller produced the most authoritative account of the Fourth Crusade, and this has been usefully supplemented by Madden's work on Venice. Powell's book of the Fifth Crusade is perhaps the finest study of a single crusade. The crusades of Frederick II and St Louis are very well covered in notable biographies by van Cleve and Richard respectively.[3] Studies of the Third Crusade have focused almost entirely on the personality of Richard I of England (1189–99) and this has produced a lively controversy with Prestwich portraying Richard, in contrast to other Angevin rulers, as a militant king and Gillingham suggesting that his father, Henry II, was every bit as great a soldier.[4]

There are some very useful studies of particular campaigns and battles. Asbridge has analysed the defeat of the principality of Antioch at the 'Field of Blood' in 1119. In 1148 the Second Crusade first besieged and then withdrew from Damascus. Our sources are very cryptic on the reasons for the attack and hint at dark motives for the withdrawal. Modern historians have criticized the initial decision because Damascus generally was friendly to Jerusalem, but Hoch has suggested that the precariousness of the Damascus regime made the decision to attack a sensible one, while Forey pointed to good reasons for the eventual withdrawal. Barber has given us an insight into the real military problems of Jerusalem in the struggle with Saladin in an important study of the campaign on the frontier with Damascus which led to the fall of the castle at Jacob's Ford in 1179, while Kedar has produced the best account of Hattin. For the decisive battle at Nicopolis the finest study remains that of Atiya.[5]

One of the most important aspects of warfare in the crusader states was the development of fortifications and siege warfare. The nature and purpose of castles in Europe has recently become very controversial, with writers such as Coulson arguing that castles were much more than bunkers, and that indeed in many cases military concerns were barely discernible as reasons for their construction. These ideas have made a considerable impact upon studies of crusader castles, especially as we have begun to learn much more from archaeology. The key study is that of Pringle on the 'Red Tower' which inclines us to see crusader castles as primarily structures arising from the European institution of lordship which the Europeans imported into the Holy Land. However, it is undeniable that crusader castles had a real military purpose even when they served other functions. Ellenblum has shown that Belvoir, built 1168–70, was a true concentric castle in that the inner castle was built in a way which allowed its garrison to support the defenders of the outer castle. This remarkable structure anticipated the concentric castles of Europe which are associated with Edward I of England (1272–1307) and heralded a new wave of fortress-building as the kingdom faced a graver threat from Islam. At about the same time Kerak, in the exposed area east of the Dead Sea, was strengthened, and shortly after Belmont near Jerusalem, while a mighty new fortress was begun at Jacob's Ford (Vadum Iacob), but destroyed by Saladin in 1179 before it was completed. In the thirteenth century the crusaders were largely content to stand on the defensive, and it was then that the mighty fortresses of Crac des Chevaliers and Marqab reached their ultimate development. Kennedy has produced a remarkable overview of the subject, taking into account recent work and considering the castles of the thirteenth century and Islamic fortifications. There is an excellent treatment of the siege-warfare of the Latin East by Rogers.[6]

The Latins of the East were entirely dependent on the sea-power of the Italian city-states for their communications with Europe, but, curiously, there has never been a specific study of naval warfare during the crusades. Pryor's study of the maritime history of the Mediterranean is very significant and this author has also written a number of important specialist studies. He has suggested that the one Islamic power with a fleet, Egypt, found it difficult to fight the westerners because the Egyptians had not developed wooden casks to carry water. They still relied on heavy earthenware jars which were much more difficult to fill at stops along the coast, and had a much greater empty weight which meant they could store less, and this limited their range. Rose includes a chapter on maritime crusading war in her general book on medieval naval warfare. Saladin attempted to break the naval stranglehold of the Italian cities, but by his time Egyptian naval power had declined beyond recovery because he seems to have found it difficult to recruit good sailors.[7]

The authoritative work on the weapons and armour of the crusaders and their enemies is contained in Nicolle's remarkably comprehensive study which covers the period 1050–1350.[8] The essays in Parry and Yapp's volume provide an excellent introduction to the variety of military methods in Islam, while Y. Lev is useful for the Fatimids, Gibb for the Ayyūbids and Humphreys for the Mamluks. Bowlus has provided a very useful insight into the limitations of horse-archers as instruments of war

which has great importance for our understanding of the effectiveness
of Islamic armies. There has been a lively debate over the nature of the
Turcopoles who are often mentioned as an element in Frankish armies.
The term is of Byzantine origin meaning soldiers who were the sons of
mixed marriages between Turks and Christians. It is generally agreed that
they were light cavalry, as Harari has shown, but his suggestion that they
were actually Franks has not met with general agreement and Savvides
has argued that they were native light horse hired by the crusaders. The
evidence is very ambivalent, but in any case, as France has shown, the
use of *Turcopoles* represented one of many adaptations of their military
methods made by the Franks to meet conditions in the East.[9]

Ellenblum's recent archaeological work shows that Frankish settlement
in the countryside of Jerusalem was more intensive than we have tended to
think, and that it was closely associated with native Christian settlements.
This evidence that native Christians were friendly and prepared to work
with the Latins offers a possible explanation for the otherwise curious
fact that the Latins managed to raise an army of 20,000 for the battle of
Hattin, a figure greatly in excess of contemporary armies in Europe.[10]

the sources for the study of crusading warfare

To understand crusading warfare it is necessary to understand the
shortcomings of the western sources and to make some headway in
grasping Islamic material also, because the ways in which their enemies
lived and fought influenced the crusaders. There were actually interesting
parallels between the crusaders and their enemies, in that Islam was
dominated by a small and alien elite, the Turks, whose lifestyle resembled
that of the similarly tiny elite who ruled Europe and the crusader states.
But such similarities should not be allowed to obscure the different ways
in which their societies were organized or the very different ways in
which they fought.

We can gain an insight into the mentality of the elite who dominated
European society through the *chansons de geste*. These poems, of which
the most famous is the *Chanson de Roland*, reveal a delight in war and
its blunt methods and stratagems. In *The Song of William of Orange* the
mayhem of war is vividly portrayed, and there is a certain admiration
for the low cunning required, as shown by what may be a reference to
a particular tactic in the clash of arms: 'Rainouart was both valiant and
wise. He made a circle round [his enemy in battle] in the French style,
and struck him such a blow on the back of his neck that his eyes started
from his head, and threw him down dead.'[11] Such attitudes did have

an influence upon the writing of sources for the crusades. The *Gesta Francorum et aliorum Hierosolimitanorum* is an anonymous work which may have been written by a layman, a knight from South Italy who travelled with Bohemond. Quite in the style of the *chansons* the author lauds his hero, 'the valiant Bohemond', rejoices in the bravery of his companions, and even complements his enemies: 'What man, however experienced and learned, could dare to write of the skill, prowess and courage of the Turks.'[12] But this was not the dominant influence on the writing of western accounts. The process of writing was largely in the hands of clergy whose attitudes tend to dominate contemporary historical writing. Moreover, this clerical elite was often writing to an agenda which has to be discerned if we are to reach an understanding of events.

Amongst the sources for the First Crusade there are a few very valuable letters written during the crusade which reveal strictly contemporary attitudes.[13] However, all our narrative accounts date from after the capture of Jerusalem in 1099. This staggering event made an enormous impression upon the peoples of Europe. Even the *Gesta Francorum*, which was written by 1105 at the latest, conforms to this pattern. It is perhaps the story of a simple knight at some level, but as we have it the text displays a keen awareness of God's agency. Clerical writers developed this emphasis enormously. Raymond of Aguilers went on the crusade as the chaplain of the count of Toulouse, but used the *Gesta Francorum*. He wrote in order to present the 'Holy Lance', discovered at Antioch, as the great manifestation of God's will.[14] Fulcher of Chartres, another eyewitness, also made use of the *Gesta Francorum*; he was deeply anxious to portray events as God's work and to protect the reputation of Godfrey de Bouillon and other members of the house of Boulogne which he served.[15] A generation later Guibert of Nogent, appalled by its rustic style, rewrote it as his *Gesta Dei per Francos*, but this entailed only a minimal rearrangement of the material which remained clearly the Anonymous's work.[16] As a result of the reflections of these and other writers, the emphasis of the works is spiritual and simply misses much about military matters. Godfrey de Bouillon played a limited part on the crusade, but he became the first ruler of Jerusalem and was virtually sanctified by the time that Robert of Rheims portrayed him as 'a monk at prayer rather than a soldier'.[17] The clerical chronicles routinely tell us that the 'army of God' was outnumbered by its enemies and ascribe vast numbers to the forces of Islam, in order to emphasize that this was God's work. In the same vein the fortifications of eastern cities and fortresses were magnified to such an extent that it has long been assumed that they must have been the inspiration for the later builders of western castles. Such spiritualizing of the First Crusade tended to portray it less as a military campaign and more as a religious exercise to invoke God's grace.

In addition, all these numerous writers who used the *Gesta Francorum* reproduce its gaps, notably the complete absence of any record of events between early April and late May 1098.[18] Albert of Aachen's work (written in the Rhineland) was independent of the *Gesta* tradition. He was not an eyewitness, but he may have written as early as 1102, using the eyewitness accounts of returning crusaders. His account is particularly interesting because it is full of military detail, and contains the best account of the siege of Jerusalem.[19] It is interesting that both the Anonymous and Albert report what were clearly stories circulating in the crusader camp and these found their way into the vernacular tradition in the *Chanson d'Antioche* which, in its present form, is a late twelfth-century 'Song of the Crusade'.[20]

The First Crusade was the focus of thinking about the nature of crusading. It was the model from which all later definition and practice, such as that of Innocent III (1198–1216) proceeded. But the disasters which crusading met in the twelfth and thirteenth centuries, culminating in the fall of Acre in 1291, generated another kind of literature, some of it critical, if not of the crusade itself then of the means by which it was achieved. To a degree this was about military matters. Odo of Deuil wrote a history of the Second Crusade in which he participated. But he was also concerned to explain the problems the French army faced and to set out lessons. Thus he urged that large numbers of non-combatants should not be allowed to accompany the army as they were a hindrance; crusading, he argued, was a matter for the committed soldier who had the means to sustain himself. He particularly urged that attention be paid to problems of supply and logistics which dogged the Second Crusade. The disasters of 1187 led Ralph Niger to question whether God wanted His people to labour for the liberation of Jerusalem, but such radical questioning was unusual. The failure of the thirteenth-century crusades led to bitter criticism of the papacy and the various methods it adopted to foster the liberation of Jerusalem, and this came to a head at the Council of Lyons in 1274. By that time the papacy was clearly wedded firmly to the traditional strategy of attacking Islam through Byzantium, and was prepared to achieve this by friendship or conquest of the ancient empire, but this was vitiated by developments in Mediterranean politics.[21] After the fall of Acre a series of strategic analyses were produced to suggest how the situation might be recovered. This was not entirely new. Richard I of England seems to have urged the crusade to attack Egypt which was the centre of power of Saladin's family, the Ayyūbids, and subsequent crusades took this as their objective, but there was no writing upon strategy at that time. Of the plans called forth by the disaster of 1291, Pierre Dubois's is the best known, but that of Sanudo was perhaps the most impressive. He was a Venetian of a family which ruled many of the Aegean islands, and his highly practical plan drew on his naval experience and knowledge of the Eastern Mediterranean.[22] There was much to be said for these strategic plans, but they floundered on the costs of achieving them and the outbreak of difficult political conditions in Europe, notably the Hundred Years War after 1337, which absorbed the finances and energies of rulers.

The history of the European settlers in the Holy Lands, the Latins, was begun by Albert of Aachen who carried the story down to 1119, and Fulcher of Chartres whose last events are for 1127.[23] Both were well-informed about military events, although Fulcher, as a loyal servant of the house of Jerusalem, was very careful to present their deeds in the most favourable light. The parallel account for Antioch is Walter the Chancellor's *The Antiochene Wars* which has a vivid account of the battle of the Field of Blood at which the Antiochenes were decisively defeated in 1119.[24] The most important history of events in the Holy Land for the twelfth century is the work of William of Tyre, a native of the Latin East, who died in 1184/85.[25] He was deeply interested in military matters and often provides fascinating detail, but he was also a party to the factional struggles of the 1170s and 1180s and this colours his account markedly. The destruction of the kingdom at the battle of Hattin in 1187 was a major military event, but our knowledge of how and why it happened is obscured by the savage partisanship which accompanies every account. At the time of the battle King Guy was bitterly hated by a substantial group of his nobles, and after Hattin the survivors of both parties were anxious to blame their enemies for the disaster.[26] Thereafter the history of the Latin East is primarily recorded in Old French continuations of William of Tyre's work, which reflect tensions and troubles in the divided rump of the Latin Kingdom. The plethora of narratives of individual crusades reflects the rising literary output of thirteenth century Europe and the intense interest in the crusade to the eastern Mediterranean. In addition the numerous western chroniclers reported events in the East, though they are not always well-informed. With exceptions, such as the crusade of Theobald of Champagne (1239–41), there is a substantial body of material to provide a good knowledge of the military events of the period down to the capture of Acre by the Mamluks in 1291. In addition, the involvement of kingdoms in crusading has provided record sources so that we can cost, for example, the crusade of St Louis.[27]

It is the centrality of crusades and crusading to European medieval history that creates problems for the historian. Understanding the crusade does not depend upon mastering a specific range of localized material, like the sources for English constitutional history, but on perceptive use of an enormous range of different sources of different kinds. To understand crusading warfare the historian must explore all this material, and look at other sources bearing upon the nature of war. In addition it is important to see what Wellington called 'the other side of the hill': Islamic warfare and, therefore, Islamic sources.

These pose very substantial problems for the historian of the crusades. Ultimately Islam 'won' in the sense that Acre fell in 1291. The conflict between Christianity and Islam soon after assumed a new form created by Ottoman expansionism from the fourteenth century onwards which is well chronicled in both West and East. However, sources for the earlier period are rather scanty. Islamic writers seem to have preferred not to recall the painful events of 1095–99 and some of those that do, like the *Damascus Chronicle of the Crusades*, reflect a very local viewpoint.[28] One very valuable source for warfare is the book of memoirs written by Usama, a member of the ruling house of Shaizar, who provides a vivid picture of war against the crusaders in the twelfth century.[29] Usama was interested in the westerners and their doings, and because he was a Shi'ite, he did not overly emphasize the religious aspects of the fighting against them. Indeed in some respects he quite admired them. Quite different were the later Arab chroniclers who wrote in the thirteenth century when the spirit of *jihād* against the invaders was well and truly established. At the time of the First Crusade *jihād* barely existed in the Muslim world and it only revived slowly.[30] Saladin was at pains to embody the spirit of *jihād* and this is reflected in a whole corpus of writing produced by writers associated with him, such as Ibn al-Athir, and after that it became a truism.[31] In the age of the Mamluk Sultans who took over Egypt and dominated much of Syria in the thirteenth and fourteenth centuries the crusaders faded as a threat and the Mongols were infinitely more dangerous and, therefore, commanded more attention. However, the Mamluks were always at pains to present themselves as the upholders of *jihād*.

Mamluk Egypt produced many manuals of war for instruction in their special mounted exercises, known as *furusiyya*. These exercises became highly formalized in the later Middle Ages, but the manuals often reflect earlier conditions and in some cases may be based on older books. It is unfortunate that the very important *Nihayat al-Sul*, written c. 1371, has not been published; but some of these works are known and have been translated.[32] The Arab sources for the crusades are at least as diverse as those of the West but they have been much less studied and published; and this, together with western ignorance of Arabic, has inhibited writing about the crusades from an Arab standpoint. Perhaps the best examination of the variety of material, including such media as inscriptions and ceramics, is that presented by Carole Hillenbrand in a truly ground-breaking book.[33] The Islamic literary sources focus a good deal on the conduct of war, and though descriptions of battle are sometimes flowery and conventionalized, they contain much useful material. One very valuable composition appears to be an account of the Cairo armoury at the time of Saladin, which contains our first clear reference to a counterweight trebuchet.[34]

It is often forgotten that there were others besides the Europeans and the Muslims involved in the fighting in the Middle East in the age of the crusades. Armenians played an especially important role in the thirteenth century when their kingdom of Cilicia became a major force.[35] They were particularly important as castle-builders, but their armies are not well-known, though there is some information for the twelfth century in the work of Matthew of Edessa, whose work suggests that the Armenians were primarily horse-archers. In Cilicia they built remarkable fortresses from which they controlled the plains which stretch towards the Mediterranean, and archaeology has now revealed how magnificent they were as well as suggesting that they may have influenced the crusaders.[36] Even less known are the forces of the other Christian inhabitants of the Middle East, who tend to be described by crusader sources as Syrians, and in this respect the work of Michael the Syrian, Jacobite Patriarch of Antioch (1166–99), has some value and suggests that they were primarily foot-archers.[37] It is a pity we know so little about their methods of making war because, as we have seen, recent archaeological work suggests that they played a more important role in the crusader kingdom of Jerusalem and may well have provided soldiers for its rulers.[38]

Those who are interested in crusading warfare need, therefore, to consider a substantial and highly differentiated range of evidence. But to appreciate the ways in which the Latins and the crusaders made war we need to consider even wider evidence about how their very different styles of warfare emerged and changed in the clash of arms. European evidence is remarkably oblique. European chronicles are full of war, but it is not often that they say much about its techniques, methods and logistics. This was not simply because the writers were usually clerics, for they were not removed from the secular world. Indeed, a writer like Gilbert of Mons, who was chancellor to Baldwin of Hainaut, was very much involved in war and politics.[39] His account of twelfth-century warfare was, however, unusually explicit. For the most part writers made assumptions about what their audiences knew, particularly about the infrastructure of war. Alas we are not always party to such assumptions!

styles of war

the western style of war

European state structures were weak and depended on subsistence agriculture. Standing armies, except for the small personal followings gathered around kings and lords, could not be afforded.[40] The powerful built castles to control the peasantry and equipped themselves and small groups of retainers with horses, armour, swords and lances in the style of what we call knights. They were well-trained to fight on horse or foot. Some held land in return for service, but others were swords for hire for whom a military career offered prospects. Gilbert of Mons shows us poor knights coming to fight for the count of Hainaut when his lands were invaded in 1184, and asking only rations in return – they doubtless hoped for loot and ransoms.[41] For European war was rarely *guerre à l'outrance*. For the most part it consisted of local raiding for limited objectives.[42] The pattern of castles accentuated this. Ravaging and plundering weakened the enemy's resistance and capturing his soldiers was a useful means of extracting wealth. Suger complained that King Louis VI was handicapped in his war with Henry I of England by his inability to pay ransoms for captured knights.[43] In the shifting pattern of small and loosely organized political units, they might find themselves fighting relatives, or this year in alliance with last year's enemies. In such circumstances the leaders of society were disposed to be merciful to those whom they captured, if only because they themselves might be victims on another occasion, and this was the basis of 'chivalric' behaviour which became elaborated into the laws of war in the later Middle Ages.[44] Foot-soldiers, however, were often massacred if they found themselves on the losing side; and even amongst the leaders, merciless war, like that waged by Frederick I against the cities of the Lombard plain, was not unknown, while civil wars could be savage.[45] The knights were an armed elite who could be raised quickly for the kind of local warfare characteristic of a decentralised society, and they were mounted and therefore mobile. Europe lacks vast plains where ponies can be easily grazed, so that the focus of horse-raising was stall-feeding to produce larger animals which could bear heavily equipped men.

Because climate, geography and topography in western Europe often favoured infantry, the elite were accompanied to war by foot-soldiers, humbler men prepared to take the risks of war, amongst whom were *sergeants*, who held petty lands of lords in return for military service. Infantry were mostly spearmen and archers, sometimes supplemented by mercenaries, who became increasingly popular and important in the armies of the twelfth century, and by crossbowmen.[46] Mobility gave cavalry the initiative in war but they were not necessarily the decisive arm.

Large armies were made up of separate retinues of cavalry and footmen and so lacked cohesion. Since, as Suger remarked, 'the outcome of battle is an uncertain thing', this was an added disincentive to risk battle.[47] Moreover, the ethos of war was overwhelmingly individual because personal prowess counted for more than tactical ability or logistic skill in small-scale encounters, and pride of birth was resistant to discipline.[48] Also armies were so expensive to maintain that they were dispersed as soon as possible, which added to their incoherence. Even sieges raised organizational problems. The need for hand-to-hand fighting favoured the besieged, and protracted operations meant the besiegers needed equipment and regular supply.[49] Therefore the staple of war was ravaging to destroy the enemy's economic base. It was widely understood that in battle, close formation, in which knights or foot-soldiers could support one another, was desirable – it was simply difficult to achieve on the basis of incoherent forces whose members were not used to working with one another. As a result, when it did come to battle, western armies tended to eschew manoeuvre and, as quickly as possible, close with the enemy.

the warfare of the middle east

Cities, with a flourishing money-economy, dominated the Middle East. The Seljuk Sultanate of Baghdad and the Fatimid Caliphate of Cairo were centralized and their rulers depended on ministries, *Diwans*, which collected and spent revenues centrally.[50] Nizam al-Mulk's *Book of Government* records much about the support of armies in Syria at the end of the eleventh century.[51] Standing forces were larger than in the West, but represented only the cores of armies that, as in Europe, were *ad hoc* gatherings. Once the acute fragmentation which afflicted Syria, Palestine and Egypt was brought to an end under Saladin, large armies became possible, like the 30,000 gathered for the campaign of 1187 in which he destroyed the kingdom of Jerusalem. But he had difficulty holding together his composite forces even though he made constant efforts to infuse them with the spirit of *jihād*.[52] The make-up of Islamic armies was different from those of the westerners. Infantry were much less important because they could be isolated and cut off from water in the arid lands of the Middle East, and light cavalry, whose horses could easily be raised in the arid plains, were vital. From the ninth century, Turkish mounted archers, recruited from the Steppe, were prominent in Islamic armies and from the mid-eleventh century they took over political control of much of the Middle East and extended it to Egypt in the twelfth century. Their mounted archers were highly effective with both mobility and the ability to strike from a distance. They were not the only horse-archers in the area. Fatimid Egypt employed Armenians in this role and used Bedouin and other Arab tribes as light cavalry, though the core of its army was formed by heavy cavalry and excellent infantry recruited from the Sudan.[53] But the Turks were the best light cavalry, while the heavy cavalry became more important in the course of the wars against the crusaders in the twelfth century. Saladin's *ghulams* were never as heavily equipped as the best of the crusader knights, but they were not very different. In 1250 the Circassian and Turkish 'slave-soldiers' or Mamluks in Egypt slew Saladin's descendant, Turanshah, and set up the Mamluk regime which created a standing army based on well-armoured and equipped cavalry. They were able to fight off the Mongol onslaught, and in 1291 captured Acre, extinguishing the crusader states.[54]

Tactically, Islamic commanders used mounted archers to encircle and thus shake the resolve of an enemy and thin their ranks, destroying isolated individuals or groups to open gaps in enemy formations. Victory against any resolute enemy depended on charging home, but the Muslim style of war, in contrast to that of the West, allowed for considerable manoeuvre in the approach to battle.

the military problems of the crusades and the settlers in the latin east

Divided command dogged almost all crusades. The First Crusade was a collection of five major armies and many lesser forces run by a committee of leaders. On the Second (1147–49) Louis VII of France (1137–80) and Conrad III of Germany (1138–52) did not meet until the German army had been defeated in Asia Minor. On the Third, Richard I of England (1189–99) and Philip II of France (1180–1223) bickered, and after Philip's departure Richard quarrelled with other leaders. Venice commandeered the Fourth Crusade (1202–04). On the Fifth (1217–21), crusaders came and went so frequently that military decisions were made by the papal legate.[55] Only the crusades of Frederick II and Louis IX of France (1228–29,

1248–54, 1270) had a single leader. Differences between the leaders of the French and Hungarian contingents and the arrogance of the French cavalry all contributed to the defeat at Nicopolis in 1396.[56]

The problem was that crusader leaders, raised in the chivalric code of individual valour, were reluctant to accept subordination to any single person. This did not improve the coherence of crusading forces which suffered from all the general weaknesses of medieval European armies. In the case of the First Crusade, good leadership, good luck and the divisions of its enemies enabled it to survive to the point where it became an efficient fighting force.[57] The siege of Nicaea, 14 May to 19 June 1097, placed no special strains on the collective leadership. An ill-judged Turkish relief effort on 16 May was repelled easily because the lightly-armed enemy attacked in a confined space. The sheer number of the crusaders, about 50–60,000 strong, enabled them to brush aside the Turks of Asia Minor at Dorylaeum on 1 July. However, on this occasion a western knight recorded his surprise at the tactics of the enemy army: 'Our men could not understand whence could have come such a great multitude of Turks, Arabs, Saracens and other peoples whose names I do not know.'[58] During the siege of Antioch, 21 October 1097 to 3 June 1098, they slowly extended their siege in an effort to strangle the city. With the aid of a fleet and food from the Byzantines on Cyprus and the Armenians in the mountains they managed to supply their army, though in early 1098 they almost starved to death. In battle they learned the value of solidity of formation, of guarding their flanks, and of establishing a rearguard against the Turkish tactics of encirclement. On 2 February 1098, under threat from an Aleppan army, they chose Bohemond as sole commander and he led a successful ambush of the enemy army. After the capture of Antioch, Bohemond claimed the city. This caused dissension amongst the leaders and eventually a relatively small army of about 12,000 marched south and captured Jerusalem from Fatimid Egypt in July 1099. The Fatimids had been taken by surprise because they regarded the crusaders as allies against the Seljuk Turks. They concentrated a great force at Ascalon. The crusaders marched towards them adopting a formation in which each squadron of cavalry was protected by footmen. This complex formation was only possible because they had become a disciplined force, and this was the reason for their triumph at the battle of Ascalon.[59]

Of later crusades, the Third was together long enough during the siege of Acre to become a formidable force capable of defeating Saladin.[60] That of Louis IX was entirely French and unusually homogeneous, but its commander was fatally flawed.[61] On the Second Crusade Louis VII's vanguard abandoned the main force, leaving it open to Turkish attack in the mountains of southern Anatolia while the crusading fleet had attacked Lisbon, delaying its arrival in the Holy Land.[62] Crusades to the Eastern Mediterranean remained wedded to western methods of war throughout their relatively short lives, though their commanders understood the need for solid formations to counter the enveloping tactics of the Turks.

Because there was no 'land-bridge' to Europe, the condition of survival for the European settlers in the Holy Land was the naval supremacy of the Italian cities. Their fleets helped to supply the First Crusade. Egypt, the only Islamic naval power in the Mediterranean, attacked a crusader fleet at Jaffa during the First Crusade.[63] However, factionalism weakened the Fatimid state in the twelfth century and by 1174 Saladin had reunited it with Syria. The Italian cities received privileged quarters in the crusader cities that served as bases for trade. This stimulated their maritime power and helped to sustain their naval supremacy, enhanced when Richard I of England conquered Cyprus in 1191.[64] The only serious Islamic challenge before the Ottomans was mounted unsuccessfully by Saladin.[65] This acquiescence in European naval supremacy was not due to technical factors, because Islam enjoyed a flourishing trade with the Far East. Perhaps this promoted disinterest in trade with Europe. Moreover, the Europeans interfered very little with the Islamic trade routes across the southern Mediterranean. Above all, Islam defeated the crusaders on land, negating the need to revive naval power.

The most important military problem of the settlers was that they were few. The Kingdom of Jerusalem contained about 120,000 westerners and perhaps the same number lived in the other principalities.[66] The plethora of castles which they created were the consequence of the seigneural structure of their society. Fortified cities anchored the crusader states just as they anchored the Islamic states. However, under Islamic pressure a new wave of building and refortifying of castles was launched after 1160 which represented an adaptation of castle design to the circumstances of war in the East (see above, pp. 60–1).

Siege warfare was vital to the settlers in the twelfth century because they needed to capture the well-fortified Levantine ports. Siege warfare demanded machinery, but the westerners enjoyed no technical advantages over Islam and, indeed, never mastered 'Greek fire'. What is striking about crusader sieges is their persistence and organization. The Franks prepared carefully, with a Venetian alliance, for the siege of Tyre in 1124. Once the siege had begun the army of the kingdom had to dig fortifications against a relief force as well as to create a strong camp from which machines and attacks could be launched against the city. A similarly massive preparation brought the long siege of Ascalon, from January to August 1153, to a successful conclusion.[67]

The key tactical adaptations of the Franks to the conditions of war in the East were readiness for battle and the employment of massed cavalry charges as a battle-winning tactic.[68] This was more than a matter of having big horses and heavier army. The First Crusade had encountered well-armoured Islamic heavy horse. Rather, it was a willingness to take the battle to the enemy at all costs, springing from a particular mind-set and combination of circumstances. The Franks were a minority whose existence depended on a psychological supremacy. Usama refers to their caution, but overall their hallmark was aggression. In 1119, Roger Prince of Antioch and his army were trapped when Il-ghazi's larger army infiltrated the mountains and passes around the plain in which he had encamped on his way to relieve the siege of al-Atharib. Roger chose the option of attack, and suffered heavy defeat. In 1149 Raymond of Antioch challenged the power of Nūr al-Dīn only to go down to total defeat at *Fons Muratus*. At the Spring of the Cresson on 1 May 1187 about 140 Templars and Hospitallers attacked 7000 of their enemies. These were defeats, but in 1177 Baldwin IV took the enormous risk of confronting Saladin and won at Montgisard.[69] The settlers were constantly at war and so gained experience in fighting together. As a result the armies of the crusader states were more disciplined and coherent than those of the West. In the face of a more mobile enemy their cohesiveness enabled them to employ their magnificent horses in what Muslim sources call their 'famous charge'. This sudden, disciplined onslaught had to be timed precisely if it was to be successful, as at Marj as-Suffar on 25 January 1126. In all conditions this posed a severe threat to Islamic armies which were forced to avoid presenting a suitable target. In Europe, cavalry was not disciplined enough to risk a mass charge, a tactic which only evolved there in the thirteenth century. Another indication of their discipline was the fighting march. Frankish forces in certain circumstances refused to confront their enemies when they met them in the field but formed into column of march which fought off the enemy in a kind of mobile siege. This could only have been achieved by disciplined and coherent forces.[70] The highly disciplined military orders – the Templars, Hospitallers and Teutonic Order – enhanced their strength.

The Kingdom of Jerusalem continued to exist until 1291, because the Third Crusade restored it as a coastal strip centred on Acre.[71] However, it was always heavily dependent upon outside aid. The military culture of this period was dominated by the need to defend a few well-fortified cities, notably Acre, Tripoli and Antioch and some remarkable castles, notably

Marqab, Crac des Chevaliers, 'Atlit and Arsuf. The Franks could no longer challenge the Muslim powers in the open field and so sought to extend their influence by raids, consolidated by new fortresses and agreements with neighbours. The quarrels of the Ayyūbid family offered the prospect of a reconquest, but the kingdom was not strong enough on its own to profit. In 1229 Frederick II negotiated a restoration of the kingdom and a ten-year truce, but he was an absentee king whose despotic ideas divided the kingdom which was unable to solidify its control.[72] At the battle of La Forbie in 1244 the army of the kingdom tried to exploit quarrels between its Muslim powers, but was catastrophically defeated by the Ayyūbids of Egypt. Thereafter the kingdom became totally dependent on crusades from the West, and when they failed to arrive after the departure of Louis IX in 1254 it dissolved into factional squabbles and fell to the superior military power of the Mamluks in 1291.[73]

conclusion

In a military sense the crusades were an extension of the military culture of western Europe into the Middle East. To understand their successes and failures it is necessary to examine a wide range of sources for the period after 1095 and to set them in the context of the development of war in Europe. In addition there is an obvious need to understand the military culture of the Islamic Middle East. Nor should it be forgotten that the crusades took place in a theatre of diplomacy. It is often said that the First Crusade only succeeded because Islam was divided, as if this were a chance conjunction of events, but the crusaders were there because Alexius I Comnenus (1080–1118) had asked them to come. A wider appreciation of the diplomatic context is now emerging, but a diplomatic history of the crusades has yet to be written.[74] The crusade was also a universal instrument for the extension of papal authority and its military institutions were broadcast all over Europe. In particular the military religious orders were widely imitated, and in Spain and the Baltic provided nuclei for crusading thrusts. Crusading was therefore a part of European warfare, which produced adaptations to local circumstances. These were most extensive and manifest in the Eastern Mediterranean but happened elsewhere. The evidence indicates that European military leaders, faced with conditions which produced unwieldy armies, were able to adapt intelligently to different circumstances and different enemies, even when they lacked any kind of technical advantage. The fact that they ultimately failed in the Middle East, the most spectacular theatre of all, should not be allowed to detract from that achievement.

notes

1. There is a bibliography by E. U. Crosby, *Medieval Warfare. A Bibliographical Guide* (New York, 2000), and see also J. France, 'Recent Writing on Medieval Warfare from the Fall of Rome to c.1300', *Journal of Military History*, 65 (2001), 441–73; J. France, *Western Warfare in the Age of the Crusades, 1000–1300* (London, 1999); H. Nicholson, *Medieval Warfare: Theory and Practice of War in Europe, 300–1500* (Basingstoke, 2004); J. F. Verbruggen, *The Art of Warfare in Western Europe during the Middle Ages. From the Eighth Century to 1340*, trans. S. Willard and R. W. Southern (Woodbridge, 1997).

2. R. C. Smail, *Crusading Warfare, 1097–1193*, 2nd edn, ed. C. Marshall (Cambridge, 1995); C. Marshall, *Warfare in the Latin East 1192–1291* (Cambridge, 1992); P. W. Edbury, 'Warfare in the Latin East', in *Medieval Warfare. A History*, ed. M. Keen (Oxford, 1999), pp. 89–112; N. Housley, *Religious Warfare in Europe, 1400–1536* (Oxford, 2002).

3. T. S. Asbridge, *The First Crusade* (London, 2004); J. France, *Victory in the East. A Military History of the First Crusade* (Cambridge, 1994); D. E. Queller, *The Fourth Crusade* (Leicester, 1978); T. F. Madden, *Enrico Dandolo and the Rise of Venice* (Baltimore, 2003); J. M. Powell, *Anatomy of a Crusade, 1213–1221* (Philadelphia, 1986); T. C. van Cleve, *The Emperor Frederick II of Hohenstaufen, Immutator Mundi* (Oxford, 1972); J. Richard, *Saint Louis*, ed. S. Lloyd from a 1983 French original (Cambridge, 1992).

4. John Gillingham is the chief authority on Richard and the Third Crusade, especially in his 'Richard I and the Science of War in the Middle Ages', in *War and Government in the Middle Ages*, ed. J. Gillingham and J. C. Holt (Woodbridge, 1984), pp. 78–91, and *Richard Coeur de Lion: Kingship, Chivalry and War in the Twelfth Century* (London, 1994). For another view of Richard see R. V. Turner, *The Reign of Richard Lionheart, Ruler of the Angevin Empire* (Harlow, 2000). For a vigorous debate on Richard as a soldier see the opposing views of J. O. Prestwich, 'Richard Coeur de Lion: *rex bellicosus*', in *Riccardo Cuor di Leone nella storia e nella leggenda* (Rome, 1981) and J. Gillingham, 'Conquering Kings: Some Twelfth Century Reflections on Henry II and Richard I', in *Warriors and Churchmen in the High Middle Ages: Essays Presented to Karl Leyser*, ed. T. Reuter (London, 1992), pp. 163–78.

5. T. S. Asbridge, 'The Significance and Causes of the Battle of the Field of Blood', *Journal of Medieval History*, 23 (1997), 301–16; A. J. Forey, 'The Failure of the Siege of Damascus in 1148', *Journal of Medieval History*, 10 (1984), 13–23; M. Hoch, 'The Choice of Damascus as the Objective of the Second Crusade', in *Autour de la première croisade: actes du Colloque de la Society for the Study of the Crusades and the Latin East: Clermont-Ferrand, 22–25 juin 1995*, ed. M. Balard (Paris, 1996), pp. 359–70; M. Barber, 'Frontier Warfare in the Latin Kingdom of Jerusalem: the Campaign of Jacob's Ford, 1178–79', in *The Crusades and their Sources: Essays Presented to Bernard Hamilton*, ed. J. France and W. G. Zajac (Aldershot, 1998); B. Z. Kedar, 'The Battle of Hattin Revisited', in *The Horns of Hattin*, ed. B. Z. Kedar (Jerusalem, 1992), pp. 190–207; A. S. Atiya, *The Crusade of Nicopolis* (London, 1934).

6. C. Coulson, 'Cultural Realities and Reappraisals in English Castle-study', *Journal of Medieval History*, 22 (1996), 171–207; D. Pringle, *The Red Tower* (London, 1986); R. Ellenblum, 'Frankish Castle-Building in the Latin Kingdom

of Jerusalem', in *Knights of the Holy Land. The Crusader Kingdom of Jerusalem*, ed. S. Rozenberg (Jerusalem, 1999), pp. 142–7; A. J. Taylor, *The King's Works in Wales 1277–1330* (London, 1974); H. Kennedy, *Crusader Castles* (Cambridge, 1995); R. Rogers, *Latin Siege Warfare in the Twelfth Century* (Oxford, 1997).

7. J. H. Pryor, *Geography, Technology and War. Studies in the Maritime History of the Mediterranean 649–1571* (Cambridge, 1992); J. H. Pryor, 'The Venetian Fleet for the Fourth Crusade and the Diversion of the Crusade to Constantinople', in *The Experience of Crusading*, vol. 1: *Western Approaches*, ed. M. Bull and N. Housley (Cambridge, 2003), pp. 103–26; J. H. Pryor, '"Water, water everywhere, Nor any drop to drink." Water Supplies for the Fleets on the First Crusade', in *Dei gesta per Francos. Études sur les croisades dédiées à Jean Richard – Crusade Studies in Honour of Jean Richard*, ed. M. Balard, B. Z. Kedar and J. Riley-Smith (Aldershot, 2001), pp. 21–8; S. Rose, *Medieval Naval Warfare 1000–1500* (London, 2002); A. Ehrenkreutz, 'The Place of Saladin in the Naval History of the Mediterranean Sea in the Middle Ages', *Journal of the American Oriental Society*, 75 (1955), 100–16.

8. D. Nicolle, *Arms and Armour of the Crusading Era 1050–1350*, 2 vols (New York, 1988).

9. *War, Technology and Society in the Middle East*, ed. V. J. Parry and M. E. Yapp (London, 1975); Y. Lev, *State and Society in Fatimid Egypt* (Leiden, 1991); H. A. R. Gibb, 'The Armies of Saladin', in *Studies in the Civilization of Islam*, ed. S. J. Shaw and W. R. Polk (New Haven, 1982), pp. 74–90; R. S. Humphreys, *From Saladin to the Mongols* (Albany, 1977); C. R. Bowlus, 'Tactical and Strategic Weaknesses of Horse-archers on the Eve of the First Crusade', in *Autour de la première croisade*, ed. Balard, pp. 159–66; Asbridge, 'Significance and Causes of the Battle of the Field of Blood'; A. G. C. Savvides, 'Late Byzantine and Crusader Historiographers on Turkish Mercenaries in Greek and Latin Armies. The Turcopoles/Tourkopoloi', in *The Making of Byzantine History. Essays Dedicated to D. M. Nicol*, ed. R. Beaton and C. Roueché (Aldershot, 1993), pp. 122–36; Y. Harari, 'The Military Role of the Frankish Turcopoles', *Mediterranean History Review*, 12 (1997), 75–116.

10. J. France, 'Crusading Warfare and its Adaptation to Eastern Conditions in the Twelfth Century', *Mediterranean History Review*, 15 (2000), 49–66; R. Ellenblum, *Frankish Rural Settlement in the Latin Kingdom of Jerusalem* (Cambridge, 1998).

11. *The Song of Roland*, trans. G. Burgess (Harmondsworth, 1990); *The Song of William of Orange*, in *William Count of Orange. Four Old French Epics*, ed. G. Price et al. (Dent, 1975), p. 195. On the value of chivalric literature to the study of war see especially Nicholson, *Medieval Warfare*.

12. Anonymous, *Gesta Francorum et aliorum Hierosolimitanorum*, ed. R. Hill (Edinburgh, 1962), p. 21.

13. *Epistulae et chartae ad historiam primi belli sacri spectantes: Die Kreuzzugsbriefe aus den Jahren 1088–1100*, ed. H. Hagenmeyer (Innsbruck, 1902), translated into English in *The First Crusade*, ed. A. C. Krey (Gloucester, Mass., 1958).

14. Raymond of Aguilers, *Liber*, ed. J. H. and L. L. Hill (Paris, 1969).

15. Fulcher of Chartres, *Historia Hierosoloymitana*, ed. H. Hagenmeyer (Heidelberg, 1913). His work continues the story of the kingdom down to 1127.

16. Guibert de Nogent, *Dei gesta per Francos et cinq autres textes*, ed. R. B. C. Huygens, Corpus Christianorum: Continuatio mediaevalis 127A (Turnhout, 1996). For

the view of the *Gesta* as the work of a simple knight, see the introduction to her edition by R. Hill, pp. ix–xvi; C. Morris, 'The *Gesta Francorum* as Narrative History', *Reading Medieval Studies*, 19 (1993), 55–71, contests this view sharply, while K. B. Wolf, 'Crusade and Narrative: Bohemond and the *Gesta Francorum*', *Journal of Medieval History*, 17 (1991), 207–16, argues for the subtlety of the storytelling. J. France,'The Anonymous *Gesta Francorum*, the *Historia Francorum qui ceperunt Iherusalem* of Raymond of Aguilers and the *Historia de Hierosolymitano Itinere* of Peter Tudebode: An Analysis of the Textual Relationship between Primary Sources for the First Crusade', in *The Crusades and their Sources. Essays Presented to Bernard Hamilton*, ed. J. France and W. G. Zajac (Aldershot, 1998), pp. 39–70, argues that the present text is the result of later editing.

17. *Roberti monachi Historia Iherosolimitana*, Recueil des historiens des croisades, ed. Académie des Inscriptions et Belles-Lettres (Paris, 1841–1906), Historiens Occidentaux [henceforth cited as RHC Occ.] vol. 3, pp. 717–882: here p. 731.

18. J. France, 'The Fall of Antioch during the First Crusade', in *Dei Gesta per Francos*, ed. Balard et al., pp. 13–20, has suggested that during this period the crusaders made a truce with Antioch which, after the fall of Jerusalem, chroniclers preferred to delete from the record.

19. Albert of Aachen, *Alberti Aquensis Historia Hierosolymitana*, in RHC Occ., vol. 4, pp. 265–713. A new edition with English translation is being prepared by S. B. Edgington, to whom I owe thanks for giving me access to her work and her ideas.

20. S. Duparc Quioc, in her edition of *La Chanson d'Antioche*, 2 vols (Paris, 1976–8), takes the view that the *chanson* is a revised version of an early twelfth-century song, but it has been suggested by R. F. Cook, in *Chanson d'Antioche, chansons de geste: le cycle de la croisade est-il épique?* (Amsterdam, 1980), that the whole work was written in the later twelfth century. See the comments of S. B. Edgington, 'The First Crusade: Reviewing the Evidence', in *The First Crusade: Origins and Impact*, ed. J. Phillips (Manchester, 1997), pp. 62–3.

21. Odo of Deuil, *De Profectione Ludovici VII in orientem*, ed. V. G. Berry (New York, 1947), and see J. France, 'Logistics and the Second Crusade' (forthcoming); E. Siberry, *Criticism of Crusading 1095–1274* (Oxford, 1985); J. France, 'Thinking about Crusader Strategy' (forthcoming).

22. Pierre Dubois, *The Recovery of the Holy Land*, ed. W. I. Brandt (New York, 1956). There is no good translation of Sanudo but there is a useful study by C. J. Tyerman, 'Marino Sanudo Torsello and the Lost Crusade: Lobbying in the fourteenth century', *Transactions of the Royal Historical Society*, 32 (1982), 57–73.

23. See above, notes 15 and 19.

24. Walter the Chancellor, *The Antiochene Wars*, ed. and trans. T. S. Asbridge and S. B. Edgington (Aldershot, 1999).

25. William of Tyre, *Chronicon*, ed. R. B. C. Huygens, 2 vols, Corpus Christianorum: continuatio mediaevalis, 63–63A (Turnhout, 1986); E. A. Babcock and A. C. Krey, trans, *A History of the Deeds Done Beyond the Sea*, 2 vols (New York, 1943).

26. There is a brilliant analysis of the factional struggle in Jerusalem before 1187 by P. W. Edbury, 'Propaganda and Faction in the Kingdom of Jerusalem: The Background to Hattin', in *Crusaders and Muslims in Twelfth-Century Syria*, ed. M. Shatzmiller (Leiden, 1993), pp. 173–89. For the difficulty of establishing events see Kedar, 'Battle of Hattin Revisited'. Some of the texts and useful further references are translated into English by P. W. Edbury, *The Conquest of Jerusalem and the Third Crusade* (Aldershot, 1996).

27. W. C. Jordan, *Louis IX and the Challenge of the Crusade. A Study in Rulership* (Princeton, 1979), pp. 65–104.

28. Ibn al-Qalanisi, *Damascus Chronicle of the Crusades* ed. A. R. Gibb (Luzac, 1932); Kemal al-Din, 'Chronicle of Aleppo', in RHC Historiens Orientaux, ed. Académie des inscriptions et Belles-Lettres (Paris, 1872–1906), vol. 3.

29. Usama, *An Arab-Syrian Gentleman and Warrior in the Period of the Crusades*, ed. P. K. Hitti (New York, 1929).

30. For an early instance of *jihād* being advocated against the invaders see N. Christie and D. Gerish, 'Parallel Preachings: Urban II and al-Sulami', *Al-Masaq*, 15 (2003), 139–48. N. Christie is preparing an edition of this early text.

31. There is a useful introduction to these and other texts in English in *Arab Historians of the Crusades*, ed. F. Gabrieli (New York, 1989).

32. G. Tantum, 'Muslim Warfare. A Study of a Medieval Muslim Treatise on the Art of War', in *Islamic Arms and Armour*, ed. R. Elgood (London, 1979), pp. 187–201; G. Scanlon, *A Muslim Manual of War* (Cairo, 1961).

33. C. Hillenbrand, *The Crusades. Islamic Perspectives* (Edinburgh, 2000).

34. C. Cahen, 'Un traité d'armurerie compose pour Saladin', *Bulletin d'études orientales de l'Institut français de Damas*, 12 (1947/48), 103–63.

35. *The Cilician Kingdom of Armenia*, ed. T. S. R. Boase (Edinburgh, 1978).

36. N. J. G. Edwards, *Fortifications of Armenian Cilicia* (Washington DC, 1992); Matthew of Edessa, *Chronicle*, ed. A. E. Dostourian (London, 1993); J. France, 'Fortifications East and West' (forthcoming).

37. Michael the Syrian, *Chronique*, ed. J. B. Chabot (Brussels, 1963, reprint of 1899–1910 original).

38. See Ellenblum, *Frankish Rural Settlement*.

39. Gislebertus Hanoniensis, *Chronicon*, ed. L. Vanderkindere (Brussels, 1904); an English translation by Laura Napran is in preparation.

40. France, *Western Warfare*, pp. 1–15.

41. Gislebertus, *Chronicon*, p. 173.

42. M. Strickland, *War and Chivalry. The Conduct and Perception of War in England and Normandy 1066–1217* (Cambridge, 1996).

43. Suger of St Denis, *The Deeds of Louis the Fat*, ed. R. C. Cusimano and J. Moorhead (Washington, DC, 1992), pp. 26–7.

44. M. H. Keen, *The Laws of War in the Later Middle Ages* (London, 1965).

45. France, *Western Warfare*, pp. 43–7.

46. Ibid., pp. 64–76; S. D. B. Brown, 'The Mercenary and His Master: Military Service and Monetary Reward in the Eleventh and Twelfth Century', *History*, 74 (1989), 20–38; K. A. Fowler, *Medieval Mercenaries* (Oxford, 2001).

47. Suger, *The Deeds of Louis the Fat*, p. 26.

48. C. B. Bouchard, *Strong of Body Brave and Noble. Chivalry and Society in Medieval France* (Ithaca, 1998); R. W. Kaeuper, *Chivalry and Violence in Medieval Europe* (Oxford, 1999).
49. France, *Western Warfare*, pp. 107–27; Rogers, *Latin Siege Warfare*; J. Bradbury, *The Medieval Siege* (Woodbridge, 1992).
50. P. M. Holt, *The Age of the Crusades* (London, 1986), provides an excellent introduction to the history of the Muslim Middle East.
51. Nizam al-Mulk, *The Book of Government or Rules for Kings*, trans. H. Darke (London, 1960).
52. M. C. Lyons and D. E. P. Jackson, *Saladin. The Politics of Holy War* (Cambridge, 1982).
53. Y. Lev, 'Regime, Army and Society in Egypt, 9th–12th Centuries', in *War and Society in the Eastern Mediterranean, 7th–15th Centuries*, ed. Y. Lev (Leiden, 1997), pp. 115–52.
54. D. Nicolle, *The Medieval Warfare Source-Book*, vol. 2 (London, 1996); R. Amitai-Preiss, *Mongols and Mamluks: The Mamluk-Ilkhanid War 1260–81* (Cambridge, 1995); J. M. Smith, 'Mongol Society and the Military in the Middle East. Antecedents and Adaptations', in *War and Society in the Eastern Mediterranean*, ed. Lev, pp. 249–66.
55. Powell, *Anatomy of a Crusade*; Oliver of Paderborn, *The Capture of Damietta*, trans. J. J. Gavigan, ed. E. Peters (New York, 1980).
56. N. Housley, *The Later Crusades. From Lyons to Alcazar 1274–1580* (Oxford, 1992), pp. 75–8.
57. France, *Victory*, pp. 367–73.
58. Anonymous, *Gesta Francorum*, p. 19.
59. France, *Victory*, pp. 367–73.
60. S. Painter, 'The Third Crusade: Richard the Lionhearted and Philip Augustus', and E. N. Johnson, 'The Crusades of Frederick Barbarossa and Henry VI', in *A History of the Crusades*, ed. K. M. Setton, 2nd edn (Madison, Wisc., 1969–89), vol. 2, *The Later Crusades: 1189–1311*, ed. R. L. Wolff and H. W. Hazard, pp. 45–122; P. Munz, *Frederick Barbarossa. A Study in Medieval Politics* (London, 1969); J. Gillingham, *Richard the Lionheart* (London, 1978); J. W. Baldwin, *The Government of Philip Augustus. Foundations of French Royal Power in the Middle Ages* (Berkeley, 1986).
61. Joinville, *Life of St Louis*, in *Chronicles of the Crusades*, trans. Shaw, pp. 163–353; Richard, *Saint Louis*.
62. Odo of Deuil, *De Profectione*, pp. 114–21; *The Conquest of Lisbon*, ed. C. W. David (New York, 2001).
63. Raymond of Aguilers, *Liber*, pp. 119–21.
64. P. W. Edbury, *The Kingdom of Cyprus and the Crusades, 1191–1374* (Cambridge, 1991).
65. Ehrenkreutz, 'Place of Saladin in the Naval History of the Mediterranean', pp. 100–16.
66. J. Prawer, *Crusader Institutions* (Oxford, 1980), p. 106.
67. William of Tyre, *Chronicon*, Bk 13, chs 1–14; Bk 17, chs 21–30.
68. France, 'Crusading Warfare and its Adaptation', 49–66.
69. Asbridge, 'Field of Blood', pp. 301–16; J. Richard, *The Crusades c.1071–1291*, trans. J. Birrell (Cambridge and New York, 1999) p. 171; D. Pringle, 'The Spring

of the Cresson in Crusading History', in *Dei Gesta per Francos*, ed. Balard et al., pp. 231–40; B. Hamilton, *The Leper King and his Heirs. Baldwin IV and the Crusader Kingdom of Jerusalem* (Cambridge, 2000), pp. 132–58.

70. Smail, *Crusading Warfare*, pp. 182, 156–64.
71. *Chronicle of the Third Crusade: A Translation of the Itinerarium peregrinorum et gesta Regis Ricardi*, trans. H. J. Nicholson (Aldershot, 1997).
72. Van Cleve, *Frederick II*. See also D. Abulafia, *Frederick II. A Medieval Emperor* (London, 1988).
73. S. Runciman, 'The Crusader States, 1243–91', in *History of the Crusades*, ed. Setton, vol. 2, pp. 522–98.
74. R. J. Lilie, *Byzantium and the Crusader States, 1096–1204*, trans. J. C. Morris and E. Ridings (Oxford, 1994); J. P. Phillips, *Defenders of the Holy Land: Relations between the Latin East and the West 1119–87* (Oxford, 1996); M. Purcell, *Papal Crusading Policy 1244–91* (Leiden, 1975).

part II
approaches to the evidence

4

the material culture of the crusades

maria georgopoulou

The term 'material culture' defies the well established categories of art history and archaeology. Institutionally the term and the field of study that it has generated since the 1980s imply connections with anthropology, archaeology, the history of collecting and museums, and an interdisciplinary approach.[1] Within the strict parameters of the term, material culture stands as a counterpart to art as it studies the products of the industrial arts; it is interested on the banal and the quotidian as opposed to High Art. Rather than thinking about the hand of a master, the study of material culture begs for understanding of the organization of the so-called industrial arts, the collective lives of craftsmen, the modes of production and the ways in which the artefacts reached the market and the home. In short, material culture deals with commodities rather than Art.

When we deal with the past, however, the boundaries between art and material culture are often blurred. As this volume does not contain a separate chapter on the art of the crusades, I will include in this chapter not only objects that were produced for the market but also things that are traditionally associated with high art, namely illuminated manuscripts. Monumental painting and sculpture will be largely excluded as their study addresses, I believe, a whole different array of issues of patronage and artistic affiliation. My approach is that of an art historian with emphasis placed on the historical circumstances surrounding works of art. I am, nevertheless, committed to viewing the arts in a broad sense ranging from luxury objects that are now proudly displayed in museums and galleries all over the world, to archaeological objects that were less expensive and circulated more widely. So my method espouses archaeology as well as art history within the context of economic history.

The importance of the material culture for understanding the cultural horizons of the crusader period hardly needs justification: religious icons, manuscripts, architecture, everyday things that adorned the home and were used to prepare food and drink, and instruments that cultivated the land or were used in other trades must have played a crucial role in identifying social status and in making one's life comfortable. When the written sources are silent about tastes or individual thoughts about art and beauty, artefacts may tell us a lot about the choices of the people who populated the crusader states.

The study of the material culture of the crusades may therefore be divided between archaeology and art history. The special attention that has been given to the study of archaeological artefacts in large excavation projects at Caesarea Maritima, 'Atlit and Acre, and also in smaller sites, has substantially enriched our knowledge of the material, which because of its nature does not occupy a prominent position in museums.[2] The studies of Adrian Boas, Ronnie Ellenblum, Denys Pringle and Edna Stern among others have shown the significance of local manufacturing techniques that persisted in crusader metalwork, glassware, pottery and construction techniques.[3]

Crusader art is a rather young field and started with the study of architecture in the late nineteenth century.[4] Not surprisingly, the political situation in the Middle East influenced the theoretical constructs that informed the view of the crusader material. Architecture, sculpture, and to some extent manuscript illumination were interpreted as belonging to a colonial French artistic enterprise. The field has been dominated by studies in architecture, sculpture and manuscript illumination.[5] In the last 15 years, studies have expanded the array of objects and artefacts studied under the rubric of crusader art to offer more nuanced methodological views on the products of this period. Recently emphasis has been given to pieces that are hybrid in nature and cross regional boundaries. As such they resist the identification of their patron and producer with any one particular ethnic and/or religious group. These studies insist on the vitality of a local artistic idiom informed by the indigenous cultural heritage intermingled with the veneer of Muslim art that had been predominant in the area of the Holy Land since the seventh century AD.[6] They suggest that the local artists and artisans played a much more important role than hitherto suggested in the literature. These authors no longer frame crusader art as a colonial art but study it from the lens of postcolonial studies.

We know that the Franks asserted their hegemony on the land and their superiority over the indigenous population through political and economic measures. Such an act conditioned a response from the local population. How did they construct their group identity vis-à-vis their Frankish overlords and vis-à-vis other Christian groups? Material culture, art and architecture must have played a crucial role in this process: the things used in daily life, the form and distinct function of a place of worship, the rituals taking place therein, as well as the things that one could buy in the markets would have a tremendous impact in delineating the cultural identity of the people. So, were we to understand how these people behaved as patrons and users of art and architecture, we would know much more about their self-fashioning and their aspirations. Research into the material culture and other portable objects reveals a common artistic language shared by all – oriental Christians and Muslims but presumably also Franks – at least in the secular sphere. Our tendency to separate the religious from the secular objects is informed by categories imposed in the modern period and poses several problems that the field of material culture, especially through the finds in excavations, refutes. Certain grand religious projects like the refurbishment and decoration of churches or castles must have employed artists and artisans imported from Europe or Byzantium. The case of the mosaics of the Church of the Nativity in Bethlehem and that of the construction of the castle of Crac des Chevaliers are instructive in this regard.[7] The majority of things used by the crusaders, however, must have been local products that were made suitable for the newcomers with the insertion of their language and possibly images that were familiar to them. Thus, it is not surprising that when it comes to identifying things related to the crusades we are bound to look for references to chivalry and pilgrimage, glimpses of a Gothic style, or the use of Latin.

In this chapter I will consider the material culture of the crusades from the following two perspectives: first, from the point of view of the ideology of the crusades, and, second, from the point of view of the geopolitical realities of the time.

crusade and pilgrimage

The rhetoric of the crusades was intimately connected with the notion of holy war and strove to insert the crusades within the grand narratives of biblical and world history. When Pope Urban II preached the crusade to the Holy Land in the ecclesiastical Council of Clermont (1095) he pointed to the fact that participation in the holy war had as a reward religious privileges. The journey to the East had as its objective the deliverance of the holy sites, so the pope's speech explicitly transferred the rewards and concept of pilgrimage to the holy war: it would bring salvation and deliverance, and the holy warriors would do penance for all their sins. Taking up the cross had a literal meaning for the crusaders: it appeared on their garments, weapons and horses. It is this literalness of the crusading material culture that I would like to emphasize here.

The concept and realities of pilgrimage were of great significance for the formation of the material culture of the crusaders because the physical appearance and materiality of the environment were intimately connected with the way in which the crusaders experienced their surroundings. The tokens that pilgrims and crusaders brought back home from the Holy Land derived their symbolic significance and healing powers from their very substance, their contents (oil or water from the holy sites) as well as their decoration and inscriptions.[8] The best known pilgrims' tokens are lead flasks known as *ampullae* that were produced in large quantities from the sixth century through to the time of the crusades.[9] On the example shown in Plate 1 the Church of the Holy Sepulchre is portrayed as it was rebuilt by the crusaders in the middle of the twelfth century, with emphasis placed on the large ashlar blocks that form its walls and the dome over the Tomb of Christ known as the Anastasis. In addition to the images evoking the holy sites that commemorated the life of Jesus, inscriptions from the Bible made these flasks palpable souvenirs of holiness.

As expected, much of the official art of the period focuses on religious themes. Some of the surviving illuminated manuscripts are liturgical in nature, such as the famous psalter of Queen Melisende (London, British Library, MS Egerton 1139) dating to 1131–43. Its 24 full-page miniatures of the New Testament show a close affinity with miniatures of Byzantine lectionaries that seem to have been used as models but betray a manipulation of the image to fit the new full-page illustration of the psalter, as we can see in the large golden leaf portion that is left bare in the psalter image of the Prayer in Gethsemane (Plate 2).[10] Similar issues of borrowings and bilingualism are seen in the opening folio that portrays a traditional Byzantine image of a Deesis (Christ flanked by the Virgin Mary and St John the Baptist) signed in Latin by a painter whose name is Greek: Basil. The eclecticism of the illuminator(s) is further attested in the eight full-page initials, which show a mixture of western and Islamic motifs, and finally in the portrayal of saints who in their flat style remind the viewer of English miniatures. The English calendar of saints' feasts contained in the end of the manuscript securely connects it to two Englishmen: William, prior of the Holy Sepulchre, who in 1128 became the first Archbishop of Tyre; or Ralph, royal chancellor in the 1140s. Yet

Plate 1. Pilgrim *ampulla* (Staatliche Museen zu Berlin Preußischer Kulturbesitz, Inv.-Nr. 25/73 (VS)), photo: Staatliche Museen zu Berlin – Preußischer Kulturbesitz; Museen für Spätantike und Byzantinische Kunst / Gudrun Stenzel / Bildarchiv Preußischer Kulturbesitz.

the hybridity of the images poses questions about the scriptorium that produced it.[11]

Often the illuminated religious manuscripts explore the ideas and realities of holy war by equating the deeds of the crusaders with the sacred

Plate 2.   Prayer in Gethsemane, from the psalter of Queen Melisende (London: British Library, MS Egerton 1139, fol. 7r); by permission of the British Library.

history of the Bible. One folio from the luxurious illuminated manuscript known as the Arsenal Bible (Plate 3),[12] which has been attributed to the patronage of the French king, Louis IX, shows the biblical armies bearing all the military accoutrements of the crusader armies: coats of arms, armouries, shields and swords can be easily identified with specific European armies. In this Old French abridged version of the Old Testament, biblical history is conflated with current military history to elevate the crusaders into holy warriors and to equate their army with that of the chosen people.[13] Similarly the biblical kings Saul, David and Solomon take on attributes of the Latin Kings of Jerusalem. On the frontispiece of I Kings, Saul is crowned on a faldstool known as the *sella curulis*, the throne of king Dagobert and later of the Capetian kings of France. On the frontispiece of II Kings David's coronation follows the French custom: he is anointed by the archbishop who also confers on him the crown and sceptre, which here is replaced by the *labarum* (sign of the Cross) of Constantine the Great, who was instrumental in the recovery and refurbishment of the *loca sancta* in Palestine.

A large number of illuminated manuscripts have been attributed to thirteenth-century Acre, the capital of the Latin Kingdom of Jerusalem after the loss of Jerusalem. Its scriptoria were also active in producing books of a non-religious nature participating fully in the writing of history that became current in thirteenth-century European culture. Two types of books were popular enough in the crusader states of the Latin East to receive illustrations of great value: the *Histoire Universelle* and the *Histoire d'Outremer*. The former is a world chronicle that related the history of the world from the time of the Creation to that of Julius Caesar and attempted to correlate the chronology of the Old Testament with the writings of ancient historians. It is the earliest compilation of a historical text in the vernacular and implies a lay audience. Four illustrated manuscripts have survived from Acre and are currently in the national libraries of Dijon (1260–70), Brussels (1270–80), London (1286?), and Paris (1287). They probably followed a common French prototype although they predate European manuscripts. Painted in a style that betrays knowledge of French painting, they also display affinities with Byzantine painting. In one folio of the luxurious *Histoire Universelle* in the British Library (Plate 4), London, Penthesilea and the Amazons are shown with the Trojans, who pose as the ancestors of the French.[14] The text of the *Histoire d'Outremer* was also written in Paris and it contains the continuation of the history of William of Tyre until the 1270s. Its images derive from the *Histoire Universelle*. Seven copies survive from Acre and many later ones from Paris.

Plate 3. Frontispiece to the Book of Joshua, from the Arsenal Bible (Paris: Bibliothèque de l'Arsenal, MS 5211, fol. 69v); Bibliothèque nationale de France.

Plate 4. Penthesilea and Amazons with Trojans, from the *Histoire Universelle* (London, British Library, MS Add. 15268, fol. 122r); by permission of the British Library.

In addition to these objects numerous fragments of pottery celebrate the crusading spirit by showcasing knights and their ladies on a white background (Plate 5).[15] Recent studies by David Jacoby and Veronique François have focused on the availability of romances and their illustration on pottery, and Hugo Buchthal has suggested that some of the illustrations of the London *Histoire Universelle* were inspired by jousting tournaments in the crusader states.[16] The pottery of Cyprus also follows similar prototypes.[17]

material culture within the world of the eastern mediterranean

In order to understand the position of the material culture of the crusades within the larger political, economic and social context of the Levant we must remember that the crusader states were made up of complex, multiethnic, and polyglot societies. Traditionally the crusades have been seen as the meeting of two worlds: the West/Europe and the East. This eastern culture was not uniform, however: it comprised peoples of different ethnicities (Syrians, Greeks, Arabs, Copts, Armenians, and so

Plate 5.   Ceramic plate showing a knight; courtesy Israel Antiquities Authority.

on) and religions (Eastern Christians and Muslims). The Holy Land in the twelfth and thirteenth centuries was a cosmopolitan region, where a variety of languages were spoken, where people lived peacefully among different religious groups, and where one's ethnic identity was construed in terms different to those of western Europeans.

Obviously the material culture reproduced the same scheme. Indeed, in the wake of multiculturalism there has been an increase in the number of scholars who look at the art of the crusades not as a polemical cultural construct between East and West but as an experiment in symbiotic cultural relationships.[18] The plurality of artistic voices – Latins and Muslims, of course, but very importantly the indigenous Christians (Jacobites, Armenians, Nestorians, Copts, and Orthodox) – have by now been established for a variety of works of art. The primary objects that have come to the fore are hybrids: Christian religious icons from Mount Sinai, religious manuscripts written in Arabic, Syriac or Coptic, and Islamic damascened brasses with Christian images. The icon of Saints

George and Theodore on horseback with a donor is a case in point (Plate 6).[19] Sharon Gerstel has proposed that their militant, riding posture is associated with the posture of the fighting crusaders and may also have implications for the propagation of a chivalric ideal that permeated cultural boundaries.[20] A small figure of a donor prostrates at the saints' feet. An inscription clearly written in Greek spells out his name and complicates the meaning of this otherwise typical icon: 'Prayer of your servant, George from Paris' (probably meaning Parisiou). Even if the identity of this George is Greek, as the language of the inscription and the presence of his beard suggest, the personal tone of the inscription anchors this icon in time and place and thus differentiates it from the majority of painted Byzantine icons until that time.[21]

Powerful cultural signs like this icon were, it seems, affected by the presence of the Latin crusaders. This was one among many cultural encounters between crusaders and indigenous people. Different customs and cultures mixed on the soil of the Holy Land; they can be seen in domestic architecture and furniture, food, fashion, clothing, language, religious practices, and so on. All these elements were recorded by the westerners as curiosities, and some of them entered their life as well. What at first seemed like an exotic East, little by little became more familiar, less threatening and easier to embrace.

It is this cultural amalgamation that is hard to grasp in the study of individual artefacts. Traditionally, medieval art historians have interpreted the formal qualities of works of art produced in ethnically diverse societies as carriers of ethnic, religious and political meanings. In other words, it is generally assumed that the style of works of art construes and is construed by the cultural identity of different ethnic and religious groups, which in this way set and affirm their own separate identity vis-à-vis each other. Such considerations exemplify dichotomies between East–West, Christian–Muslim, and so on. Recent scholarship has shown that these methodological constructs do not always constitute a viable framework for the study of the art created in multiethnic communities; the *a priori* imposition of stylistic boundaries hinders the understanding of artistic products which transcend the norm.

In contrast to most art historians who are trained to look only at a particular segment of the Mediterranean world and consider a western European, Byzantine or Islamic agent as the only possible manufacturer and consumer of goods in a particular region, economic historians from the time of Robert Sabatino Lopez and S. D. Goitein have shown that the world of trade in the eleventh, twelfth and especially in the thirteenth centuries was multifaceted.[22] The experience of the crusades and the

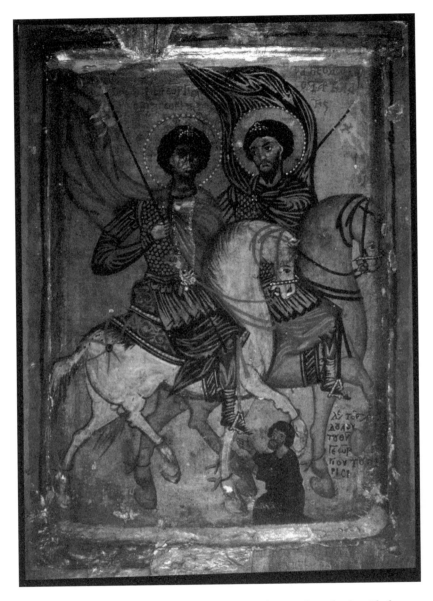

Plate 6. Icon of Saints George and Theodore Stratelates on horseback, with donor, from the Monastery of St Catherine at Mount Sinai: reproduced through the courtesy of the Michigan-Princeton-Alexandria Expedition to Mount Sinai.

close contact between Europeans and Middle Easterners that these wars and ensuing settlements forged was instrumental for the emancipation of the Mediterranean as an international commercial region.

Throughout the Mediterranean, objects were manufactured by artisans of various ethnicities and religious confessions living side by side in the same city. In the crusader and the neighbouring Muslim states the marketplace was the most important site where Muslims, Christians of various rites (Latin, Greek/Melchite, Jacobite, Nestorian, Armenian, and so on) and Jews came into contact. Thus, the conditions in the marketplace may be used as a gauge for understanding the relationship between the different ethnic groups in the area. The crafts were not separated in quarters nor were ethnic groups segregated. The ethnic origin or religious identity of the maker of an object was not the only defining factor in the artefact's appearance. Nor was place of manufacture necessarily related to separate clienteles divided along confessional lines. The material culture of the crusades has therefore to be placed within this Mediterranean context which was larger than the borders of the crusader states.

Despite the loss of Jerusalem to the Muslims in 1187, European presence in the Levant had been consolidated by the thirteenth century, especially after the establishment of Venetian and other Italian emporia on the coast of Palestine following the Fourth Crusade. The European settlers and the Venetian and Genoese middlemen who had special quarters in the cities of the Levant acted as catalysts for the growth of local and international trade. In addition to the vibrant markets of the Middle East, the western and central Mediterranean provided the necessary markets for products of the East. Thus, we see a boom in the production of objects for sale locally and across the sea: metalwork, glass, textiles, and above all pottery. All these materials had been traded before, but after 1200 their production was both intensified and differentiated to gear its objects – it seems – to various clienteles. Production centres were scattered throughout the Mediterranean: in the Holy Land, the Middle East (Aleppo and Damascus), Cairo, Cyprus, Corinth, Sicily, France and Spain – not to mention Constantinople, which was under Latin rule from 1204 to 1261.

Insofar as the crusader states functioned as emporia and entrepôts for international trade, the Muslim states of the area should be included in any study on commercial or cultural exchange in the thirteenth century. Not only was Jerusalem part of the Ayyūbid state after 1187, but the Muslim states contained large Christian populations and provided the agricultural hinterland, the cultural background, and the necessary market mechanisms to support the coast-oriented crusader states. For instance, although the majority of the approximately 100,000 inhabitants of Damascus, the largest city in the area, were Muslims, considerable Christian (Melchite and Jacobite) as well as Jewish communities resided in the city.[23] According to estimations based on tax records, the second largest Muslim city in the area, Aleppo, had between 12,000 and 15,000 non-Muslim inhabitants in the Ayyūbid period (1169–1250).[24]

The new political and economic situation ushered by the crusades in the twelfth and thirteenth centuries increased the traffic of goods, encouraged competition among markets and states, and by the middle of the thirteenth century it had created a robust system of Mediterranean trade that connected East and West. The dissemination of protomaiolica pottery from southern Italy in various parts of the eastern Mediterranean and mainland Greece is a case in point. Whereas the rare finds of this type in Constantinople pose an interesting problem for its overall dissemination and commercial success, the type appears in regions as disparate as Corinth, 'Atlit and Lucera in Italy, only emphasizing a shared material culture fostered by trade and fashion in the major ports of the Mediterranean (Plate 7).[25] Numerous archaeological finds on land and in shipwrecks counteract the frustrating absence of particular references to manufactured goods in the extant Italian merchants' manuals. The famous commercial manual of Francesco Pegolotti includes spices, foodstuffs, raw materials, precious luxuries and textiles, but does not mention manufactured goods of metal, ceramic or wood. Glass is sometimes mentioned in these manuals, indicating that it may have been a significant element of Mediterranean trade in the thirteenth century but lost its importance by the end of the century when Venice's glass industry took off.[26] If pottery was present in the hulls of ships why did the merchants not focus on it? Was it insignificant because of the large quantity traded, or its low price? In fact, the recent publications of shipwreck finds and ongoing excavations have shown the significance of dated pottery for our understanding of the aesthetic and monetary value attached to objects.[27]

issues of manufacture and style

Before dealing directly with objects that were produced by and for the western crusaders it is instructive to look briefly at the indigenous material culture. The Oriental Christians who populated the crusader states spoke predominantly Arabic but used in their church the liturgical languages of Greek, Syriac and Coptic. One of the most conspicuous features of Syriac, Christian Arabic, and Coptic illuminated Gospel manuscripts

Plate 7. Protomaiolica plate from 'Atlit; courtesy Israel Antiquities Authority.

of the thirteenth century is the inclusion of numerous details of daily life (furniture, textiles, artefacts and buildings), which in fact faithfully reproduce the world around them. These details and the style of the illuminations document an affinity with Islamic material culture and a shared stylistic idiom.[28] Not surprisingly, these manuscripts echo the unique material culture of their place of production, which had a pronounced Islamic character. At the same time the insistence on the faithful reproduction of their surroundings in an almost personal, domestic way, must have been a continuation of a practice older than Islam: that of the lived experience of the holy pilgrimage sites. Similarly to the Syriac manuscripts, the official imagery of the Latin Kingdom reproduces visually accurate representations of the main monuments of Jerusalem: the Tower of David, the Dome of the Rock, and the Holy Sepulchre, as we can see on a lead seal of John of Brienne (Plate 8).[29]

Plate 8. Lead seal of John of Brienne, 1212–25; by permission of the Staatliche Münzsammlung, Munich.

Similar care to reproduce the holy sites appears on two gilt enamelled glass beakers at the Walters Art Gallery in Baltimore. They appear as products of an Islamic atelier in Aleppo or Damascus c. 1260 and were located until the beginning of the twentieth century in Egypt. Carl Johann Lamm places the height of Aleppo's glass industry after the attack of Genghis Khan in 1220/21. A different place of origin cannot be precluded, however, as the chemical composition of the Aleppo glass cannot for the moment be distinguished from that of Damascus, Tyre or Hebron.[30] The scenes are set between two horizontal bands, the upper one decorated with inscriptions in Arabic. On the larger beaker (19 cm high and 12 cm in diameter) the inscription reads: 'Glory to our master, the sultan, the royal, the learned' with the name of the sultan omitted and not enough titulature to identify him with certainty (Plate 9).[31] It has been suggested that when the name is omitted the pieces were not commissioned by a known patron but were made for the market.[32] Haloed figures dressed like monks or clerics are flanked by large green plants and stand between two domed buildings on the main body of the beaker, identifiable as the Church of the Holy Sepulchre and the Dome of the Rock, which had been named by the crusaders as Templum Domini. Interesting iconographic comparisons can be made with Oriental Christian manuscripts.[33] The companion piece shows a haloed man riding a donkey, two similar domed buildings, a standing haloed person, and a smaller figure (possibly a child) climbing on one of the buildings reaching to the plant in front of him. All these details suggest a representation of the Entry of Jesus to Jerusalem.

These two beakers may be unique in their iconography among Islamic glassware, but they fit within a larger category of objects that defy the strict dichotomies between East and West: a group of 18 gold and silver inlaid metal vessels which are Islamic in style but display Christian themes (rows of saints or ecclesiastics and scenes from the life of Christ). Their iconography betrays a relationship with a Christian clientele and arguably the adjacent crusader states. Most of them were made outside the crusader kingdoms, in the large cities of the neighbouring Ayyūbid (that is, Islamic) states in the mid-thirteenth century, so they are not usually treated within the context of crusader art. These pieces are associated with the markets of Muslim cities in every technical and stylistic aspect: shape (incense burners, ewers, boxes and trays), manufacturing technique, composition, treatment of the human or animal figures and decorative details.[34] The two studies that have dealt with these objects view them as atypical and interpret them either as unique examples made during a period of entente between crusaders and Muslims, or as problematic pieces within the wider Islamic artistic production.[35] Their relatively large number, I argue, is indicative of a far wider production than previously thought, and they ought to be studied within a larger framework that incorporates the artistic production and the market mechanisms of the crusader and the neighbouring Muslim states. When we explore their shapes, technique, style and iconography in relation to the various local traditions – both Christian and Muslim – we may uncover possible Byzantine, Syrian, Jacobite, Jewish or other sources that have been

Plate 9. Beaker depicting buildings (the Walters Art Museum, no. 47.17); by permission of the Walters Art Museum, Baltimore.

overlooked by historians of Islamic art. For example, my investigation of five incense burners which belong to this group has shown that the shape of the vessels, usually thought to be exclusively Islamic, is also known in Byzantium from examples found in Egypt as well as in wall paintings in the Balkans of a slightly later period.[36] Although there is no question that the decoration is part of the well known 'princely cycle' of Islamic art and the writing is in Arabic (with the exception of a unique piece from Cyprus),[37] most of the iconographic motifs can be shown to share a common vocabulary with the decorative arts of Byzantium and the Near East. Some of the objects are quite large and seemingly have been used very little, two points indicating a ceremonial or decorative function. Others are of a lesser artistic quality that suggests mass production, or show signs of wear which imply extensive use by a less wealthy but not necessarily local clientele. Since inscriptions and other documentation are lacking, it is difficult to prove which objects were made for local consumption. The lesser quality that arguably meant a cheaper object is by no means an absolute indicator of the fact that these pieces were not made for export.

The most impressive of these pieces is a large brass canteen inlaid with silver, now at the Freer Gallery in Washington, DC (Plate 10).[38] It is a large vessel that would not have been used in everyday life, so it must have had a ceremonial function. The central medallion is decorated with the Virgin enthroned holding the Christ child on her lap. She is flanked by two figures and two hovering angels. A band with Arabic calligraphy in the Kufic angular script surrounds the medallion and gives blessings to the (unknown) owner of this object. In the next zone three medallions are inhabited by birds and three others contain scenes from the life of Christ: the Nativity, the Presentation of Jesus to the Temple, and the Entry into Jerusalem. All these scenes are quite faithful to the Byzantine ways of displaying these events despite the few anomalies that occur. If, however, we compare these scenes with those on the pilgrims' *ampullae* discussed above (Plate 1) we see that the crusader vessel lacks any reference to the Passion of Christ, the motifs most often employed on the pilgrims' flasks.[39] The *verso* of the brass canteen (Plate 11) is decorated with a series of figures standing under an arcade, obviously in a processional manner. Two of them have been identified with the Virgin and the Archangel Gabriel, in a schematic representation of the Annunciation. Closer to the centre, figures on horseback have been associated with hunters, warriors or knights. These themes that are usually found on secular Islamic and Byzantine objects, plates, bowls and textiles would be extremely suited for a crusader knight who might have commissioned this object as a souvenir from the Holy Land in the mid-thirteenth century.

Plate 10.   Brass canteen inlaid with silver, front; Freer Gallery of Art, Smithsonian Institution, Washington, DC: Purchase, F1941.10.

If indeed the patron of this vessel was a Latin, we can surmise that the workshops in the area were versatile enough to be able to create vessels of unusual shapes and with images that would fit any client. Rather than argue for the existence of a special workshop in Syria working exclusively for the Europeans of the Holy Land, I would argue that these objects were made in the market of a Muslim city for Christian patrons of local or European origin. Based on an enamel beaker in the British Museum containing a Latin inscription (*magister Aldrenandin[i] me fecit*), Carl Johann Lamm has suggested the existence of a special Latin workshop in Syria working exclusively for the Europeans of the Holy Land and has labelled this group of glasses as 'Syro-Frankish'.[40] In fact, the latest archaeological findings and technical analyses have brought into question

Plate 11.   Brass canteen inlaid with silver, verso; Freer Gallery of Art, Smithsonian Institution, Washington, DC: Purchase, F1941.10.

the whole theory of the production of glass objects for a special Frankish clientele in the area of greater Syria in the thirteenth century. Recent scholarship on these glasses which have been found in northern and central Europe favours a Venetian manufacture, because documentary evidence for a central European origin is non-existent.[41] To return to the canteen: the scenes from the life of Christ of course referred to the holy sites in the area. Arabic was the language that the majority of locals, Muslims and Christians, spoke. Thus, the Freer canteen encapsulates the Holy Land for the westerners, who never immersed themselves fully in its culture. It can be seen as an attempt to colonize the Holy Land, to make a facsimile of its treasures and return home with it.

Although no direct evidence links these pieces with the crusaders their appearance at this period suggests to me that the impetus and demand for such objects was provided by the new market mechanisms initiated in the crusader states of the Levant. Despite the widespread exchange of cultural forms and a social situation able to accommodate different peoples and demands, however, no assimilation of the indigenous population was possible with the westerners because according to crusader law, eastern Christians and Muslims were treated as second-class citizens under the Franks. The natives were able to maintain their ethnic and cultural identity vis-à-vis the western crusaders due to the familial and clan networks that had existed for centuries.

All evidence indicates that the two centuries of crusader presence in the Holy Land did not disrupt local modes of production but rather recognized the significance of maintaining the status quo. This is evident even in the mode of construction. A crusader mason can be easily detected by the presence of distinctively diagonally dressed stones, but bilingual inscriptions, masonry marks and construction techniques point to a versatile workforce that crossed ethnic and confessional lines. Although masonry marks from crusader buildings, which are taken to be autographs of the individual masons who dressed the stones, do not provide a complete corpus or confirm the makeup of particular workshops, they suggest the presence of Latins, Greeks, Armenians and Arabs among the workforce.[42] Here we have a perfect echo to the fields of artisanal production, trade, and material culture, all of which were shared by any person who had the means to participate in the dominant culture.

To conclude, it appears that despite several ways in which the Franks tried to separate themselves from the indigenous population, when it came to material culture and art, the riches of the Holy Land had the upper hand. Either because of the sanctity of space, the symbolic value of pilgrimage or the importance of inserting the crusades within biblical and historical time, local culture proved to be quite strong. Artistic production was grounded in the place of production in an almost personal, experiential way. The coexistence of Europeans and Orientals in the Holy Land brought an understanding and appreciation of a material culture that originated in the East and eventually became valued because of its origin in the Holy Land. Crusader material culture may have stopped with the loss of Acre in 1291, but the economic realities of Mediterranean trade demanded the presence of European merchants in the Near East. Because of profit, fashion or taste these merchants managed to promote the products of the Holy Land as desirable commodities whose value depended on their place of manufacture. It was the long presence of the crusaders in the Holy Land that allowed such a change in the perception of these products and in the development of a parallel system of commodification in Europe.

notes

1. *Reading Material Culture: Structuralism, Hermeneutics, and Post-structuralism*, ed. C. Tilley (Oxford and Cambridge, Mass., 1990); *The Meanings of Things: Material Culture and Aymbolic Expression*, ed. I. Hodder (London and Boston, 1989); *Approaches to Material Culture: Research for Historical Archaeologists: a Reader from Historical Archaeology*, ed. D. R. Brauner (California, Penn., 2000); *Art and Artifacts: Essays in Material Culture and Museum Studies in Honor of Jane Powell Dwyer*, ed. D. Juli (Providence, R.I., 1992); *Experiencing Material Culture in the Western World*, ed. S. M. Pearce (London and Washington, DC, 1997); *History from Things: Essays on Material Culture*, ed. S. Lubar and W. D. Kingery (Washington, DC, c. 1993); *The Material Culture Reader*, ed. V. Buchli (Oxford and New York, 2002).

2. C. N. Johns, 'Excavations at Pilgrims' Castle, 'Atlit (1932); The Ancient Tell and the Outer Defences of the Castle', *Quarterly of the Dept. of Antiquities of Palestine*, 3 (1934), 152–64; A. Boas, 'Islamic and Crusader Pottery (c. 640–1265) from the Crusader City (Area TP/4)', in *Caesarea Papers: Straton's tower, Herod's Harbour, and Roman and Byzantine Caesarea: Including the Papers given at a Symposium held ... on 25–28 March, 1988*, ed. R. L. Vann (Ann Arbor, 1992); *King Herod's Dream: Caesarea on the Sea*, ed. K. Holum et al. (New York and London, 1988).

3. A. J. Boas, *Crusader Archaeology: The Material Culture of the Latin East* (London and New York, 1999); R. Ellenblum, *Frankish Rural Settlement in the Latin Kingdom of Jerusalem* (Cambridge, 1998); R. Ellenblum, 'Construction Methods in Frankish Rural Settlements', in *The Horns of Hattin*, ed. B. Z. Kedar (Jerusalem, 1992), pp. 168–89; D. Pringle, 'Medieval Pottery from Caesarea', *Levant*, 17 (1985); E. Stern, 'Excavations of the Courthouse Site at Akko: The Pottery of the Crusader and Ottoman Periods', *Atiqot*, 31 (1997).

4. For an overview of the establishment and evolution of the field see: J. Folda, *The Art of the Crusaders in the Holy Land, 1098–1187* (New York, 1995); J. Folda, 'The Saint Marina Icon. "Maniera greca", "Lingua franca" or "Crusader Art"?' in *Four Icons in the Mesnil Collection*, ed. B. Davezac (Houston, 1992).

5. The field has been dominated by studies in architecture, scuplture and manuscript illumination, the most important of which are: P. Deschamps, 'La sculpture française en Palestine et en Syrie à l'époque des croisades', *Monuments et Memoires (fondation Piot)*, 31 (1930); C. Enlart, *Les Monuments des croisés dans le royaume de Jérusalem; architecture religieuse et civile* (Paris, 1925); H. Buchthal, *Miniature Painting in the Latin Kingdom of Jerusalem* (Oxford, 1957); J. Folda, *Crusader Manuscript Illumination at Saint-Jean d'Acre, 1275–1291* (Princeton, 1976); K. Weitzmann, 'Icon Painting in the Crusader Kingdom', *Dumbarton Oaks Papers*, 20 (1966).

6. The most vocal studies following this trend are: L.-A. Hunt, 'Art and Colonialism: The Mosaics of the Church of the Nativity in Bethlehem (1169) and the Problem of "Crusader" Art', *Dumbarton Oaks Papers*, 45 (1991), 69–85;

A. Weyl Carr, 'Art in the Court of the Lusignan in Cyprus', in *Cyprus and the Crusades*, ed. N. Coureas and J. Riley-Smith (Nicosia, 1995), pp. 239–74; M. Georgopoulou, 'Orientalism and Crusader Art: Constructing a New Canon', *Medieval Encounters: Jewish, Christian and Muslim Culture in Confluence and Dialogue*, 5 (1999), 289–321; B. Zeitler, '"Sinful Sons, Falsifiers of the Christian Faith": The Depiction of Muslims in a "Crusader" Manuscript', *Mediterranean Historical Review*, 12 (1997), 25–50.

7. Hunt, 'Art and Colonialism'; J. Folda, 'Crusader Frescoes at Crac des Chevaliers and Marqab Castle', *Dumbarton Oaks Papers*, 36 (1982), 177–210; H. Kennedy, *Crusader Castles* (Cambridge and New York, 1994); W. Müller-Wiener, *Castles of the Crusaders* (New York, 1966); E. G. Rey, *Étude sur les monuments de l'architecture militaire des croisés en Syrie et dans l'île de Chypre, Collection de documents inédits sur l'histoire de France. Première série, Histoire politique* (Paris, 1871).

8. G. Vikan, *Byzantine Pilgrimage Art*, Dumbarton Oaks Byzantine Collection Publications, 5 (Washington, DC, 1982).

9. For examples of crusader *ampullae* see: Folda, *Art of the Crusaders*, pp. 294–7; D. Syon, 'Souvenirs from the Holy Land: A Crusader Workshop of Lead Ampullae from Acre', in *Knights of the Holy Land: The Crusader Kingdom of Jerusalem*, ed. Silvia Rozenberg (Jerusalem, 1999), pp. 110–15.

10. Published by Buchthal, *Miniature Painting*, plate 7a.

11. See ibid., pp. 21–3, 123.

12. Ibid., plate 67a.

13. D. H. Weiss, 'Biblical History and Medieval Historiography: Rationalizing Strategies in Crusader Art', *Modern Language Notes*, 108 (1993), 710–37; D. H. Weiss, *Art and Crusade in the age of Saint Louis* (Cambridge and New York, 1998).

14. Buchthal, *Miniature Painting*, plate 113c.

15. Published in *Knights of the Holy Land*, ed. Rozenberg, pp. 128–9.

16. D. Jacoby, 'Knightly Values and Class Consciousness in the Crusader States of the Eastern Mediterranean', *Mediterranean Historical Review*, 1 (1986), 158–86; V. François, 'Une Illustration des Romans courtois. La vaisselle a table chypriote sous l'occupation franque', *Cahier du Centre d'Etudes Chypriotes*, 29 (1999).

17. D. Papanikola-Bakirtzis, 'Cypriot Medieval Glazed Pottery: Answers and Questions', in *The Sweet Land of Cyprus. Papers Given at the Twenty-Fifth Jubilee Symposium of Byzantine Studies, Birmingham, March 1991*, ed. A. A. M. Bryer and G. S. Georghallides (Nicosia and Birmingham, England, 1993), pp. 115–30; D. Papanikola-Bakirtzis, 'La céramique à glaçure dans la Chypre du Moyen-Age', in *La France aux portes de l'Orient Chypre XIIème-XVème siècle*, ed. J. Charles-Gaffiot (Paris, 1991).

18. See note 6 above and B. Zeitler, 'Cross-cultural interpretations of imagery in the Middle Ages', *Art Bulletin*, 76 (1994), 680–94; B. Zeitler, 'Two Iconostasis Beams from Mount Sinai: Object Lessons in Crusader Art', in *Ikonostas: proiskhozhdenie, razvitie, simvolika*, ed. A. Lidov (Moscow, 2000).

19. Published by Kurt Weitzmann, *The Icon* (London, 1982), p. 220.

20. S. E. J. Gerstel, 'Art and Identity in the Medieval Morea', in *The Crusades from the Perspective of Byzantium and the Muslim World*, ed. A. E. Laiou and R. P. Mottahedeh (Washington, DC, 2001), pp. 264–85, esp. pp. 268–73.

21. A. Cutler, 'Misapprehensions and Misgivings: Byzantine Art and the West in the Twelfth and Thirteenth Centuries', in *Mediaevalia*, 7 (1984), 51; reprinted in *Byzantium, Italy and the North: Papers on Cultural Relations* (London, 2000), article XVII. See also *Byzantium: Faith and Power: 1261–1557*, ed. H. Evans (New Haven and London, 2004).

22. Among the many influential works of these two scholars are: S. D. Goitein, *A Mediterranean society; The Jewish Communities of the Arab World as Portrayed in the Documents of the Cairo Geniza*, 6 vols (Berkeley, 1967–); and R. S. Lopez, *The Commercial Revolution of the Middle Ages, 950–1350* (Englewood Cliffs, N.J., 1971).

23. N. Ziadeh, *Damascus Under the Mamluks* (Norman, Okla., 1964), pp. 60, 63 and 86.

24. Ziadeh, *Urban Life in Syria*, p. 31.

25. For an example see *Knights of the Holy Land*, ed. Rozenberg, p. 265; see also S. Patitucci Uggeri, 'La protomaiolica del Mediterraneo orientale in rapporto ai centri di produzione italiani', *Corso di cultura sull'arte ravennate e bizantina*, 32 (1985), 337–402; D. Pringle, 'Pottery as Evidence for Trade in the Crusader States', *I comuni italiani nel regno crociato di Gerusalemme. Atti del Colloquio 'The Italian Communes in the Crusading Kingdom of Jerusalem', Jerusalem, May 24 – May 28, 1984* (Genoa, 1986), pp. 449–76; D. Pringle, 'Some more Protomaiolica from Athlit (Pilgrims' Castle) and a Discussion of its Distribution in the Levant', *Levant*, 14 (1982), 104–17; A. J. Boas, 'The Import of Western Ceramics to the Latin Kingdom of Jerusalem', *Israel Exploration Journal*, 44 (1994), 102–22; D. B. Whitehouse, 'Proto-maiolica', *Faenza*, 66 (1980), 77–89; V. François, 'Sur la circulation des céramiques byzantines en Méditerranée orientale et occidentale', in *La céramique médiévale en Méditerranée* (Aix-en-Provence, 1997), p. 235; *Byzantine Glazed Ceramics. The Art of Sgraffito*, ed. D. Bakirtzi-Papanikola (Athens, 1999); T. S. Mackay, 'More Byzantine and Frankish Pottery from Corinth', *Hesperia*, 36 (1967), 249–320; E. Stern, 'Export to the Latin East of Cypriot Manufactured Glazed Pottery in the Twelfth-Thirteenth Century', in *Cyprus and the Crusades*, ed. Coureas and Riley-Smith, pp. 325–35; C. I. Williams, 'Frankish Corinth: An Overview', in *Proceedings for the Centennial of the Corinth Excavation, Dec. 5–7, 1996* (2003), pp. 223–81.

26. Lopez, *Commercial Revolution of the Middle Ages*, p. 96; and F. Balducci Pegolotti, *La pratica della mercatura*, ed. A. Evans (Cambridge, Mass., 1936); D. Jacoby, 'A Venetian Manual of Commercial Practice from Crusader Acre', in *Comuni italiani nel regno crociato di Gerusalemme*, ed. G. Airaldi and B. Kedar (Genoa, 1986), pp. 403–28; R. Lopez and G. Airaldi, 'Il più antico manuale italiano di pratica della mercatura', *Miscellanea di studi storici*, 2, Fonti e Studi 38 (Genoa, 1983), pp. 99–117.

27. C. B. Kritsas, 'To byzantinon nauagion Pelagonnesou-Alonnesou' [The Byzantine Shipwreck of Pelagonnesos-Alonnesos]', *Athens Annals of Archaeology*, 4 (1971); G. F. Bass, 'The Shipwreck at Serçe Limani, Turkey', *Archaeology*, 32 (1979), 36–43; and G. F. Bass, J. R. Steffy and F. H. van Doorninck, Jr, 'Excavation of an 11th-Century Shipwreck at Serçe Limani, Turkey', *National Geographic Society Research Reports*, 17 (1984), 161–82.

28. L.-A. Hunt, *Byzantium, Eastern Christendom and Islam: Art at the Crossroads of the Medieval Mediterranean*, 2 vols (London, 1998); R. Nelson, 'An Icon at Mount Sinai and Christian Painting in Muslim Egypt during the Thirteenth and

Fourteenth Centuries', *Art Bulletin*, 65 (1983), 201–18; E. Dodd, *The Frescoes of Mar Musa al-Habashi: a Study in Medieval Painting in Syria* (Toronto, 2001); A. Weyl Carr, 'The Mural Paintings of Abu Ghosh and the Patronage of Manuel Comnenus in the Holy Land', in *Crusader Art in the Twelfth Century*, ed. J. Folda (Oxford, 1982), pp. 215–44.

29. The seal is illustrated in Y. Friedman, 'Pilgrims in the Shadow of the Crusader Kingdom', in Rozenberg, *Knights of the Holy Land*, p. 108, fig. 3, and H. E. Mayer, *Das Siegelwesen in der Kreuzfahrstaaten* (Munich, 1978), pl. 2, figs 17–18.

30. C. J. Lamm, *Oriental Glass of Mediaeval Date found in Sweden and the early history of lustre-painting* (Stockholm, 1941), p. 63; J. Allan and W. Henderson, 'Enamels on Ayyubid and Mamluk Glass Fragments', *Archaeomaterials*, 4 (1990).

31. E. Atil, *Renaissance of Islam. The Art of the Mamluks* (Washington, DC, 1981), p. 126; and Georgopoulou, 'Orientalism and Crusader Art'.

32. D. S. Rice, 'Inlaid Brasses From the Workshop of Ahmad al-Dhaki al-Mawsili', *Ars Orientalis*, 2 (1957), 283–4 and n. 9.

33. J. Leroy, *Les manuscripts syriaques à peintures conservés dans les bibliothèques d'Europe et d'Orient* (Paris, 1964), p. 259, pl. 60, fig. 2; p. 335, pls. 111–13; pl. 130, 134/2, and 135/2; J. Leroy, *Les manuscripts coptes et coptes-arabes illustrés* (Paris, 1974), p. 126, pl. 54, fig. 1.

34. Goitein, *Mediterranean Society*, vol. 1, pp. 99–110 and vol. 2, pp. 289–96; N. A. Ziadeh, *Urban Life in Syria Under the Early Mamluks* (Beirut, 1953).

35. R. Katzenstein and G. Lowry, 'Christian Themes in Thirteenth-Century Islamic Metalwork', *Muqarnas*, 1 (1983), 53–68; E. Baer, *Ayyubid Metalwork with Christian Images* (Leiden, 1989).

36. Georgopoulou, *Burning Incense in the Islamic and Byzantine Near East* (forthcoming).

37. A. Carr Weyl, 'Art in the Court of the Lusignan Kings', in *Cyprus and the Crusades*, ed. Coureas and Riley-Smith, pp. 239–74.

38. L. T. Schneider, 'The Freer Canteen', *Ars Orientalis*, 9 (1973), 137–56.

39. Katzenstein and Lowry, 'Christian Themes in Thirteenth-Century Islamic Metalwork'.

40. Lamm, *Oriental Glass of Medieval Date*; R. Smidt, *Das Glas* (Berlin and Leipzig, 1922); I. Krueger, 'Research in Medieval Glass. Where Are We Standing Now?', in *Annales du 13e Congrès de l'Association Internationale de l'Histoire du Verre. Pays Bas 28 août–1 septembre 1995* (Lochem, 1996), pp. 283–4.

41. S. Carboni, 'Oggetti decorati a smalto di influsso islamico nella vetraria muranese: tecnica e forma', in *Arte Veneziana e arte Islamica. Atti del primo simposio internazionale sull'arte veneziana e l'arte islamica. Venice, Ateneo Veneto 1986*, ed. E. J. Grube (Venice, 1989), p. 153; M. Verità, 'Analytical Investigation of European Enameled Beakers of the 13th and 14th centuries', *Journal of Glass Studies*, 37 (1995), 83–4.

42. D. Pringle, 'Some Approaches to the Study of Crusader Masonry Marks in Palestine', *Levant*, 13 (1981), 173–99, esp. 176–7.

5
prosopography

alan v. murray

The term 'prosopography' differs from most of the other chapter headings in this book in that it refers not to a particular subject of scholarship, but to a form of historical inquiry. The Latin term *prosopographia*, from which the modern English word is derived, was coined in humanist circles in the sixteenth century; it derives from the Greek word *prosopon*, which is related to Latin *persona* and means 'face, mask, role, person'. Prosopography is concerned with the study of the identities, lives and relationships of people in historical societies; yet while it seeks to compile and analyse information on individuals, its essential feature is that it is concerned with groups or sets of people.[1] A short serviceable definition of prosopography would be 'the compilation and analysis of data on a defined set of individuals', and it should be stressed that prosopography goes far beyond the scope of traditional historical biography. One practical reason for this is that at least until the later Middle Ages, the nature of the surviving source material means that the amount of information necessary to write narrative biography of the traditional literary or historical type is generally restricted to relatively few monarchs, saints and bishops and a handful of other individuals, and even then, often with crucial gaps in the surviving evidence.

The aim of prosopography is to compile accurate data on a defined group – that is, a set of individuals – and to interrogate this data with the objective of illuminating our understanding of a particular historical society. Groups which constitute the subjects of prosopographical study may be defined in a vast range of ways according to the nature of the source material and the aims of the investigation, but the essential point is that a given group should have at least one common characteristic. This defining characteristic may relate to social factors (such as membership of a particular social group or tenure of a particular office or profession), to geographical factors (such as birth, upbringing or activity in a particular region or place), to chronological factors (such as age group or birth or activity in a defined time period), or even connections with particular historical events (such as a crusade). Different characteristics may be selected and combined in order to define groups whose constituents might be regarded as profitable subjects from the point of view of historical inquiry. Prosopographers might wish to study, for example, the entourage of a particular monarch, inhabitants of a particular town, members of a particular religious order or graduates of a particular university. Obviously, some characteristics may be so general or broad that the amount of data relating to the groups defined by them may be too large for practical study; however, by refining and combining characteristics – and especially by introducing chronological and geographical parameters – it is possible to define prosopographical groups of manageable proportions, such as members of a religious order in one geographical area in a given time period, or graduates of a given university in one particular discipline. For the study of the crusades, obvious groupings relate to participants in a particular expedition, or crusaders originating from particular regions or countries. Within a defined group, the prosopographer attempts to compile information which is as complete as possible in a number of discrete categories across its entire membership. Forms of names used by individuals are one obvious category, not only because the name was basic to a person's identity, but also because medieval name-giving habits meant that a person's name – particularly in the noble classes – often gives important clues about his or her family ties. There is no set scheme of categorization, which will vary depending on the nature of the target group, the source material evaluated and the aims of the particular study; thus, a study of university masters or graduates would probably wish to compile data on the degrees they held, although this would rarely be true of other social or professional groups. The most common categories compiled might include parentage, other kinship and marital relationships, social group, feudo-vassalic relationships, dates of birth and death, geographical origin, and titles and offices held. However, the realities of source materials in the Middle Ages mean that it will be rare that information will be available across the board in all categories. It is therefore important to supplement such basic data with other information, such as that relating to involvement in particular events, but particularly with the descriptive terminology applied in source materials to a given individual, which can often reveal a great deal about social status, geographical origins and other characteristics.

The data compiled on defined groups can be used to answer a vast range of questions which might form the starting points for historical inquiry. Some such questions might be: What were the geographical origins of participants in the First Crusade? What were the social origins of the French episcopate under the Capetians? What was the age structure of Benedictines in England? How many graduates of the University of Paris in the thirteenth century originated from Scotland? Notwithstanding the last two questions, it should not be assumed that prosopography is primarily a quantitative science. Although statistical information is frequently compiled as basic data or used for illustrative purposes, the main aim of prosopographers is to produce analytical discussions of their given topics which are detailed, discursive and nuanced.

Prosopography can thus be regarded as a particular branch of social history which is linked to genealogy, demography and onomastics, contributing to the results of scholarship in these areas while also making use of their techniques. The nature of the evidence used by prosopography also means that it may need to draw on knowledge of diplomatics (the study of documents), palaeography (study of writing), sigillography (study of seals), epigraphy (study of inscriptions), and heraldry (study of armorial devices). Prosopography aims to overcome the limitations of the restricted amount of information available on the vast majority of individuals in the Middle Ages by casting its net to encompass as wide a sample of subjects as possible. The idea of collectivity is not only significant in the definition of subjects of prosopographical research, but is also of crucial importance *within* subject groups, in that one of the main aims of prosopography has always been to identify the nature of relationships, networks and affinities which linked and affected individual people, and ultimately, the workings of societies and institutions. Thus, in the case of the putative study of the entourage of a particular medieval monarch, it would be important to identify and analyse not only common features characterizing different individuals, but also any bonds between them.

The first sustained use of prosopographical techniques in modern scholarship was carried out by nineteenth-century classicists in connection with the study of the ruling classes of the Roman Empire. It was particularly well suited to gathering and collating information from a vast range of sources which were often fragmentary in nature (such as inscriptions or papyri), and where many names were shared by numerous different individuals. This work has continued to produce a great range of reference works and case studies of the Roman and Byzantine Empires up to the present. In similar fashion, prosopography of the medieval period was long concerned with social and governmental elites such as monarchs and their families, and secular and ecclesiastical office holders. This focus was not only because these were the groups for which the greatest amount of evidence was available, but also because their study had the greatest relevance to the history of institutions. The greatest strides in medieval prosopography have undoubtedly been made by German scholars, many of them based at the universities of Freiburg and Münster, such as Gerd Tellenbach, Karl Schmid, Otto Gerhard Oexle and Karl Ferdinand Werner. Their work on the Merovingian, Carolingian and Ottonian periods was remarkable in that while making use of traditional sources such as chronicles, hagiography, diplomas and charters, they also opened up the evidence of liturgical sources such as necrologies and confraternity books originating from the great southern German abbeys such as St Gallen, Reichenau, Fulda and Remiremont, and stressed the importance of name-giving habits and their interpretation. The explosion of prosopographical work since the Second World War can be measured in the publication of numerous sources and studies, as well as the scope of scholarly journals.[2]

There is insufficient space in this chapter even to summarize the development of medievalist prosopographical research in recent decades, but three significant features can be highlighted. Firstly, scholarship is still largely dominated by the study of elite (and often overlapping) groups such as royal and princely dynasties, ecclesiastical and secular office-holders, cathedral chapters, landowners, courtiers, nobilities and so on. Yet research has also come to take in a much wider range of social groups. Members of religious orders and university masters and students have been one major area of expansion, but research of recent years has extended to such diverse groups as merchants and artisans, and even poachers and prostitutes, while that part of prosopographical inquiry concerned primarily with names and name-giving habits has also ranged over all social classes. Secondly, there has been a growing emphasis on the separation of evidence and its interpretation. It has been viewed as increasingly important that the user of any prosopographical resource should be presented with as much of the original evidence as possible in order that the writer's analysis can be checked independently as a safeguard against what might be called over-interpretation. In an ideal world, every separate piece of evidence should be collected and presented in discrete fashion even if a scholar's interpretation regards them as relating to the same medieval individual. The publication costs of print media meant that it was often difficult to present evidence in ideal, or even adequate fashion, but new vistas have been opened up by the third significant development in prosopographical research, that is the growing possibilities of electronic technology. The collection of large amounts of diverse data which need to be stored in an often highly structured format is a task which lends itself to realization by means of proprietary or customized electronic databases.[3] For a considerable time now, databases have been used for data collection and maintenance in prosopographical research, even if interpretative results have still largely been presented in print format, but it is likely that in future evidential electronic databases may be published as complete or partial works of research in themselves, as is the case with the prosopography of post-Conquest English landholders compiled by K. S. B. Keats-Rohan.[4] The other significant characteristic of electronic databases is that they now permit the undertaking of prosopographical projects in cases where the sheer amount of data involved might otherwise have been beyond the capacities of individual scholars or research groups.

In the study of the crusades, prosopography has been predominantly concerned with the composition of individual crusade expeditions, with traditions of crusading in particular countries, regions or families, and with the societies of states established by the crusades in the Levant, Greece, and the Baltic region.[5] These main areas in actual fact cover a multitude of diverse topics, and the amount of research on each of them varies greatly. Many individual topics overlap: for example, since the majority of the early Frankish population of Outremer during the first two decades of the twelfth century were immigrants who had arrived in the East with the First Crusade (1096–99), it is obvious that any study of the early society of the kingdom of Jerusalem, the principality of Antioch or the county of Tripoli must necessarily be concerned with the recruitment of the crusade itself. Similarly, a diachronic study of a particular family's interest in crusading will need to be concerned with the detail of several individual crusade expeditions, as well as with its genealogy and with the local history of its places of residence in the West.

One of the most basic tasks of prosopographical research on the crusades is to establish as completely as possible the composition of individual crusading expeditions. In this respect, modern scholarship could look back on a long historiographical tradition which could be regarded as going back almost as far as the beginning of the crusades themselves. Within a few years of the capture of Jerusalem in 1099, chroniclers in western Europe were writing narrative accounts of the First Crusade which recorded large numbers of names of participants in the expedition. As one might expect, much detail preserved by them relates to leaders of the expedition or those whose subsequent careers made them important, such as Godfrey of Bouillon or Bohemond I of Antioch, or those who were distinguished for deeds of valour, such as the German Wicher, celebrated for killing a lion and for cutting a Turk in two, or Letold, the Fleming famed as the first crusader to mount the walls of Jerusalem on the day of its capture (15 July 1099).

The chroniclers also record a great many names of other individuals, in some cases in the form of muster-rolls listing participants in battles. In doing so, they tended to display a bias of interest towards participants from their own homelands or in contingents with which they themselves were associated. Thus Albert of Aachen, writing in the Rhineland, gives a great deal of information on crusaders from Lotharingia, Germany and the Low Countries; Raymond of Aguilers, associated with Raymond of Saint-Gilles, is primarily interested in crusaders from Languedoc, Provence and Auvergne, while our best information on the Normans of southern Italy comes from the anonymous author of the *Gesta Francorum*, who had gone on crusade with Bohemond.[6] This form of bias often produced descriptive terminology which is invaluable in allowing us to narrow down geographical origins. Thus Guibert of Nogent describes a crusader who later became lord of Tiberias as '*miles egregius … Gervasius vocabatur apud castrum Basilicas pagi Suessonici nobiliter oriundus*' ('the distinguished knight … called Gervase, nobly born in the castle of Bazoches of the country of Soissons'), enabling an identification of his birthplace as Bazoches-sur-Vesle in the modern French *département* of Aisne.[7] The style of writing about the earliest crusade established a pattern according to which later medieval writers were concerned to record numerous names of those participants, especially those who died on crusade or who distinguished themselves in battle; among numerous examples of the genre which are rich in such prosopographical information one might highlight Roger of Howden and the anonymous *Historia de expeditione Friderici imperatoris* for the Third Crusade, Geoffrey of Villehardouin for the Fourth, and John of Joinville for the crusades of Louis IX of France.

In the course of hundreds of years in which original sources were copied, edited, translated and often incorporated in condensed or excerpted into new works, changes wrought in transmission often affected the accuracy of their prosopographical information considerably. Thus a surprisingly large number of names of participants of the First Crusade are preserved in an illustrated fourteenth-century genealogical history roll (MS Leeds, University Library, Brotherton Collection 100), which contains an account of the history of Outremer in French, but their precise identification is not immediately obvious without knowledge of the contemporary accounts.[8] For example, the second king of Jerusalem is correctly identified as *Baudouin de Bourc* after his place of origin of Bourcq near Vouziers in the southern Ardennes; yet at the same time a quite separate literary tradition had developed which turned the king into *Baudouin de Sebourg* and associated him with Hainaut.[9]

The single most popular text dealing with the crusades in the Middle Ages was probably the *Historia Iherosolimitana* by Robert, a monk of Reims, which was repeatedly copied, used as a source book, and also translated.[10] However, in the German translations of this work the Latin versions of personal names are often changed beyond recognition; thus in one of the late-fifteenth-century printed editions, the French crusaders Achard of Montmerle (Lat. *Achardus de Montemerlo*) and Roger of Barneville (Lat. *Rogerus de Bardavilla*, or in some manuscripts, *Pardavilla*) are germanized into *Archadus von Moerelberg* and *Rogerius von Partdorff*, again making accurate identification difficult.[11]

Deficiencies of this type were exacerbated by a prevalent trend in the later medieval and early modern historiography of the crusades, which often had the aim (whether explicit or implicit) of recording and glorifying the contributions of particular countries, regions or families. This led to a tendency towards selective treatment, over-interpretation and distortion of evidence which characterized much published scholarship up to the nineteenth century, and in some cases, beyond. Thus the German humanist Froben Christoph, Count of Zimmern (1519–66) incorporated into his family chronicle (the *Chronicle of Zimmern*), an account of the First Crusade. He proclaims that one of his aims was to record the deeds of the southern German nobility, which he states had been unjustly neglected by other authors who had concentrated on crusaders from France and the Low Countries; yet the list of German crusaders he presents includes several figures who are anachronistically derived from later crusading expeditions, several who are simply invented, and at least one who was created by transmogrifying a French knight called Walter Sans-Avoir into a fictitious German called Walter, Duke of Teck, whom Froben Christoph could claim as a member of a dynasty to which his own ancestors were related.[12]

It should be remembered that in Europe at least up to the time of the First World War, the crusades were (with few exceptions) uncritically viewed as an enterprise which was Christian and meritorious.[13] It was only in the late nineteenth century that a more scholarly attitude emerged. One of the earliest practitioners of exemplary prosopographical technique was Reinhold Röhricht, who attempted to compile comprehensive lists of German crusaders and pilgrims for the whole of the Middle Ages along with listings of source materials.[14] Nevertheless, in much published work there was still frequently a tendency to over-interpret or ignore evidence, especially when it came to demonstrating participation of particular regions in the crusades. Thus even as late as the end of the twentieth century, a paper published in the acts of the conference commemorating the Council of Clermont could assert an origin in the Auvergne for a crusader called 'Eustache d'Agrain', who later became Count of Sidon and Caesarea.[15] Yet it had long been established that Eustace Granarius (Fr. Grenier), to give more accurate forms of his name, originated in the diocese of Thérouanne in Flanders.[16]

It can be seen that the correct identification of crusaders is fundamental to prosopographical study. One of the main reasons for many of the deficiencies of much of the earlier scholarship was an over-reliance on narrative sources. In many of the older published editions of chronicles and similar accounts, individual crusaders are often identified wrongly, inadequately or not at all. It is essential that the evidence of narrative sources should be supplemented by that of documents such as charters and letters which generally have a far greater immediacy than narrative sources. Charters issued by crusaders, being written records of transactions such as gifts or sales of property, give much information about matters such as finance and motivation, as well as the personal connections of the crusader, which become apparent in the lists of individuals appended as a record of witnesses. The formulaic information included in a charter also normally allows a localization of the original transaction – and consequently, these individuals involved in it – to a particular place and time.[17]

The importance of documentary evidence can be illustrated by the case of the crusader *Warnerus de Greis*, who is mentioned several times by Albert of Aachen between 1096 and 1100.[18] Albert's evidence reveals primarily that he was a relative of Godfrey of Bouillon and also figured as the leader of Godfrey's household knights who mounted a coup d'état on Godfrey's death in July 1100 in order to ensure that the succession to the kingdom of Jerusalem should pass to Godfrey's younger brother Baldwin, Count of Edessa. However, documentary evidence allows us to gain a more complete picture of Warner and his connections. Whereas Runciman, relying only on the narrative sources, describes him as a 'Burgundian count', a charter of 1095 or 1096 reveals how he sold to the church of Fosses his allod of Vaux in the county of Huy (mod. Belgium), which he had received in the division of his patrimony with his brother Henry, in order to go to Jerusalem with Duke Godfrey. This single piece of evidence enables us to correctly locate his geographical origins at the village of Grez-Doiceau on the western frontiers of the diocese of Liège, while the witness lists of other charters issued around the same time show him in the company of other men from the Liège-Ardennes region who are known to have accompanied Godfrey and Baldwin to the East. These connections, as well as his comital rank, probably explain why he was accepted as leader by those who held key positions within Godfrey's household in Jerusalem.[19]

The publication in the later nineteenth and twentieth centuries of a vast number of documentary sources relating to the western countries allowed more comprehensive and critical diachronic study of crusade participation from particular regions.[20] An even more fruitful approach was that which studied the contributions of individual noble and knightly families, which have been illuminating in showing how some of them, such as the Lusignans of Aquitaine or the Rotrous of the Perche, developed real traditions of crusading over the generations, demonstrating a commitment which frequently involved great personal and financial sacrifice.[21]

For the purposes of both teaching and research there is a need for a study of each major crusade which ideally should comprise analytical discussion as well as a catalogue listing of all known participants. It is therefore surprising that the first study of an entire crusade on modern prosopographical principles was not published until 1978, with the appearance of Longnon's study of the participants of the Fourth Crusade. His work not only gives an identification of all 'companions of Villehardouin' recorded in the sources, but also attempts to clarify the nature of the ties which linked individual crusaders with the leaders of the expedition and with each other.[22] Nevertheless, even before the publication of Longnon's book, partial studies of the armies of the First Crusade had begun, which came to take in the contingents led by Robert of Normandy, Bohemond, Godfrey of Bouillon and others.[23] A series of studies of motivation by Riley-Smith, dealing with the earliest Frankish settlement of Palestine, also produced many valuable prosopographical findings concerning the crusade which preceded it, and his work culminated in a full-length study of crusaders from the First Crusade up to the end of the reign of Baldwin II, which draws on his study of a vast number of charters issued in the West and includes a listing of a great number of known, probable and possible crusaders.[24] He has subsequently utilized information on known participants as a way of addressing the issue of casualty rates in the course of the crusade.[25]

Apart from the monographs by Riley-Smith and Longnon dealing with the First and Fourth Crusades respectively, the only other study of complete participation in a single expedition is that undertaken for the

Fifth Crusade by Powell.[26] Each of these major studies has been able to establish the identities of hundreds of participants in each crusade, and to give significant discussion about recruitment, motivation and networks. It remains the case that the First Crusade has been the object of more intensive prosopographical investigation than any other expedition. There are partial studies of the composition of the Second Crusade,[27] the Third Crusade,[28] and the crusade of Nicopolis,[29] as well as some of the lesser expeditions.[30] However, although there are a vast number of biographical studies of individual crusaders, particularly those who figured as leaders of expeditions, it would appear that most of the other expeditions to the Eastern Mediterranean region are still waiting for detailed prosopographical treatment.

The greatest area of prosopographical research connected with the crusades has in fact been on the societies of the Frankish states in Outremer, Cyprus and Greece. Within this, by far the largest body of work has concerned the kingdom of Jerusalem.[31] There are considerably smaller numbers of studies on the principality of Antioch,[32] the county of Tripoli,[33] the kingdom of Cyprus,[34] and the various Frankish states in Greece.[35]

The prosopographical study of Outremer and Cyprus could be said to have started with the publication of a monographic study, the *Familles d'Outremer*, by Charles Du Fresne Du Cange.[36] One reason why such a voluminous and detailed work could appear at such a relatively early date was the existence of a unique genealogical text known as the *Lignages d'Outremer*, which Du Cange used as his principal source material.[37] The transmission of the *Lignages* is complex. The original version of the work is thought to have been compiled between 1265 and 1270 by a writer who was connected with the Ibelin family. The scope of this first version was relatively modest, being confined to the Ibelins and other Frankish families related to them, about 20 lineages in all. In 1309 this material was reorganized and greatly expanded, while a third and final redaction was completed in 1369.[38] The second and third redactions of *Lignages* were organized on a new, hierarchical principle, with most chapters dealing with single families or lordships. They contain the names of around 1000 individuals in the kingdom of Jerusalem from the twelfth and thirteenth centuries, even though at the time of the second redaction all the Frankish mainland possessions in Outremer had been lost to the Muslims.

The first redaction of the *Lignages* may have made use of genealogies or family traditions originally dating from the twelfth century, but it is questionable as to how accurate their information was for that period as the information has come down to us, since in several test cases it can be shown that the testimony of the *Lignages* is contradicted by documentary evidence. For example, the chapter which deals with the succession of the lordship of Tiberias (Galilee) claims that William of Bures, lord from 1119, had a wife called Eschiva, and four sons, called Hugh, William, Hosto and Ralph, none of whom are known from documentary sources. The *Lignages* simply do not mention Walter of Saint-Omer, who is well-documented as Prince of Galilee between 1159 and 1170, and who is known to have had a wife called Eschiva and a son called Hugh.[39] In this case, there is an evident conflation of two distinct generations, and it often seems that a desire to portray an unbroken succession stretching back to the time of the first three crusades often suggests a greater genealogical continuity in the tenure of lordships than actually was the case.

Du Cange's work not only followed the basic organizational structure of the *Lignages* in attempting to provide an account of the rulers, aulic officers, lords, patriarchs, archbishops and bishops of each of the Frankish states, but drew heavily on its evidence. However, as the *Familles d'Outremer* appeared before the publication of the majority of narrative and documentary sources, it is of limited value and needs to be used with great caution. However, the appearance of a new critical edition by Nielen, as well as her earlier work on its transmission, means that the *Lignages* are now available as an important research tool in their own right, which may well spur on research on the nobility of Outremer in the thirteenth century.[40]

It was only with the publication of many important editions of documents from the later nineteenth century onwards that a firm foundation was established for the prosopography of Outremer, although it should be stressed that this work is by no means complete.[41] The nature of the available sources has meant that it has concentrated on the holders of particular lordships or secular offices,[42] or on families and individuals.[43] However, much of the earlier work, especially that by Pirie-Gordon, La Monte and Rüdt de Collenberg, suffered from an over-reliance on the evidence of the *Lignages*; it was only with a greater emphasis on the testimony of documents, particularly in the work of Mayer, that many earlier errors were corrected.

Although much of this work was useful in establishing family genealogies and the succession of lordships, there was still a need for more all-embracing work that would reveal more about Frankish society as a whole. And in fact, since the 1980s our understanding of the kingdom's politics, institutions and society have been transformed by a range of studies which have attempted to examine the ruling classes as a whole in segmental rather than linear fashion, that is by studying the group over a period of time, such as a particular reign or longer.

One of the most basic questions was that concerning the factors that determined whether crusaders returned to their homes in the West after the capture of Jerusalem in 1099 or whether they remained as settlers in the East, and this question was addressed by Riley-Smith in his studies dealing with motivations and relationships involved in the initial period of settlement.[44] Subsequent work by Riley-Smith and Phillips has stressed the importance of continuing immigration by groups and individuals in the period right up to the overthrow of the kingdom by Saladin in 1187, and the continuing ties between the Franks of Outremer and their kinsmen and friends in the West.[45]

It is perhaps understandable that a great deal of (not only prosopographical) research on the kingdom has been drawn to the decades before the defeat of the kingdom by Saladin in 1187: the reign of Amalric (1163–74) and the Frankish attempts to conquer Egypt, that of the gallant leper-king Baldwin IV (1174–85), and fractious reigns of his heirs Guy and Sibylla (1185–90/92). However, the high drama of this period has meant that research has tended to focus on the individual personalities of the monarchs and the major political players rather than on the ruling classes as a group.[46] Yet some prosopographical studies shine through in their significance. It was long thought that the internal struggles which plagued the kingdom after the accession of Baldwin IV were the result of hostility between two factions: a party of long established 'native barons', such as Raymond III of Tripoli, and a 'court party' of newcomers from the West. Yet an outstanding study by Edbury has demonstrated that the idea of factions of fixed composition can no longer serve as an explanation for internal instability after 1174.[47]

In comparison with this richness of research on the twelfth-century kingdom, the thirteenth century has received little study, and indeed cries out for attention. Only recently has an attempt been made to study the burgess class of Jerusalem; this is one of the few areas where there is sufficient data for non-noble and non-clerical groups in the twelfth century, although for the thirteenth century, a considerable amount of source material is also available.[48] Studies on women have tended to focus on ruling queens and royal consorts.[49]

The Church, however, has received greater attention. The historian William of Tyre was unique among the higher clergy in that he was born in Outremer, whereas as far as origins can be ascertained, the patriarchs, archbishops and bishops were almost invariably recruited from immigrants. Prosopographical research on the Latin Church has largely concentrated on some on the senior secular clergy rather than the monastic Church.[50]

A final and quite innovative area of research on the kingdom of Jerusalem has been the study of personal names, a subject which has been relatively neglected in connection with Outremer even though it has long been a staple topic of wider prosopographical research. Nielen has studied the range of names which feature in the *Lignages d'Outremer*, but the most comprehensive treatment of the subject has been in a recent monograph by Shagrir, who has attempted to ascertain a complete picture of the forenames used by the Frankish population of the Latin kingdom over the entire duration of its existence. The starting point of her anthroponymic analysis was to ask to what extent the Franks preserved European patterns and traditions in their new homeland, or whether they assimilated features from their eastern environment. While the Latin kingdom shared in the general western trend by which the name stock of the period moved to a more 'Christian' character, it did not participate in the general decline in the number of names used, retaining a greater range, which may reflect the diversity of lands from which Frankish society originated.[51] The conclusions of this work show how much can still be achieved through prosopographical research on an area as much studied as the Latin kingdom.

The final area which remains to be discussed is the so-called Baltic or 'Northern' crusades. After the initial conquest of Livonia and Prussia, the pattern of crusading which developed was not one of large general expeditions, as in the crusades in the Mediterranean region, but rather one in which crusaders travelled from their home countries (predominantly Germany, the Low Countries, England, Scotland and France) either as individuals with their retinues, or in relatively small groups, and then joining in the annual campaigns against the Lithuanians organized by the Teutonic Order. This rather fragmented pattern of crusading would at first sight seem much less conducive to the collection and analysis of prosopographical data, and for long scholarly work on the Baltic crusades tended to feature in regional studies or essays on individual crusaders or expeditions.[52] However, it is striking that despite the scattered nature of the sources, the numerous crusading expeditions to Prussia have been the subject of a remarkable study by Paravicini. This draws on a vast and diverse array of materials, the great majority of them unpublished archival sources, and ranging from travel accounts to heraldry, in order to produce detailed documentation and analysis of hundreds of individual journeys to Prussia. Paravicini's study is exemplary not only in the range of source materials it draws on, but also in the diversity of questions it uses these to illuminate: not only, for example, the identity, status and age structure of crusaders, but also the financing of their journeys, methods and speed of travel, their entertainment and commemorations of crusading.[53]

Paravicini's work represents the most impressive single piece of prosopographical research yet undertaken in connection with the crusades, and is thus an appropriate note on which to end this survey. It can be seen that prosopographical approaches and techniques have done a great deal to further our understanding of the nature of the crusading movement and of the societies it engendered, particularly with regard to the major expeditions to the East in the twelfth and thirteenth centuries, the kingdom of Jerusalem in the twelfth century, and the crusades in the Baltic region. In other areas, notably the later kingdom of Jerusalem, the other Frankish states in the Levant, and most of the expeditions in the later Middle Ages, a great deal remains to be undertaken – and to be achieved.

notes

1. For a more detailed treatment of definitions of prosopography and the history of the term, particularly with regard to the medieval period, see: G. Beech, 'Prosopography', in *Medieval Studies: An Introduction*, ed. J. M. Powell (Syracuse, 1976), pp. 151–84; Neithard Bulst, 'Zum Gegenstand und zur Methode von Prosopographie', in *Medieval Lives and the Historian: Studies in Medieval Prosopography*, ed. N. Bulst and J-P. Genet (Kalamazoo, Mich., 1986), pp. 1–16, and K. F. Werner, 'L'apport de la prosopographie à l'histoire sociale des élites', in *Family Trees and the Roots of Politics: The Prosopography of Britain and France from the Tenth to the Twelfth Century*, ed. K. S. B. Keats-Rohan (Woodbridge, 1997), pp. 1–21.

2. In addition to the specialist journal *Medieval Prosopography: History and Collective Biography* (Kalamazoo, Mich., 1980–), one can mention two other journals with a strong prosopographical interest: *Francia: Forschungen zur westeuropäischen Geschichte* (Sigmaringen, 1973–) and *Frühmittelalterliche Studien* (Berlin, 1967-). There is also a purely electronic publication *Prosopon: Newsletter of the Unit for Prosopographical Research*, accessible at <www.linacre.ox.ac.uk/prosop/home.stm>.

3. On computer applications, see, for example, J-P. Genet and M. Hainsworth, 'Entre statistique et documentation: Un système de programmes pour le traitement des données prosopographiques', in *Medieval Lives and the Historian*, pp. 359–79, and D. Geuenich, 'Eine Datenbank zur Erforschung mittelalterlicher Personen und Personengruppen, in ibid., pp. 405–17. Numerous descriptions of computer applications can be found in the periodicals *Medieval Prosopography* and *Le Médiéviste et l'ordinateur*.

4. [CD] *Continental Origins of English Landholders 1066–1166: A Prosopography of Post-Conquest England*, comp. K. S. B. Keats-Rohan (Oxford, 2001).

5. For bibliography on individual crusades, regions, families and individuals, see the relevant sections in H. E. Mayer, *Bibliographie zur Geschichte der Kreuzzüge* (Hannover, 1960); H. E. Mayer and J. McLellan, 'Select Bibliography of the Crusades', in *A History of the Crusades*, ed. K. M. Setton, 2nd edn (Madison, Wisc., 1969–89), vol. 6, *The Impact of the Crusades on Europe*, ed. H. W. Hazard and N. P. Zacour, pp. 511–664; and Z. Hunyadi, 'A Bibliography of the Crusades and the Military Orders', in *The Crusades and the Military Orders: Expanding the Frontiers of Medieval Latin Christianity*, ed. Z. Hunyadi and J. Laszlovsky (Budapest, 2001), pp. 501–88. Bibliography cited in the remainder of this chapter is meant to be representative rather than exhaustive, and studies of single individuals are largely excluded unless they have a wider prosopographical relevance. Prosopographical study of the military monastic orders, although beyond the scope of this chapter, is also relevant to the societies of the states established by the crusades in the Levant and the Baltic countries.

6. Other important prosopographical information for the First Crusade is provided by Peter Tudebode, Orderic Vitalis and Guibert of Nogent. Fulcher of Chartres, who is otherwise well-regarded as a valuable eyewitness source, gives comparatively little detail on individuals, probably because his work was originally conceived as a history of the *Gesta* (deeds) of Baldwin I of Jerusalem.

7. Guibert de Nogent, *Dei Gesta per Francos et cinq autres textes*, ed. R. B. C. Huygens, Corpus Christianorum: Continuatio mediaevalis 127A (Turnhout, 1996), Bk 7 lines 2160–1, p. 350.

8. O. Pickering, 'The Crusades in Leeds University Library's Genealogical History Roll', in *From Clermont to Jerusalem: The Crusades and Crusader Societies, 1095–1500*, ed. A. V. Murray (Turnhout, 1998), pp. 251–66.

9. P. R. Grillo, 'Romans de croisade, histoires de famille. Recherches sur le personnage de Baudouin de Sebourg', *Romania*, 110 (1989), 383–95.

10. *Roberti monachi Historia Iherosolimitana*, Recueil des historiens des croisades, ed. Académie des Inscriptions et Belles-Lettres (Paris, 1841–1906), Historiens Occidentaux [henceforth cited as RHC Occ.], vol. 3, pp. 717–882; F. Kraft, *Heinrich Steinhöwels Verdeutschung der Historia Hierosolymitana des Robertus Monachus: Eine literarhistorische Untersuchung* (Straßburg, 1905); B. Haupt, *Historia Hierosolymitana von Robertus Monachus in deutscher Übersetzung* (Wiesbaden, 1972), pp. 223–30; S. Fuchs, 'Die St. Galler Übersetzung der *Historia Hierosolymitana* des Robertus Monachus' (unpublished MA dissertation, University of Frankfurt am Main, 1990).

11. *Historie von der Kreuzfahrt nach dem Heiligen Lande* (Augsburg, 1482), fols 49r, 82v.

12. A. V. Murray, 'The Chronicle of Zimmern as a Source for the First Crusade: The Evidence of MS Stuttgart, Württembergische Landesbibliothek, Cod.Don.580', in *The First Crusade: Origins and Impact*, ed. J. P. Phillips (Manchester, 1997), pp. 78–106; A. V. Murray, 'Walther Duke of Teck: The Invention of a German Hero of the First Crusade', *Medieval Prosopography*, 19 (1998), 35–54.

13. See Chapter 9 by Jean Richard in this volume.

14. R. Röhricht, *Die Deutschen im Heiligen Lande: Ein chronologisches Verzeichnis derjenigen Deutschen, welche als Jerusalempilger und Kreuzfahrer sicher nachzuweisen oder wahrscheinlich anzusehen sind (ca. 650–1291)* (Innsbruck,

1894); R. Röhricht, *Deutsche Pilgerreisen nach dem Heiligen Lande* (Innsbruck, 1900).

15. C. Lauranson-Rosaz, 'Le Velay et la croisade', in *Le Concile de Clermont de 1095 et l'appel à la croisade* (Rome, 1997), pp. 32–64, here 52.

16. C. Moeller, 'Les flamands du Ternois au royaume latin de Jérusalem', in *Mélanges Paul Fredericq* (Bruxelles, 1903), pp. 189–202; A. V. Murray, 'A Note on the Origin of Eustace Grenier', *Bulletin of the Society for the Study of the Crusades and the Latin East*, 6 (1986), 28–30.

17. Collections of documents of relevance to crusade expeditions are too numerous to list individually. For a detailed discussion of the importance of charter evidence, see G. Constable, 'Medieval Charters as a Source for the History of the Crusades', in *Crusade and Settlement*, ed. P. W. Edbury (Cardiff, 1985), pp. 73–89.

18. Albert of Aachen, *Alberti Aquensis Historia Hierosolymitana*, RHC Occ., vol. 4, pp. 265–713, here pp. 299, 300, 301, 310, 383, 514, 520–4.

19. S. Runciman, *A History of the Crusades*, 3 vols (Cambridge, 1951–54), vol. 1, p. 313; A. V. Murray, 'Daimbert of Pisa, the *Domus Godefridi* and the Accession of Baldwin I of Jerusalem', in *From Clermont to Jerusalem: The Crusades and Crusader Societies, 1095–1500*, ed. A. V. Murray (Turnhout, 1998), pp. 81–102.

20. For example, H. Brassat, *Die Teilnahme der Friesen an den Kreuzzügen ultra mare vornehmlich im 12. Jahrhundert* (Berlin, 1970), pp. 17–32; A. Macquarrie, *Scotland and the Crusades, 1095–1560* (Edinburgh, 1985); C. J. Tyerman, *England and the Crusades, 1095–1588* (Chicago, 1988); M-L. Favreau-Lilie, *Die Italiener im Heiligen Lande vom ersten Kreuzzug bis zum Tode Heinrichs von Champagne (1098–1197)* (Amsterdam, 1989); *Les Champenois et la croisade*, ed. Y. Bellenger and D. Queruel (Paris, 1989); M. Balard, 'Les Picards et la croisade au XIIe siècle', in *Orient et Occident du IXe au XVe siècle*, ed. G. Jehel (Paris, 2003), pp. 13–28.

21. J. S. C. Riley-Smith, 'The Crusading Heritage of Guy and Aimery of Lusignan', in *Cyprus and the Crusades*, ed. N. Coureas and J. S. C. Riley-Smith (Nicosia, 1995), pp. 31–45; K. Thompson, 'Family Tradition and the Crusading Impulse: The Rotrou Counts of the Perche', *Medieval Prosopography*, 19 (1998), 1–34; M. R. Evans, 'The Ferrers Earls of Derby and the Crusades', *Nottingham Medieval Studies*, 44 (2000), 69–81.

22. J. Longnon, *Les Compagnons de Villehardouin: Recherches sur les croisés de la Quatrième Croisade* (Geneva, 1978). See also J. Dufournet, 'Villehardouin et les Champenois dans la quatrième croisade', in *Les Champenois et la croisade*, ed. Bellenger and Queruel, pp. 131–47.

23. C. W. David, *Robert Curthose, Duke of Normandy* (Cambridge, Mass., 1920), pp. 221–9; E. M. Jamison, 'Some Notes on the *Anonymi Gesta Francorum*, with Special Reference to the Norman Contingent from South Italy and Sicily in the First Crusade', in *Studies in French Language and Medieval Literature presented to Professor Mildred K. Pope* (Manchester, 1939), pp. 195–204; G. Airaldi, 'I Lombardi alla Prima Crociata', in *I Comuni italiani nel Regno crociato del Gerusalemme*, ed. G. Airaldi and B. Z. Kedar (Genova, 1986), pp. 477–96; B. Figliuolo, 'Ancora sui Normanni d'Italia alla prima crociata', *Archivio storico per le province napoletane*, 104 for 1986 (1988), 1–16; A. V. Murray, 'The Army of Godfrey of Bouillon, 1096–1099: Structure and Dynamics of a Contingent

prosopography

on the First Crusade', *Revue Belge de Philologie et d'Histoire*, 70 (1992), 301–29; M. Bull, *Knightly Piety and the Lay Response to the First Crusade: The Limousin and Gascony, c. 970-c. 1130* (Oxford, 1993).
24. J. S. C. Riley-Smith, 'The Motives of the Earliest Crusaders and the Settlement of Latin Palestine, 1095–1100', *English Historical Review*, 98 (1983), 721–36; Riley-Smith, 'The Latin Clergy and the Settlement in Palestine and Syria, 1098–1100', *Catholic Historical Review*, 74 (1988), 539–57; J. S. C. Riley-Smith, 'Families, Crusades and Settlement in the Latin East, 1102–1131', in *Die Kreuzfahrerstaaten als multikulturelle Gesellschaft. Einwanderer und Minderheiten im 12. und 13. Jahrhundert*, ed. H. E. Mayer (München, 1997), pp. 1–12; J. S. C. Riley-Smith, *The First Crusaders, 1095–1131* (Cambridge, 1997).
25. J. S. C. Riley-Smith, 'Casualties and the Number of Knights on the First Crusade', *Crusades*, 1 (2002), 13–28.
26. J. M. Powell, *Anatomy of a Crusade, 1213–1221* (Philadelphia, 1986).
27. J. S. C. Riley-Smith, 'Family Traditions and Participations in the Second Crusade', in *The Second Crusade and the Cistercians*, ed. M. Gervers (New York, 1992), pp. 101–8; J. P. Phillips, 'The Murder of Charles the Good and the Second Crusade: Household, Nobility, and Traditions of Crusading in Medieval Flanders', *Medieval Prosopography*, 19 (1998), 55–75; V. Hrochová, 'La participation tchèque aux deuxième et troisième croisades', in *Le partage du monde*, ed. M. Balard and A. Ducellier (Paris, 1998), pp. 279–86.
28. H. van Werveke, 'La contribution de la Flandre et du Hainaut à la Troisième Croisade', *Le Moyen Age*, 78 (1972), 55–90; Hrochová, 'La participation tchèque aux deuxième et troisième croisades'.
29. C. Tipton, 'The English at Nicopolis', *Speculum*, 37 (1962), 528–40; B. Schnerb, 'Le contingent franco-bourguignon à la croisade de Nicopolis', *Annales de Bourgogne*, 68 (1996), 59–75.
30. For example: G. Despy, 'Des nobles hainuyers à la croisade contre les Albigeois', in *Recueil d'études d'histoire hainuyère offertes à Maurice-A. Arnould*, ed. J-M. Cauchies and J-M. Duvosquel, 2 vols (Mons, 1983), vol. 2, pp. 51–8; C. Keck, 'L'entourage de Simon de Montfort pendant la Croisade albigeoise et l'établissement territorial des crucesignati', in *La Croisade Albigeoise*, ed. M. Roquebert (Balma, 2004), pp. 235–44 (the Albigensian Crusade); R. Köhn, 'Die Teilnehmer an den Kreuzzügen gegen die Stedinger', *Niedersächsisches Jahrbuch für Landesgeschichte*, 53 (1981), 139–206 (crusades against the Stedinger); R. Bleck, 'Ein oberrheinischer Palästina-Kreuzzug 1267', *Basler Zeitschrift für Geschichte und Altertumskunde*, 87 (1987), 5–27 (Upper Rhine Crusade of 1267).
31. See A. V. Murray, 'The Prosopography and Onomastics of the Franks in the Kingdom of Jerusalem, 1099–1187', in *Onomastique et parenté dans l'Occident médiéval*, ed. K. S. B. Keats-Rohan and C. Settipani (Oxford, 2000), pp. 283–94; A. V. Murray, *The Crusader Kingdom of Jerusalem: A Dynastic History, 1099–1125* (Oxford, 2000); A. V. Murray, 'The Origins of the Frankish Nobility of the Kingdom of Jerusalem, 1100–1118', *Mediterranean Historical Review* 4 (1989); A. V. Murray, 'Dynastic Continuity or Dynastic Change? The Accession of Baldwin II and the Nobility of the Kingdom of Jerusalem', *Medieval Prosopography* 13 (1992), 1–28; as well as the discussion below.
32. Comte Chandon de Briailles, 'Lignages d'Outre-Mer: Les seigneurs de Margat', *Syria*, 25 (1946–48), 231–58; H. E. Mayer, *Varia Antiochena: Studien zum Kreuz-*

fahrerfürstentum Antiochia im 12. und frühen 13. Jahrhundert (Hanover, 1993); A. V. Murray, 'How Norman was the Principality of Antioch?' Prolegomena to a Study of the Origins of the Nobility of a Crusader State', in *Family Trees and the Roots of Politics: The Prosopography of Britain and France from the Tenth to the Twelfth Century*, ed. K. S. B. Keats-Rohan (Woodbridge, 1997), pp. 349–59.

33. J. Richard, *Le comté de Tripoli sous la dynastie toulousaine, 1102–1187* (Paris, 1945); J. Richard, 'Les comtes de Tripoli et leurs vassaux sous la dynastie antiochénienne', in *Crusade and Settlement*, ed. Edbury, pp. 213–24; W. Antweiler, *Das Bistum Tripolis im 12. und 13. Jahrhundert. Personengeschichtliche und strukturelle Probleme* (Düsseldorf, 1991).

34. W. H. Rüdt de Collenberg, 'Etat et origine du haut clergé de Chypre avant le Grand Schisme d'après les registres du XIIIe et du XIVe siècles', *Mélanges de l'Ecole Française de Rome. Moyen Age – Temps modernes*, 91 (1979), 197–332; W. H. Rüdt de Collenberg, 'The Fate of the Frankish Noble Families Settled in Cyprus', in *Crusade and Settlement*, ed. Edbury, pp. 268–72; B. Arbel, 'The Cypriot Nobility From the Fourteenth to the Sixteenth Century: A New Interpretation', *Mediterranean Historical Review*, 4 (1989), 175–97; N. Coureas, 'The Latin Elite on Cyprus: Trying to Keep Apart', *Journal of Mediterranean Studies*, 10 (2000), 31–45.

35. J. A. C. Buchon, *Recherches et matériaux pour servir à une histoire de la domination française aux XIIIe, XIVe et XVe siècles dans les provinces démembrées de l'empire grec à la suite de la quatrième croisade*, 2 vols (Paris, 1840); J. Longnon, 'Les Autremoncourt, seigneurs de Salona en Grèce', *Bulletin de la Société historique de Haute-Picardie*, 15 (1937), 235–76; Longnon, 'Les premiers ducs d'Athènes et leur famille', *Journal des Savants*, 1973, pp. 61–80; A. Bon, *La Morée franque: Recherches historiques, topographiques et archéologiques sur la principauté d'Achaie, 1205–1430*, 2 vols (Paris, 1969); R-J. Loenertz, 'Généalogie des Ghisi, dynastes vénitiens dans l'Archipel (1207–1390)', *Orientalia Christiana Periodica*, 28 (1962), 121–72, 322–35; R.-J. Loenertz, 'Les seigneurs tierciers de Négropont de 1205 à 1280', *Byzantion*, 35 (1965), 235–76; T. Evergates, 'The Origin of the Lords of Karytaina in the Frankish Morea', *Medieval Prosopography*, 15 (1994), 81–114; D. Jacoby, 'Venetian Settlers in Latin Constantinople (1204–1261): Rich or Poor?', in *Ricchi e poveri nella società dell'Oriente greco-latino*, ed. C. A. Maltezou (Venice, 1998), pp. 181–204.

36. C. Du Fresne Du Cange, *Les familles d'Outremer*, ed. E-G. Rey (Paris, 1869).

37. *Lignages d'Outremer*, in RHC Lois: Assises de Jérusalem: ou, Recueil des ouvrages de jurisprudence composés pendant le XIIIe siècle dans les royaumes de Jérusalem et de Chypre, ed. le Comte Beugnot, 2 vols (Paris, 1841–1843), vol. 2, pp. 435–74.

38. M-A. Nielen-Vandevoorde, 'Un livre méconnu des *Assises de Jérusalem*: Les *Lignages d'Outremer*', *Bibliothèque de l'Ecole des chartes*, 153 (1995), 103–30; M-A. Nielen, 'Families of Outremer: A Source of Traditional Naming Customs', in *Personal Names Studies of Medieval Europe: Social Identity and Familial Structures*, ed. G. T. Beech, M. Bourin and P. Chareille (Kalamazoo, Mich., 2002), pp. 131–9.

39. *Lignages d'Outremer*, p. 455; R. Röhricht, *Regesta Regni Hierosolymitani* with *Additamentum* (Innsbruck, 1893–1904), nos 414, 417, 447, 448, 488a, 522.

40. *Lignages d'Outre-Mer: Introduction, notes et édition critique*, ed. M-A. Nielen (Paris, 2003).

41. The major editions of documents are based on the principle of provenance, and relate to the archives of ecclesiastical institutions in the Holy Land: E. de Rozière, *Cartulaire du Saint-Sépulcre*, in *Patrologiae cursus completus, series latina*, ed. J. P. Migne, 221 vols (Paris, 1834–64), vol. 155, cols 1105–202; Marquis d'Albon, *Cartulaire général de l'ordre du Temple* (Paris, 1913); H-F. Delaborde, *Chartes de Terre Sainte provenant de l'abbaye de Nôtre-Dame de Josaphat* (Paris, 1880); J. Delaville Le Roulx, *Cartulaire général de l'Ordre des Hospitaliers de Jérusalem, 1100–1310*, 4 vols (Paris, 1894–1906); J. Delaville Le Roulx, 'Chartes de Terre-Sainte', *Revue de l'Orient latin*, 11 (1905–08), 181–91; C. Kohler, 'Chartes de l'abbaye de Nôtre-Dame de la Vallée de Josaphat (1108–1291)', *Revue de l'Orient latin*, 7 (1900), 108–222; Comte de Marsy, 'Fragment d'un cartulaire de l'ordre de Saint-Lazare en Terre-Sainte', *Archives de l'Orient latin*, 2 (1884), 121–57; G. Bresc-Bautier, *Le Cartulaire du chapitre du Saint-Sépulcre de Jérusalem* (Paris, 1984); R. Hiestand, 'Zwei unbekannte Diplome der lateinischen Könige von Jerusalem aus Lucca', *Quellen und Forschungen aus italienischen Archiven und Bibliotheken* 50 (1971), 1–57. Calendared versions of the majority of documents from Outremer are given in Röhricht, *Regesta Regni Hierosolymitani* with *Additamentum*, whose numbers (generally cited with the abbreviation RRH) are usually given as a form of quick reference in much published work. The only significant collection of documents from Outremer organized according to issuer rather than provenance is the edition of documents of the kings of Jerusalem currently being prepared by H. E. Mayer.

42. H. Pirie-Gordon, 'The Reigning Princes of Galilee', *English Historical Review*, 27 (1912), 445–61; J. L. La Monte, 'The Viscounts of Naplouse in the Twelfth Century', *Syria*, 19 (1938), 272–8; J. L. La Monte, 'The Lords of Caesarea in the Period of the Crusades', *Speculum*, 22 (1947), 145–61; J. L. La Monte, 'The Lords of Sidon in the 12th and 13th Centuries', *Byzantion*, 17 (1944–45), 183–211; M. E. Nickerson, 'The Seigneurie of Beirut in the 12th Century and the Brisebarre Family of Beirut-Blanchegarde', *Byzantion*, 19 (1949), 141–85; J. L. La Monte and N. Downs, 'The Lords of Bethsan in the Kingdom of Jerusalem and Cyprus', *Medievalia et Humanistica*, 6 (1950), 57–75; H. E. Mayer, 'Die Herrschaftsbildung in Hebron', *Zeitschrift des Deutschen Palästina-Vereins*, 101 (1985), 64–82; H. E. Mayer, 'The Origins of the County of Jaffa', *Israel Exploration Journal*, 35 (1985), 35–45; H. E. Mayer, 'The Origins of the Lordships of Ramla and Lydda in the Latin Kingdom of Jerusalem', *Speculum*, 60 (1985), 537–52; H. E. Mayer, *Die Kreuzfahrerherrschaft Montréal (Sobak): Jordanien im 12. Jahrhundert* (Wiesbaden, 1990); H. E. Mayer, 'The Crusader Principality of Galilee between Saint-Omer and Bures-sur-Yvette', in *Itinéraires d'Orient: Hommages à Claude Cahen*, ed. R. Curiel and R. Gyselen (Bures-sur-Yvette), 1994, pp. 157–67; M. Rheinheimer, *Das Kreuzfahrerfürstentum Galiläa* (Frankfurt am Main, 1990).

43. J. L. La Monte, 'The Lords of Le Puiset on the Crusades', *Speculum*, 17 (1942), 100–18; W. H. Rüdt de Collenberg, 'Les premiers Ibelins', *Le Moyen Age*, 71 (1965), 433–74; H. E. Mayer, 'Carving Up Crusaders: The Early Ibelins and Ramlas', in *Outremer: Studies in the History of the Crusading Kingdom of Jerusalem presented to Joshua Prawer*, ed. B. Z. Kedar, H. E. Mayer and R. C. Smail (Jerusalem, 1982), pp. 101–18; H. E. Mayer, 'John of Jaffa, his Opponents, and His Fiefs', *Proceedings of the American Philosophical Society*, 128 (1984),

134–63; H. E. Mayer, 'Manasses of Hierges in East and West', *Revue Belge de Philologie et d'Histoire*, 66 (1988), 757–66; Murray, 'A Note on the Origin of Eustace Grenier'; P. W. Edbury, *John of Ibelin and the Kingdom of Jerusalem* (Woodbridge, 1997).

44. Riley-Smith, 'The Motives of the Earliest Crusaders and the Settlement of Latin Palestine'; Riley-Smith, 'The Latin Clergy and the Settlement in Palestine and Syria'.

45. Riley-Smith, *The First Crusaders*; Riley-Smith, 'Families, Crusades and Settlement in the Latin East'; J. P. Phillips, *Defenders of the Holy Land: Relations Between the Latin East and the West, 1119–1187* (Oxford, 1996).

46. B. Hamilton, 'The Elephant of Christ: Reynald of Châtillon', in *Religious Motivation: Biographical and Sociological Problems for the Church Historian*, ed. D. Baker, *Studies in Church History*, 15 (1978), 97–108; B. Hamilton, 'Miles of Plancy and the Fief of Beirut', in *The Horns of Hattin*, ed. B. Z. Kedar (Jerusalem, 1992), pp. 136–46; H. E. Mayer, 'The Beginnings of King Amalric of Jerusalem', in ibid., pp. 121–35; H. E. Mayer, 'Die Legitimität Balduins IV. von Jerusalem und das Testament der Agnes von Courtenay', *Historisches Jahrbuch*, 108 (1988), 63–89; J. S. C. Riley-Smith, *The Feudal Nobility and the Kingdom of Jerusalem, 1174–1277* (London, 1973).

47. P. W. Edbury, 'Propaganda and Faction in the Kingdom of Jerusalem: The Background to Hattin', in *Crusaders and Muslims in Twelfth-Century Syria*, ed. Maya Shatzmiller (Leiden, 1993), pp. 173–89.

48. C. Tischler, *Die Burgenses von Jerusalem im 12. Jahrhundert. Eine Prosopographie über die nichtadligen Einwohner Jerusalems von 1120 bis 1187* (Frankfurt am Main, 2000).

49. B. Hamilton, 'Women in the Crusader States: The Queens of Jerusalem 1100–1190', in *Medieval Women*, ed. D. Baker, *Studies in Church History: Subsidia*, 1 (1978), pp. 143–74; B. Hamilton, 'The Titular Nobility of the Latin East: The Case of Agnes of Courtenay', in *Crusade and Settlement*, ed. Edbury, pp. 197–203; H. Houben, 'Adelaide "del Vasto" nella storia del Regno di Sicilia', in *Bianca Lancia D'Agliano: Fra il Piemonte e il Regno di Siicilia*, ed. R. Bordone (Alessandria, 1992), pp. 121–45; S. Lambert, 'Queen or Consort: Rulership and Politics in the Latin East, 1118–1228', in *Queens and Queenship in Medieval Europe*, ed. A. J. Duggan (Woodbridge, 1997), pp. 153–69.

50. R. B. C. Huygens, 'Guillaume de Tyr étudiant: un chapitre (XIX,12) de son Histoire retrouvé', *Latomus*, 21 (1962), 811–29; H. E. Mayer, 'Guillaume de Tyr à l'école', *Mémoires de l'Académie des sciences, arts et belles-lettres de Dijon*, 117 (1985–86), 257–65; Mayer, *Bistümer, Klöster und Stifte im Königreich Jerusalem*; H. E. Mayer, 'Fontevrault und Bethanien. Kirchliches Leben in Anjou und Jerusalem im 12. Jahrhundert', *Zeitschrift für Kirchengeschichte*, 102 (1991), 14–44; H. E. Mayer, 'Einwanderer in der Kanzlei und am Hof der Kreuzfahrerkönige von Jerusalem', in *Die Kreuzfahrerstaaten als multikulturelle Gesellschaft*, pp. 25–42; H. E. Mayer, 'Frederick of Laroche, bishop of Acre and archbishop of Tyre', *Tel Aviver Jahrbuch für deutsche Geschichte*, 22 (1993), 59–72; R. Hiestand, 'Zum Leben und zur Laufbahn Wilhelms von Tyrus', *Deutsches Archiv für Erforschung des Mittelalters*, 34 (1978), 345–80; P. W. Edbury and J. G. Rowe, 'William of Tyre and the Patriarchal Election of 1180', *English Historical Review*, 93 (1978), 1–25; B. Z. Kedar, 'Gerard of Nazareth, a Neglected Twelfth Century Writer in the Latin East', *Dumbarton Oaks Papers*, 37 (1983),

55–77; B. Z. Kedar, 'The Patriarch Eraclius', in *Outremer*, ed. Kedar et al., pp. 177–204; J. S. C. Riley-Smith, 'Latin Titular Bishops in Palestine and Syria, 1137–1291', *Catholic Historical Review*, 64 (1978), 1–15; R. Hiestand, 'Der lateinische Klerus der Kreuzfahrerstaaten: geographische Herkunft und politische Rolle', in *Die Kreuzfahrerstaaten als multikulturelle Gesellschaft*, pp. 43–68; M. Matzke, *Daibert von Pisa. Zwischen Pisa, Papst und erstem Kreuzzug* (Sigmaringen, 1998); K-P. Kirstein, *Die lateinischen Patriarchen von Jerusalem: Von der Eroberung der heiligen Stadt durch die Kreuzfahrer 1099 bis zum Ende der Kreuzfahrerstaaten 1291* (Berlin, 2002).

51. M-A. Nielen, 'Families of Outremer: A Source of Traditional Naming Customs'; I. Shagrir, *Naming Patterns in the Latin Kingdom of Jerusalem* (Oxford, 2003).

52. For example: L. Toulmin-Smith, *Expeditions to Prussia and the Holy Land Made by Henry Earl of Derby*, Camden Second Series, 52 (London, 1894); F. R. H. Du Boulay, 'Henry of Derby's Expeditions to Prussia 1390–1 and 1392', in *The Reign of Richard II*, ed. F. R. H. Du Boulay and C. Barron (London, 1971), pp. 153–72; Macquarrie, *Scotland and the Crusades*; Tyerman, *England and the Crusade*; *Studien über die Anfänge der Mission in Livland*, ed. M. Hellmann (Sigmaringen, 1989).

53. W. Paravicini, *Die Preußenreisen des europäischen Adels*, 2 vols to date (Sigmaringen, 1989-). See also W. Paravicini, 'Die Preussenreisen des europäischenAdels', *Historische Zeitschrift*, 232 (1981), 25–38; W. Paravicini, 'Edelleute, Hansen, Brügger Bürger: Die Finanzierung der westeuropäischen Preussenreisen im 14. Jahrhundert', *Hansische Geschichtsblätter*, 104 (1986), 5–20; W. Paravicini, 'Heraldische Quellen zur Geschichte der Preussenreisen im 14. Jahrhundert', in *Werkstatt des Historikers der mittelalterlichen Ritterorden*, ed. Z. H. Nowak (Toruń, 1987), pp. 111–34.

6

gender theory

deborah gerish

Gender theory explores ways in which humans describe and socially organize sexual difference. All societies engage in this process, thereby establishing definitions of normality and deviance. In many instances, the process also rests on perceived relationships between 'nature' and 'culture', or the arrangements people have crafted to control and counteract the natural world, with culture seen as both superior and masculine. Almost universally, these social organizations and norms have led to patriarchal systems that favour males over females. Political institutions, law and language inscribe and enforce patriarchy.

Two examples of this process became the cornerstones for later developments in medieval Europe. First, the creation account in Genesis explained male superiority by deriving (at least in English translation) the term 'woman' from the word 'man'. Then, in the story of the Fall, Yahweh reinforced Adam's dominance when punishing Eve. Generations of Jews and Christians could look back to these texts as they established customs, formed states, developed theology and wrote laws. Second, in fourth-century Athens, Aristotle turned his observations about sexual differences into theories wherein females were defective males, lacking physical and mental characteristics that defined the free male citizen. Once European scholars rediscovered Aristotle's works in the mid-twelfth century, they had classical proof to further support what they found in the Bible, which they had already incorporated into their society. Language, social arrangements, theology and philosophy formed a positive feedback loop that touched every facet of human existence. Thus gender studies can examine any and all areas of medieval society – from sexuality, marriage and childrearing to economic, legal, political and military arrangements. While historians of the crusades have explored all these areas, not many have incorporated gender *theory* into their work. The field is wide open for ground-breaking research that will also appeal to scholars in other disciplines as well as to medievalists.

Gender theory has its roots in women's history, itself a product of women's movements since the nineteenth century. Nineteenth- and twentieth-century activists such as Susan B. Anthony and Elizabeth Cady Stanton wanted to draw upon examples from the past, but they found little historical research on women to support their liberal proposals. They quickly filled the gap by producing several histories of women; the earliest study of women in crusading, by Celestia Bloss, dates from this period.[1] When feminism resurfaced in the 1960s, a new generation of liberals redis-covered earlier women's histories and expanded upon them. Because these scholars aimed at raising consciousness and came from various disciplines, their historical treatment of women's issues sometimes lacked sophistica-tion. Such researchers wanted to write women back into history, in what was often called 'herstory', and these studies typically celebrated extraor-dinary women who operated within existing social arrangements.

Not all feminists were liberals, however, and the liberal approach did not sit well with radical and Marxist/socialist feminists, who felt that because various social arrangements caused sexism, women's conditions could not improve until these systems were dismantled. Again, historical studies of women served the agendas of activists.

Radical feminists distinguished between sex and gender in their work – a development that has shaped nearly all studies of women since. Sex was determined biologically, delineating someone as male or female, but societies constructed masculine and feminine gender roles. This important theoretical breakthrough was soon sidetracked into discussions of men's and women's essential natures, or the attributes rooted in biology. Questions like 'Are women naturally more nurturing than men?' and 'Are men naturally more aggressive than women?' interested radical and psychoanalytical feminists, but often led to dead ends in historiography. Essentialist assumptions in historical studies now invite scorn, no matter what else the researcher does well. Yet the sex/gender distinction has proved extremely valuable for historians, since it caused them to question fundamental assumptions about sex differences and simultaneously allowed for the influence of societal components. The realization that 'feminine' and 'masculine' might mean different things in different times and places opened a floodgate for anthropologists, sociologists and historians, who could now see societies building and then reinforcing patriarchal systems. Scholars also realized that gender roles could change over an individual's lifetime, and that a person's social status and ethnicity might affect these roles as well. Historical research now invokes the triad of sex, class and race when discussing gender. (Medievalists need to add a fourth factor: religious affiliation. Any consideration of gender in medieval Europe must incorporate these four elements, for they all shaped patriarchal institutions.)

Marxist/socialist feminists accepted the triad and, like radicals, they denounced the patriarchy that oppressed women, but they saw its origin specifically in the economic and political arrangements of capitalism. Though nowadays few would accept Friedrich Engels's thesis connecting sexism to the rise of private property, Marxist feminists recognized that capitalism and patriarchy reinforce each other. Marxist feminist historians following Mary Ritter Beard and Alice Clark originally believed that since the Industrial Revolution, women have been relegated to the private sphere of home and children, while men worked in the more highly valued public sector. Research in this vein often explored relationships among women in their own private world, as though women existed almost independently of men or the state. It also attempted to redress denigration of the private by showing how women's contributions to the family economy may not have achieved recognition in the public sector but were nevertheless valuable in their own right. More recently, historians have realized that these spheres are not in fact completely separated. Private family relationships can affect affairs of state when, say, women influence their politically active male kin to favour a particular policy, while public laws touch on family matters such as inheritance, marriage, divorce, and so on. Moreover, Marxists have long recognized that women's contributions to the family economy are necessary to support a 'public' capitalist economy. The distinction between private and public can be particularly thorny for medievalists, who have long recognized the blurred line between these spheres.

Another type of feminism has had less impact on historical studies of gender, but it poses a tantalizing question for crusades research. Simone de Beauvoir's existential feminist theories posited that males designated themselves as 'selves' and females as the 'Other' who could threaten the self. Because men perceived women as a danger, they had to establish control over them. Women internalized male perceptions of themselves until they were indeed the second sex. Beauvoir suggested that men turn women into the Other because only females can give life, while males can risk their lives and take it away from others in fighting or hunting. This last insight may prove particularly useful for studying medieval constructions of masculinity and nobility, especially as related to crusading.

Poststructural feminists, like existential feminists, agreed that men see women as Other, but many would disagree with de Beauvoir's view that otherness is inherently negative: because women are the second sex, they can best understand patriarchy and challenge a world that celebrates sameness, maleness and rationality (usually viewed as a distinctly masculine trait). Poststructural feminism borrowed a great deal from Jacques Derrida's ideas on deconstruction and Jacques Lacan's reworking of Freudian psychoanalysis, both of which hinge upon language. Given space constraints here, I shall simplify and focus on the parts most useful for historians. To Lacan, a symbolic order governs human societies through rituals, signs and other unspoken rules that ended up being expressed in language. Children mature by learning these linguistic rules that reflect the symbolic order. However, any patriarchal society's language is inherently masculine, so girls cannot really identify with it in the way that boys can. The language women learn only expresses what men think, not what women feel. Derrida would agree: western linguistic structures and the western symbolic order combine to prefer spoken over written language (logocentrism), male over female (phallocentrism), and binary opposites over multiple alternatives (dualism). Taken together, these three 'isms' mark the western world's drive to reach a single, unitary truth that renounces differences and privileges patriarchy to the exclusion of anything that is not male, white and rational. Language props up this symbolic order. And because people can only destroy the symbolic order using the words that help support it, there is no easy way out. Yet the system contains flaws, in that it cannot exclude everyone who fails to meet the criteria. Derrida's work inspired literary critics to deconstruct texts – to look for the 'others' who were marginalized, misrepresented or persecuted. Historians, especially social and cultural scholars, have used these techniques as well, seeking to analyse mentalities or perceptions rather than political institutions. Postmodern historians have produced some of the most exciting recent research, though the specialized vocabulary used to convey their findings can make their writing challenging to understand. Postmodern deconstruction particularly lends itself to discussions of gender, ethnicity and class; medievalists can apply it to religious affiliation too.

As should be obvious from the above discussion, gender theory is multidisciplinary and highly diverse. These characteristics make it simultaneously challenging and exciting for the historian. The challenge lies in preparation: anyone who wants to utilize gender theory must be prepared to read in many areas of the social sciences and humanities, both for philosophical approaches and methodologies. Moreover, gender studies require a commitment to theory, so that the historian uses these methods appropriately. Some of the humanities and social sciences have always embraced philosophical musings about what their practitioners hope to achieve, and how and why. History has not always done so, yet as Joan Scott points out in her introduction to *Feminism & History*, this can be dangerous, for conclusions reached in gender studies often depend upon the researcher's opinion of how the past can best serve the present.

The excitement inherent in gender theory comes, not coincidentally, from the same place as its challenge. A working knowledge of all the methodological and theoretical options will inevitably broaden understanding of the historian's craft. Debates about gender in history raise three philosophical questions that historians have long disputed.[2] First, where does human agency fit into explanations of social developments and historical change? Do people (acting singly or in groups) really have the ability to change the world around them, or are they mere pawns moved by extrapersonal structures such as Hegelian or Marxist cycles? Second, what is the relationship between text and context, language and society? Does language reflect reality or create it? Finally, should historians study the past to improve the present? If so, how can we best improve gender relations today?

This last question is particularly tricky for historians, who have long viewed their discipline as one that does *not* attempt to enhance the present or future. Scholars trained in the Rankean traditions of positivism and objectivity have often looked askance at those who are active in any political or social movement. Rankeans have also preferred political and institutional history to research about social constructions of masculinity and femininity, sexuality and family history, socio-sexual norms and deviations. Although the tendencies toward positivism, objectivity, and traditional political research have all drawn heavy fire since the 1930s, they have not completely disappeared from history departments in the US and Europe. Consequently, more traditional historians sometimes see gender history as a fad. For example, gender historians might ask how crusading affected the lives of wives who administered family lands while their husbands travelled to Spain, Jerusalem or the Baltic. Was this a liberating or an oppressing experience? Were these women able to exert some control over property, or did they simply take on extra responsibilities without any new resources? Often these questions draw fire from traditionalists who might never have considered such issues, who see little or no relevance in them, and who believe the gender historians' political beliefs render them incapable of handling the subject objectively. For these reasons, gender theory has not made much of an impression on crusade studies.

But there are other factors at work too. When historians today look at the crusades, they see men – calling for holy war, planning spiritual and practical elements of campaigns, donating property or imposing taxes to finance an expedition, leading marches, fighting in battles, and then ruling the states established in these endeavours. This decided male emphasis comes directly from medieval sources. In most cases, women could not do any of the jobs listed above. Usually they took on support positions: they prayed, donated money, took care of family interests at home while their men were away, or if they actually joined a campaign, they performed menial duties. Men perceived that women were as likely to disrupt a holy war as to further it, for their bodies could tempt male crusaders and undermine an entire campaign. Medieval understandings of warfare, sexuality and gender greatly circumscribed women's and men's roles in crusading and their representation in sources.

Such attitudes have not changed fundamentally over time. War remains a male domain today; typically men fight and women perform background tasks that free warriors for combat. This may further explain why gender theory has not received much attention from crusade historians. Given the long-lived attitudes that keep women off the battlefield, it is not surprising that historians today have continued the perspective of medieval narrators; the first scholarly book-length study of women in the crusades was not published until 2003.[3] Trade books and textbooks on the crusades typically mention just the extraordinary cases of women who fought or who undercut crusading efforts.[4] Only two narratives of the crusades mention women in their tables of contents, and these are aimed at a popular rather than a scholarly audience.[5] Bibliographies and a recent collection of secondary sources similarly say little or nothing about women, let alone gender history.[6] It was not until early 2004 that the first detailed historiographical essay on the roles of women in the crusade movement was published.[7]

A fairly narrow definition of 'crusade studies' has further hampered considerations of gender. Historians have increasingly become aware of how crusading affected nearly everyone within medieval Europe and in the places contested by crusade. Yet for the most part, historians who ask how women fit into crusading have started from traditionally masculine roles, approached crusades only as a series of military campaigns, or looked only at the Latin East. These limitations are not meant to be taken as criticism: these studies have broken new ground. They remain useful for researchers who want to incorporate gender theory into their work as they consider how medieval understandings of gender affected what women *or* men did within the crusading movement.

Most existing research on gender in the crusades really looks at women rather than constructions of gender. These studies generally fall into several categories: (1) women in military campaigns; (2) women in papal policy and canon law; (3) women on the home front; (4) women and military orders; (5) women in regions affected by crusading, especially the Latin East. The work that does not fit into my arbitrarily designated classes looks at the gendering of Muslims and non-Catholics, or popular images of male and female crusaders.

The largest body of research considers how women fought or otherwise became involved in various campaigns. (Indeed, this was the issue that first inspired Bloss in the nineteenth century, as noted above.) It has consistently received the most attention from historians: even those studies that predate gender theory provide useful references, such as Walter Porges's narrative about women and non-elite males on the First Crusade.[8] Benjamin Kedar considered why women travelled on a ship carrying male crusaders to the Latin East.[9] James Brundage explored ecclesiastical fears of sexual contact during the First Crusade.[10] James Powell provided several treatments of women on the Fifth Crusade.[11] A more theory-driven approach appeared in Laura Brady's exploration of women in the First and Second crusades. She argued that male writers developed a love–hate relationship with women on campaign: chroniclers recognized that women could provide invaluable services, but they feared that females would tempt them into unchastity and other unsuitable behaviours.[12] Helen Nicholson has also incorporated theory in a sophisticated way in her work on women in the Third Crusade.[13] In the only collection of articles published so far on women and crusading, six historians out of thirteen discussed this issue. Matthew Bennett, Keren Caspi-Reisfeld, Susan Edgington, Michael Evans and Sarah Lambert explore how male writers portrayed women in battle; Lambert's piece is particularly sophisticated in its use of theory.[14] Yvonne Friedman expanded an earlier study of women captives in the Latin East to describe the treatment of Roman Catholic, Muslim and Jewish prisoners.[15] There is only one study at this time on women acting in Baltic campaigns; Rasa Mažeika has shown that here males did not denigrate or fear female participants as they did in the Levant.[16] Her work also demonstrates the value of comparative studies, which hopefully will become easier to manage as research on the northern crusades expands.

Ecclesiastical policies and canon law comprise another major category of study in gender, sexuality, and crusading. Christopher Tyerman and

Constance Rousseau have looked at how popes and upper clergy saw females participating in crusading. Tyerman's comments on women are brief, but because his whole book traces the development of the movement, it is valuable reading in this area.[17] Rousseau indicates that popes initially perceived no real role for women in crusading until Innocent III recognized that wives could persuade their husbands to take the cross, instead of impeding the men's efforts to fight.[18] James Brundage has led the field in explorations of crusading in canon law, including the impact on marriage, sexuality, and penitence.[19] Maureen Purcell's work on female crusaders has shown that canon law did recognize such a position for women, but only briefly.[20] All the studies cited here represent excellent and exhaustive work on canon law and papal policy; for various reasons, however, they do not incorporate gender theory, which could add many nuances to our understandings of medieval gender.

Women's real experiences on the home front have garnered attention too. In an innovative study, Miriam Tessera has considered Hildegard of Bingen's spiritual advice to Philip of Flanders and how it focused on penitence rather than military goals.[21] Penelope Adair and Thérèse de Hemptinne have focused on women who stayed in Europe while their husbands crusaded.[22] Bernard Hamilton has explored how a queen affected her husband's crusading efforts.[23] Even more recently, Jonathan Riley-Smith has discussed female influence on crusading within noble families, arguing that in France women could maintain crusading traditions within their natal families and even export them to their husband's families.[24] Jonathan Phillips has found that this process did not hold in Flanders, at least during the Second Crusade, when regional issues prevented crusading families from sending members to the East.[25]

Historians have also considered several aspects of women and the military religious orders. Malcolm Barber's detailed treatment of the Templars includes a short section on how women interacted with the order.[26] Timothy Miller's work on the Hospitallers similarly discusses women's roles.[27] His article sparked a debate about whether females actually nursed or not, which in turn has led to wonderful studies showing that, for all the fighting orders, stated policy did not always dictate accepted practice.[28] Helen Nicholson has been especially interested in showing that the military orders acted like cenobitic orders in officially circumscribing female roles but then opening their doors to female patrons or continuing to enjoy secular pursuits involving women. She and Marian Dygo have recently embarked upon another promising avenue of study that can make good use of theory: how female saints fit into the world of the male military orders.[29]

Research on women's experiences in crusading states has taken several directions. Some work starts from laws, such as Brundage's and Richard's research on marriage codes.[30] Queens have received attention from several scholars: Bernard Hamilton has collected important material on all First Kingdom queens, paying special attention to Agnes of Courtenay, and Hans Eberhard Mayer has analysed the activities of Melisende and Agnes in some detail.[31] The most theory-driven work comes from Sarah Lambert, who has treated the effects of gender in royal policy.[32] P. M. Holt and Sylvia Schein have examined noblewomen in the Latin East; Schein's work draws upon colonial theory and attempts to compare eastern women to their counterparts in Europe.[33] Finally, Heath Dillard had the means to examine Castilian women at all social ranks; this work would offer valuable insights to anyone interested in comparative studies of the Iberian Peninsula and the Latin East, though there are few eastern sources on non-noble women.[34]

Another research category with almost unlimited potential for theory and innovation explores gendering of non-Christians and non-Catholics. Niall Christie considers both of these groups in his synthesis of literature on Muslim women, which contains numerous valuable references to primary and secondary sources.[35] Natasha Hodgson uses theory creatively to show how Christian writers portrayed Kerbogha's mother in their accounts of the First Crusade.[36] Marc Carrier and Peter Frankopan discuss gender implications for western views of Greek culture.[37] Louise Mirrer's work on male Christian gendering of women, Jews and Muslims in the multicultural Iberian Peninsula is fascinating and highly sophisticated.[38]

Finally, Elizabeth Siberry has taken gender and crusading studies in new directions in her work on what might be considered popular culture. She has explored themes in medieval lay poetry on crusading and Victorian treatments of the movement.[39]

In short, many scholars have produced excellent studies of women in the crusades, but there is room for more work in different geographical areas and historical periods. Little has been done in the area of gender studies, nor has gender theory made much of an impact except as noted above. The following questions came to me as I examined numerous studies of medieval men and women (whether they crusaded or not), but this list is by no means exhaustive. Works listed in the endnotes may well lead readers in new directions.

The first potential research topic concerns the three orders and gender roles: the phenomenon of crusading suggests as many as six socially constructed genders in medieval Europe, based on a combination of order and biological sex. For example, medieval intellectuals considered that men could fight for Christianity but women could only pray, even in defence of Christendom.[40] Yet the intellectuals themselves, as clerics, did not fight but prayed to support crusading. Conceivably male and female religious comprised two additional genders, who theoretically circumvented the typical reproductive functions of men and women. (The same might be true for peasants, who worked instead of praying or fighting, yet who reproduced.)

If there were more than two genders in medieval society, men and women within the Church deserve much more study in relation to crusading. We might consider whether it was more masculine to pray or to fight, since monks considered their calling superior to any lay activity.[41] Were monks men or more than men, especially in the days when Benedictine imagery depicted monks fighting Satan through prayer? Similarly, gender constructions might well have affected nuns by making them less likely to go on pilgrimage or crusade than monks or priests.[42] Male superiors might also have discouraged nuns from founding or moving to houses in regions affected by crusade. In other words, crusading may have offered other ways to gender expressions of spirituality. There have been debates about the Church fathers' ability to conceive of spirituality in feminine terms; Caroline Bynum's work suggests that this was no longer a problem by the twelfth century.[43] Crusading may have affected or counteracted this process in several ways, and certainly crusading shaped clerical views of the laity.[44] Male clergy acted out their concern over sexuality by limiting or prohibiting female participation in crusading; more work can be done in this area.

Within lay society, crusading also intersected with social status, especially if we consider the possibility of more than two genders. Research on chivalry has shown that nobles or those wishing to be considered nobles saw crusading as their prerogative.[45] Yet by and large, only literary studies have considered what it meant to be a 'masculine' noble, and crusading tends to be incidental in these works.[46] Popes prohibited the poor from taking the cross, yet large numbers of them did so anyway;[47] were they trying to tap into masculine power that had associations with rank as well as gender?

Perhaps the least explored area of crusade studies concerns female experiences of crusading. To what extent did crusading reinforce sexual difference and male superiority?[48] How did intellectual, literary or chronicle sources deal with women warriors in general?[49] Male chroniclers mentioned noblewomen who persuaded male kin to take the cross, but female persuasion was something of a topos.[50] Other types of sources may reveal a different pattern. Social rank must have affected women's experiences when they became involved with crusading or pilgrimage in any way. What did medieval writers say about peasant women in the popular crusades, if they mentioned them at all? How might queens or noblewomen in realms established by crusade differ from their counterparts in the heart of Europe?[51] How did writers perceive noblewomen who stayed home to safeguard family property?[52] What did crusaders' wives, women crusaders or pilgrims of any rank say for themselves?[53] Thus there remain many questions about men's reactions to women who became involved in crusading, and whether they perceived these female actions as part of feminine spirituality and/or feminine power.

Questions of context also warrant further research: regional differences and urbanization would have shaped men's and women's experiences in crusading.[54] High levels of urbanization existed in the Iberian Peninsula and the crusader states, and even nobles lived in towns, while other places affected by crusading did not share these characteristics. Were there variations in social constructions of gender for people in the Baltic, the Latin Kingdom of Constantinople and southern France? Did these variations depend on location, on the level of urbanization, or other factors?

Researchers can also explore religious affiliation, ethnicity, social status and sex intertwined in the Latin West and in crusading regions. There are numerous topics associated with these issues. To what extent did crusaders' gender roles depend on the enemy's ethnicity and/or religious affiliation: was it manlier to fight a Muslim or a heretic? Enemies of the faith could be gendered in a variety of ways – as honourable masculine enemies, as effeminate or feminine cowards, as genderless children.[55] Heretics might be gendered in similar ways, and condemnations of their sexual behaviour certainly said something about sexual deviance.[56] How did legal treatment of religious or ethnic minorities in crusading regions reflect constructions of gender and concerns about sexuality?[57] What did Roman Catholic writers have to say about masculine and feminine social roles in non-western cultures?[58]

As the preceding discussion indicates, research topics grow exponentially in number and scope if scholars take a broader definition of 'crusading': one that embraces more than just the military ventures, or that re-imagines these campaigns as involving more than just the actual fighting. Related issues include heresy, pilgrimage, gender roles within the Church, intellectual understandings of feminine and masculine natures, the relationship between political power and gender, urban gender roles and crusading, and the economic impact of crusading on those who took the cross and those who stayed home. There is plenty of room for regional comparisons, either between different areas affected by crusading or between the center of Europe and the new states on its periphery. Work on changes over time, or the interplay of sex, social rank, ethnicity and religious affiliation, would further expand these topics.

Finally, researchers can ask gender-related questions of 'traditional' crusading sources. Troubadour lyrics about crusading may show differences if compared by the sex of the writer. Town or manorial records could reflect the economic impact of crusading on men and women; they might also show if women became involved in city- or manor-sponsored crusading activities. Various documentary and literary sources (chronicles, saints' lives, papal and conciliar decrees, law codes, romances, epics, charters issued to military orders) indicate attitudes about crusaders, enemies of the faith and non-Latin allies through gendered language and portrayals of appropriate gender roles in Latin and non-Latin culture. The iconography and patronage of crusade-related art and architecture, broken down by donor's sex, may also yield interesting results. Works cited below and in the endnotes may suggest additional topics or approaches.

The further reading section at the end of this volume also provides titles on gender theory. Readers new to this area will want to begin with the works of Tong, Wiesner-Hanks, Scott and Fay et al. before reading in other disciplines such as literary criticism, sociology or anthropology. Space did not permit a full bibliography on gender history for the Middle Ages. Wiesner-Hanks includes suggested readings with each chapter that are very helpful, and several recent studies demonstrate a growing interest in gender studies related to masculinity.[59] Very little work has been done in this area for the Middle Ages as a whole, and at this time there is nothing specifically related to crusading.

More application of gender theory to crusading will, I believe, add greatly to our view of medieval Europe and the women and men who lived in it – partly because the crusading movement pervaded every facet of life, and partly because so many people were not expected to take part in it directly. The overriding goal of gender history, to understand what it means to be masculine or feminine in a given place and time, asks a question that remains relevant for the world today. Given that gender studies has achieved a place for itself in the academy since its early days, historians can no longer afford to dismiss gender theory as a passing craze. They should instead consider how gender theory can add sophistication and depth to the questions they ask about human experiences for both females and males.

notes

1. C. A. Bloss, *Heroines of the Crusades* (Muscatine, Iowa, 1853).
2. A fourth question has generally concerned anthropologists and sociologists more than historians: how can we best explain the origins of patriarchy? As should be obvious from the preceding discussion, each subtype of feminism has its own explanation. Yet while historians often align themselves with one subtype or another, their research generally analyses how patriarchy operated in a given place and time, rather than trying to figure out how it came to exist.
3. S. Geldsetzer, *Frauen auf Kreuzzügen, 1096–1291* (Darmstadt, 2003). This book appeared after this chapter had been written.
4. M. Billings, *The Crusades*, 2nd edn (Stroud, 2000); B. Hamilton, *The Crusades* (Stroud, 1998); H. E. Mayer, *The Crusades*, trans. J. Gillingham, 2nd edn (Oxford, 1988); J. Phillips, *The Crusades, 1095–1197* (Harlow, 2002); J. Richard, *The Crusades, c. 1071–c. 1291* (Cambridge, 1999); J. Riley-Smith, *The Crusades: A Short History* (New Haven, 1987); J. Riley-Smith, ed., *The Oxford Illustrated History of the Crusades* (Oxford, 1995); S. Runciman, *A History of the Crusades*, 3 vols (Cambridge, 1951–54).
5. R. C. Finucane, *Soldiers of the Faith: Crusaders and Moslems at War* (New York, 1983); R. Pernoud, *The Crusaders* (Edinburgh, 1963).
6. T. F. Madden, *The Crusades: The Essential Readings* (Oxford, 2002), does not consider gender or women at all. Hans Eberhard Mayer's seminal bibliographies predated the entry of gender studies into the academy and do not include sections on either women or gender: *Bibliographie zur Geschichte der Kreuzzüge* (Hanover, 1960) and 'Literaturbericht über die Geschichte der Kreuzzüge', *Historische Zeitschrift*, 3 (1969), 641–736. James F. McEaney, *Crusades: A Bibliography with Indexes* (Hauppage, NY, 2002), includes 'women' as a category in his subject index but offers only two article citations.
7. C. Maier, 'The Roles of Women in the Crusade Movement: A Survey', *Journal of Medieval History*, 30 (2004), 61–82. This essay appeared after this chapter was completed.
8. W. Porges, 'The Clergy, the Poor, and the Non-Combatants on the First Crusade', *Speculum*, 21 (1946), 1–21.
9. B. Z. Kedar, 'The Passenger List of a Crusader Ship, 1250', *Studi Medievali*, series 3, 13 (1972), 267–79.
10. J. A. Brundage, 'Prostitution, Miscegenation and Sexual Purity in the First Crusade', in *Crusade and Settlement: Papers Read at the First Conference of the Society for the Study of the Crusades and the Latin East and Presented to R.C. Smail*, ed. P. W. Edbury (Cardiff, 1985), pp. 57–65; reprinted in J. A. Brundage, *The Crusades, Holy War, and Canon Law* (London, 1991).
11. J. M. Powell, *Anatomy of a Crusade, 1213–1221* (Philadelphia, 1986) and 'The Roles of Women in the Fifth Crusade', in *The Horns of Hattin*, ed. B. Z. Kedar (Jerusalem, 1992), pp. 294–301.
12. L. Brady, 'Essential and Despised: Images of Women in the First and Second Crusades, 1095–1148' (unpublished MA thesis, Department of History, University of Windsor, 1992).
13. H. J. Nicholson, 'Women on the Third Crusade', *Journal of Medieval History* 23 (1997), 335–49.

14. M. Bennett, 'Virile Latins, Effeminate Greeks and Strong Women: Gender Definitions on Crusade?'; K. Caspi-Reisfeld, 'Women Warriors during the Crusades, 1095–1204'; S. B. Edgington, '"Sont çou ore les fems que jo voi la venir?" Women in the *Chanson d'Antioche*'; M. R. Evans, '"Unfit to Bear Arms": The Gendering of Arms and Armour in Accounts of Women on Crusade'; S. Lambert, 'Crusading or Spinning'; all in *Gendering the Crusades*, ed. S. B. Edgington and S. Lambert (Cardiff, 2002) [hereafter cited as *Gendering*].

15. Y. Friedman, 'Women in Captivity and Their Ransom During the Crusader Period', in *Cross-Cultural Convergences in the Crusader Period: Essays Presented to Aryeh Grabois on His Sixty-Fifth Birthday*, ed. M. Goodich, S. Menache and S. Schein (New York, 1995), pp. 75–87, and 'Captivity and Ransom: The Experience of Women', in *Gendering*, pp. 121–39.

16. Rasa Mazeika, 'Women Warriors in the Baltic Crusade Chronicles', in *From Clermont to Jerusalem: The Crusades and Crusader Societies, 1095–1500*, ed. A. V. Murray (Turnhout, 1998), pp. 229–48.

17. C. Tyerman, *The Invention of the Crusades* (Basingstoke, 1998).

18. C. M. Rousseau, 'Home Front and Battlefield: The Gendering of Papal Crusading Policy (1095–1291)', in *Gendering*, pp. 31–44.

19. J. A. Brundage, 'The Crusader's Wife: A Canonistic Quandary', *Studia Gratiana*, 12 (1967), 427–41, 'The Crusader's Wife Revisited', *Studia Gratiana*, 14 (1967), 243–51, *Medieval Canon Law and the Crusader* (Milwaukee, 1969).

20. M. Purcell, 'Women Crusaders: A Temporary Canonical Aberration?', in *Principalities, Powers and Estates: Studies in Medieval and Early Modern Government and Society*, ed. L. O. Frapell (Adelaide, 1979), pp. 57–64.

21. M. R. Tessera, 'Philip Count of Flanders and Hildegard of Bingen: Crusading against the Saracens or Crusading against Deadly Sin?' in *Gendering*, pp. 77–93.

22. P. Adair, '"Ego et uxor mea . . .": Countess Clemence and Her Role in the Comital Family and in Flanders (1092–1133)' (unpublished PhD dissertation, Department of History, University of California, Santa Barbara, 1994); T. de Hemptinne, 'Les épouses de croisés et pèlerins flamands aux XIe et XIIe siècles: l'exemple des comtesses de Flandre Clémence et Sibylle', in *Autour de la première croisade*, ed. M. Balard (Paris, 1996).

23. B. Hamilton, 'Eleanor of Castile and the Crusading Movement', *Mediterranean Historical Review*, 10 (1995), 92–103.

24. J. Riley-Smith, 'Family Traditions and Participation in the Second Crusade', in *The Second Crusade and the Cistercians*, ed. M. Gervers (New York, 1992) and *The First Crusaders, 1095–1131* (Cambridge, 1997).

25. Jonathan Phillips, 'The Murder of Charles the Good and the Second Crusade: Household, Nobility, and Traditions of Crusading in Medieval Flanders', *Medieval Prosopography*, 19 (1998), 55–76.

26. Malcolm Barber, *The New Knighthood: A History of the Order of the Temple* (Cambridge, 1993).

27. T. S. Miller, 'The Knights of Saint John and the Hospitals of the Latin West', *Speculum*, 53 (1978), 709–33.

28. A. J. Forey, 'Women and the Military Orders in the Twelfth and Thirteenth Centuries', *Studia Monastica*, 29 (1987), 63–92; H. J. Nicholson, 'Templar Attitudes Towards Women', *Medieval History*, 1 (1991), 74–80, 'Margaret de Lacy and the Hospital of St. John at Aconbury, Herefordshire', *Journal*

of Ecclesiastical History, 50 (1999), 629–51, 'The Military Orders and Their Relations with Women', in *The Crusades and the Military Orders: Expanding the Frontiers of Medieval Latin Christianity*, ed. Z. Hunyadi and J. Laszlovsky (Budapest, 2001), 'Women in Templar and Hospitaller Commanderies', in *La Commanderie: Institution des ordres militaires dans l'Occident médiéval*, ed. A. Luttrell and L. Pressouyre (Paris, 2002); Jane Oliver, 'The Rule of the Templars and a Courtly Ballade', *Scriptorium*, 35 (1981), 303–6.

29. M. Dygo, 'The Political Role of the Cult of the Virgin Mary in Teutonic Prussia in the 14th and 15th Centuries', *Journal of Medieval History*, 15 (1989), 63–80; H. J. Nicholson, 'The Head of St. Euphemia: Templar Devotion to Female Saints', in *Gendering*, pp. 108–20.

30. J. A. Brundage, 'Marriage Law in the Latin Kingdom of Jerusalem', in *Outremer: Studies in the History of the Crusading Kingdom of Jerusalem*, ed. B. Z. Kedar, H. E. Mayer and R. C. Smail (Jerusalem, 1982), pp. 258–71; J. Richard, 'Le statut de la femme dans l'Orient Latin', in *La Femme 2: Recueils de la société Jean Bodin pour l'histoire comparative des institutions*, 12 (Brussels, 1962), pp. 377–88.

31. B. Hamilton, 'Women in the Crusader States: The Queens of Jerusalem', in *Medieval Women*, ed. D. Baker, *Studies in Church History: Subsidia*, 1 (1978), pp. 143–74, and 'The Titular Nobility of the Latin East: The Case of Agnes of Courtenay', in *Crusade and Settlement*, ed. P. W. Edbury (Cardiff, 1985), pp. 197–203; H. E. Mayer, 'Studies in the History of Queen Melisende', *Dumbarton Oaks Papers*, 26 (1972), 93–189, 'Die Legitimtät Balduins IV. von Jerusalem und das Testament der Agnes von Courtenay', *Historisches Jahrbuch*, 108 (1988), 63–89; and 'The Beginnings of King Amalric of Jerusalem', in *The Horns of Hattin*, ed. B. Z. Kedar (Jerusalem, 1992), pp. 121–35.

32. S. Lambert, 'Queen or Consort: Rulership and Politics in the Latin East, 1118–1228', in *Queens and Queenship in Medieval Europe*, ed. A. J. Duggan (Woodbridge, 1997), pp. 153–69.

33. P. M. Holt, 'Baybar's Treaty with the Lady of Beirut in 667/1279', in *Crusade and Settlement*, ed. Edbury, pp. 242–5; S. Schein, 'Women in Medieval Colonial Society: The Latin Kingdom of Jerusalem in the Twelfth Century', in *Gendering*, pp. 140–53.

34. H. Dillard, *Daughters of the Reconquest: Women in Castilian Town Society, 1100–1300* (Cambridge, 1984).

35. N. Christie, 'Crusade Literature', in *Encyclopaedia of Women and Islamic Culture*, ed. S. Joseph et al. (Leiden, forthcoming).

36. N. Hodgson, 'The Role of Kerbogha's Mother in the *Gesta Francorum* and Selected Chronicles of the First Crusade', in *Gendering*, pp. 163–76.

37. M. Carrier, 'Perfidious and Effeminate Greeks: The Representation of Byzantine Ceremonial in the Western Chronicles of the Crusades (1096–1204)', *Annuario dell'Instituto Romeno di Cultura e Ricerca Umanistica Venezia*, 4 (2002), 47–68; P. Frankopan, 'Perception and Projection of Prejudice: Anna Comnena, the *Alexiad*, and the First Crusade', in *Gendering*, pp. 59–76.

38. L. Mirrer, 'Representing "Other" Men: Muslims, Jews, and Masculine Ideals in Medieval Castilian Epic and Ballad', in *Medieval Masculinities: Regarding Men in the Middle Ages*, ed. C. A. Lees (Minneapolis, 1994), pp. 169–86, *Women, Jews and Muslims in the Texts of Reconquest Castile* (Ann Arbor, 1996).

39. E. Siberry, 'Troubadours, Trouvères and Minnesingers and the Crusades', *Studi Medievali*, series 3, 29 (1988), 19–43, 'The Crusader's Departure and Return: A Much Later Perspective', in *Gendering*, pp. 177–90.

40. A. Blamires, *The Case for Women in Medieval Culture* (Oxford, 1997).

41. E. Siberry, *Criticism of Crusading, 1095–1274* (Oxford, 1985).

42. G. Constable, 'Opposition to Pilgrimage in the High Middle Ages', *Studia Gratiana*, 19 (1976), 125–46, reprinted in G. Constable, *Religious Life and Thought (11th–12th Centuries)* (London, 1979); J. Lane, 'The Quest for the Holy Sepulchre: The Crusades and Beyond', paper given at the Sewanee Medieval Colloquium at Sewanee, Tennessee, 2001.

43. For patristic understandings of spirituality, see P. Allen, RSM, *The Concept of Woman: The Aristotelian Revolution 750 BC–AD 1250* (Montreal, 1985); E. A. Clark, 'Ideology, History, and the Construction of "Woman" in Late Ancient Christianity', *Journal of Early Christian Studies*, 2 (1994), 155–84; G. Cloke, '*This Female Man of God': Women and Spiritual Power in the Patristic Age, AD 350–450* (London, 1995); B. Newman, *From Virile Woman to Woman Christ: Studies in Medieval Religion and Literature* (Philadelphia, 1995). For high medieval spirituality, see C. Walker Bynum, *Jesus as Mother: Studies in the Spirituality of the High Middle Ages* (Berkeley, 1982), *Holy Feast and Holy Fast: The Religious Significance of Food to Medieval Women* (Berkeley, 1987), and *Fragmentation and Redemption: Essays on Gender and the Human Body in Medieval Religion* (New York, 1992); J. Tibbetts Schulenberg, 'The Heroics of Virginity: Brides of Christ and Sacrificial Mutilation', in *Women in the Middle Ages and the Renaissance*, ed. M. B. Rose (Syracuse, 1986), pp. 29–72.

44. M. Green, 'Female Sexuality in the Medieval West', *Trends in History*, 4 (1990), 127–58.

45. *Medieval Knighthood V*, ed. S. Church and R. Harvey (Woodbridge, 1995); G. Duby, *The Chivalrous Society* (Berkeley, 1977), *The Three Orders: Feudal Society Imagined* (Chicago, 1978), and 'The Courtly Model', in *A History of Women in the West: Silences of the Middle Ages*, ed. C. Klapisch-Zuber (Cambridge, Mass., 1992); J. France, 'Patronage and the Appeal of the First Crusade', in *The First Crusade: Origins and Impact*, ed. J. Phillips (Manchester, 1997), pp. 5–20; *The Ideals and Practice of Medieval Knighthood II*, ed. C. Harper-Bill and R. Harvey (Woodbridge, 1988); R. W. Kaeuper, *Chivalry and Violence in Medieval Europe* (Oxford, 1999); P. L'Hermite-Leclercq, 'The Feudal Order', in *A History of Women in the West*, ed. Klapisch-Zuber; M. Keen, *Chivalry* (New Haven, 1984) and *Nobles, Knights, and Men-at-Arms in the Middle Ages* (London, 1996); C. S. Jaeger, *The Origins of Courtliness: Civilizing Trends and the Formation of Courtly Ideals, 939–1210* (Philadelphia, 1985) and *Ennobling Love: In Seach of a Lost Sensibility* (Philadelphia, 1999).

46. R. H. Bloch, *Medieval Misogyny and the Invention of Western Romantic Love* (Chicago, 1991); *Courtly Ideology and Woman's Place in Medieval French Literature*, ed. E. J. Burns and R. Krueger (Chapel Hill, 1985); E. J. Burns, *Bodytalk: When Women Speak in Old French Literature* (Philadelphia, 1993) and 'Refashioning Courtly Love: Lancelot as Ladies' Man or Lady/Man?' in *Constructing Medieval Sexuality*, ed. K. Lochrie, P. McCracken and J. A. Schultz (Minneapolis, 1997), pp. 111–34; J. W. Ferrante, *Woman as Image in Medieval Literature: From the Twelfth Century to Dante* (New York, 1975); R. W. Hanning, 'The Social Significance of Twelfth-Century Chivalric Romance', *Medievalia et Humanistica*, 3 (1972), 3–29; S. Knight, 'The Social Function of the Middle

English Romances', in *Medieval Literature: Criticism, Ideology & History*, ed. D. Aers (Brighton, Sussex, 1986), pp. 99–122; C. Marchello-Nizia, 'Amour courtois, société masuline et figures du pouvoir', *Annales: Économies, Sociétés, Civilisations*, 36 (1981), 969–82; S. Westphal-Wihl, 'The Ladies' Tournament: Marriage, Sex, and Honor in Thirteenth-Century Germany', *Signs: Journal of Women in Culture and Society*, 14 (1989), 371–98.

47. W. Porges, 'The Clergy, the Poor, and the Non-Combatants on the First Crusade', *Speculum*, 21 (1946), 1–21; R. Somerville, 'The Council of Clermont and the First Crusade', *Studia Gratiana*, 20 (1976), 325–37.

48. J. A. Brundage, 'Sexual Equality in Medieval Canon Law', in *Medieval Women and the Sources of Medieval History*, ed. J. T. Rosenthal (Athens, Ga, 1990), pp. 66–79; E. M. Makowski, 'The Conjugal Debt and Medieval Canon Law', *Journal of Medieval History*, 3 (1977), 99–114.

49. J. M. Blythe, 'Women in the Military: Scholastic Arguments and Medieval Images of Female Warriors', *History of Political Thought*, 22 (2001), 242–69; B. C. Hacker, 'Women and Military Institutions in Early Modern Europe: A Reconnaissance', *Signs*, 6 (1981), 643–71; M. McLaughlin, 'The Woman Warrior: Gender, Warfare and Society in Medieval Europe', *Women's Studies*, 17 (1990), 193–209; H. Solterer, 'Figures of Female Militancy in Medieval France', *Signs*, 16 (1991), 522–49; L. K. Stock, '"Arms and the (Wo)man" in Medieval Romance: The Gendered Arming of Female Warriors in the *Roman d'Eneas* and Heldris's *Roman de Silence*', *Arthuriana*, 5 (1995), 56–83.

50. S. Farmer, 'Persuasive Voices: Clerical Images of Medieval Wives', *Speculum*, 61 (1986), 517–43.

51. Studies include: M. Erler and M. Kowaleski, eds, *Women and Power in the Middle Ages*, (Athens, Ga, 1988) and *Gendering the Master Narrative: Women and Power in the Middle Ages* (Ithaca, 2003); *Women and Sovereignty*, ed. L. O. Fradenburg (Edinburgh, 1992); J. Gillingham, 'Love, Marriage and Politics in the Twelfth Century', in his *Richard Coeur de Lion: Kingship, Chivalry and War in the Twelfth Century* (London, 1994); M. Howell, 'Royal Women of England and France in the Mid-Thirteenth Century: A Gendered Perspective', in *England and Europe in the Reign of Henry III (1216–1272)*, ed. B. Weiler (Aldershot, 2002); K. A. LoPrete, 'The Gender of Lordly Women: The Case of Adela of Blois', in *Pawns or Players?: Studies on Medieval and Early Modern Women*, ed. C. Meek and C. Lawless (Dublin, 2003); *Medieval Queenship* (New York, 1998), ed. J. Carmi Parsons; E. M. Searle, 'Emma the Conqueror', in *Studies in Medieval History Presented to R. Allen Brown*, ed. C. J. Holdsworth, C. Harper-Bill and J. L. Nelson (Woodbridge, 1989), pp. 281–8; J. A. Truax, 'Anglo-Norman Women at War: Valiant Soldiers, Prudent Strategists or Charismatic Leaders?', in *The Circle of War in the Middle Ages: Essays on Medieval Military and Naval History*, ed. D. J. Kagay and L. J. A. Villalon (Woodbridge, 1999), pp. 111–25; W. J. Wilkins, '"Submitting the Neck of Your Mind": Gregory the Great and Women of Power', *Catholic Historical Review*, 77 (1991), 583–94.

52. Adair, '"Ego et uxor mea . . ."'; T. de Hemptinne, 'Les épouses de croisés et pèlerins flamands aux XIe et XIIe siècles: l'exemple des comtesses de Flandre Clémence et Sibylle', in *Autour de la premiere croisade*, ed. M. Balard (Paris, 1996).

53. S. Schein, 'Bridget of Sweden, Margery Kempe, and Women's Jerusalem Pilgrimages in the Middle Ages', *Mediterranean Historical Review*, 14 (1999),

44–58; K. T. Utterback, 'The Vision Becomes Reality: Medieval Women Pilgrims to the Holy Land', in *Pilgrims and Travelers to the Holy Land*, ed. Br. F. Le Beau and M. Mor (Omaha, 1994), pp. 159–68.

54. *The Medieval City under Siege*, ed. I. A. Corfis and M. Wolfe (Woodbridge, 1995); Dillard, *Daughters of the Reconquest*; D. Herlihy, 'Land, Family and Women in Continental Europe, 701–1200', *Traditio*, 28 (1962), 89–120; E. Lourie, 'A Society Organized for War: Medieval Spain', *Past and Present*, 35 (1966), 64–76; B. F. Reilly, *The Kingdon of Leon-Castilla under Queen Urraca, 1109–1126* (Princeton, 1982).

55. Mirrer, 'Representing "Other" Men'; J. de Weever, *Sheba's Daughters: Whitening and Demonizing the Saracen Woman in Medieval French Epic* (New York, 1998).

56. R. Abels and E. Harrison, 'The Participation of Women in Languedocian Catharism', *Mediaeval Studies*, 41 (1979), 215–51; M. Barber, 'Women and Catharism', *Reading Medieval Studies*, 3 (1977), 45–62; A. Blamires, 'Women and Preaching in Medieval Orthodoxy, Heresy, and Saints' Lives', *Viator*, 26 (1995), 135–52; J. Boswell, *Christianity, Social Tolerance, and Homosexuality* (Chicago, 1980) and *Same-Sex Unions in Premodern Europe* (New York, 1994); S. F. Kruger, 'Conversion and Medieval Sexual, Religious, and Racial Categories', in *Constructing Medieval Sexuality*, ed. Lochrie et al., pp. 158–79.

57. D. Nirenberg, *Communities of Violence: Persecution of Minorities in the Middle Ages* (Princeton, 1996).

58. M. Carrier, 'Perfidious and Effeminate Greeks: The Representation of Byzantine Ceremonial in the Western Chronicles of the Crusades (1096–1204)', *Annuario dell'Instituto Romeno di Cultura e Ricerca Umanistica Venezia*, 4 (2002), 47–68; N. Daniel, *Islam and the West: The Making of an Image* (Edinburgh, 1960) and *Heroes and Saracens: An Interpretation of the Chansons de Geste* (Edinburgh, 1984); L. Mirrer, *Women, Jews and Muslims in the Texts of Reconquest Castile* (Ann Arbor, 1996).

59. *Masculinity in Medieval Europe*, ed. D. M. Hadley (London, 1999); R. Mazo Karras, *From Boys to Men: Formations of Masculinity in Late Medieval Europe* (Philadelphia, 2003); *Medieval Masculinities: Regarding Men in the Middle Ages*, ed. C. A. Lees (Minneapolis, 1994); *Conflicted Identities and Multiple Masculinities: Men in the Medieval West*, ed. J. Murray (New York, 1999).

7
frontiers
nora berend

The 'frontier' became an analytical concept in medieval history-writing in the twentieth century, and has been used especially since the second half of that century. In the historiography of the Middle Ages, two main lines of thought concerning frontiers developed largely independently of each other. One addresses the development of frontiers, understood to be linear or zonal, around villages, estates and kingdoms; the other focuses on 'frontier societies', seen as societies possessing special characteristics. The works that first influenced medievalists, leading them to start employing the concept of the 'frontier', were written at the end of the nineteenth and in the early twentieth centuries.

The 'frontier' played a significant part in nineteenth- and twentieth-century European political geography: many discussions centred on the role and development of state frontiers, their expansion and the 'natural frontiers' that states should achieve in order to survive.[1] In the early twentieth century, Lucien Febvre wrote an article that rapidly became a classic, drawing attention to the way the terminology and reality of frontiers developed over time.[2] He established the 'frontier' as worthy of historical investigation. From the 1940s on, work has proliferated on the development of medieval frontiers, understood to be boundary-lines, or more frequently zones, in analyses of the formation of states and provinces.

It was a historian of the United States, Frederick Jackson Turner, who exercised a formative influence on medievalists that led to the development of the concept of 'frontier society'.[3] According to him, the westward movement of white settlers in search of new lands in America brought savagery and civilization face to face with each other. The pioneers left behind all the political and social structures and customs that they had brought from Europe and the development of new institutions, ways of

148

thought and habits began. He saw the American frontier as the main influence on the formation of American institutions and character. These ideas were altered to some extent by Walter Prescott Webb and others, and the 'frontier thesis' spread in its modified form. Although during the late twentieth century Turner's thesis has been criticized and discarded by historians of the United States, the impact of his ideas on medievalists started to grow. Primarily medieval historians in the United States adopted the concept of the frontier for medieval European history, quickly coining the terminology of 'frontier societies'. Early uses in medieval studies of a Turnerian 'frontier' denoting expansion include articles written in 1913 and 1958, but it is especially from the 1960s that historians have employed 'frontier' and increasingly 'frontier society' in order to describe expansion or interaction.[4]

'Frontier' in its meaning of a political boundary has been the object of numerous historical studies. As historians have shown, stable linear state frontiers emerged in the early modern and modern period; therefore medieval Europe has often been seen as an era when frontiers did not exist. Medievalists rarely question the chronology of the birth of political state boundaries (although some scholars argue that in a few areas, notably Iberia, linear state boundaries started to emerge already in the Middle Ages[5]). They have, however, drawn attention to the existence of 'frontier zones': most medievalists argue that during the Middle Ages boundaries of units larger than estates or villages (for example of principalities or kingdoms) were zones rather than lines. For example, as one study shows, Normandy was not surrounded by a precise linear frontier, but by a more fluid frontier zone.[6] Scholars also explored how boundaries around estates and villages developed in the various European countries. Studies written in French, Italian, German, Spanish and many other languages include work on dating the emergence of the first linear boundaries around estates in various countries, on the custom of delimitations, on the markers used to designate limits, on disputes concerning borders, and on rituals associated with borders. These have shown how descriptions in charters include very detailed boundary lines delimited by trees, roads, rocks and man-made markers. The first appearance of the word 'frontier' in Latin and various vernacular languages has also been traced for numerous medieval kingdoms.

Historians have recourse to the terms 'frontier' and 'frontier society' in the sense of interaction or process in many divergent ways, and the use of this terminology is more controversial than that of 'frontier' as political boundary. First it was applied to German eastward migration and western European expansion, and as a consequence the crisis of the fourteenth century was interpreted as the 'closing of the frontier', that is the end of expansion. Although the association of 'frontiers' to expansion remained a consistent element of frontier studies, subsequently 'frontier' was used to denote an increasingly wide variety of historical circumstances. Closest to the original Turnerian hypothesis, 'frontier' is used to analyse human interaction with nature in uninhabited regions: the medieval colonization of new areas, agricultural expansion, the extension of cultivation to new lands, and monastic, especially Cistercian, settlement and innovation.

Most medievalists, however, employ the term to discuss cultural and religious developments, the interaction between groups of people and societies rather than between man and nature. The interaction in the focus of frontier studies is frequently a military one. The military aspects of frontiers that scholars have studied include the rise of border lords along the Arab-Byzantine frontier; warfare between the Irish and the English in the British Isles, and between Christians and Muslims in Iberia. Medievalists started early on to draw attention to the fact that even in regions characterized by warfare, peaceful interaction also existed between the two sides involved in conflict. Thus negotiations, arbitration, and even trade characterized this interaction along with war. Some scholars argue that life in frontier zones was different from life in the central areas due to these dynamics of peaceful and military interaction. Thus frontier regions supposedly provided a greater freedom from central control and institutions to those living there and were therefore places that fostered self-reliance and were conducive to more fluid social conditions and gave rise to loyalties that cut across traditional divides. In some cases life in frontier zones could even lead to acculturation and religious syncretism, with the inhabitants, originally belonging to different cultures, forming a symbiosis that differed from their respective centres. Frontiers are also important in the historiography of nomad–sedentary interaction in eastern and central Europe. Nomads regularly raided neighbouring sedentary societies, but they also served as military allies and even settled in neighbouring states. These interactions affected the sedentary societies in the borderlands of Christendom, such as Hungary, Georgia and Rus', as they had to face military confrontations with nomads, but also find ways for diplomatic contact.

Some historians have seen 'frontier interaction' as affecting the entire society: especially in analyses of the British Isles, Anglo-Irish and Anglo-Scottish relations have often been understood in that way. 'Frontier society' served to denote not only interaction with another society, religion or culture, but also a society where conquerors subjugated a native population (sometimes described as a colonial society). 'Frontier interaction' even provided the framework for an interpretation of medieval Europe: Robert Barlett wrote about the creation of Europe through the expansion of Christendom's frontiers. He argued that western European conquerors and settlers brought many institutions and customs to the peripheries in northern, eastern and southern Europe, where they interacted with the local populations. This was the chief formative force in the development of European society, leading to 'the foundation of an expansive and increasingly homogeneous society'.[7] 'Frontier' and 'frontier society' acquired abstract and vague meanings as well. 'Frontiers' are occasionally used to indicate 'mental frontiers': a sense of identity and perceptions of difference. 'Frontier society' served even more loosely, for example to denote societies developing in response to new challenges and opportunities instead of adopting existing customs and systems, and to designate areas where new institutions, norms and social forms emerge.

The range of meanings is therefore very large, and although there are distinctions between 'frontier' and 'frontier society' in many works, occasionally even these distinctions are blurred. The terms can designate a region or area; a type of society; and a process of development. They have been employed to describe processes from expansion against nature through military confrontation with another society to acculturation. Whereas American historians found fault with every aspect of Turner's thesis about the American frontier, most medievalists have shunned a terminological debate and continue to use 'frontier' and 'frontier society' in its varied meanings. Yet some medievalists have started to question the use of these concepts, from the most radical refusal of the usefulness of the 'frontier' concept, namely that 'frontier' in any other than a political boundary sense is too vague and useless as an analytical tool, to criticisms of particular aspects of the use of this concept. The concept of frontier society has been criticized for its focus on western European motivations and actions, on Christian expansion and influence, while excluding the other side, be it Lithuanians or Muslims. Historians also argued that many developments designated by this concept had in fact nothing to do with the 'frontier' or could be explained through the use of other terminology.

Historians of the crusades have employed the concept of the 'frontier' and of 'frontier society' in its many different meanings. Frontiers and frontier society were most frequently used in the history of the crusades for Iberia and the Baltic areas; indeed analysis of Iberia played a prominent role in introducing the concept of frontier societies to medieval studies itself. 'Frontier' has been used primarily in the following meanings in crusader studies. It denoted military frontiers that had to be defended and where confrontation took place. It signalled types of life and processes of development: areas of interaction (including military and peaceful interaction) between adherents of different religions, especially Christians and Muslims, and 'frontier zones' of coexistence. 'Frontier society' also occurs, as a type of society that was created once the crusaders conquered areas and established their power over native populations. The nature of such societies itself has been much debated: whether it was colonial, oppressive of the indigenous populations, or based on peaceful interaction and even acculturation. 'Frontier' occasionally occurs in its abstract meanings, mostly as 'mental frontiers' between adversaries such as Christians and Muslims or Christians and pagans. Finally, the concept of 'frontier crusade' has been coined, focusing on the specificities of later medieval crusades, linked to a shift in control of crusading to societies on the frontiers of Christendom.

Military frontiers, important in frontier studies in general, have been especially pertinent to the history of the crusades. Crusading has been called a frontier activity, resulting in conquests and the need to defend borders. Thus frontier defence can be construed as a key aspect of crusades. Yet the treatment of such defence is often controversial. Debate over the defence of the frontiers of the crusader states has been especially intense. Traditionally, the function of crusader castles was thought to have been the defence of the frontiers of these polities. Otto Smail challenged this view, arguing that castles could only imperfectly fulfil the role of frontier defence on the one hand, and had other, often more important, functions on the other hand, including being centres for Latin control and colonization, bases for power. Many castles were not built on the frontier, and many 'frontier' sectors were not fortified. In any case, fortresses could not stop invading armies, and indeed Muslim armies often penetrated deep into Latin territory. He claimed that there was no consciously planned frontier defence system, although the importance of some castles on the frontier was recognized; these could be centres of sustained attack against Muslims.[8] Malcolm Barber, on the other hand, insisted on the 'importance of the frontier in the relations between the Latin settlers and their Muslim enemies',[9] claiming that Smail exaggerated in his argument that the Franks did not build castles to defend their frontiers. According to Barber, the policy driven by the military religious orders was to consolidate and even expand the eastern frontier. Control over this frontier became crucial to the survival of the crusader states during the reign of Baldwin IV, and both sides recognized this. Ronnie Ellenblum also contributed to this debate on frontier defences in the Latin

Kingdom of Jerusalem, using archaeological data.[10] He demonstrated that more fortresses were constructed in areas that were relatively safe from Muslim attacks than in areas exposed to danger. He distinguished three phases of building activity; whereas in the first two castles were built as central places, settlement kernels to provide ecclesiastical, administrative and commercial services, in the third (after 1168) they were built on the borders. At the same time, existing fortresses were reinforced. This was a new policy, and Muslim response to it was the siege of these fortresses. In his article 'Were There Borders and Borderlines in the Middle Ages?', however, Ellenblum challenged the very idea that medieval kingdoms had borders, and that there was an association between castles and borderlines, using the example of the Latin Kingdom of Jerusalem. According to him, medieval political entities did not have linear borders, or even border-zones; rather, suzerainty (power over people) was the key issue: kings ruled over people rather than over territories from centres of political power. Thus castles served not as parts of a fortified borderline, but as centres with spheres of influence. Analysing the account of Ibn Jubayr, Ellenblum concludes that as he passed from Muslim to Frankish territory, Ibn Jubayr did not cross a border, but rather encountered several distinct points of demarcation: the boundary between safety and danger (the point beyond which the Franks could capture Muslims); a different boundary in a valley where cultivation was divided between Franks and Muslims; and yet a different point where duties had to be paid on goods.[11]

The frontier defence of other crusader areas are also discussed. When crusading is defined as a frontier activity, establishing borders with Muslims, it follows that these borders needed to be defended. For example, Theresa M. Vann analysed the frontier strategies of twelfth-century Castile. According to her, Castilians created an in-depth defence system, investing in fortifications, then maintaining this perimeter by militias raised by the frontier settlers. They also aimed to expand, or when necessary recapture a line of fortresses that constituted a screen of defence, as demonstrated by the castles guarding the routes to Toledo.[12] The militarized frontier with its chain of fortresses in late medieval Hungary has been the topic of a whole array of studies. These were lines of defence against the Ottomans, built up over time as a sophisticated system to stop or hinder the attackers. Whereas at first it was the southern border of the kingdom of Hungary that was defended by these means, from the middle of the sixteenth century, after the fall of Buda, a new strategy developed. Separate castle regions were created, each around a central frontier fortress. Border fortress generalcies (*Grenzoberhauptmannschaften*) controlled the frontier defence. The line of border fortresses from the Adriatic Sea to Transylvania consisted of a chain of about 120 fortresses of differing size. The supply of war material, food and payment for the soldiers was organized from Austria. In the seventeenth century, as payment to soldiers was often delayed or partial, the soldiers became semi-civilians, involved in local production, while border lords and their subjects, including peasant-soldiers, took a more active part in defence against Ottoman incursions. Whereas for a long time Hungarian historiography has tried to demonstrate the unique nature of the Hungarian-Ottoman military frontier, this view has now come under attack, with recent work demonstrating that the number of Ottoman soldiers present and the nature of Ottoman administration in Hungary was not unique, but similar to other frontier regions of the Ottoman Empire.[13]

The military nature of frontiers more generally has also often been discussed in crusade studies. The type of castle-building, the method of warfare (such as constant raids or skirmishes), the creation of special institutions such as the military orders are linked not only specifically to the defence of physical frontiers, but to the 'frontier' nature of a zone or even of the whole society. However, not all historians analyse these developments in the framework of 'frontiers'. Least controversially, the military orders are understood to have developed due to the nature of frontier areas: warfare and interaction with another society engendered frontier institutions that differed from those in central areas. Military orders are often thought of as groups who were permanently ready to wage war, adapting their strategy and practices to local needs. Members of military orders thus become 'frontiersmen' whose main task was the defence of frontiers. Thus the emergence of military orders both in the Latin East and Iberia has been interpreted in the light of the frontier concept, and the function of military orders in central and eastern Europe has been discussed in terms of border defence. In this vein, Ann Williams defined the members of the Order of St John as frontiersmen patrolling the frontiers between Islam and Christendom for five centuries, their main priorities being in the Eastern Mediterranean during the later Middle Ages. These frontiers included sea frontiers that were amorphous and 'almost pulled the enemy in to raid and devastate the coast';[14] Malta was to be a fortified frontier outpost here, to prevent Ottoman raids on the coasts of Italy and Iberia and subsequent Ottoman conquests. During the seventeenth century, the Mediterranean was a fluid frontier between Islam and the West, where trade and war equally occurred. Similarly numerous articles in Spanish discuss the local military orders as institutions that defended and advanced the frontier in Iberia.

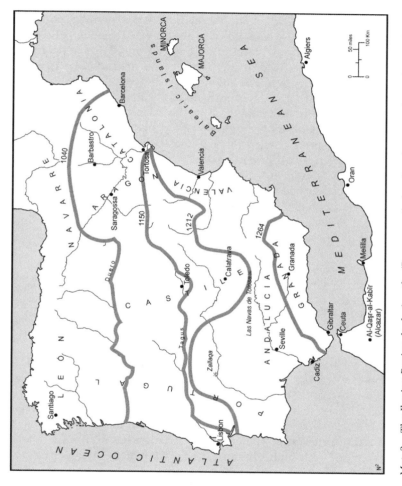

Map 3. The Iberian Peninsula during the 'Reconquest', showing the approximate frontier lines between the Christian and Muslim regions in 1040, 1150, 1212 and 1264, after Angus MacKay, *Spain in the Middle Ages: From Frontier to Empire, 1000–1500* (Basingstoke: Macmillan, 1977), p. xiv.

The view that the primary task of military orders was frontier warfare has been modified by scholars focusing on other aspects of the orders' activities. For example, Nikolas Jaspert studied the Templars in Catalonia. He argued that frontier areas of Christendom had both a military function and a role in introducing civil and administrative structures; thus the Templars 'served the specific needs of a frontier society in the military, economic and spiritual field'.[15] The Templars were given estates, parish churches and fortifications; their task was not only to defend but also to settle the frontier area. Yet as Christian conquest advanced, the Templars' activities ceased to be linked to the frontier, and instead came to be focused within the kingdom. The colonization of newly-acquired land, thus service on the frontiers, was entrusted to military orders even in areas where there were no crusades, as in the British Isles.[16] Carlos de Ayala Martínez argued that the military orders helped strengthen the Castilian-Leonese monarchy less through their contribution in military action, and more through providing a political justification for kings through the *reconquista*: they helped to strengthen the image of the war against Muslims as a crusade. By their presence on the frontier, military orders facilitated the permanent legitimization of the crusade, an important propaganda reference for kings.[17] The orders also played a role in the integration of frontier territories through colonization and the implantation of a legal system.

Describing other institutions as 'frontier' ones has been more controversial. New religious orders such as the Cistercians, Franciscans and Dominicans, active in frontier regions in the service of expansion through mission and contributing to the ecclesiastical organization of new lands, are sometimes described as having 'frontier' characteristics. Thus Lawrence McCrank saw the Cistercians as bringing a frontier religion to the newly Christianized lands of Catalonia.[18] Robert I. Burns interpreted the parish as a frontier institution, a means of introducing social and religious organization to newly conquered lands in Valencia. This type of approach has been criticized by Peter Linehan, who pointed out that religion and religious organization were the same in Iberia as in 'non-frontier' areas, for example France.[19] Militarization has been seen as a key characteristic not simply of frontier regions, but of 'frontier societies' affected by the crusades, permeating the entire society and determining its development. Elena Lourie's article 'A Society Organised for War: Medieval Spain' formulated this thesis forcefully for medieval Iberia.[20] According to her, after 711, the Muslim conquest of the Peninsula, the development of Spanish society was determined by responses to military danger. The privileges given to settlers, the creation of military orders, the ideology of the reconquest all developed due to the confrontation with Muslims. This thesis was very influential, but eventually new research modified the understanding of most of the evidence, therefore undermining the main argument. The ideology of the reconquest did not appear in 711, but developed gradually in the eleventh and twelfth centuries. Muslim–Christian interaction was more complex than simply military confrontation. There was fighting between co-religionists on both sides and alliances that cut across the confessional divide. Indeed, scholars like Eduardo Manzano Moreno, Richard Fletcher and Ann Christys now argue that before the eleventh century there was no Muslim–Christian frontier: the population of the Duero valley intermingled, and the movement of people, especially of military adventurers both Muslim and Christian shows that those ready to seize opportunities sought their fortunes entirely without regard to the religious adherence of their allies and enemies. Examples of such adventurers include Mahmud ibn 'Abd al-Jabbar of Mérida in the ninth century and Rodrigo Diaz de Vivar, el Cid, in the eleventh century.[21]

Many historians refer to the importance of the military element and the frontier in determining the development of the crusader states of the Latin East. Joshua Prawer wrote about preferential rights given to settlers in frontier settlements and of Frankish settlement in the Latin East as being part of the crusades, as a key aspect of fortifying and defending the frontier.[22] Jonathan Riley-Smith argued that the Latin East was a frontier region, and challenged the notion that the only form of power in a frontier region could be marcher lordships. According to him, this was a frontier feudal society where military service was crucial to the functioning of society, as the needs of government and defence were acute.[23] In his book *Frankish Rural Settlement in the Latin Kingdom of Jerusalem*, Ronnie Ellenblum offered an alternative approach. According to him, Frankish settlement was not crusader settlement, no central authority encouraged emigration to borderlands and settlement had no role in frontier defence. He argued that previous studies assumed that the crusades created a frontier with both physical obstacles and a human enemy; that then the frontier was filled with settlers who were pioneers and conquerors. This society then created a 'frontier myth', immortalizing the first crusaders and exhorting newcomers to live up to the standards of the pioneers. In contrast, Ellenblum claimed that this was a migrant society, settled to cultivate the land, and did not prioritize war against Muslims. He interpreted crusade ideology as based on the concept of a cultural (not territorial) frontier. However, he emphasized that the end of this society was characteristic of frontiers: the confrontation with the Turks was a frontier phenomenon, and the Frankish frontier failed in the face of the enemy's almost unlimited manpower.[24]

Analyses of how the military aspect of crusades permeated the life of all concerned include studies on the Baltic as well. For example, Carsten Selch Jensen has considered cities on the frontiers surrounded by enemies, that served as the starting-point of military campaigns, and where the presence of crusaders was permanent. At the same time, they could also be the seat of missionary bishoprics established to convert pagans. Open to attacks, they had to be defended, sometimes with the active participation of townspeople who were perhaps not crusaders. 'The crusades were an enterprise that influenced the whole of society in the regions subjected to crusading warfare, warriors and merchants alike.'[25]

The multifaceted nature of interaction during crusading has often been described as characteristic of 'frontier' relations. Most historians point out that 'frontier societies' created in crusade areas (or the influence of 'frontiers' in those regions) entailed more than warfare, and included peaceful interaction. That is, despite and even during military campaigns, not only negotiations and diplomacy but even trade between the two sides continued. For example, Rasa Mažeika analysed the duality of this interaction during the wars between the Teutonic Order and Lithuania; Stephen Rowell wrote about the astute use of Lithuanian diplomacy in the same wars.[26] José Enrique López de Coca Castañer analysed the institutions on the Castilian-Granadan frontier of the fifteenth century. Even though neither side recognized the fact, this frontier was virtually stable for a longer period. Whereas in their ideology both Christians and Muslims advocated holy war, in practice various institutions developed to regulate interaction. The two sides made truces and set up peacekeeping mechanisms across the frontier against robbery and kidnapping for example, appointed deputies to settle quarrels involving parties on both sides of the frontier, licensed merchants to trade across the frontier, and made arrangements for the redemption of captives. These agreements, however, were only kept until the Muslims were defeated. The view that frontiers were scenes of more than military interaction, however, is beginning to come under criticism.[27] Francisco García Fitz wrote of the Castilian-Muslim frontier of the eleventh to thirteenth centuries as a 'hot frontier'; according to him, its characteristics were intense confrontation, violence and brutality associated with a permanent warfare. He argued against an interpretation that sees peaceful relations as well as war as characteristics of the frontier, and claimed that habitual violence, insecurity and anxiety were the norm due to a continuous fight against the political, economic and psychological support system of the enemy.[28] The Baltic region has been described as a 'frontier area between different economic systems, between different religions and different denominations of Christianity, and between very different linguistic and ethnic groups'.[29] Coexistence and confrontation are the main themes here as well. However, writing about the Baltic as a frontier area where crusading was an important aspect of life does not mean that every historian writing about the Baltic crusades links them to the 'frontier'. Norman Housley also categorized a number of the features of late medieval crusades as 'frontier characteristics'.[30] For example, the enemy's ways were known. Sixteenth-century Dalmatian *uskok* (pirate) towns saw themselves as engaged in holy war on Christendom's frontier, and linked their identity and justification for war to religion. In the case of late medieval frontier areas, be they Hungary, the *uskoks*, Lithuania or Granada, warfare and the ideology of holy war coexisted with pragmatic everyday relations between the foes, and peaceful relations between the two sides could include trade, diplomacy, adjudication, peacekeeping mechanisms and even cultural exchange. There was no polarization between peaceful interaction such as trade on the one hand and crusade on the other; and the latter was often orchestrated by central authority. Even when warfare was local, it often entailed the hope of drawing on the resources from the centre (from a central authority or the papacy). Even though frontier interaction included political and diplomatic relations and trade as well as warfare, at the same time many of the powers, as divergent as Rhodes, Cyprus or Hungary, represented themselves as 'bulwarks of Christendom' in order to gain support and counter criticism from Christians.

Scholars working on different theatres of crusading also concluded that long-term contacts between two sides led not simply to peaceful interaction but even to cultural exchange, acculturation and assimilation. Instances of these include the Iberian frontier ballads and common cults of saints by Muslims and Christians in Iberia. Alliances across the frontier were commonplace, and even borrowing and religious syncretism were not rare, as Angus MacKay demonstrated. There was such 'cultural confusion' that the frontier 'hardly existed':[31] Muslims crossed the frontier to worship at the shrine of a Christian saint, literature was written by moriscos in romance dialect using Arabic characters. Rasa Mažeika analysed similar trends where enemy gods were treated as real forces by the two sides in the wars between the Teutonic Order and Lithuanians, and she also pinpointed an instance of the common mindset between pagans and crusaders: the importance of honour to both Teutonic Knights and Lithuanians.[32]

Interaction and acculturation continued in the new societies established after the conquest of various areas by crusaders. The states established by crusaders have sometimes been characterized as 'frontier societies', that is, societies where interaction with conquered indigenous populations created specific dynamics, allegedly different from those operating in other societies. It should be pointed out, however, that the multicultural nature of conquest societies was already analysed in early scholarship without recourse to the terminology of 'frontier society'. Scholars' opinions changed over time on issues such as cultural interaction in the Latin East, the treatment of indigenous populations in the Latin Kingdom of Jerusalem, and the adoption by the Franks of some of the customs of the conquered majority. The earlier view that westerners adopted many oriental customs and became 'Orientalized', mingling with the indigenous populations, leading to the emergence of a new nation from the blending of conquerors and the conquered, was discarded by Smail and Prawer. They argued that the Franks formed a distinct ruling elite, clearly differentiated from the people they conquered; a numerically small military elite imposed itself over the native population and exploited them, creating a colonial society. Ronnie Ellenblum in turn attacked this view, claiming that Franks settled in areas inhabited by native Christians, and created a Franco-Eastern Christian or Franco-Syrian frontier society which was Christian under Frankish hegemony.

Crusade and conquest have also been seen as creating division rather than acculturation. The concept of the frontier explicitly or implicitly informs essays that depict first the lack of a frontier between adherents of different Christian confessions, or between Christians and non-Christians, and then the creation of a frontier due to the crusades; the crusades, then, are seen as the key factor in introducing divisions where they had not existed. Thus John H. Lind charted the change from a Russian-Scandinavian symbiosis that included alliances between dynasties prior to and during the first half of the twelfth century, to a growing division and confessional hostility after the start of the Baltic crusades in the 1140s, manifest in the adoption of abusive terminology and stereotyping and finally leading to the depiction of those of another Christian denomination as enemies.[33] Anti Selart argued that in the thirteenth century, 'Livonia and North-Western Russia were a common area of politics, where the borders between confessions were not so significant as sometimes imagined.'[34] While there was competition between various Catholic powers (the Teutonic Order, Denmark and Sweden), Catholics, Orthodox and pagans cooperated as a matter of course in politics. From the end of the century, however, such cooperation was used to accuse opponents in internal conflicts. These accusations were rhetorical, to gain the ear of the pope; at the same time, everyday life continued to be based on trade and politics. Locals, such as the townspeople of Riga, out of practical considerations, had to continue to cooperate with Lithuanians and Russians. A new frontier, between Christians and pagans, was defined when crusading ideology was applied to the region east of the Elbe, a topic examined by Friedrich Lotter.[35] Whereas until the early twelfth century Christians and pagans, Saxons and Slavs mixed and cooperated, a divide was established on the basis of faith with the recourse to the rhetoric of crusade. Lands east of the Elbe were represented in clerical propaganda as areas that had been Christianized earlier, and then lost through pagan invasions, thus drawing a parallel to the 'Holy Land' to provide justification for conquest. Historians of Iberia showed how 'frontiers' expressed and created an array of divisions. Miguel Ángel Ladero Quesada analysed the development of borders between the Christian kingdoms in Iberia in the thirteenth century, demonstrating that their emergence was parallel to the reconquest and that they also played an important role in the consolidation of monarchies.[36] As Pascal Buresi pointed out, this territorialization, the development of well-defined frontiers between the Christian Iberian kingdoms and the centralization of power was also accompanied by the emergence of a feeling of community of Christendom against Islam.[37] Changes in the vocabulary of frontiers mirrored a change of mentality: a distinction developed between frontiers between Christian kingdoms in Iberia on the one hand, and frontiers between Christendom and Islam on the other. Papal influence led to the definition of frontiers as frontiers of Christendom to be pushed as far as possible. Muslims, on the other hand, envisaged one frontier only: that with the infidel, associated with holy war.

'Frontier' is also sometimes employed in crusade studies to express the irreconcileable hostility that existed between two sides. Vera Matuzova described the chronicler Peter von Dusburg's account of pagan Prussians. Peter, a member of the Teutonic Order, justified the crusade against the Prussians by giving a negative image of them; he focused on the difference between 'them' and 'us', providing a stereotypical image of the other rather than trying to know and describe the Prussians. She characterized this attitude by calling it a mental frontier: 'A mental frontier is a borderline between two mentalities that cannot interpenetrate each other.'[38] Reflecting on the apparent contradiction between religious enmity and everday coexistence, Charles Halperin argued that a specific mechanism characterized religious frontiers in the Middle Ages: the 'ideology of silence'.[39] Even though Christian thought could not accept the truth of other religions, where Christians had to coexist with Muslims because they did not have sufficient power to subjugate them, a tacit acceptance followed, where there was no mention of the tension between the ideology of religious exclusivism and the reality of religious plurality. Authors such as Pierre Guichard or John Tolan do not use the concept of 'frontier' or 'mental frontier' explicitly when they talk about the perceptions of the 'other', describing the negative stereotyping, hostility, contempt and hatred that served to instil into Christians a sense of radical difference from the Muslims.[40]

Recently, scholars have started to pay attention to medieval ideological uses of 'frontiers' as well. This includes studies on medieval terminology. War against Muslims and pagans was often described as the 'dilatatio' or expansion of the boundaries of the Christian faith, of Christians, or of Christendom. The word 'frontera' appeared as a consequence of the confrontation between Christians and Muslims in Iberia; designating a military front, it then started to take on the meaning of 'frontier'. Philippe Sénac analysed the emergence of this terminology, and paid special attention to Ramiro I's testament (1059), where the term 'frontier' made its first appearance. He concluded that 'frontier' did not simply denote the area in the vicinity of the Muslims, but indicated an idological context: the legitimization of royal power through war against the Muslims.[41] Philippe Josserand showed how frontiers could become a subject of conflicting interpretations, and how they were at stake in the power struggle between monarchs and popes. Whereas the papacy defined Iberian frontiers as part of the frontiers of Christendom that military orders had to defend and expand, serving the interests of the Church, Iberian kings used these orders to serve royal interests, linking the war against Muslims to royal territorial aims.[42] Thomas Lindkvist drew attention to how Swedes used crusading ideology in order to legitimize wars on the eastern frontier.[43] It has often been assumed that Sweden, as a frontier region in the Christian community, took part in crusading and missionary activity; indeed, later Swedish sources talk about medieval crusades. Yet these included warfare before the 1140s which never resulted in conquests, and were simply plundering raids legitimized by crusading ideology. On the other hand, Swedes even had recourse to the notion of a Catholic frontier against other Christians, notably Russia; their wars were driven primarily by Swedish interests, and legitimized by crusading ideology. As discussed in my own work, the ideology of standing on Christendom's frontier, waging a war in defence of the whole of Christendom, was also used from the thirteenth century on in Iberia and Hungary and from the fourteenth century in Poland, and became typical of late medieval wars.[44] This ideology was based on the papal propagation of the idea of Christendom's borders; it was developed at royal courts in order to put pressure on the popes to claim ecclesiastical revenues and royal control over ecclesiastical personnel. Scholars also analysed the development of a particular identity among the soldiers of the frontier fortresses (*végvárak*) of late medieval Hungary. The notion that Hungary was the bulwark of Christendom became a recurrent motif from the fifteenth and sixteenth centuries on, although in fact condominium (joint rule including dual taxation and jurisdiction), adaptation and cultural borrowing as well as military resistance characterized the period of the Ottoman conquest.

While 'frontier' often implies two antagonistic sides, whereas 'frontier zones' and 'frontier societies' suggest a mixing of different populations, both have been used as a framework for studies of entire post-conquest societies. This has been particularly true of Iberia, but effected other areas of crusade as well. The whole course of Iberian history has often been described as a development 'from frontier to empire', to use the formulation of Angus MacKay: starting from the pushing of the 'Muslim frontier' southward, through the defence of a succession of newly-created frontiers and repopulation of frontier villages, to the organization and characteristics of Iberian kingdoms throughout the entire medieval and early modern period, Spanish history is thus seen to be stamped by the 'frontier' experience. These scholars see the wars against the Muslims and the expansion of the frontier southward as the defining element of Iberian history. Institutional developments, the incorporation of Islamic heritage and the imposition of new Christian control, the adoption of the hydraulic irrigation system, extensive stock-raising and transhumance, the repartition of lands after conquest and many other issues that are not directly or not at all related to crusading are explained in this way.

Numerous works by American historians, for example by Robert I. Burns and Charles Julian Bishko, exemplify this approach. Bishko wrote about the frontier as a new space where population had to settle and culture had to be transplanted; a region where the dynamics of life modified social and economic structures. He also wrote extensively on ranching as a particular economic form tied to 'frontiers'.[45] Burns pointed out that in Spain, the moving frontier with Islam played a prominent role, as well as the interaction of cultures. He analysed Crusader Valencia's development in detail in many works. He defined both Spain as a region and the process taking place there as a 'frontier' in several respects. 'Frontaria' was used in contemporary sources to denote the region where warfare was endemic. The area provided resources and was a magnet for surplus populations from elsewhere. It was also a socio-economic frontier, which influenced the core by bringing wealth and strategic advantages to it. It was also a region where an interaction of two cultures took place. Finally, the 'Valencian frontier created a new man, recognizably different from the Catalan or the Aragonese or the Occitan, in his speech, in his habits, in his laws, in his character, in his relation to his environment'.[46] Burns also argued that religion was especially important on the frontier: religious ideology presented the conquests as part of a crusade; in the conquered areas ecclesiastical organization and Christian institutions had to be introduced, accompanied by a 'hardening' of attitudes to avoid acculturation to Muslims.

Work in Spanish along these lines is even more numerous; Manuel González Jiménez's article in English is an example of such traditional approach to Iberian medieval history by Spanish historians. He identified the frontier as the key to Iberian history, expressing the process of Iberia's lengthy transformation. This frontier was more than a political and military boundary; rather, it was linked to the ideology of the Reconquest. Frontiers with Islam were regarded as impermanent. In practice, with the advance of the Reconquest, new frontiers were created, mirroring different phases of settlement, yet created by 'the same mentality',[47] in other words the will to safeguard both defence and settlement. From the late eleventh century, rulers attempted to create a frontier society, where everything was subordinated to the main aim of organization for war. Thus Iberia produced a society of warrior-shepherds and militant peasants; war was also a basic element of the economy. Laws were introduced to regulate military obligations; murderers were allowed to settle provided they would fight. The exposed nature of the frontier also led to a shortage of population and the birth of the military orders.

A wide variety of studies focuses on some particular aspect of Iberia's frontier experience. For example, Jean-Pierre Molénat investigated the differences between linguistic, political and religious frontiers through the example of Toledo. Toledo in the eleventh to thirteenth centuries was on the Christian side of the frontier in terms of political, military and religious affiliation, yet its inhabitants were on the Muslim side in terms of the linguistic divide between Arabic and romance languages. The religious rather than the linguistic frontier determined identity in this case.[48] Recently several historians challenged the traditional interpretation of Iberian history as one equal with the Reconquest, and as the history of expanding Christian frontiers. Instead, they advocate the thesis of a feudal expansion. Thus for example Eduardo Manzano Moreno demonstrated how the Duero valley was not a depopulated desert; later on local aristocratic lords had networks and loyalties on both sides of the frontier. The ideological division in the sources was not a true mirror of the mixed alliances, rebellions and internal strife in reality. Ana Rodríguez López in her analysis of the reign of Ferdinand III of Castile similarly shifted the focus from Reconquest to feudal expansion. At the same time, the concept of frontiers became an analytical tool for historians analysing Muslim Iberia (al-Andalus) as well, drawing attention to such features as the defensive attitude and the specific organization of frontier territories.[49]

Analyses of post-crusade societies employing the concept of 'frontiers' also include studies of other areas. For example, Robert Bartlett argued that the Latin-Frankish (Anglo-Norman) elite that came to rule through conquest in Palestine as well as in the British Isles resembled each other and were used to the same institutions, regardless of the vast diversity of the indigenous populations they had conquered. Europe in many areas was surrounded by 'indefinite boundaries capable of expansion',[50] yet the newly conquered lands rather than being a frontier where anything goes, were often pure or even exaggerated versions of the social and political structures characteristic of the core areas at the time. S.C. Rowell contrasted different views of the frontier in his treatment of Žemaitija (Samogithia), a region between the Teutonic Order's state and the Grand Duchy of Lithuania, the Lithuano-Prussian forest frontier of the fifteenth and sixteenth centuries. For the central government, it was a line to be defined through treaties, whereas for the local inhabitants it was a region; the inhabitants of the borderlands on both sides of the frontier in many respects formed one interlinked community. Although the boundary between Poland-Lithuania and Prussia was established at the peace treaty of 1422, demarcated and confirmed subsequently, disputes over political affiliation and taxation recurred due to over-eager local officers. At the same time, local inhabitants from both sides used the frontier woods to get commodities like timber, and raided across the border, poaching, thieving and smuggling. An ethnically diverse population also migrated in both directions.[51]

Finally, some scholars used the frontier concept to designate particular forms of crusade or developments characteristic of particular areas of crusade. William Urban drew comparisons between American and Baltic frontiers. He argued that different frontier experiences existed in both. Livonia was the meeting point between the expanding cultures of Russia, Scandinavia, Germany and Lithuania. The indigenous populations were divided, had no overall leader, and did not have the military technology to match those of the invaders. The invaders established trading and missionary centres, forged alliances with some of the indigenous against the others and finally conquered the new lands. They were driven by a 'crusading ethos' as well as by economic and political interests. Yet the interior remained mostly undisturbed beyond a defensive line of fortifications for two centuries. Those who benefited from the conquest were the nobility rather than free peasants. Prussia was the scene of violent military confrontation, where westerners were pitted against fewer and less well armed indigenous; it led to the emergence of 'a class of self-made warriors'[52] and the settlement of Germans, Poles and Pomeranians. According to Urban, the Livonian frontier experience resembled that in New Spain and New France, the Prussian one that of British settlers in America. Lithuania was yet another type of frontier, a 'battleground between two … expanding cultures'.[53] Urban pointed to a common element between these divergent frontier experiences nonetheless: every adult male knew how to use a weapon, and the society was organized for war. 'Frontier theories can provide alternative interpretations', offering an interpretive framework without reference to nationalism and class struggle, or which at least 'opens the way for a discussion of the myths … at the heart of popular history'.[54]

Norman Housley analysed a change in crusading linked to frontier areas. He argued that crusading before 1291 was defined and led by people from the heartland of Europe: the papacy, western European aristocracy, monks. Although crusades were led in 'frontier societies' (that is, ones where Christians lived in close proximity to pagans or Muslims), crusader ideology was imported into rather than formed in these areas. Housley has identified two key issues in pre-1291 crusading where the frontier made its impact on crusades: 'frontiersmen' in Iberia and Germany worked to have local wars with Muslims and pagans recognized as crusades; and the interaction between the Latin East and western Europe was one between frontier and heartland. In the later Middle Ages, however, frontier societies played a more important role in the crusades not simply as theatres of warfare, but by inventing new forms of crusading: the Lithuanian Reisen and the naval leagues against the Anatolian Turks. Holy war on a religious frontier applied especially to conflict with the Ottomans.[55] The specificities of late medieval crusades are also analyzed without having recourse to the frontier concept. For example, Axel Ehlers demonstrated how the Teutonic Knights created a permanent holy war against Lithuania; they managed it themselves, did not have renewed papal authorization but used older privileges. In this way they created a new form of crusade.[56]

Frontier crusades have been characterized as wars alternating with periods of coexistence and trade; as featuring constant raids such as on the frontier of Granada; as waged by local powers such as Venice or Cyprus in the case of anti-Turkish leagues in order to maintain the balance of power in the region, but at the same time also drawing on papal involvement and western participants which broadened the scope of such crusades. Robert I. Burns, although he used the 'frontier' as an explanatory concept for medieval European history as a whole (950–1350), talking of frontier experience through expansion, and examined the importance of frontiers to various areas, pointed out that the 'crusade frontier' of Europe[57] had an impact on Europeans, and influenced the papacy. Thus frontiers provide a comparative framework for many scholars, who use the frontier as a tool to compare experiences and places in different periods.

Overall, the 'frontier' concept is used in crusade studies in a patchy way; crusading as such is not the primary area where the concept has been most applied in medieval history, even though it is often linked to the analyses of warfare and military confrontation. Some historians have recourse to it, while others write of the same phenomena linked to the crusades without using the concept of the frontier. Thus interaction, 'the other', conquest or expansion have all been addressed outside the framework provided by the frontier concept. For example, Archibald Lewis wrote a book on the expansion of nomadic and western European societies without recourse to the concept of the frontier, using simply 'expansion' when discussing the crusades.[58] Yet others write of frontiers without connecting them to the crusades: thus 'frontier' is often involved in the description of Iberian developments in general. Indeed, frontier and frontier society are most often used for Iberian history, but not primarily the history of the crusades there. The other crusading theatre where the concept has found widespread application is the Baltic region. The 'frontier' as borderline or region is often employed in studies of military defence in studies on the crusades. However, the distinction between 'frontier' and 'frontier society' (the latter now being replaced by the term 'borderlands' in American historiography) has not always been made in crusade studies; indeed, one of the key areas of study under either is interaction. The 'frontier' concept led scholars to focus on interaction, in not only its military but also peaceful forms and on the varieties of coexistence; it has come to designate interaction either between opponents or within the societies created by crusaders. It also served as a tool for comparison between different areas of crusade. As with any category, such comparison can be fruitful or it can be deceptive, as many 'frontier experiences' are so diverse as to have no meaningful similarities, so the concept of the 'frontier' can become a straitjacket for fitting these divergent realities into one category. In its most original applications, the concept led historians to pinpoint the specificities of later medieval crusades, which emerged in crusading theatres in the contact zones between Christians and Muslims and Christians and pagans.

notes

1. F. Ratzel, *Politische Geographie* (reprinted Osnabruck, 1974).
2. L. Febvre, 'La frontière: le mot et la notion', *Revue de Synthèse Historique*, 45 (1928), 31–44.
3. F. J. Turner, 'The Significance of the Frontier in American History', originally delivered in 1893, then incorporated into *The Frontier in American History* (New York, 1962), pp. 1–38.
4. J. W. Thompson, 'Profitable Fields of Investigation in Medieval History', *American Historical Review*, 18 (1913), 490–504; A. Lewis, 'The Closing of the Medieval Frontier 1250–1350', *Speculum*, 33 (1958), 475–83.
5. J. Gautier-Dalché, 'Islam et chrétienté en Espagne au XIIe siècle: contribution à l'étude de la notion de frontière', *Hespéris*, 46 (1959), 183–217; A. Bazzana, P. Guichard and P. Sénac, 'La frontière dans l'Espagne médiévale', *Castrum 4: Frontière et peuplement dans le monde méditerranéen au Moyen Age* (Rome and Madrid, 1992), pp. 36–59.
6. D. J. Power, 'What did the Frontier of Angevin Normandy Comprise?' *Anglo-Norman Studies*, 17 (1995), 181–201.
7. R. Bartlett, *The Making of Europe: Conquest, Colonization and Cultural Change 950–1350* (Princeton, 1993), p. 3.
8. R. C. Smail, *Crusading Warfare, 1097–1193*, 2nd edn (Cambridge, 1995).
9. M. Barber, 'Frontier Warfare in the Latin Kingdom of Jerusalem: The Campaign of Jacob's Ford 1178–79', in *The Crusades and their Sources: Essays Presented to Bernard Hamilton*, ed. J. France and W. G. Zajac (Aldershot, 1998), pp. 9–22, at p. 14.
10. R. Ellenblum, 'Three Generations of Frankish Castle-building in the Latin Kingdom of Jerusalem', in *Autour de la première croisade: Actes du colloque de la Society for the Study of the Crusades and the Latin East*, ed. M. Balard (Paris, 1996), pp. 517–51.
11. R. Ellenblum, 'Were There Borders and Borderlines in the Middle Ages? The Example of the Latin Kingdom of Jerusalem', *Medieval Frontiers: Concepts and Practices*, ed. D. Abulafia and N. Berend (Aldershot, 2002), pp. 105–19.
12. T. M. Vann, 'Twelfth-Century Castile and its Frontier Strategies', in *The Circle of War in the Middle Ages: Essays on Medieval Military and Naval History*, ed. D. J. Kagay and L. J. A. Villalon (Woodbridge, 1999), pp. 21–31.
13. G. Ágoston, 'Ottoman Conquest and the Ottoman Military Frontier in Hungary', in *A Millennium of Hungarian Military History*, ed. L. Veszprémy and B. K. Király (Boulder, Colo. and Highland Lakes, N.J., 2002), pp. 85–110; *Ottomans, Hungarians and Habsburgs in Central Europe: The Military Confines in the Era of the Ottoman Conquest*, ed. G. Dávid and P. Fodor (Leiden, 2000).
14. A. Williams, 'Crusaders as Frontiersmen: The Case of the Order of St John in the Mediterranean', in *Frontiers in Question: Eurasian Borderlands, 700–1700*, ed. D. Power and N. Standen (London, 1999), pp. 209–27, at p. 224.

15. N. Jaspert, 'Bonds and Tensions on the Frontier: The Templars in Twelfth-Century Western Catalonia', in *Mendicants, Military Orders, and Regionalism in Medieval Europe*, ed. J. Sarnowsky (Aldershot, 1999), pp. 19–45, at p. 44.
16. H. Nicholson, 'The Knights Hospitaller on the Frontiers of the British Isles', in *Mendicants, Military Orders*, ed. Sarnowsky, pp. 47–57.
17. C. de Ayala Martínez, 'Las órdenes militares castellano-leonesas y la acción de frontera en el siglo XIII', in *Identidad y representación de la frontera en la España medieval (siglos XI–XIV)*, ed. C. de Ayala Martínez, P. Buresi and P. Josserand (Madrid, 2001), pp. 123–57.
18. L. J. McCrank, 'The Cistercians of Poblet as Medieval Frontiersmen: An Historiographic Essay and Case Study', in *Estudios en Homenaje a don Claudio Sanchez Albornoz en sus 90 años*, ed. María de Carmen Carlé et al., 3 vols (Buenos Aires, 1983), vol. 2, pp. 313–60.
19. R. I. Burns, 'The Parish as a Frontier Institution in Thirteenth-Century Valencia', *Speculum*, 37 (1962), 244–51; P. Linehan, 'Segovia: A "Frontier" Diocese in the Thirteenth Century', *English Historical Review*, 96 (1981), 481–508.
20. In *Past and Present*, 35 (1966), 54–76.
21. E. Manzano Moreno, 'The Creation of a Medieval Frontier: Islam and Christianity in the Iberian Peninsula, Eighth to Eleventh Centuries', in *Frontiers in Question*, ed. Power and Standen, pp. 32–54; R. A. Fletcher, 'Reconquest and Crusade in Spain c. 1050–1150', *Transactions of the Royal Historical Society*, 5th series, 37 (1987), 31–47; A. Christys, 'Crossing the Frontier of Ninth-Century Hispania', in *Medieval Frontiers*, ed. Abulafia and Berend, pp. 35–53.
22. J. Prawer, *Crusader Institutions* (Oxford, 1980).
23. J. Riley-Smith, *The Crusades: A Short History* (London, 1990), ch. 4.
24. R. Ellenblum, *Frankish Rural Settlement in the Latin Kingdom of Jerusalem* (Cambridge, 1998).
25. C. S. Jensen, 'Urban Life and the Crusades in Northern Germany and the Baltic Lands in the Early Thirteenth Century', in *Crusade and Conversion on the Baltic Frontier, 1150–1500*, ed. A. V. Murray (Aldershot, 2001), pp. 75–94, at p. 93.
26. R. Mažeika, 'Of Cabbages and Knights: Trade and Trade Treaties with the Infidel on the Northern Frontier, 1200–1390', *Journal of Medieval History*, 20 (1994), 63–76; C. Rowell, 'A Pagan's Word: Lithuanian Diplomatic Procedure 1200–1385', *Journal of Medieval History*, 18 (1992), 145–60.
27. J. E. López de Coca Castañer, 'Institutions on the Castilian-Granadan frontier 1369–1482', in *Medieval Frontier Societies*, ed. R. Bartlett and A. MacKay, 2nd edn (Oxford, 1989), pp. 127–50.
28. F. García Fitz, 'Una *frontera caliente*. La guerra en las fronteras castellano-musulmanas (siglos XI–XIII)', in *Identidad y representación*, ed. Ayala Martínez et al., pp. 159–79.
29. K. V. Jensen, 'Introduction', in *Crusade and Conversion*, ed. Murray, pp. xvii–xxv, at p. xviii.
30. N. Housley, 'Frontier Societies and Crusading in the Late Middle Ages', in *Intercultural Contacts in the Medieval Mediterranean*, ed. B. Arbel (London, 1996), pp. 104–19.
31. A. MacKay, 'Religion, Culture, and Ideology on the Late Medieval Castilian-Granadan Frontier', in *Medieval Frontier Societies*, ed. Bartlett and MacKay, pp. 217–43, at p. 222.

32. R. Mažeika, 'Granting Power to Enemy Gods in the Chronicles of the Baltic Crusades', in *Medieval Frontiers*, ed. Abulafia and Berend, pp. 153–71.
33. J. H. Lind, 'Consequences of the Baltic Crusades in Target Areas: The Case of Karelia', in *Crusade and Conversion*, ed. Murray, pp. 133–50.
34. A. Selart, 'Confessional Conflict and Political Co-operation: Livonia and Russia in the Thirteenth Century', in *Crusade and Conversion*, ed. Murray, pp. 151–76, at p. 151.
35. F. Lotter, 'The Crusading Idea and the Conquest of the Region East of the Elbe', in *Medieval Frontier Societies*, ed. Bartlett and MacKay, pp. 267–306.
36. M. Á. Ladero Quesada, 'Sobre la evolución de las fronteras medievales hispánicas (siglos XI a XIV), in *Identidad y representación*, ed. Ayala Martínez et al., pp. 5–49.
37. P. Buresi, 'Nommer, penser les frontières en Espagne aux XIe–XIIIe siècles', in *Identidad y representación*, ed. Ayala Martínez et al., pp. 51–74.
38. V. I. Matuzova, 'Mental Frontiers: Prussians as Seen by Peter von Dusburg', in *Crusade and Conversion*, ed. Murray, pp. 253–59, at p. 258.
39. C. J. Halperin, 'The Ideology of Silence: Prejudice and Pragmatism on the Medieval Religious Frontier', *Comparative Studies in Society and History*, 26 (1984), 442–66.
40. P. Guichard, *Al-Andalus, 711–1492: Une histoire de l'Andalousie arabe* (Paris, 2001); P. Guichard, *L'Espagne et la Sicile musulmanes aux XIe et XIIe siècles* (Lyons, 2000); J. V. Tolan, *Saracens: Islam in the Medieval European Imagination* (New York, 2002).
41. P. Sénac, '"Ad castros de fronteras de mauros qui sunt pro facere". Note sur le premier testament de Ramire Ier d'Aragon', in *Identidad y representación*, ed. Ayala Martínez et al., pp. 205–21.
42. P. Josserand, '"In servitio Dei et domini regis". Les Ordres Militaires du royaume de Castille et la défense de la Chrétienté latine: frontières et enjeux de pouvoir (XIIe–XIVe siècles)', in *Identidad y representación*, ed. Ayala Martínez et al. pp. 89–111.
43. T. Lindkvist, 'Crusades and Crusading Ideology in the Political History of Sweden, 1140–1500', in *Crusade and Conversion*, ed. Murray, pp. 119–30.
44. N. Berend, 'Défense de la Chrétienté et naissance d'une identité. Hongrie, Pologne et péninsule Ibérique au Moyen Âge', *Annales: Histoire, Sciences Sociales*, 58, no. 5 (2003), 1009–27.
45. C. J. Bishko, *Studies in Medieval Spanish Frontier History* (London, 1980).
46. R. I. Burns, 'The Significance of the Frontier in the Middle Ages', in *Medieval Frontier Societies*, ed. Bartlett and MacKay, pp. 307–30, at p. 323.
47. M. González Jiménez, 'Frontier and Settlement in the Kingdom of Castile (1085–1350), in *Medieval Frontier Societies*, ed. Bartlett and MacKay, pp. 49–74, at p. 52.
48. J. P. Molénat, 'La frontière linguistique, principalement à partir du cas de Tolède', in *Identidad y representación*, ed. Ayala Martínez et al., pp. 113–22.
49. Manzano Moreno, 'The creation of a medieval frontier'; A. Rodríguez López, *La consolidación territorial de la monarquía feudal castellana: Expansión y fronteras durante el reinado de Fernando III* (Madrid, 1994).
50. R. Bartlett, 'Colonial Aristocracies of the High Middle Ages', *Medieval Frontier Societies*, ed. Bartlett and MacKay, pp. 23–47, at p. 43.

51. S. C. Rowell, 'The Lithuano-Prussian forest frontier, c. 1422–1600', in *Frontiers in Question*, ed. Power and Standen, pp. 182–208.
52. W. Urban, 'The Frontier Thesis and the Baltic Crusade', in *Crusade and Conversion*, ed. Murray, pp. 45–71, at p. 63.
53. Ibid., p. 64.
54. Ibid., p. 69.
55. Housley, 'Frontier Societies and Crusading'.
56. A. Ehlers, 'The Crusade of the Teutonic Knights against Lithuania Reconsidered', in *Crusade and Conversion*, ed. Murray, pp. 21–44.
57. Burns, 'The Significance of the Frontier', p. 317.
58. A. R. Lewis, *Nomads and Crusaders AD 1000–1368* (Bloomington and Indianapolis, 1988).

8
crusades and colonization in the baltic[1]

sven ekdahl[2]

introduction

The term 'crusade' has traditionally been used primarily to refer to the martial enterprises that went out from Christian Europe during the high Middle Ages with the goal of reconquering Muslim Palestine (1096–1291). Yet then and later there were other enterprises that have been likewise designated as crusades. They included the Christianizing and subjection of heathen Slav, Finnish-Ugric and Baltic tribes south of the Baltic Sea, in Finland and in Livonia – the modern states of Estonia and Latvia – enterprises that the pope legitimized and accomplished by peaceful means or by force. Parallel to these enterprises, or as result, occurred the colonization and incorporation of these territories into Latin Europe. In all cases the most important carriers of the expansion were the Roman Catholic Church, the European aristocracy up to kings and emperors and the merchants of the expanding cities. Except in Livonia, farmers came in as settlers. This was a complex, important and often cruel chapter of European history, which Pope John Paul II once appropriately described as a hard road of suffering, of both light and darkness: *'Fu un cammino duro e sofferto, con le sue luci e le sue ombre'*.[3]

Later generations' judgements on this epoch have been varied and contradictory. Roman Catholic and Russian Orthodox Christians, Protestants, Marxists with or without Soviet connections, communists, national socialists, nationalists, romantic admirers of the military orders and opponents of war have all felt drawn to this topic and delivered different interpretations and evaluations. Hence modern concepts and personal judgements have often been projected onto the Middle Ages, resulting in anachronistic conclusions.

Map 4. North-eastern Europe during the Baltic crusades.

Description and evaluation of the Baltic crusades is difficult because recorded history is written by the winners. The 'heathen' peoples of the Baltic did not have a written culture, no chroniclers to be their spokespersons to future generations, and therefore information about them, apart from archaeological finds, derives only from their detractors, the Christians, resulting in a distorted perspective. Only the Orthodox Russians, with whom the Roman Catholic Church, the military orders and the crusaders frequently struggled for human souls, power, money, trade routes and territories, had a written culture like that of the Latin West. In heathen Lithuania the gradually developing diplomatic correspondence took place not in Lithuanian, but in the Belorussian, Polish, German and Latin languages. The first Lithuanian chronicles appeared only at the beginning of the sixteenth century, in Belorussian.

Although the crusades to the Holy Land were unsuccessful, in the Baltic the Christian conquerors were able to remain and establish the foundations of later states. So, for example, today's states of Estonia and Latvia can, due to the crusades which Christianized and colonized them, look back on a long affiliation to the Roman West rather than the Byzantine east Slavonic cultural region – whether they now like this or not.

the crusades in the baltic

The first target for Christian expansion was the Wends, various Slavic tribes which had settled south of the Baltic Sea. The papal bull authorizing the 1147 crusade against them allowed crusaders to redeem their crusading vow in northern Europe rather than in the Holy Land.[4] The crusaders included Germans, Danes and Poles. In the twelfth and thirteenth centuries Denmark was the most powerful country on the Baltic Sea, competing with the Germans for supremacy over the southern Baltic coast and with Sweden for supremacy in Finland. In the early thirteenth century the Danes conquered the northern part of Estonia and held it until the year 1346, when it was sold to the Teutonic Order, which had crushed a rebellion there three years previously.[5] Sweden, meanwhile, conquered and colonized Finland, which became part of the Swedish realm until 1809. Today, Finnish 'nationalists' protest that their country was forcibly conquered by the crusaders.[6]

The Germans began to move into Livonia towards the end of the twelfth century. German merchants, attracted by the large Russian market (buying Russian products such as wax, flax, hemp, skins and furs and exporting others such as salt, herrings, cloth and metals), found a new trade route, the river Düna (Latvian: Daugava; Russian: Dvina), that gave direct contact with important cities in White Russia. In the year 1201 Riga was founded on the mouth of the Düna as the leading base of the Church and the German merchants and settlers in the Baltic.[7] Missionary work began to convert the Livs, a Finnish-Ugric tribe that lived in the area; but had to be supported with military force to protect the new converts against their warlike neighbours. As crusaders formed only a temporary force, in 1202 a permanent army was established, the military religious

Order of Swordbrothers.[8] After a heavy defeat by the Lithuanians in 1236, the order and its property were incorporated into the Teutonic Order, which was already fighting against the heathen in Prussia. The Teutonic Order's expansion efforts eastwards from Livonia were ended only by a defeat against the Novgorodians under Aleksandr Nevskii (better known to English readers as Alexander Nevsky) on the ice of Lake Peipus in 1242. A frontier between the two cultural areas developed.[9]

the conquest of prussia by the teutonic order

The Teutonic Order was created in 1190 during the siege of Acre in the Third Crusade as a hospital community, and a few years later converted from a charitable order into a military order.[10] After an intermediate sojourn in Hungary (today Romania), in the winter of 1225–26 the Order accepted the offer of a Polish prince, the Duke of Masovia, to help in his struggle against the heathen Prussians, a Baltic tribe. Starting from 1231, with the support of crusade privileges and crusaders by the mid 1280s it had succeeded in subjecting Prussia. But following its takeover of Christian Pomerellia and the city of Danzig (Polish: Gdańsk) in 1309, the Order came into conflict with Christian Poland.

At the end of the thirteenth century the Order began the conquest of Lithuania, which the Order attacked both from Livonia and Prussia for more than a century in an 'eternal crusade'.[11] This time the Order was fighting not individual small tribes, which could be separately defeated, but a large and well organized territorial state under the skilful guidance of the grand dukes of the Gediminid family, regarded as the military equals of the Order.[12] Between 1305 and 1409 the Teutonic Order undertook over 300 larger and smaller military expeditions from Prussia and Livonia to Lithuania, in which foreign crusaders usually took part.[13] The Lithuanians answered with appropriate military campaigns into the Order's territory, demonstrating that they were by no means only 'victims'.[14] The knight-brothers made effective use of diplomacy, and alliances between the Teutonic Order and the 'heathen' were not uncommon,[15] but they never succeeded in subjecting the Lithuanians or conquering their country. After the peaceful Christianization of Lithuania (1387), which took place independently of the Teutonic Order, the country could no longer be *de jure* the goal of crusades. Although the Order denied that the Lithuanians' conversion was genuine, its catastrophic defeat by the Polish-Lithuanian army at Tannenberg (Polish: Grunwald; Lithuanian: Žalgiris) on 15 July 1410 ended the supremacy of Prussia and German expansion eastwards.[16] Some further wars followed the initial peace of 1411, but in 1422 the east border of Prussia was fixed for centuries to come, until 1919. A long civil war, which broke off in 1454, ended after Polish intervention with a peace in 1466, by which the Teutonic Order in Prussia lost large parts of its territory. The last Prussian grand master converted to Protestantism in 1525 and the *Order-Staat* was converted into a hereditary duchy dependent on Poland. In Livonia the *Order-Staat* continued in existence somewhat longer until 1561/62, when its inheritance was divided between Poland-Lithuania, Sweden, Denmark and Moscow after three devastating Russian incursions.

the colonization of livonia and prussia

According to rough estimates, the population of Livonia at the time of the confrontation with Christianity and the crusaders was between 220,000 and 300,000, of whom not quite half were Ests.[17] In Prussia, according to the calculations of a Polish historian, there was in around 1300 a native population of 90,000, and around 1400, approximately 140,000 Prussians and 130,000 Germans.[18] Thus, contrary to what is sometimes stated in popular literature, the 'heathen' in Prussia were not exterminated, although they certainly paid a very high price. Their disappearance from history was a result of the gradual assimilation of the survivors with the many immigrant settlers from Germany. Prussia was 'Germanized'.

This was not the case in Livonia, because – due to the lack of a land route from Germany, and the costs of travel by sea – no German farmers settled here. The country was therefore colonized with native farmers. The rural population remained and its languages were preserved as Estonian and Lettish, unlike the Prussian language, which became extinct in the seventeenth century.

Before the Christianization and colonization of the heathen peoples in the Baltic there were certain differences in settlement, economics and social conditions that influenced religion, morals and customs. The new teachings brought new and unfamiliar ways of life, and frequently a substantial deterioration in their social and economic situation. The new converts to Christianity gained their new lords' protection against external enemies, but lost their political liberty. They had to accept hitherto unknown taxes and payments, such as Church tithe and interest. Their children were often taken as hostages in order to prevent their abandoning Christianity. In addition they had to fight against their own unconverted compatriots in the field, and carry out work in church- and castle-building. In Livonia the farmers' personal liberty was gradually more and more restricted, while in Prussia the unfree farmers had to bear the heaviest lot. 'To the various old burdens laid upon them by old and new landlords was now added the payment of tithe. No wonder that resistance against the new lords was especially long-lived among the peasantry and some heathen beliefs remained tenacious until the time of the Reformation', writes Reinhard Wenskus, a German authority on the subject.[19]

On the one hand there were advances in agriculture and in technology, which were previously unknown in the Baltic, including not least the introduction of writing. The inhabitants of the Baltic now encountered Latin European culture, which most of their descendants regard in a positive light. However, many people in the Baltic countries today still hark back to a pre-Christian identity, and not only in the naming of their children. Old myths and customs are experiencing a renaissance, involving more than simply folklore.

The Teutonic Order's achievements in settlement were very impressive. In Prussia approximately 100 cities and 1400 villages were created. Around the turn of the fourteenth century there were 266 castles in Prussia and Livonia, including those of bishops, monasteries and (in Livonia but not in Prussia) vassals.[20] The most important and imposing castle was Marienburg (Polish: Malbork) in Prussia. Yet the price of Christianization and colonization in human lives was very high, particularly for the defeated.[21]

views of the crusades and colonization in the baltic

the negative judgement of the enlightenment

During the Middle Ages the Teutonic Order's activities in the Baltic aroused both approval and criticism, but our analysis of reactions will begin with start of the Reformation, when the Reformer Martin Luther referred in his writing to the contradiction between the worldly commitments and the religious pretensions of the Teutonic Order.[22] In German historiography up to the mid-nineteenth century the Order was judged predominantly negatively.[23] For the age of the Enlightenment this seemed natural, since the Order, disregarding philanthropy and tolerance, had forced innocent humans to become Catholic. Johann Gottfried Herder, for example, would not even acknowledge the Order's services in colonization, and drew comparisons with what the Spaniards had done to the Peruvians.[24] Other well-known names include historians such as Ludwig von Baczko and August von Kotzebue. According to Baczko the Order exterminated the majority of the inhabitants,[25] while Kotzebue compared its campaigns to those of Cortes and Pizarro: 'behind the ravaging lion, the Order, crept the jackal, the priesthood, and greedily consumed what remained of the lion's spoil'. The Teutonic Order's craze for conquest and conversion exterminated a courageous people, whose survivors were handed over as serfs to the nobles, the 'hungry relations' of the knight-brothers.[26]

the image of the teutonic order in the nineteenth century

In mid-nineteenth century Prussia, prompted by the influence of romanticism, German idealistic philosophy and the teachings of Darwin, there was a reversal in the evaluation of the Teutonic Order, the crusades and colonization. The knight-brothers were now regarded as predecessors and forerunners of the Prussian state. Both the champions of the Prussian state and the Polish nationalists were united in this view, although their evaluation (positive and negative) differed diametrically. Even today Johannes Voigt's indispensable multivolume 'History of Prussia' lays down a scholarly basis for the study of the history of the *Order-Staat*.[27] Voigt believed that the cruel side-effects of the war against the heathen could not be excused, but he praised the cultural achievements of the *Order-Staat*, which had brought 'German education' to the country. Thus he assisted the development of the 'culture-carrier theory'.[28] That glowing nationalist of Prussian mould, Heinrich of Treitschke, stressed Germanic superiority over the Slavic race, the marvels of German-ness and the great Prussian past. The establishment of the Teutonic Order's state of Prussia was, in his eyes, a great national act, and in his essay 'the Teutonic Order's country of Prussia' (1862) he described the German eastern settlement as the 'rapid out-flowing of German spirit over the north and the east, the enormous work of our people as conqueror, teacher and disciplinarian of our neighbours'.[29] The greatest victory of the Slavs (the Lithuanian Baltic people is not mentioned) was at Tannenberg, but it was only gained through betrayal in the Order's own ranks.[30] The mood of a wide circle in Prussia at that time could not have been expressed more clearly. According to Treitschke, Prussia was thoroughly and beneficially germanized and developed into a colony of the whole of Germany. Matters were different in Livonia, where a thin layer of Germans was placed over the large mass of natives. The 'unfounded nationality' of a 'nation of unfree farm labourers [*Knechten*]' was preserved there.[31]

The Teutonic Order was judged completely differently by the native population in the former 'target countries', although they could not express their national feeling. The modern states of Estonia and Latvia formed part of the Russian realm as the Baltic Sea provinces of Estonia, Livonia and Kurland, while the divided Lithuania was also Russian. Everywhere 'national' feelings were suppressed, just as in the Russian and Prussian subsections of Poland, which had disappeared from the map of Europe with the partition of the country at the end of the eighteenth Century. Only Poles in the Austrian subsection (Galicia) were able to express both their national pride and their negative evaluation of the crusades and the Teutonic Order.[32] Important work by Polish historians on the history of the Grand Duchy of Lithuania also appeared at this time. In Galicia opposition was focused on Germans (and Russians!) through producing symbolic celebrations of the victorious battle of 1410, which had brought about the fall of the Teutonic Order and the rise of Poland-Lithuania and had thus led to the transformation of political conditions in east-central Europe. Well-known examples of these symbols are Jan Matejko's painting of the battle, 'Grunwald' (1878), over 40 square metres in size, which only barely escaped destruction by the Nazis in the Second World War;[33] Henryk Sienkiewicz's novel *Die Kreuzritter* (1900, filmed 1960),[34] and the great Grunwald celebrations in Kraków in 1910, when a mounted statue of the victorious Polish king was unveiled.[35] For the Poles 'Grunwald' became the most important symbol in the fight against the German empire and for national release. It played a similar role for the Lithuanians. They, however, regarded the victor of the battle as being not the Polish king Jagiełło (Lithuanian: Jogaila), but the Lithuanian Grand Duke Vytautas (Polish: Witold).

twentieth-century historiography

the teutonic order in the propaganda of the third reich

The 'culture-carrier theory' was to play a particularly important role in the debate during the time of national socialism, but was also important for a long time after and to some extent still is today. According to the original version of this theory, the Germans brought culture and civilization to the raw and ignorant 'East'. In the National Socialist Third Reich further components were added.[36] With 'sword and plough' a new realm of farmers drawn from the German race was to be established by force in the east of Europe as a 'bulwark against the Slavic tide'. Adolf Hitler had not only spoken in *Mein Kampf* of the 'road of the former knight-brothers', along which the 'new Reich' must march again,[37] but also stated in a table discussion on 12 May 1942:

if one wishes to make good the errors of the past century in the east, one must pursue radical German national policies. Just as the German military Order did not act with kid gloves, but employed both the Bible and the sword, so also our men sent to the east as fighters for the faith of the National Socialist world view must if necessary employ our national interests with brute force.[38]

However, Adolf Hitler was far from being an ideological admirer of the Order, since his attitude was anti-aristocratic, anti-Prussian and anticlerical. He wanted to go his own way, not to be steered by the past. For him, historical parallels often played a less important role than – for example – the mythical contents of the Wagner operas.[39] He also found no reason to keep the surviving Teutonic Order in existence. Napoleon had dissolved it in Germany in 1809 and Hitler followed his example in Austria (1938) and in Czechoslovakia (1939). The Order's property was confiscated.[40] Yet it would be a mistake to believe that because it was dissolved during the Third Reich the Teutonic Order was not used for propagandistic and symbolic purposes. Even if Hitler did not particularly commit himself to the Order's traditions, he nevertheless saw their value to the population of Prussia, for as in Bismarck's time the Prussians still regarded themselves as bearers of the traditions of the former *Order-Staat*. Hitler therefore allowed the old military Order to be used in propaganda.[41]

In an indirect appeal to subliminal feelings, Alfred Rosenberg spoke of founding 'a federation of men, we mean a German Order',[42] and Robert Ley called into life the National Socialists' *Order-Burgen* and *Junkerschulen*.[43] In a speech of 1939, Heinrich Himmler saw himself as under a great obligation to the Teutonic Order: 'I have a firm intention to take over what was good in this Order – bravery, outrageous loyalty to an ideal which we admire, adaptability, riding off into the distance, riding off towards the east.' If necessary, they would proceed with 'most brutal force and most brutal energy'.[44] For Himmler the SS was a reincarnation of the Teutonic Order, the breeding ground of the aristocracy of a new master race. Hence it was not surprising that the murderous actions of the *Einsatzgruppen*, of the Security Service (SD) and the Security Police (SiPo) were carried out in occupied Poland in the autumn of 1939 under the pseudonym 'Tannenberg'.[45]

The most salient example of how the Teutonic Order was used by National Socialist ideology was the so-called 'acquisition of the Teutonic Order's banners' in 1940.[46] When the German troops occupied Kraków, they found at Wawel Castle 18 reproductions of the Order's banners captured at Tannenberg, which were initially erected in the office of governor-general Hans Frank.[47] Then came the idea of 'bringing them back' from Kraków to Marienburg in Prussia, to demonstrate a connection between the Teutonic Order and the Third Reich. Hitler had no objections to this great act of propaganda, and on 21 May 1940 the flags were handed over to the reichs-governor Georg Forster at Marienburg.[48] According to the report in the *Völkischer Beobachter*, he stressed that 'the battle of nations of the last 500 years will be brought to a conclusion with the complete Germanization of this country'.[49]

Erich Maschke,[50] Hermann Aubin[51] and Erich Keyser were among prominent German historians whose writings supported German eastern settlement and represented the ideology of the Third Reich. In 1942 Keyser stressed that the new 'eastern researchers' should not be content to refer to the historical acts and achievements of the Germans as culture-carriers. Rather, they should examine the biological racial composition of the different peoples of the East.[52]

evaluation by marxists and communists in soviet russia

In the 1920s, the leading Soviet Marxist historian M. N. Pokrovskii, in his internationally aligned and at the same time one-sided, materialistically-shaped writings, polemized against current national Russian and pan-Slavic historiography.[53] He called the belief in continual German aggression towards the East 'a ritual legend' and did not shrink from criticizing the glorification of Aleksandr Nevskii in Russian historiography. Likewise he turned against the thesis that Russia had had cultural duties to fulfil in Asia, because that was only tsarist propaganda.[54]

At the end of the 1930s, and particularly after the German attack on the Soviet Union in 1941, such opinions had to be converted into a Soviet patriotically-shaped historiography, including fierce condemnation of the German eastern settlement. Soviet historians were now commanded to respect Aleksandr Nevskii's victory over the knight-brothers in 1242 as the crucial battle against the German *Drang nach Osten*, the drive to the East.[55] This propaganda received its most famous artistic expression in Sergej Eisenstein's film *Aleksandr Nevskii*, with music by Sergej Prokofiev (1938): through Nevskii the Russian people escaped the fate of the Prussians, Letts and Ests, whom the German barons and supporters had enslaved in serfdom.[56] This mixture of Marxist-Leninist theories with Soviet patriotism was a reaction against the victory of national socialism in Germany and its glorification of the Teutonic Order.

The voluminous Soviet book 'History of the Middle Ages' bears testimony to this change and the break with Pokrovskii; first published in Moscow in 1938, then revised in 1941 and thoroughly revised in 1952. A German translation appeared in 1958 in East Berlin (GDR).[57] In volume 1, chapter 15, written by J. A. Kosminski and M. M. Smirin, German colonization and the aggressive 'drive to the east' are violently criticized.[58]

According to this interpretation: the territorial princes strove to increase their possessions at their neighbours' expense, while the impoverished German knights were also interested in these 'predatory expeditions of conquest', because – the predatory enterprises in the Muslim Orient having failed – they now wanted to make conquests and win booty in the crusades in eastern Europe. Furthermore,

> a driving force for the aggressive campaigns to the east was the German Church, which made a most lucrative income from the hunt for tithes, goods and serfs and saw in the conversion of the heathen the opportunity for more. The papacy, which was one of the main supervisors of the campaigns to eastern Europe, helped them energetically, since it hoped to be able to expand its sphere of influence and increase its income. The cities, which wanted to capture raw material and sales markets, also took part in the annexations. The feudal lords tried to settle the conquered areas with German farmers, whereby they either exterminated the resident Slav population or forced them on to the worst estates.[59]

After this general introduction the authors describe among other things 'the conquest of the eastern Baltic Sea area' and 'the Teutonic Order and the annexation of Prussia' in the spirit of the materialistic historical viewpoint and adding patriotic Soviet remarks.[60] They state: 'Russia was for Western Europe the protective wall against the Mongols', but the Swedes and Germans, inspired by the papacy, exploited this critical moment for the Russians and the whole of Western Europe by dealing 'the Russian principalities a traitorous stab in the back.' Novgorod was strong enough, however, under Prince Aleksandr Yaroslavich ('Nevskii') to give the aggressors 'a brush-off' in 1240 and 1242.[61] It is remarkable that the book speaks only of 'Slavs' and never of 'Balts', although the Baltic tribes are given their names. Because the Soviet Union had done exactly what it accused the Teutonic Order of doing, establishing 'colonies' in the Baltic and subjecting the population, the subject of the non-Slavic races was very sensitive.

The 'official' imperialistic-chauvinistic political historiography after the Second World War, which preached the world mission of Russia and availed itself only of Marxist phraseology, shaped Soviet-Russian books and essays on the crusades and military orders during the following half century. Examples include the work of Vladimir Pashuto on 'The Struggle of the Prussian People for Independence (to the End of the Thirteenth Century)',[62] 'The Struggle of the Peoples of Russia and the Eastern Baltic against the Aggression of the German, Swedish and Danish Feudatories in the 13th–15th Centuries',[63] and on Aleksandr Nevskii.[64] The well-known historian Igor Shaskol'skii has described 'Aleksandr Nevskii's Struggle against Crusade Aggression from the late 1240s to the 1250s'[65] and *Russia's Struggle against Crusade Aggression on the Baltic Coast in the 12th–13th Centuries*.[66] The title of the last book is, however, somewhat misleading, because it deals with Swedish expansion into Finland and the resulting entanglement with Novgorod. For Shaskol'skii it was clear that the papal Curia was the 'main organizer of crusade aggression in the years 1240–1242 against Russia'.[67] He published a summary of his opinions in 1990 in a Polish conference volume.[68]

This view of Russia and the Soviet Union as saviours in the face of the German *Drang nach Osten* appeared in summarized form in a set of newspaper articles and essays that appeared in 1960 on the occasion of the Grunwald celebrations in the Soviet Union and its satellite states.[69] However, with more careful reading, it is possible to determine some nuances in the different countries of the Eastern Bloc, such as the GDR.[70]

From around the second half of the 1980s some Russian historians freed themselves from ideological obligation, among them Vera Matuzova and Evgeniya Nazarova, who in 2002 published an important source volume on the crusades and Russia.[71]

estonian, lettish and lithuanian 'national' views between the world wars

As Sweden had long developed a social and cultural upper layer in Finland, certain tensions existed between them and the representatives of the (in numerical terms) far larger Finnish group of peoples. The contrast between the Baltic Germans and the native population was much more pronounced in the Russian Baltic provinces of Estonia, Livonia and Kurland.[72] As no assimilation and 'Germanization' had taken place there as it had in Prussia, the linguistic and social, cultural and material barrier between the Germans, among them not least the noble landowners, and the Ests and Letts who mainly worked in agriculture, was never overcome. When after the First World War in 1918 these peoples attained their liberty for a few years, these accumulated feelings were directed against the German upper class, and also projected back against the medieval Teutonic Order.[73] Up until then the Baltic Germans had controlled the writing of history[74] and – particularly since the time of Russification toward the end of the nineteenth century – had considered themselves to be 'culture-carriers', but now their evaluations were questioned in bitter debates by representatives of the national movements. Their very critical attitude towards the military orders was due largely to the national movement's deep roots in Protestantism:[75] one example is a book published in 1925 by Peter Olinš on the Teutonic Knights in Latvia.[76] Both the Letts and the Ests, however, largely avoided the topic of 'crusades and Teutonic Orders', because this was felt to be a 'German' affair. They were concerned instead with the 'national' topic of the rural population and the development of agriculture, which had been left out of the German-Baltic historiography.[77]

In Lithuania the situation between the wars was somewhat different, because the country had never been a German 'colony' and there was no German social and cultural upper class. The century-long struggle against the crusaders and knight-brothers and the victory at Žalgiris (Tannenberg, Grunwald) were for the Lithuanians, just as for the Poles, central to their search for a national identity. These struggles were portrayed in the volume *The History of Lithuania* (1936), compiled by Adolfas Šapoka, and in many other books.[78] Generally the Teutonic Order was described in a very negative way: in Catholic schools it happened that Lithuanian heathendom was praised while the knight-brothers were blamed for going over to Lutheranism.[79] Nevertheless that generation of historians, including names such as Antanas Kučinskas, Juozas Jakštas and Zenonas Ivinskis, achieved a high level of scholarship.[80]

the period of soviet rule in the baltic

After the Soviet occupation of the Baltic republics in 1939, school books and scholarly literature on the Christianization, crusades and colonization in the Baltic were dominated by the only historiography that was permitted within Moscow's sphere of influence, which emphasized the struggle of the great Russian people against the feudal exploiters. In Lithuania, because the Soviet ruling powers feared the development of national consciousness, historians were forbidden to study the great epochs and events of their own past: so they could research and publish on the battle of Žalgiris only if they gave the Russian troops a decisive role in the battle.[81] A 'national' historical view was permitted only if it did not upset this picture of Russia as hero. They could also write in defence of the heathens of pre-Christian times.[82]

It was characteristic that in the Soviet Union the celebrations commemorating the victory over the Teutonic Order in 1410 were centrally organized and not left to the people of the present-day Soviet republic, because this could have led to undesirable outbursts of national feeling.[83] Thus in Lithuania only a simple stone could be set up in Vilnius to commemorate 'the year 1410' whereas the Poles could build an enormous monument on the old battleground.[84] A further instance occurred in 1980, the commemoration of the 550th anniversary of the death of the Lithuanian Grand Duke Vytautas (Witold): the Soviet secret service KGB had the pontoon bridge to the island castle of Trakai removed, and closed the entrance to the castle of the Lithuanian grand dukes in Vilnius, so that no national celebrations could take place there.[85]

Historiography in the Soviet republics during this half century was tied to Moscow. The great friendship of the Ests, Letts and Lithuanians with the Russians was repeatedly asserted. In 1953 a work was published in Riga in which the German conquerors were called 'dogs', following Karl Marx.[86] A further example from Estonia was an essay on 'The East Baltic Tribes in the Struggle against German-Scandinavian Aggression in the 12th–13th Centuries'.[87] Yet in a sense there was a continuity with the interwar historiography, when the military orders had been negatively evaluated in all three republics. The old preference for agrarian history as an Estonian and Latvian 'national' topic could be continued during the time of Soviet rule. The work of the Estish historian Sulev Vahtre also shows that it was possible to a certain degree to write a national history in a Marxist context.[88] His work considered the rebellion of the Ests against the Germans and Danes in 1343.[89]

In Lithuanian historiography there is a distinction between the time of severe 'supervision' by the Soviet Union, from 1944 to approximately 1966, and the somewhat relaxed situation thereafter up to the regaining of national independence around 1990. Some works described the Lithuanians' struggle against the Order of Swordbrothers and the Teutonic Order, while there were also studies of the large Prussian rebellion of 1260–74.[90]

research in exile

During the Soviet occupation of the Baltic, only historians who had gone into exile could carry on free research, although they suffered from having no access to archives and libraries in the Soviet Union and in Poland. These researchers directed their criticism not only against the Germans, but also against the Russians. Thus a history of the Lettish people by Arveds Schwabe, a well-known former professor of the University of Riga (published in Stockholm in 1953) also condemned the 'première agression russe contre les pays baltes' and the century-long Russian Drang nach Westen (drive to the West) which had taken place at the expense of the Baltic peoples.[91] Similar opinions appear, for example, in books by Constantine R. Jurgéla, an historian of Lithuanian descent active in the US.[92] In the United States in particular a lively historical literature of exile was developed by the Ests, Letts, Lithuanians and Poles living there; in addition there are researchers from the Baltic and east-central Europe in the UK and other countries.

poland: a special case

Because it was already Christian, Poland could not be the goal of crusades, but from 1309 it waged repeated wars against the Teutonic Order in Prussia, which left deep traces in the historiography. As already mentioned, from the second half of the nineteenth century the Order became a negative symbol for the Poles, while the victory at Grunwald in 1410 was for them, just as for the Lithuanians, a unifying symbol of national identity. That was also the case in the period between the world wars and has remained so in both countries until the present day. Above all the development during Soviet domination after the Second World War is of special interest.

The historians in the communist-governed Polish People's Republic, part of the Warsaw Pact, enjoyed a freer position in relation to the Soviet Union than their colleagues in other Eastern Bloc countries, which is why 'national' criteria were no rarity here. Indeed the party and government tried to use the strong national feeling of the Polish population for their own purposes and in their own favour, as with the Grunwald celebrations of 1960 and the millennium celebrations of 1966.[93] It suited them that the Poles had always been very critical in their judgement of the Teutonic Order. Examples of negative but scholarly representations include a long essay by Henryk Łowmiański on the Order's military campaigns into Lithuania,[94] and a long monograph on the war with the Teutonic Order of 1409–11 by Stefan M. Kuczyński, who had given historical instruction to his compatriots in the underground resistance during the Second World War.[95] The officially publicized polemical view appeared particularly clearly in summary form in connection with the celebrations of 1960 and 1966. An editorial in the party newspaper *Trybuna Ludu* stated:

> the battle [at Grunwald] finally ended the wide military predominance of aggressive German feudalism pressing towards the East, which directed its spear not only against Poland, but against the whole Slavic world and the Baltic peoples. This victory restrained the desire for eastern conquest for several centuries and changed the balance of power in Europe at that time to the advantage of the development of the countries of Eastern Europe.[96]

The battle at Grunwald was the most important event in the resistance against the German craze for conquest and only the years 1944–45 brought the first equivalent victory for many centuries.[97]

Polish researchers' investigations covered not only their country's relations with the Teutonic Order's state of Prussia, but also the Teutonic Order's expansion in the entire Baltic area and its history from the thirteenth to the mid-sixteenth centuries. In 1988 an international conference on this subject was held in Toruń (German: Thorn), whose proceedings were published two years later.[98] Participants were prominent historians from the Soviet Union including the Soviet republics of Estonia, Latvia and Lithuania, as well as from the Polish People's Republic, as it concerned an eastern European subject. The German Democratic Republic (GDR/DDR) was, however, not represented. The stimulus for the conference was probably the unstable political situation in eastern Europe at the end of the 1980s, so that the Polish organizers were hoping for a kind of scholarly 'reinsurance' in case of a possible future Soviet over-reaction.

the german-polish confrontation in the historiography

The inappropriate association of the Teutonic Order with the ideas and the objectives of national socialism led after the Second World War to different sides raising the unhistorical accusation against the Order, that it had been (with Prussia and the German Empire) a forerunner of the Third Reich, an 'SS of the Middle Ages'.[99] These accusations took up and resumed National Socialist propaganda, but with diametrically opposite evaluations. Such ideas were not only advanced by communists and nationalists in the Soviet Union and its satellite states within the Warsaw Pact area, but were also represented in left-wing and partially Catholic circles in the Federal Republic of Germany.[100] The Order and its history became an object in the debates of the Cold War, a ball in the area of conflict between the free West and eastern Europe controlled by the Soviet Union. For the one it had been 'cornerstone of Europe'[101] and 'border guardian of the West against eastern heathendom',[102] for the other a representation of absolute evil.

In consequence, in some of the extremely bitter debates interest was focused on the battle at Tannenberg. The battle was exploited in many ways as a means to achieve current political goals, as the monuments to the battle, for example, witness. Thus not the least purpose of the large Polish Grunwald monument of 1960 was the need to emphasize the acknowledgement of the new Polish western border after the Second World War, the Oder-Neisse frontier.[103] Such an objective also moulded much scholarly work of this period that dealt with the history of the Teutonic Order.

In the Federal Republic of Germany there was a much larger range of evaluations of the eastern colonization than in Poland. The original version of the 'culture-carrier theory', without the dire additions of the Third Reich, had many supporters, for example the historians Walther Hubatsch and Walter Kuhn,[104] and there were also isolated extreme advocates of a position reminiscent of the ideology of the Third Reich. Hermann Aubin belonged to those who still represented national racial (*völkische*) views and made no secret of it,[105] while after the war Erich Maschke gave up his earlier similar opinions of the Teutonic Order as an historical example and model of concepts of 'Führer' leadership and the elite, and turned to, for example, social historical questions.[106]

On the other hand, in the 1960s a reaction began in the Federal Republic of Germany and in Austria, which made Polish opinions its own and directed violent attacks against the Teutonic Order. This occurred not least in certain Catholic circles. One critic of the Order expresses this attitude as follows:

> in our opinion the Teutonic Order, in its fight against the old Prussians and Lithuanians, wrote the darkest side of western Church history; the Lithuanians and the Poles even today recall their encounter with the Teutonic Order with horror. In our opinion, on the German side everything that keeps this memory awake should be avoided, because in our opinion the Teutonic Order can be washed no whiter than the SS.[107]

A violent polemic took place in the media between German and Austrian historians friendly towards the Order and critics of the crusade, reminiscent of the medieval argument between the lawyers of Poland and the Teutonic Order at the Council of Constance (1414–18).[108]

Between the extreme positions an abundance of solid scholarly work on the Teutonic Orders developed, understandably mostly from the German viewpoint. For example, one may refer to the comprehensive representation by Hartmut Boockmann, *The Teutonic Order: Twelve Chapters from its History*, which endeavours to be reliable and balanced, including well-referenced research and bibliography.[109] A work entitled 'The Teutonic Order's Struggle against the Heathen' should be mentioned here,[110] as well as two anthologies on *Heathen Mission and Crusade Thought in the German Eastern Politics of the Middle Ages*[111] and *The German Eastern*

Settlement as a Problem of European History.[112] The opinions represented therein reflect different views among German researchers.

Some works dealing with ideology should also be mentioned, foremost being Wolfgang Wippermann's important book about the Teutonic Order's image in German historiography and journalism (1979), whose closing chapter is dedicated to the function of the 'ideology of the *Order-Staat*' in the historical-political consciousness of Poland.[113] The Swedish historian Sven Ekdahl, who works mainly in Germany, has also discussed these questions.[114]

The dialogue between German and Polish historians became even livelier after the conclusion of the German-Polish contract in Warsaw in 1970, because in that treaty the Federal Republic of Germany recognized the new Polish west border (developed following the Second World War), the Oder-Neisse frontier.[115] The German Democratic Republic had done this already in 1950. Thus the most important condition for a rapprochement of the historians of both countries had been created. The problem of the Christianization, subjection and colonization of the Baltic and the history of the Teutonic Order was now discussed at many conferences and the proceedings were published. This positive climate led to a rapprochement of positions, not least also through the common work of the German-Polish school book commission.[116] When in 1990 reunified Germany – the Federal Republic of Germany and the GDR – finally acknowledged the Oder-Neisse frontier,[117] relations became still closer. Today there is a constructive exchange of ideas and research between the historians of both countries.

During the era of the GDR dictatorship the history of the Teutonic Order had been a taboo topic in that part of Germany, on which there were only two opportunities to speak: in newspaper articles on the occasion of the Grunwald celebrations in Poland in 1960 and in a magazine essay by the historian Wolfgang Küttler in 1971.[118] After the reunification of the two German states there was therefore a large pent-up demand for information on this range of topics from the population of the former GDR.

Küttler's essay demonstrates that immense problems face Marxist historians in inserting the phenomenon of the Teutonic Order and its 'state' into their theoretical historical model. They have not yet succeeded in explaining the multilayered structure of this 'state', particularly since Marxism is incapable of self-criticism. It proceeds on a fixed pattern into which everything must fit, which in this case does not work. To quote Wolfgang Wippermann:

In many ways seeming so 'modern', the 'functionary state' of the Teutonic Order does not fit into the general picture of feudalism. In this case a state that was characterised by an 'early mercantile' administrative and economic system became subjected to one still purely 'feudal', that is, Poland. But the Marxist stage theory not only proves problematic if one wishes to consult it for an explanation of the rise and fall of the *Order-staat*, for also Marx's whole general conception that economic basis determines the social essence does not seem to apply here. There were probably actually few historical features which were fundamentally moulded by what Marx called 'the superstructure'. The actual basis of the Order and its 'state' was the concept of combat against the heathen.[119]

current trends in historiography

The large political, social, economic and cultural changes after the decay of the Soviet Union around 1990 meant that historians of the countries concerned could establish new valuations and priorities. Many seized this possibility and endeavoured to consider the crusades and colonization in the Baltic from new points of view. Other researchers, who were used to following orders from Moscow, were left in something of a hole because they were suddenly required to come up with their own ideas. In order to escape from this dilemma, they took refuge in detailed regional studies. Here it should be mentioned that throughout the whole Eastern Bloc there was usually a separation between research and teaching. The Academies of Sciences were responsible for research and the universities for teaching. This strict demarcation has now broken down, which has led to many problems and changes.

Thus there are now several trends of thought, which since the dissolution of the monolithic Soviet Bloc have become strongly pronounced in different ways in the different countries depending upon their tradition.

lithuania

The Marxist-Leninist work of the Soviet period has been rejected by the new generation of researchers in Lithuania, and instead they are aligning themselves around the big names of the 'national' historiography from the interwar period, whose work is being reprinted. In addition, new paths are being taken. The break with Marxism does not mean, however, that the Teutonic Order is being revaluated. Occasionally criticism of the Order, its actions and the Christianization and colonization of the

Baltic are called 'communist propaganda',[120] but these are exceptions. Otherwise, the evaluation of the Order is mostly negative.[121] The image of the knight-brothers in fairy tales and children's books is also dark.[122] It is the same with the older generation of historians. According to Edvardas Gudavičius, the renowned representative of a 'genuine' Marxist social history without Soviet additions, the Teutonic order prevented Lithuania's access to the sea, and obstructed the unification of the Baltic tribes. Therefore the suppression of the military orders was a historical necessity. Lithuanians took an active part and did not permit the German colonies to capture the whole east Baltic.[123]

However, no serious Lithuanian historian denies that there were also often favourable relations between the *Order-Staat* and the Grand Duchy of Lithuanian and that the Teutonic Order played an important role in the history of their country in many fields of culture, technology, economics and trade.

The centres of research in Lithuania are the universities of Vilnius, Kaunas and Klaipéda (German: Memel)[124] as well as the Academy of Sciences and the Lithuanian Institute of History in Vilnius.

latvia

Three different research directions can be identified, all represented in the capital Riga.[125] The first is the old conservative Marxist-Leninist line with its emphasis on agrarian history. Its now rootless representatives now concentrate mainly on local Latvian history covering a short timespan.[126] Then there is a continuation of the 'national' historical research of the interwar years, today represented by Indriķis Šterns, an emeritus historian from the US, who in 2002 published a monumental book on the Baltic crusades in the context of his research into the history of Latvia.[127] According to the English summary, 'this volume is written entirely from original sources, and often offers an interpretation of facts, events and personalities different from the popular German view'.[128] Finally we have a third new research direction from the University of Riga and Professor Ilgvars Misāns: orientated away from both Marxism and nationalism, breaking away from a focus on the history of the Latvian people and showing greater understanding of Christian ideology and the complete European situation in the high and the late Middle Ages.[129] A work by Eva Eihmane written from this viewpoint treats 'the Baltic crusades in the context of the European crusades in the twelfth and thirteenth centuries'.[130]

estonia

The research situation in Estonia resembles that in Latvia. The long-prevailing concentration on the history of the Estish people, that is agrarian history, omitting medieval topics in which the Germans were the leading participants – including the crusades in the Baltic – has now been broken by the new generation of historians, the pupils of Priit Raudkivi, Sulev Vahtre and Jüri Kivimäe. The centres of research are the university in Tartu (German: Dorpat), the Ajalooinstitute in Tallinn (German: Reval) and the Tallinn town centre archives. An informative essay by Juhan Kreem gives details.[131]

russia

The Academies of Sciences in Moscow and St Petersburg (formerly Leningrad) were and are the most important mechanisms for the study of the crusades and of the confrontation of the Russian states with Latin Europe. The research tradition represented by Vladimir Pashuto, Igor Shaskol'skii and others still continues, but there are also historians who have freed themselves from ideological ties. However, Russian historians will not necessarily be prepared to break away from traditional concepts and to adopt the many and various opinions of the western European historians.[132] Furthermore, the Russians regard the crusaders and the Teutonic Order with critical eyes. Aleksandr Nevskii will continue to be regarded and admired by the predominant majority of the population as rescuer and bulwark of the nation against the Swedes and Germans. For understandable reasons, the orthodox Russians are far less ready to accept 'Latin Europe' than are the peoples of the Baltic states. The various essays and discussions by the Danish historian John Lind should be mentioned in the context, as he has considered this topic several times. A set of articles by the Muscovite journalist Yuri Klitsenko[133] in the scholarly sections of the newspapers *Pravda* and *Isvestija* are particularly informative because they represent the Russian orthodox patriotic viewpoint.[134]

This overview shows that in the former 'target countries' there are today many different views of the crusades and conversion in the Baltic. If research in Sweden, Finland, Denmark, Poland and Germany is also taken into consideration, the number increases substantially.

In the western world and particularly in the Anglo-Saxon countries, careful research into the crusades, which have become widely topical after the events of 11 September 2001, will surely continue to develop, bypassing former political, cultural and linguistic barriers in the Baltic and in eastern Europe, and the scholarly dialogue between 'East' and 'West' over the events in the Middle Ages will intensify. Not least is the contribution of William Urban through his many books and essays, most recently a revised edition of *The Livonian Crusade* (2004).[135] As some of his works are now also being translated into the respective languages of the countries concerned, in the future they will be available not only to scholars but also to interested laypeople in the former 'target countries'.

It will be interesting to observe in years to come the reaction to Urban's books in those countries, because he regards himself not only as a historian, but also as a mediator of a political, religious and moral message.[136] As a modern crusader against Marxism, communism, Islam and, to some degree, orthodox Christianity, he represents as it were a 'western' point of view and shows much understanding of the crusades of the Order of Swordbrothers and the Teutonic Order, which, incidentally, has been well-received in Germany.[137] His judgement of his historian colleagues in his essay 'Rethinking the Crusades' reads: 'in short, an ageing collection of anti-colonial sentiments has merged with mild political correctness (opposition to violence, scepticism toward Western religious tradition and practices, concern for social issues reflecting race, gender, class, and ethnicity) to dominate the current historiography of the Crusades'.[138] The realities of the world today, however, have in his view undermined the interpretation of the crusades as a consequence of imperialism and power politics. Characteristically the crusades 'were a moral cause, often based on Christian principles',[139] and the crusaders achieved their victories 'only by suffering and struggle against determined, entrenched enemies who have powerful belief systems of their own'.[140] Urban suggests that historians should 'look for connections between our efforts to resolve today's most difficult international problems and the crusaders' experiences as medieval peacekeepers', because then they 'may find more justification for the crusaders' efforts'.[141] Thus 'the time is ripe for a reassessment of the Crusades in light of our present concerns'.[142]

In other words, Urban can be seen as an advocate of both the medieval and the modern crusade ideology, and thus he is certainly on a confrontation course with many Russian colleagues. In an article entitled 'The Medieval Peacekeepers' – so Urban designates the crusaders – in the Muscovite daily, *Pravda*, in April 2003, Yuri Klitsenko turned to the counterattack.[143] According to his viewpoint, 'American imperialism' must after 11 September 2001 justify its expansive foreign policy and reconsider how history is to be taught now, that is, the purposes and goals of the crusades must be re-evaluated. 'The ideology of the crusades may become one of the directions in educating youth in the spirit of war patriotism.' However, for people in Russia these 'new crusaders' are recommending decidedly new values: 'to ignore traditional values and their own history. Even some Russians are ready to repeat that the aggression of the Teutonic order against Novgorod and Pskov is only an imagination of the orthodox Church, and remains of Stalinist propaganda.'[144]

Klitsenko has summarized his opinions in a letter of May 2004:

> Any rethinking of the crusades is not possible without hearing the voices of Muslims, Jews and Orthodox Christians, Catholic Poles and Lithuanians. In 'Srednevekovite mirotvortsii' ['The Medieval Peacekeepers'] I wrote that I disagree with Professor William Urban. I tried to persuade him that the film *Alexander Nevsky* is not 'communist propaganda', crusaders were not 'medieval peacekeepers' and US soldiers are not 'holy apostles'.[145]

Urban also opposes applying 'victimization theory' to the Baltic crusade,[146] arguing that the Baltic peoples did not live in peace and harmony before the Christians' arrival, but waged vigorous wars against each other, and sometimes welcomed the Christians as protectors against predatory neighbours.[147] For this reason 'we might consider looking at the crusade through the eyes of contemporaries, to see it as an international peace-keeping force'.[148] Yet this positive valuation of the *pax baltica* enforced by the crusaders and military orders ignores the many rebellions by the conquered and 'protected'. His theses will certainly encounter opposition in other countries as well as in Lithuania. On the other hand it is to be expected that the new research currents in the Baltic will partly fall back on his opinions.[149] In any case in years to come the discussion over crusades and colonization in the Baltic will certainly be greatly invigorated.

In short, future historiography promises to be extremely interesting and informative.

conclusion

Historical research is never independent; as a humanistic science it is not capable of obtaining absolute 'truth'. Each historian has a starting point in his or her own political, religious, social and cultural milieux, which each either follows or escapes. This is particularly clear when evaluating the historiography of Christianization, crusade and colonization: an author's possible political, confessional or other material or ideological dependences must always be considered. So Marxist theories may be very helpful for understanding the material and socio-historical sides of the problem and thus extending the spectrum of the inquiry, but in order to produce a full picture they should be supplemented by knowledge of and attention to the mental and religious concepts dominant during the Middle Ages. It is easy in modern times to overlook the conspicuous existence of the 'religious' component during the Middle Ages. However the reverse is also the case: anyone who ignores secular motives of the crusade movement and colonization likewise risks coming to an ideological and scholarly dead-end.

notes

1. Strictly speaking 'the Baltic' refers to the territory of the modern states of Estonia, Latvia, and – since 1991 – Lithuania. In this chapter, however, the term is also used in a much broader sense to include the crusaders' 'target countries' in the entire eastern and southeast Baltic Sea area. When considering colonization, it must be remembered that whereas 'colonies' depend on a geographically remote country, from which conquest came and to which products gained from the colony are transferred, the areas whose colonization is described in this chapter were net consumers rather than exporters of wealth from the 'home country'.

2. The author thanks Dr Helen Nicholson, Cardiff University, for the translation of this chapter. A longer version is published in English in *XIX Rocznik Instytutu Polsko-Skandynawskiego 2003/2004*, ed. E. S. Kruszewski (Copenhagen, 2004), pp. 1–42.

3. Papal greeting to Monsignore Michele Maccarrone, the president of the Pontificio Comitato di Scienze Storiche, 21 June 1986, published in *L´Osservatore Romano*, 25 June 1986, p. 4, and in the conference publication *Gli inizi del cristianesimo in Livonia-Lettonia. Atti del colloquio internazionale di storia ecclesiastica in occasione dell´VIII centenario della chiesa in Livonia (1186–1986), Roma, 24–25 Giugno* 1986, ed. M. Maccarrone (Vatican City, 1989), pp. 7–8.

4. See, for instance, E. Christiansen, *The Northern Crusades. The Baltic and the Catholic Frontier 1100–1525*, 2nd edn (Harmondsworth, 1997), pp. 50–72, esp. p. 53.

5. P. Rebane, 'Denmark, the Papacy and the Christianization of Estonia', in *Gli inizi del cristianesimo*, pp. 171–201. T. Kala, 'The Incorporation of the Northern Baltic Lands into the Western Christian World', in *Crusade and Conversion on the Baltic Frontier 1150–1500*, ed. A.V. Murray (Aldershot, 2001), pp. 3–20.

6. T. Lindquist, 'Crusades and Crusading Ideology in the Political History of Sweden, 1140–1500', in *Crusade and Conversion*, ed. Murray, pp. 119–30; D. Fewster, 'Approches to the Conversion of the Finns: Ideologies, Symbols, and Archaeological Features', in *Christianizing Peoples and Converting Individuals*, ed. G. Armstrong and I. N. Wood (Turnhout, 2000), pp. 89–102.

7. F. Benninghoven, *Rigas Gründung und der frühhansische Kaufmann* (Hamburg, 1961).

8. F. Benninghoven, *Der Orden der Schwertbrüder. Fratres milicie Christi de Livonia*, *Ostmitteleuropa in Vergangenheit und Gegenwart*, 9 (Cologne, 1965).

9. J. Lind, 'Consequences of the Baltic Crusades in Target Areas: The Case of Karelia', in *Crusade and Conversion*, ed. Murray, pp. 133–50, esp. pp. 149–50.

10. For the history of the Teutonic Order, see, for instance, W. Urban, *The Teutonic Knights. A Military History* (London, 2003); H. Boockmann, *Der Deutsche Orden. Zwölf Kapitel aus seiner Geschichte*, 4th edn (Munich, 1994).

11. W. Paravicini, *Die Preußenreisen des europäischen Adels*, 2 vols to date (Sigmaringen, 1989–); S. Ekdahl, 'Horses and Crossbows: Two Important Warfare Advantages of the Teutonic Order in Prussia', in *The Military Orders*, vol. 2: *Welfare and Warfare*, ed. H. Nicholson (Aldershot, 1998), pp. 119–51.

12. A. Nikžentaitis, 'Changes in the Organisation and Tactics of the Lithuanian Army in the 13th, 14th and the first half of the 15th century', in *Fasciculi Archaeologiae Historicae*, 7 (1994), 45–53, esp. 46–7.

13. Paravicini, *Die Preußenreisen*, 2, table on pp. 20–41.

14. A. Nikžentaitis, 'Prisoners of War in Lithuania and the Teutonic Order State (1283–1409)', in *Der Deutsche Orden in der Zeit der Kalmarer Union 1397–1521*, ed. Z. H. Nowak and R. Czaja, Ordines militares. Colloquia Torunensia Historica, 10 (Toruń, 1999), pp. 193–208.

15. S. C. Rowell, *Lithuania Ascending. A Pagan Empire within East-Central Europe, 1295–1345* (Cambridge, 1994), p. 259.

16. W. Urban, *Tannenberg and After. Lithuania, Poland, and the Teutonic Order in Search of Immortality* (Chicago, 1999, 2002, revised edn 2003); S. Ekdahl, *Die 'Banderia Prutenorum' des Jan Długosz – eine Quelle zur Schlacht bei Tannenberg 1410* (Göttingen, 1976); S. Ekdahl, *Die Schlacht bei Tannenberg 1410. Quellenkritische Untersuchungen*, I: *Einführung und Quellenlage* (Berlin, 1982); S. Ekdahl, 'Tannenberg/Grunwald – ein politisches Symbol in Deutschland und Polen', *Journal of Baltic Studies*, 22 (1991), 271–324.

17. H. von zur Mühlen, 'Livland von der Christianisierung bis zum Ende seiner Selbständigkeit (etwa 1180–1561)', in *Deutsche Geschichte im Osten Europas. Baltische Länder*, ed. G. von Pistohlkors, 2nd edn (Berlin, 2000), pp. 25–171, especially p. 120.

18. H. Łowmiański, quoting from A. Rutkowska-Płachińska, 'Tradition und Kulturumwandlung der Prussen im 14. und 15. Jahrhundert. Zur Fragestellung', in *Kultur und Politik im Ostseeraum und im Norden 1350–1450*, ed. S. Ekdahl (Visby, 1973), pp. 53–61, esp. p. 53.

19. R. Wenskus, 'Der Deutsche Orden und die nichtdeutsche Bevölkerung des Preußenlandes mit besonderer Berücksichtigung der Siedlung', in *Die deutsche Ostsiedlung des Mittelalters als Problem der europäischen Geschichte*, ed. W. Schlesinger, Vorträge und Forschungen, 18 (Sigmaringen, 1974), pp. 417–38, esp. pp. 419–22; quotation from p. 422. Also important: E. Maschke, *Der Deutsche Orden und die Preußen. Bekehrung und Unterwerfung in der preußisch-baltischen Mission des 13. Jahrhunderts*, Historische Studien, 176 (Berlin, 1928).

20. S. Ekdahl, 'The Strategic Organization of the Commanderies of the Teutonic Order in Prussia and Livonia', in *La Commanderie, institution des ordres*

militaires dans l'Occident médiéval, ed. A. Luttrell and L. Pressouyre (Paris, 2002), pp. 219–42, esp. p. 228.

21. See, for example, the views of K. Conrad, 'Der Deutsche Orden und sein Landesausbau in Preußen', in *Deutscher Orden 1190–1990*, ed. U. Arnold (Lüneburg, 1997), pp. 83–106, esp. pp. 86–7.

22. Martin Luther, *An die Herren deutsch Ordens, dass sie falsche Keuschheyt meiden und zur rechten ehelichen Keuschheyt greifen (1523)*, in Martin Luther, *Werke*, 12 (Weimar, 1891), pp. 232–44.

23. On the following, see the important book by W. Wippermann, *Der Ordensstaat als Ideologie. Das Bild des Deutschen Ordens in der deutschen Geschichtsschreibung und Publizistik* (Berlin, 1979).

24. Johann Gottfried Herder, *Ideen zur Philosophie der Geschichte der Menschheit*, quoted from his collected works (*Werke*) in 5 vols, ed. W. Dobbek, vol. 4, 4th edn (Berlin, 1969), pp. 393–4; Wippermann, *Der Ordensstaat*, pp. 104–6.

25. Ludwig von Baczko, *Geschichte Preußens*, 6 vols (Königsberg, 1792–1800), vol. 2, p. 62; Wippermann, *Der Ordensstaat*, pp. 110–44.

26. August von Kotzebue, *Preußens ältere Geschichte*, 4 vols (Riga, 1808), vol. 1, pp. 36, 68, 124–5, 134, 145, 148, 150, 173, 190; Wippermann, *Der Ordensstaat*, pp. 104–19 (giving more quotations).

27. J. Voigt, *Geschichte Preußens von den ältesten Zeiten bis zum Untergang der Herrschaft des Deutschen Ordens*, 9 vols (Königsberg, 1827–29); Wippermann, *Der Ordensstaat*, pp. 120–5.

28. Voigt, *Geschichte*.

29. H. von Treitschke, 'Das Deutsche Ordensland Preußen', *Preußische Jahrbücher*, 10 (1862), 95–151. Quotation from Wippermann, *Der Ordensstaat*, p. 156. See also Wipperman, *Der Ordensstaat*, pp. 155–67.

30. Ekdahl, 'Tannenberg/Grunwald', 279–80.

31. On Treitschke, see Wippermann, *Der Ordensstaat*, pp. 155–67.

32. For the following, see Ekdahl, 'Tannenberg/Grunwald'.

33. Ekdahl, *Die Schlacht bei Tannenberg*, plates 4–5, between pp. 16 and 17.

34. A dubbed English version of this film is entitled *Knights of the Black Cross*.

35. S. Ekdahl, 'The Battle of Tannenberg-Grunwald-Žalgiris (1410) as Reflected in Monuments of the Twentieth Century', in *The Military Orders*, vol. 3: *Their History and Heritage*, ed. W. G. Zajac (Aldershot, forthcoming).

36. On the following, see Wippermann, *Der Ordensstaat*, pp. 253–83 ('Bedeutung und Funktion des Ordensstaates in der nationalsozialistischen Ideologie und Propaganda') and Ekdahl, 'Tannenberg/Grunwald', pp. 286–9. Also see W. Wippermann, *Der 'deutsche Drang nach Osten'. Ideologie und Wirklichkeit eines politischen Schlagwortes* (Darmstadt, 1981); M. Burleigh, *Germany Turns Eastwards. A Study of Ostforschung in the Third Reich* (Cambridge, 1988); R. Tuchtenhagen, 'Die Rolle des Nordens in der deutschen historischen Osteuropaforschung', in *Osteuropaforschung in der nordeuropäischen Historiographie*, ed. R. Tuchtenhagen, Nordost-Archiv, 9 (2000) (Lüneburg, 2001), pp. 11–49.

37. See Wippermann, *Der Ordensstaat*, pp. 254–5.

38. Ekdahl, 'Tannenberg/Grunwald', p. 287.

39. Ibid., p. 286.

40. Ibid.; U. Arnold, 'Eight Hundred Years of the Teutonic Order', in *The Military Orders: Fighting for the Faith and Caring for the Sick*, ed. M. Barber (Aldershot, 1994), pp. 223–35, esp. p. 234.
41. Ekdahl, 'Tannenberg/Grunwald', p. 287.
42. A. Rosenberg, *Der Mythus des 20. Jahrhunderts. Eine Wertung der seelisch-geistigen Gestaltungskräfte unserer Zeit* (Munich, 1939), p. 546.
43. For literature, see Wippermann, *Der Ordensstaat*, p. 269.
44. Heinrich Himmler, *Geheimreden 1933 bis 1945 und andere Ansprachen*, ed. B. F. Smith and A. F. Peterson (Frankfurt am Main, Berlin and Vienna, 1974), pp. 50–1 with note on p. 284. See Wippermann, *Der Ordensstaat*, pp. 261–2, and Ekdahl, 'Tannenberg/Grunwald', p. 287 with n. 133 on p. 312.
45. Ekdahl, 'Tannenberg/Grunwald', p. 289 with n. 148 on p. 314; Burleigh, *Germany Turns Eastwards*, p. 189.
46. S. Ekdahl, *Die 'Banderia Prutenorum'*, p. 53; S. Ekdahl, *Die Schlacht bei Tannenberg 1410*, p.25; S. Ekdahl, 'Tannenberg/Grunwald', pp. 287–8 with notes on pp. 312–14.
47. See photograph in Ekdahl, *Die Schlacht bei Tannenberg*, between pp. 48 and 49.
48. Photograph in ibid., between pp. 64 and 65.
49. *Völkischer Beobachter*, 21 May 1940. See Ekdahl, 'Tannenberg/Grunwald', p. 288 and n. 137 on p. 313.
50. See Wippermann, *Der Ordensstaat*, pp. 275–80, and Burleigh, *Germany Turns Eastwards*, passim (cf. index).
51. Wippermann, *Der Ordensstaat*, p. 327, and Burleigh, *Germany Turns Eastwards*, passim.
52. E. Keyser, 'Die Erforschung der Bevölkerungsgeschichte des deutschen Ostens', in *Deutsche Ostforschung. Ergebnisse und Aufgaben seit dem ersten Weltkrieg*, ed. H. Aubin et al. (Leipzig, 1942), 1, pp. 90–104, here p. 93; Wippermann, *Der 'deutsche Drang nach Osten'*, p. 113; on Keyser also see Burleigh, *Germany Turns Eastwards*, passim.
53. M. N. Pokrovskii, *History of Russia, from the Earliest Times to the Rise of Commercial Capitalism*, new intro. by J. D. Clarkson, trans. and ed. J. D. Clarkson and M. R. M. Griffiths. 2nd edn (Bloomington, c. 1966).
54. For the following, see A. G. Mazour, *Modern Russian historiography*, rev. ed. (Westport, Conn., 1975). Cf. Wippermann, *Der 'deutsche Drang nach Osten'*, pp. 57–62, esp. pp. 61–2.
55. According to H.-H. Nolte, *Drang nach Osten. Sowjetische Geschichtsschreibung der deutschen Ostexpansion* (Frankfurt am Main, 1976), p. 90 (without giving reference).
56. Wippermann, *Der 'deutsche Drang nach Osten'*, pp. 62–70.
57. *Geschichte des Mittelalters*, vols 1–2 (Berlin [East], 1958).
58. Ibid., vol. 1, ch. 15: 'Deutschland vom 13. bis 15. Jh.' (pp. 337–55).
59. Ibid., p. 337.
60. Ibid., pp. 340–3.
61. Ibid., p. 342.
62. Владимир Т. Пашуто, 'Борьба прусского народа за независимость (до конца XIII в.)' (Vladimir T. Pashuto, 'The Struggle of the Prussian People for Independence (to the End of the Thirteenth Century)'), *История СССР* (*Istorija SSSR*), 6 (1958), 54–81.

63. V. L. Pashuto, 'Борьба народов Руси и Восточной Прибалтики с агрессией немецких, шведских и датских феодалов в XIII–XV веках' ('The Struggle of the Peoples of Russia and the Eastern Baltic against the Aggression of the German, Swedish and Danish Feudatories in the 13th–15th Centuries'), *Вопросы истории* (*Voprosy istorii*), 7 (1969), 109–28.

64. V. L. Pashuto, *Александр Невский* (*Aleksandr Nevskii*) (Moscow, 1974).

65. Игорь Р. Шаскольский, Борьба Александра Невского против крестоносной агрессии конца 40-х–50-х годов XIII в. (Igor' P. Shaskol'skii, 'Aleksandr Nevskii's Struggle against Crusader Aggression from the late 1240s to the 1250s'), *Исторические записки* (*Istoricheskije zapiski*), 43 (1953), 182–200.

66. I. P. Shaskil'skii, *Борьба Руси против крестоносной агрессии на берегах Балтики в XII–XIII вв.* (Russia's Struggle against Crusader Aggression on the Baltic coast in the 12th–13th Centuries) (Leningrad, 1978).

67. I. P. Shaskil'skii, 'Папская курия – главный организатор крестоносной агрессии 1240–1242 гг. против Руси' ('The Papal Curia – a leading Organizer of Crusader Aggression against Russia During the Years 1240–1242'), *Исторические записки* (*Istoricheskije zapiski*), 37 (1951), 169–88.

68. I. P. Szaskolskij, 'Walka Rusi przeciwko ekspansji niemieckich zakonów rycerskich w XIII wieku', in *Ekspansja niemieckich zakonów rycerskich w strefie Bałtyku od XIII do połowy XVI wieku. Materiały z konferencji historyków radzieckich i polskich w Toruniu z r. 1988*, ed. M. Biskup (Toruń [Thorn]: Instytut Historii Polskiej Akademii Nauk, Zakład Historii Pomorza, 1990), pp. 103–20.

69. See Ekdahl, *Die Schlacht bei Tannenberg*, pp. 33–4.

70. Ibid., p. 34, n. 61.

71. В. И. Матузова, Е. Л. Назарова, *Крестоносцы и Русь. Конец XII в.–1270 г. Тексты, Перевод, Комментарий* (V. I. Matuzova and E. L. Nazarova, *Crusaders and Russia: Late 1100s–1270. Texts, Translation, Commentary*) (Moscow: 'Индрик' [Indrik], 2002), Russian literature: pp. 392–402; literature in other languages: pp. 403–13.

72. For the following, see J. Kreem, 'The Teutonic Order in Livonia: Diverging Historiographic Traditions', in *The Crusades and the Military Orders: Expanding the Frontiers of Medieval Latin Christianity*, ed. Z. Hunyadi and J. Laszlovszky (Budapest, 2001), pp. 467–79.

73. I. Misāns, 'Geschichtswissenschaft in Lettland nach 1990. Zwischen Tradition und Neuorientierung', *Österreichische Osthefte*, 44 (2002), 1–2, 179–93, esp. 187–8. Also personal letter to the author (S.E.) from Professor Ilgvars Misāns, Riga, 12 February 2004.

74. G. von Rauch, *Geschichte der deutschbaltischen Geschichtsschreibung*, Ostmitteleuropa in Vergangenheit und Gegenwart, 20 (Cologne and Vienna, 1986). Also see the bibliography in *Deutsche Geschichte im Osten Europas. Baltische Länder*, ed. G. von Pistohlkors (Berlin, 1994).

75. Kreem, 'The Teutonic Order', p. 470.

76. P. Olinš, *The Teutonic Knights in Latvia* (Riga, 1925).

77. Kreem, 'The Teutonic Order', p. 467.

78. *Lietuvos istorija* (*The History of Lithuania*), ed. A. Šapoka (Kaunas, 1936). For more literature, see the Research Review in Z. Kiaupa, J. Kiaupienė

and Kuncevičius, *The History of Lithuania before 1795* (Vilnius, 2000), pp. 365–401.

79. Letter from Prof. Edvardas Gudavičius, Vilnius, to the author (S.E.), 18 February 2004.

80. For these historians' work, see the Research Review in Kiaupa et al., *The History of Lithuania before 1795*.

81. Ekdahl, 'Tannenberg/Grunwald', pp. 298–9.

82. Letter from Prof. Gudavičius to the author (S.E.), 18 February 2004, pp. 2–4.

83. Ekdahl, *Die Schlacht bei Tannenberg*, pp. 32–4.

84. Ekdahl, 'The Battle of Tannenberg-Grunwald-Žalgiris'.

85. Ekdahl, 'Tannenberg/Grunwald', pp. 298–9.

86. S. Ekdahl, 'Die Rolle der Ritterorden bei der Christianisierung der Liven und Letten', in Gli inizi del cristianesimo, pp. 203–43, esp. pp. 210–11. For Karl Marx, see Wippermann, *Der Ordensstaat*, p. 307.

87. A. K. Vassar and E. V. Tarvel, 'Die ostbaltischen Stämme im Kampf gegen die deutsch-skandinavische Aggression im 12.–13. Jahrhundert', *Eesti NSV Teaduste Akademia Toimetised. Ühiskonnateadused*, 1 (1975), 26 ff.

88. See Kreem, 'The Teutonic Order', p. 473.

89. S. Vahtre, *Jüriöö* (*St. George's Night*) (Tallinn, 1980).

90. R. Jasas, *Didysis prūsų sukilimas (1260–1274)* (Vilnius, 1959); *Lietuvių karas su kryžiuočiais*, ed. J. Jurginis et al. (Vilnius, 1964); E. Gudavičius, *Kryžiaus karai pabaltijyje ir Lietuva XIII amžiuje* (Vilnius, 1989).

91. A. Schwabe [Švabe], *Histoire du peuple letton* (Stockholm, 1953), quotations from pp. 35, 47–56.

92. See, for instance, C. R. Jurgėla, *History of the Lithuanian Nation. Introduction by C. A. Manning* (New York, 1948); C. R. Jurgėla, *Lithuania: The Outpost of Freedom* (The National Guard of Lithuania in Exile in cooperation with Valkyrie Press [St Petersburg, Florida], 1976).

93. Ekdahl, 'Tannenberg/Grunwald', pp. 289–92 with notes on pp. 314–15.

94. H. Łowmiański, 'Agresja Zakonu Krzyżackiego na Litwę w wiekach XIII–XV', *Przegląd Historyczny*, 45 (1954), 338–71. An early Polish counterpart to Wippermann's book *Der 'deutsche Drang nach Osten'* (1981) is G. Labudas's essay, 'A Historiographic Analysis of the German "Drang nach Osten"', *Polish Western Affairs*, 5 (1964), 221–65.

95. S. M. Kuczyński, *Wielka Wojna z Zakonem Krzyżackim w latach 1409–1411*, 5 edns (Warsaw, 1955; 1960; 1965; 1980; 1987).

96. *Trybuna Ludu*, 197, 17 July 1960, p. 1. Quoted by Ekdahl, 'Tannenberg/Grunwald', pp. 291–2.

97. Ibid.

98. *Ekspansja niemieckich zakonów rycerskich w strefie Bałtyku od XIII do połowy XVI wieku. Materiały z konferencji historyków radzieckich i polskich w Toruniu z. r. 1988*, ed. M. Biskup (Toruń, 1990).

99. On the following, see Wippermann, *Der Ordensstaat*, pp. 304–69, and Ekdahl, 'Tannenberg/Grunwald', pp. 292–5.

100. Ekdahl, 'Tannenberg/Grunwald' (with notes on pp. 316–17).

101. W. Hubatsch, *Eckpfeiler Europas. Probleme des Preußenlandes in geschichtlicher Sicht* (Heidelberg, 1953).

102. W. Kuhn, 'Ritterorden als Grenzhüter des Abendlandes gegen das östliche Heidentum', *Ostdeutsche Wissenschaft*, 6 (1959), 7–70; also in W. Kuhn, *Vergleichende Untersuchungen zur mittelalterlichen Ostsiedlung*, Osteuropa in Vergangenheit und Gegenwart, 16, ed. R. Schmidt and H. Weczerka (Cologne and Vienna, 1973), pp. 305–68.

103. Ekdahl, 'Tannenberg/Grunwald', pp. 289–300 (passim); Ekdahl, 'The Battle of Tannenberg-Grunwald-Žalgiris'.

104. See Wippermann, *Der Ordensstaat* (passim).

105. See Wippermann, *Der 'deutsche Drang nach Osten'*, pp. 112–16, 126–7, and Burleigh, *Germany Turns Eastwards*, ch. 6: 'The "Band of the Unbroken" and their Critics: Aspects of "Ostforschung" after 1945', pp. 300–21, passim.

106. Ibid. See also Wippermann, *Der Ordensstaat*, pp. 275–80; Maschke's articles, 'Burgund und der preußische Ordensstaat. Ein Beitrag zur Einheit der ritterlichen Kultur Europas im Spätmittelalter', in *Syntagma Friburgense, Historische Studien. Hermann Aubin zum 70. Geburtstag* (Lindau and Constance, 1956), pp. 147–72, and 'Die inneren Wandlungen des Deutschen Ordens', in *Geschichte und Gegenwartsbewusstsein. Festschrift für Hans Rothfels* (Göttingen, 1963), pp. 249–77. Both articles are reprinted in E. Maschke, *Domus hospitalis Theutonicorum. Europäische Verbindungslinien der Deutschordensgeschichte. Gesammelte Aufsätze aus den Jahren 1931–63*, Quellen und Studien zur Geschichte des Deutschen Ordens, 10 (Bad Godesberg, 1970), pp. 15–34 and 35–59.

107. Ekdahl, 'Tannenberg/Grunwald', pp. 294–5.

108. Ibid. (with notes on pp. 316–17). The Teutonic Order defended itself in the booklet *Contra-Punkte oder die Kunst, sich zu irren. Im Auftrag des Generalrates des Deutschen Ordens Sankt Mariens zu Jerusalem*, ed. P. K. Wieser et al. (Vienna, 1968); see also Chapter 2 by James Muldoon, this volume.

109. Boockmann, *Der Deutsche Orden*, pp. 255–89.

110. E. Weise, 'Der Heidenkampf des Deutschen Ordens', *Zeitschrift für Ostforschung*, 12 (1963), pp. 420–73, 622–72, 13 (1964), 401–20.

111. H. Beumann, *Heidenmission und Kreuzzugsgedanke in der deutschen Ostpolitik des Mittelalters* (Darmstadt, 1973).

112. *Die deutsche Ostsiedlung des Mittelalters als Problem der europäischen Geschichte. Reichenau-Vorträge 1970–1972*, ed. W. Schlesinger, Vorträge und Forschungen, 18 (Sigmaringen, 1973). Two important articles should be mentioned here: W. Schlesinger, 'Zur Problematik der Erforschung der deutschen Ostsiedlung' (ibid., pp. 11–30), and R. Wenskus, 'Der Deutsche Orden und die nichtdeutsche Bevölkerung des Preußenlandes mit besonderer Berücksichtigung der Siedlung' (ibid., pp. 417–38); for the German settlement in east-central Europe also see W. Kuhn, *Geschichte der deutschen Ostsiedlung in der Neuzeit*, vol. 1: *Das 15. bis 17. Jahrhundert (Allgemeiner Teil)* (Cologne and Graz, 1955), and W. Kuhn, *Vergleichende Untersuchungen zur mittelalterlichen Ostsiedlung* (Cologne and Vienna, 1973).

113. Wippermann, *Der Ordensstaat*.

114. Ekdahl, *Die 'Banderia Prutenorum'*; Ekdahl, *Die Schlacht bei Tannenberg 1410*; Ekdahl, 'Tannenberg/Grunwald'. See also his forthcoming article mentioned in note 35.

115. Ekdahl, *Die Schlacht bei Tannenberg*, pp. 61–2, n. 62.

116. See, for instance, *Zum wissenschaftlichen Ertrag der deutsch-polnischen Schulbuchkonferenzen der Historiker 1972–1987: XX. Deutsch-polnische Schulbuchkonferenz der Historiker, 1.-6. Juni 1987 in Poznań (Posen)*, ed. W. Jacobmeyer (Brunswick, 1988).
117. Ekdahl, 'Tannenberg/Grunwald', p. 297 with n. 223 on p. 320.
118. W. Küttler, 'Charakter und Entwicklungstendenzen des Deutschordensstaates in Preußen', *Zeitschrift für Geschichtswissenschaft*, 19 (1971), 1504–29.
119. Wippermann, *Der Ordensstaat*, pp. 30–1. Also see Wippermann's analysis on pp. 312–15.
120. As, for instance, in a lecture held by Bishop Dr J. Boruta SJ, 'Christentum in der Zeit von Mindaugas und Litauen' at a conference in Vilnius in 2001. It will be published in *Christianisierung Litauens im mitteleuropäischen Kontext*, ed. V. Dolinskas (forthcoming).
121. Y. Klitsenko, 'Crusader Image in Lithuanian Culture', *Isvestija* (Section *Nauka* [*Science*]), 20 May 2004. The Russian version was published 2 May 2004. See <www.inauka.ru/blogs/article47016.html/>; also letters to the author (S.E.) from Dr Tomas Baranauskas of Vilnius, one of them dated 18 February 2004.
122. Ibid.
123. E. Gudavičius, 'Lietuvos valstybės susidarymo reikšmė vokietijos "Veržimesi į rytus"', *Lituanistica*, 3 (1990), 21–30.
124. Note especially the Institute for Baltic Sea Region History and Archaeology, in Klaipėda.
125. For the following, see the instructive article by Misāns, 'Geschichtswissenschaft in Lettland nach 1990', 179–93.
126. Ibid., 180, 189.
127. Indriķis Šterns, *Latvijas vēsture 1180–1290. Krustakari* (Riga, 2002), with an English summary: 'History of Latvia 1180–1290. The Crusades', pp. 710–35; cf. Misāns, 'Geschichtswissenschaft in Lettland nach 1990', 191.
128. Šterns, *Latvijas vēsture*, p. 715.
129. See Misāns, 'Geschichtswissenschaft in Lettland nach 1990'.
130. MA thesis with a summary in English. There will be a future dissertation on this subject by E. Eihmane. The author (S.E.) thanks her and Prof. Misāns for making available to him a review article by the former, which will be published in English: 'Crusades and the Incorporation of the Baltic into the Christian Civilisation in the 12th–13th Centuries'.
131. Kreem, 'The Teutonic Order'.
132. Cf. the international religious-scientific conference 'Orthodox Byzantium and Latin West', which was held in the Pilgrim Centre of the Moscow Patriarchy on 26–27 May 2004.
133. Yuri Klitsenko is a journalist, working at the Moscow Patriarchate and ITAR-TASS news agency. He researches Russian Orthodox Church symbolism, and has also written on the image of crusaders in Russian and Lithuanian culture, Aleksandr Nevskii, and so on.
134. In a letter of 25 May 2004, Yuri Klitsenko informed the author (S.E.) about some of his shorter articles in English, available on the internet: 'Crusader Image in Lithuanian Culture'; 'The Audiovisual symbolism of the film *Alexander Nevsky*' (<http://english.pravda.ru/science/19/95/380/10208_nevsky.html>); '"Furnace play" in the films *Alexander Nevsky* and *Ivan*

the Terrible' <http://english.pravda.ru/science/19/95/380/10565_crusader. html>); 'The Symbol of Martyrdom for the faith in the Works of S. Eisenstein and S. Prokofiev'.

135. W. Urban, *The Samogitian Crusade* (Chicago, 1989); W. Urban, *The Baltic Crusade*, 2nd edn (Chicago, 1994); W. Urban, *The Prussian Crusade*, 2nd edn (Chicago, 2000); W. Urban, *The Livonian Crusade*, 2nd edn (Chicago, 2004); Urban, *Tannenberg and After*; Urban, *The Teutonic Knights*.

136. See the review by S. Ekdahl of Urban, *The Teutonic Knights*, in *Crusades*, 4 (2005) (forthcoming).

137. F. Benninghoven, 'Über Veröffentlichungen zur Geschichte des Deutschen Ordens. Ein kritischer Literaturbericht, Teil III (Schluß)', in F. Benninghoven, *Zur Geschichte des Deutschen Ordens, der Stadt Danzig, des Klosters Oliva und zur Eroberung Ostpreußens 1945. Unzensierte Nachträge zur Ostforschung* (Berlin: [private print, not for sale], 1996), pp. 10–23. On Urban's books, *The Baltic Crusade*, *The Livonian Crusade*, and *The Prussian Crusade*, ibid., pp. 10–17.

138. W. Urban, 'Rethinking the Crusades', in *Perspectives* (October 1998), 25–9, here p. 26; website: <www.historians.org/Perspectives/issues/1998/9810/ 9810TEC.CFM?pv=y>; for other articles by Urban, see his bibliography on the internet (Google: William Urban); and private correspondence to the author (S.E.) from Prof. Urban (Monmouth College, Illinois).

139. Urban, 'Rethinking the Crusades', p. 28.

140. Ibid.

141. Ibid.

142. Ibid.

143. Y. Klitsenko, 'Средневекоые миротворцы' ('The Medieval Peacekeepers'), *Pravda*, 16 April 2003. See <http://society.pravda.ru/society/2003/8/26/8 1/9800_Urban.html>; the same day the article was also published in the Russian Orthodox newspaper *Radonezh*: <www.radonezh.ru/analytic/ articles/?ID=4>; it was later published in other Russian newspapers: <http:// rus-vost.irk.ru/arhiv/2003/5/documents/mirotv.htm>; <www.zeminfo.ru/ newsline/2003_37/09_19_09_10_43.html>. Klitsenko's article became very popular in patriotic media in Russia. There is no English version.

144. Ibid.

145. Letter to the author (S.E.), 28 May 2004.

146. W. Urban, 'Victims of the Baltic Crusade', *Journal of Baltic Studies*, 29 (1998), 195–212; Urban, *The Livonian Crusade*, pp. 534–5.

147. S. Ekdahl, 'Christianisierung – Siedlung – Litauerreise. Die Christianisierung Litauens als Dilemma des Deutschen Ordens' (also in Lithuanian), in *Lietuvos krikščionėjimas Vidurio Europos kontekste. 2001 m. rugsėjo 26–27 d. tarptautinės konferencijos, skirtos Lietuvos karaliaus Mindaugo krikšto 750 jubiliejiniams metams, medžiaga/Christianisierung Litauens im mitteleuropäischen Kontext. Materialien der internationalen Konferenz, gewidmet dem 750. Jubiläumsjahr der Taufe Mindaugas', des Königs von Litauen, am 26.-27. September 2001*, ed. V. Dolinskas with G. Mikelaitis (Vilnius, forthcoming).

148. Urban, 'Victims of the Baltic Crusade', p. 197.

149. See Misāns, 'Geschichtswissenschaft in Lettland nach 1990', and the forthcoming works by E. Eihmane, Riga (see note 130).

9
national feeling and the legacy of the crusades
Jean Richard

Has national feeling played a role in promoting the history of the crusades since their own era? The sense of belonging to a national or provincial community was not alien to the mentality of the people of the eleventh, twelfth and thirteenth centuries, with more reason than those of later epochs. The local interests of some of the narrators of the First Crusade can be identified:[1] Raymond d'Aguilers's attention scarcely moved beyond the exploits and adventures of the count of Toulouse's contingent to which he belonged; others remembered more of what concerned the Norman princes' forces, or Godfrey de Bouillon's Lotharingians, and we have, for example, the echoes of the mockery hurled at the Provençaux, or, during the Second Crusade, the Germans, whom the French criticized for being slow-moving.[2] But the frictions between the various contingents, even if they sometimes led to brawls, remained marginal, and the chroniclers who mentioned them do not seem to have been driven by the desire to promote their own compatriots at the expense of the others.

The question of whether these authors intended to promote the role that their compatriots played in the crusade can be asked in connection with a text written by a man who never took part in a crusade himself: as Guibert de Nogent entitled his account of the First Crusade *Gesta Dei per Francos* (*God's Deeds through the Franks*), one might think that he wished to depict this crusade as an essentially French business. But it is necessary to remember that this word *Franci* then had, and retained in the East, the sense of 'arising from the former Carolingian empire', thus distinguishing them specifically from the Byzantines, who would have been included in the definition *Christiani*, although for those in the East they remained the *Romani*. Without doubt, Guibert did not intend to write in the narrow sense of the term about people from the kingdom of France, but did he intend to include all Christians of the West under this designation?[3] In contrast, it was certainly the exclusivist arrogance of the French that John of Würzburg was denouncing when, apropos of the epitaph of Wicher 'the Aleman', one of the participants of the crusade and one of Godfrey de Bouillon's faithful men, he complained that the Germans' role in these events was too widely forgotten.[4] As for Ambroise, describing in his *Estoire de la guerre sainte* the conflicts that divided the different leaders of the Third Crusade, he expressed his nostalgia for the time when all the crusaders, whatever their origin, were all called Franks – referring to the time of the First Crusade.[5]

National pride was really felt and even exploited. It seems certain that, in his speech at Clermont – although admittedly we do not possess a reliable version of it – Pope Urban II urged the French to set out on the crusade by recalling the great deeds of their ancestors. His distant successor, Clement IV, writing to King Louis IX on 21 September 1266 regarding the fortification of Aigues-Mortes, instanced the fact that this port would be used by 'the pilgrims of your realm who, burning more than all others with zeal for the faith, frequently go to the help of the Holy Land'.[6] The promotion of a national tradition was, then, a recurring argument in the preaching of the crusade and in its implementation. Writers could no more avoid mentioning this point to gain the attention of their readers and listeners than could *trouvères* when they sang their songs about the crusade.

Nevertheless, the crusade remained throughout the thirteenth century, as in the preceding century, the business of the whole of Christendom. The Third Crusade prompted contingents from all the countries of the West to set out on the road, including crusaders from the Scandinavian countries who did not arrive until the moment when the truce that ended to hostilities had just been concluded; which did not prevent a contemporary historian from writing an account of their expedition to celebrate their courage.[7] The crusades that followed were rarely the work of a single sovereign, even if one of them had taken the initiative in leading his subjects on an expedition. Although Emperor Henry VI involved almost solely Germans and Sicilians in his crusade, Louis IX, who had been unable to secure the participation of the king of Norway nor of any other sovereign in the crusade of 1248, was met by an English contingent and joined by Italian mercenaries, while the crusade in 1270 attracted the King of Aragon and Lord Edward of England as well as the King of France. Emperor Frederick II led some English in his crusade of

1228–29; in 1239–40 King Thibaud of Navarre was followed by Richard, Earl of Cornwall. Practically no crusade was truly national.

It was the same in the following century. Was French royalty more involved in the 'enterprise of Outremer' than other European princes? Certainly Philip the Fair, his sons and the first Valois kings all toyed with crusading projects; John the Good took the cross after the Treaty of Brétigny (1360); the Nicopolis expedition was primarily an expedition of French princes. But their English cousins joined them, and it was the popes, notably John XXII and Clement VI, who promoted these enterprises and who, moreover, were as much or more concerned about defence against the Turks as about the recovery of the holy places.[8] These projects cannot be described as having in any sense a national aspect: the 'Holy Leagues' were coalitions that included several nationalities.

Other enterprises took place within the panorama of the crusades. These aimed at other objectives than those the canonist Hostiensis, around 1250, defined as relevant to the *crux transmarina*: that is to say, expeditions led to the East to defend Christians menaced by Turkish expansion, the restitution of sovereignty over the holy places of Christendom, and expeditions where devotion to the Holy Sepulchre was an essential factor.[9] The *crux cismarina*, according to this definition, included the crusades against the Albigeois, the wars waged for the defence of the Church of Rome against Frederick II and his successors, and subsequently the crusade against the king of Aragon, waged to the profit of the Angevins of Naples and Sicily, the 'Urbanist' crusade during the Great Schism, directed by Bishop Henry Despenser against the supporters of the pope of Avignon in Flanders, the crusades against the Hussites and many others. Here a national aspect is more easily discerned; if these enterprises became 'crusades', it was because they were encouraged, even incited by the papacy, but they often took their origin from conflicts between dynastic or national interests and their history is part of national historiographies. Even more so the wars waged in Europe against the Moors: even though combatants from north of the Pyrenees took part, these wars belong to the history of the *reconquista*, which is part of the history of Spain.

Did epic literature, which became the literature of chivalric romance, make more appeal to national sentiment? This is expressed clearly in the *Chanson de Roland*, but it is of minor importance and the mention of 'French of France our land' does not carry any implication promoting these French above others. The works belonging to the Crusade Cycle, when they take as their theme episodes from the war waged overseas against the Saracens, make the latter the born enemies of the Christian heroes, who are generally French or Franks of Outremer of French origin, but who are not set against those of different origin. The poets who took more and more liberty with that very theme of the crusades did not set themselves to extol any special heroism of the French people. They exalted great figures, beginning with Charlemagne (in the *Pèlerinage de Charlemagne à Jérusalem*); they recalled the great deeds of the members of great families linked to the events of the crusades, and this could result in the glorification of these families who sometimes had commissioned these works. But neither Baudouin de Sebourc nor the Bâtard de Bouillon were evoked as belonging to the French nation.[10] The epic could have a dynastic colour, but it did not have a national colour. This is particularly remarkable when we consider those *chefs d'oeuvre*, destined for long popularity, the romances of Tasso and his imitators.[11] The principal hero of *Gerusalemme liberata* might belong to the Este family, but the poet did not use this as an excuse to glorify the role played by the Italians in the First Crusade.

In the fifteenth century, we find an excellent example of an historical work whose title could suggest a special attempt to promote the French role in the crusade: this is the work of Sébastien Mamerot, written in 1474 for Louis de Laval and entitled *Les passages d'Outremer faits par les François contre les Turcs*. But, richly illustrated by Michel Colombe, this is a manuscript rather than a book of history, and it is an isolated text that does not in fact seek to exalt the actions of crusaders from the kingdom of France in particular. The first true history of the crusades composed after the Middle Ages, by Benedetto de'Accoltis, published in Venice in 1532 and inspired largely by the work of William of Tyre, was itself also alien to all national favouritism. It was the Christians of the West as a group, and more particularly the Franks of the East, that interested the author. Yet arguably, this sense of a still-unified Christendom bore some sort of relationship to national feeling.

At the beginning of the seventeenth century, there appeared the first great historical work of modern times, a collection of narrative sources dedicated to the crusades: the *Gesta Dei per Francos* of Jacques Bongars, which was published in 1611, shortly after the death of King Henri IV of France.[12] The author, a Frenchman, dedicated it to 'Louis XIII, son of Henry the Great', and the book opened with a eulogy of the most Christian king; but his interests lay in 'the history of expeditions to the east and the Frankish kingdom of Jerusalem', evoking 'so many families of princes who were present in these most perilous, and thus all the more glorious, expeditions', without any hint of a desire to distinguish the French above other crusaders. It was the same for the *Histoire de la guerre sainte faite par les Français et autres chrétiens pour la délivrance de la Judée et du Saint-Sépulcre*, written by Duchet, a man of Champagne (Paris, 1620). As for the great work of P. Louis Maimbourg, his *Histoire des Croisades*, published in 1675 and republished many times, also opened with a dedication to the King of France, then Louis XIV. 'Your majesty', wrote the author, 'will be able to take pleasure in seeing the most valiant princes of their time and above all princes of his august blood, whom the glory that they acquired by a thousand fine deeds has rendered immortal.' He did not skimp on his flattery ('if Louis the Great had lived in the era of the crusades, there would have been no need for the involvement of other Christian princes'). But 'the heroes who must appear in this theatre' were all the kings of Europe and especially the emperors; Maimbourg did not give greater importance to his compatriots, not even the Capetian kings who took part in the crusades.[13]

A 'national' view began to appear during the eighteenth century, but it was not to glorify the role played by the French that Voltaire referred to it in his *Essai sur les moeurs*. In his view – which was that of the philosophers of the 'Siècle des Lumières', echoing the English adherents of the Enlightenment and little inclined to pass favourable judgement on enterprises promoted by the Roman pope – the crusades were useless expeditions, organized by the popes and by the Catholic Church to satisfy an instinct for domination, and they served as a vehicle for a display of fanaticism.[14] Voltaire could not avoid mentioning the role played by St Louis (for this philosopher was always a faithful subject of the King of France), but it was to regret that this sovereign had lost his troops and wasted his resources in these expeditions instead of profiting his kingdom through his wisdom ... . For Voltaire, the crusade venture had been harmful to the kingdom of France.[15] The crusades were then an object of almost universal criticism among French writers. It was nevertheless an historian (but one who flattered himself that he had an enlightened mind), Jean-Baptiste Mailly, who undertook in 1774 to write an *Esprit des croisades*. He wrote because he considered the crusades to be one of the major events of the history of France and even a factor in the progress of society, although he joined in criticizing the fanaticism inherent in these expeditions. With Mailly, the crusades began to regain their place in national history.[16]

But did the general public always follow the philosophers? Tasso's *Gerusalemme liberata* was always held in the same high favour among readers, and artists found there the subjects of innumerable paintings, as much in the classical era as in the era of 'troubadour' art. There was still nothing here to give a privileged place to national tradition. At the very most religious paintings evoked St Louis' crusades to illustrate the saint-king's life, but these always remained within hagiographical tradition.

The revival of historical study of the crusades that took place at the start of the nineteenth century simultaneously in Germany with Wilken and in France with Michaud does not seem to have owed a great deal to national sentiment. We know that the starting point for the monumental *Histoire des croisades* by Joseph-François Michaud was an historical introduction that he had been requested to provide for a novel set within the 'troubadour' tradition, a tale of a romance between a brother of Saladin and a noble Christian lady[17] – reminiscent of the loves of Renaud and Armid, and of Tancred and Clorinde, of which Tasso had sung. But Michaud suddenly realized that he had found a 'fair and rich subject', and it was thus that, abandoning romantic literature, he devoted himself entirely to the history of the crusades. It was then the beginning of the Napoleonic Empire, but Michaud remained on the margins of the imperial era. He dealt with the crusades as a whole, beyond the date of 1291, but limited himself to the crusades to the East, leaving Wilken, for example, to deal with the crusade against the Wends because this would probably be of more interest to a German readership. This did not mean that Michaud restricted his investigations to crusades undertaken by the French, but he felt himself more at ease in this region that was most familiar to him.[18]

Yet it was not Michaud's *Histoire* that made the crusades respected by the French public. It has been suggested that it was the fall of the Napoleonic Empire, which deprived France of the glory that it had acquired from the emperor's campaigns, which led the French to throw themselves on to another great epic that could feed national pride. In fact, the memory of the greatness won at the time of the Revolutionary and Napoleonic Wars continued to haunt the French imagination and to inspire authors, in particular poets from Béranger to Victor Hugo. The Napoleonic legend remains the great national epic.

It was at the time of the Napoleonic Empire that an incident occurred to which Gary Dickson has recently drawn attention.[19] In 1806 the Classe de lettres anciennes et de l'histoire de l'Institut national (the former and future Académie des inscriptions et Belles-Lettres) organized a competition on a subject connected with the role of the crusades. The prize was divided between two contestants, one of whom, the young Choiseul d'Aillecourt, was not content with concluding that the crusades had been a factor in human progress, but saw in them a great endeavour of faith and heroism. Dickson has pointed out the possibility that Choiseul's essay, published in 1809, was read and interested many later historians.

It was at about this time that the crusades took up a position that they had never previously held. The French Restoration government does not appear to have taken an active part in this revival, but we discover that it was not completely indifferent to it. It was Jules Polignac, then prime minister of France, who obtained for Michaud the financial grant that enabled him to travel about the East for almost two years in order to complete his research. It was also at this time that the first work destined to come to the aid of the Christians of the East was born, which became the *Oeuvre des écoles d'Orient*, later the *Oeuvre d'Orient*; Michaud announced its foundation in one of his first volumes.[20] This *oeuvre* is essentially French. But the full realization of the place that the crusades now hold in French national feeling belonged to the time of King Louis Philippe.

This king – who had fought at Jemmapes in the armies of the Republic before emigrating from France – wished to heal the fractures that divided the French people. He devised a project to reunite the French around an evocation of 'all the glories of France'. He devoted to this purpose the château of Versailles, which would no longer act as a royal residence but should become a museum of French history. The project was adopted in 1833; it envisaged that a complete iconography would develop within the body of the main building and in the wings of the château. These should contain works illustrating special themes, notably the crusades and the conquest of North Africa, undertaken by Charles X and still in progress. The object of this realization was to make the French unite in recalling the glorious pages of their history, from the beginning of the Middle Ages to the July Monarchy.[21]

It is interesting to note that a particular hall was allocated for the crusades. Certainly, as Mailly had previously thought, the crusades represented one of the most important pages in the history of France; but we have seen how the historians of the philosophical school had striven to disparage them. Louis Philippe's counsellors looked beyond this criticism, and considered that the history of the crusades was particularly rich in glorious events.

The hall of the crusades was not completed until after the formal opening of the gallery of French history (1837). Originally conceived as comprising of a single room only, it subsequently extended further. The hall was to offer the visitor a series of paintings, commissioned from numerous artists, following a scheme decided on by the committee set up by the king. The period before 1096 was represented by several paintings commemorating the exploits of the Normans in southern Italy, and, very fleetingly, French involvement in the *reconquista*. Far more developed was the illustration of the First Crusade, which was followed by the battles fought by the Franks in the Holy Land, including several scenes not connected with war. The Second Crusade was broadly represented, as was the Third Crusade, but only the victories were included; this was why there was no scene to show the defeat at Hattin. The taking of the cross and crusade preaching also received attention. The crusades of the thirteenth century were also depicted, and it is no surprise that the capture of Constantinople, the conquest of Damietta by John of Brienne (1219), and the crusades of St Louis were singled out for illustration. We must not forget that the intention was to recall the glories of France; the exploits of the Franks in the Holy Land were assimilated to those of the French of France. A series of paintings was devoted to the history of the military orders, especially the Hospitallers, who were willingly absorbed as a 'French order' because of their early history and their recruitment. If the illustration of the history of the crusades only occasionally went beyond 1291 (although the combatants of Nicopolis were not forgotten), the material concerning Rhodes and Malta went as far as the 1565 siege of the latter by the Turks. As well as paintings representing historical scenes, there were portraits, chosen for their symbolic value: the great barons of France who could have taken part in the crusades appeared there. Nevertheless, space was given to some foreign figures, such as Conrad III, Frederick Barbarossa and Richard the Lionheart (who in fact was not regarded by the French as a foreign prince). The choice and production of these paintings relied on information taken from the books by Michaud and by Vertot, the latter being author of a history of the order of the Hospital.[22] So there was an attempt at historical accuracy.

The interior decoration of the hall was to resemble the hall of a medieval castle: shields painted with coats of arms were placed on the ceilings and cornices. For the shields, the king decided to use the coats of arms of the families who had taken part in the crusades. This decision had political motives: Louis Philippe had succeeded to the throne in 1830 by evicting the elder branch of the House of Bourbon, to which the majority of the noble families remained attached. By offering them the opportunity to glorify the memory of their forebears, the king was allowing them a means of aligning themselves with the national unity that was the purpose of setting up the museum, without giving it any political colouring.

Out of concern for historical accuracy, the committee that was in charge of completing the hall required interested parties to supply in support of their application authentic documents giving evidence that their ancestors had indeed taken part in these expeditions. Lacabane, director of the École des Chartes, was given responsibility for verifying their authenticity. Taking this task to heart, he took care to have all the papers that were submitted to him transcribed into a register. This collection now grew to an unforeseen extent: the demands and claims from the noble families anxious not to be forgotten in this commemoration flowed in and contributed towards extending still further the gallery of the crusades.

Among the documents that were presented to Lacabane, a very great number were recognizances of debts owed to Genoese merchants who had advanced money to crusaders in order to finance their journey, basically for the crusades of the thirteenth century. These documents could not be faulted from a palaeographical viewpoint and they were accepted by the expert, who did not begin to suspect their authenticity until much later.[23]

It goes without saying that very few families had preserved documents some five centuries old. Those who hoped to prove their ancestors' participation in the crusades and who were having great difficulty in supplying the required authentic evidence were approached by a certain Courtois, who ran a genealogical practice. He said that he could acquire, generally at Genoa, a great number of recognizances of debts, and he offered them, in return for suitable payment, to noble families who wished to ensure that their coats of arms appeared in the museum of Versailles. Those whose families would not have attained the rank of nobility until after the crusades also took advantage of this opportunity. Even the most conscientious historians were for the most part convinced that these documents were genuine; a debate began which lasted until the twentieth century. But, under the Second Empire, proof of the forgery began to be discovered, and in our time it has been proved: the great majority of the documents that came from Courtois's office were false. Many families who really had supplied combatants to the crusades had been led, in perfect good faith, to have recourse to the services of this genealogist, who had shown a true talent as a palaeographer and a historian.[24]

The affair of the 'crusade forgeries' is very instructive. The passion with which families searched for proofs of their ancestors' participation in the crusades shows clearly that, despite the questioning of the crusade ideal by Voltaire and his imitators, the French nobility remained attached to the idea that the crusade had been a mass of great exploits accomplished in God's service. In the previous century, the count of Boulainvilliers had maintained this against his detractors; Choiseul d'Aillecourt, who was descended from a very ancient family, had written this;[25] and in the modern era, every lineage which aspired to belong to the aristocracy had to have taken part in the crusades. Having had ancestors in the crusade was proof that the family had belonged to the nobility in feudal times; the certainty of having taken part in the crusade became part of the self-image of a great family, even long before the King of France thought of taking advantage of this conviction. The conjunction between the publication of an historical work, that by Michaud, which enjoyed great popularity, and the fashion for the Middle Ages in the era of romanticism, with the celebration of the crusaders' exploits in the museum of French history, anchored the aristocratic world and subsequently other groups in the belief that the kingdom of France and its subjects had played the leading role in the epic events of the crusade.

Another possible factor, connected to the first, was the new interest that the France of the era of the Catholic revival evinced for the East. Men such as Châteaubriand or Lamartine carried out pilgrimages to Jerusalem; the French government had an interest in the Christian East, although we will see below that here the evocation of the crusades was mixed with other perspectives.

This revival of interest in the crusades had an impact on the scholarly study of history. It is interesting to read the report that Count Arthur Beugnot read at the Académie des Inscriptions et Belles Lettres when he was asked about the possibility of resuming from a new angle the publication of historical sources for the crusades that had been begun in the previous century by the Benedictines of Saint-Maur. This new publication would parallel the *Recueil des Historiens des Gaules et de la France* (and it was no coincidence that these were parallel projects), which had been entrusted to Dom Berthereau.[26]

> France has played such a glorious part in the wars of the crusades that the historical documents that contain the accounts of these memorable expeditions seem to belong to France's domain. It is her duty to bring them together, to coordinate them and by publishing them to raise a monument that preserves in its original accuracy the memory of the greatest upheaval that Christian society experienced during the Middle Ages.

Having referred to 'the popularity that accounts of wars undertaken to reconquer and defend the holy places have enjoyed for so long a time', he concluded: 'Everything commits France not to allow others to acquit the debt that she has contracted.' The Academy decided to begin work on the *Recueil des Historiens des Croisades*.

The new generation of historians who began work around 1840 were convinced of the views expressed by Beugnot. One of the best examples is Count Louis de Mas-Latrie (1815–99) who, on leaving the École des Chartes, wrote a review of the final edition of Michaud's *Histoire*. He did justice to the author yet regretted that the latter had not been sufficiently attached to the 'new nationality' that had been born in the East. In his eyes this new nation was a French nation.[27] At the end of his first trip to Cyprus, whose historian he later became, Mas-Latrie remarked on the importance of the remains left on the island from the Lusignan kingdom, and did not fail to underline their specifically French character. His interest in Cyprus – and in the Franks of the Holy Land – owed a great deal to the fact that he saw in them a reflection of French feudal society and that their Gothic art was full of French influences. When the island passed under English domination in 1878, he rejoiced to see it escape from Ottoman torpor, but he could not avoid a regret that it had not fallen on France to bring about this reawakening. He wrote this in his book *L'île de Chypre: sa situation présente, ses souvenirs du Moyen Age*, which was dedicated to the first English governor of the island, revealing that his national sentiment did not prevail over his wider awareness of the profit that western Christian civilization would draw from this new state of affairs.[28]

Within this interest for the crusades and the Latin settlement in the East, was there also space for France's African enterprise, begun with the capture of Algiers? Michaud had referred to the latter in the last edition of his *Histoire*,[29] but only in order to analyse the Muslim reaction in the face of the crusades' success by drawing a parallel with the repercussions of the events of 1830. He did not compare this occupation with that of the Holy Land, nor did he dream of linking them; for him, this modern military operation had simply been the removal of a nest of pirates that had for too long infested the Mediterranean. The people of the nineteenth century hardly ever drew parallels between colonial expansion and the crusades; although giving a colonial village in Algeria the name 'Damietta' could certainly lead us to think that some of the colonists wished to recall a feat of arms performed by the crusaders and so to associate the settlement in the Holy Land with that in which they were involved. Even more so when France became established in Tunisia; but here it was the memory of St Louis, who died at Carthage, which emerged, and that only after 1830 when the bey of Tunis authorized the king of France to raise a monument on the site in memory of his ancestor.[30]

Alongside these comprehensive studies, we must consider the very numerous works which endeavoured to discover the role that people of various lands, not simply France but also Belgium and other European countries, had played in this great movement. Here local history, which arises from a sense of belonging to a small locality, took its place within the perspective of national history. It sometimes aroused controversy, as in the case when a scholar wished to increase the number of participants on a crusade by reference to suspect documents from the Le Mans region.[31]

The French situation has received particular attention here because it is typical and because the association of national feeling and the history of the crusades appeared in France earlier and perhaps more widely than elsewhere. Medieval France had left a particularly strong mark on crusade history through the extent of its participation in crusading expeditions and through the French character of the Latin settlements in the East. Other countries had not experienced this association to the same degree. But other factors played a role. For the Spanish, the very construction of national territory itself was linked to one of the aspects of the crusade movement: the reconquest of the Iberian Peninsula from the Moors was part of the crusade movement and the historians of Spain and Portugal could not omit dealing with it in their national histories; any more than German historians writing the medieval history of the German world could avoid giving space to the crusade against the pagan Slavs and to the *Drang nach Osten*, the 'push to the East' into the Baltic lands, which was also associated with the crusade idea. Although the specific elements of the French situation were not present, others replaced them.

England had its hero: Richard the Lionheart. It is enough to recall the work of Walter Scott to testify that this highly-coloured figure had not been forgotten.[32] But the Lionheart was part of a complete historical tradition which also featured other characters who had themselves held a high rank among the crusaders: Henry II Plantagenet was at one time the hope of the eastern Franks; Richard of Cornwall and Edward I had been among the most effective defenders of the Holy Land and they had their chroniclers who were included in the great editions of texts published in the nineteenth century. The English interest in the history of the crusades is undeniable and English research has contributed greatly to this history. But the English without doubt identified themselves less with the heirs of the crusaders than did the French. Other factors drew them towards the medieval history of the East; and here it is necessary to mention the particular interest that England has shown for travel accounts and among these for pilgrimage reports, which brought about the birth of the Palestine Pilgrims Text Society.

In Italy, where the epic took over the crusading theme by giving it such popularity that paintings of scenes from Tasso's *Gerusalemme liberata* even appeared on the sides of Sicilian wagons, the crusade movement took on distinctive traits: the maritime cities that had participated in it had founded veritable empires, whose history was mingled with glorious memories and was still linked to local patriotism. Genoa boasted that its subjects had taken part in the conquest of Jerusalem in 1099; the doges of Venice had their palace decorated with paintings recalling the greatest hours of the conquest of the Venetian Empire: the capture of Zara and of Constantinople, and so on. The armies of the French Revolution had brought an end to these autonomous states and the great accomplishment of the Italian nineteenth century was the *Risorgimento* and the construction of Italian unity. Yet the local feeling of the former republics remained no less lively, and expressed itself vigorously in the field of scholarship: the publication of chronicles and of documentary sources blossomed, testimony both of scholars' attachment to the memory of their city's past and of their interest in the period of the crusades. In unifying Italy, the House of Savoy did not attempt to curb this expansion of history which made the peninsula one of the most active fields in crusade historiography.[33] In their accounts of the crusades, Italian historians were also anxious to record their ancestors' participation.

For Germany, the first great study of the crusades, written by F. Wilken, does not appear to have been specially influenced by national feeling, not more than Michaud's book, with which it was contemporary.[34] But it is known that the German patriotic revival movement that followed the Napoleonic Wars translated into an expansion of historical study of the German past. These studies held a place in the construction of a new Germany, and it is hardly necessary to mention the motto which Georg Pertz, in 1819, gave the *Monumenta Germaniae Historica* project: *Sanctus amor patriae dat animum*: 'Holy love for the fatherland gives courage'. This patriotic sentiment nourished the medieval studies undertaken under the impetus of Leopold von Ranke, among them the *Geschichte der ersten Kreuzzuges* that Heinrich von Sybel published in 1841.[35] The passionate interest that German scholars showed for the Middle Ages extended to the crusades. In fact, the emperors had personally participated in the crusades, and the death of Frederick Barbarossa in the waters of the Cydnus (the River Göksu, 1190) continued to haunt imaginations. Chivalric literature composed by the *Minnesänger* dealt broadly with the theme of expeditions to Outremer,[36] and had its echo in modern romantic literature: Wagner's Lohengrin came from the lineage of Godfrey de Bouillon. The history of the Teutonic order attracted historians very early on. Above all, it was the development of a school of German philology that aroused the anxiety of one Paul Riant who, in his 'Note sur la Société de l'Orient Latin', explained that he had been led to found this society to prevent the history of the crusades, which still seemed to him in 1875 to remain as ever primarily the domain of French scholarship, from becoming the exclusive prerogative of German erudition.[37]

Were these fears justified? Membership of the Société de l'Orient Latin was open to foreign scholars, and the Swiss Titus Tobler cooperated with Paul Riant in founding it. Many great historians of the crusades, such as Reinhold Röhricht, Hagenmeyer and Desimoni, not forgetting the Russian Khitrovo, have collaborated in its publications.

So is the national angle now tending to fade away? Alphonse Dupront, in his lectures on the 'crusade myth' which were not published until several years after his death, noted that the very concept of the crusade, which had survived until the eighteenth century, vanished when westerners became aware of the decline of the Ottoman Empire, which had still been regarded as threatening Europe in the seventeenth century, and which then became the 'Eastern Question'.[38] The Greek insurrection posed the problem of how this empire could coexist with the new nationalities that aroused such passionate support among liberal opinion. What interested governments was not the liberation of Christian brothers but the preservation or dismemberment of the sultans' empire, as well as this empire's incapacity to assure the security of its Christian subjects. From 1649 onwards, the kings of France established themselves as protectors of the Maronite Church; the French government resumed this tradition and intervened following the serious incidents of 1860, where it acknowledged the role that Emir Abd el-Kader held as protector of the Christians of Damascus by awarding him the grand cross of the Legion of Honour. The problem of the holy places also arose and in 1854 was the origin of the Crimean War. To acknowledge the aid that France had brought the Turkish Empire, the sultan gave France as a gift the church of St Anne of Jerusalem, a memento of the crusaders. A few years later, the marshal of Mac-Mahon, in the name of the French Republic, offered to redecorate the crypt of the Bethlehem basilica. France wished to present itself in this way in the Holy Land, recalling the crusade tradition, in support of the privileged position that it claimed and that was upheld by numerous religious works. A glance through the publications of the Société de l'Orient Latin suffices to reveal that the historians of the crusades were always very much aware of these contemporary questions.

Germany was not outdone. Lutheran piety played its part in devotion to the Holy Land: in 1869 the crown prince of Prussia went on pilgrimage to Jerusalem; Kaiser Wilhelm II went in 1898 to inaugurate the church of Saint Saviour in the course of a spectacular visit. Whereas at Damascus he praised Saladin as the greatest hero of Islam (it was the Hohenzollern Empire's policy to conciliate the Muslims), he also dreamed of finding Frederick Barbarossa's remains, to take them back to Germany.[39] Thus memories of the crusades mingled with other very different viewpoints in an expansionism that translated into the construction of the Baghdad railway. The creation in 1903 of a Deutsches evangelisches Institut für Altertumsforschung des heiligen Landes zu Jerusalem (German Evangelical Institute for the Archaeological Investigation of the Holy Land at Jerusalem) corresponded to the establishment of an École Biblique, a 'Bible School', set up at Jerusalem by the French Dominicans, but it was biblical antiquity rather than the era of the crusades that attracted these scholars. National interests had ceased to inspire historical research on the latter.

The 1914–18 war concluded with the birth of new states in the Middle East, which were initially placed under the mandate of France and Britain. Once again, contact with memories and evidence of the crusading past caused national feeling to emerge, with the notion that the countries under the mandate had renewed their participation with the crusades. General Allenby's entry into Jerusalem in 1917 was depicted in some newspapers of the time as the crusaders' return to the holy city.[40]

It was perhaps in Syria and Lebanon that this national feeling was most noticeable. Whereas the British mandate in Palestine prompted historians to study questions concerning Jewish and Christian Antiquity, the areas placed under the French mandate attracted more attention for their medieval memories. Admittedly, Maurice Barrès had written his *Enquête aux pays du Levant* before the war, but it was not published until 1923; just after the war, in 1918, Louis Madelin published *L'expansion française de la Syrie au Rhin*.[41]

Camille Enlart, who had previously studied Gothic and sixteenth century art in Cyprus, undertook under the aegis of the French High Commission in Syria and Lebanon a study of the crusaders' monuments, which was continued by Paul Deschamps.[42] Both scholars were aware that they were walking in the footsteps of their crusading ancestors. The example of René Grousset, whom some historians have attempted to depict as the eulogist of French colonialism, was unique. Historian of Asia, he attempted to get to the bottom of the history of the Latin states of the East, which appeared to him to be a crucial moment in civilisation, which he had already referred to his *Le reveil de l'Asie* and would take up again in *L'Empire du Levant*, which he subtitled 'The History of the

Eastern Question'. He was thus led to outline a parallel between the formation of the French colonial empire and the Frankish settlement in the East in the Middle Ages.[43] For his part, Jean Longnon published *Les Français d'Outremer au Moyen Age*, giving more attention to the territories conquered from the Byzantine Empire.[44]

This reappearance of national feeling in the history of the crusades could be regarded as belated. Already divergent currents and debates were arising, springing as much from the anti-colonial ideology that triumphed in the years following 1950 and from a wish to give value to non-western cultures, as from attempts to re-evaluate mentalities through psychological analysis, and from the debates between different historical schools of thought. Gaston Dodu had already before the start of the twentieth century introduced an anticlerical interpretation in an institutional study of the kingdom of Jerusalem;[45] Steven Runciman, who tried to take the Byzantine point of view in his monumental *History of the Crusades*, even came to write: 'the chief benefit obtained by western Christendom from the crusades was negative', and concluded thus: 'the Holy War itself was nothing more than a long act of intolerance in the name of God, which is the sin against the Holy Ghost'.[46] It would be possible to give many more examples. The severe judgements brought against the crusades in the name of ideologies that are in other respects very diverse and even contradictory, testify that national feeling is now, at least to all appearances, absent from most of these studies.

At least to all appearances .... What draws so many authors to study the history of the crusades is without any doubt the appeal of an historical phenomenon of great scope which can be considered from many different perspectives; but it is also because it was an epic that involved people stirred by great feelings, who made great sacrifices, who accomplished great exploits, and who belong to the past of each of our countries and who, unconsciously or not, make us desire to know this past better. It cannot be denied that, under new guises, national feeling remains one of the mainsprings of the interest aroused by the history of the crusades.

notes

1. A. V. Murray, 'Questions of Nationality in the First Crusade', *Medieval History*, 1.3 (1991), 61–73.
2. Johannes Kinnamos (extracts with Latin translation under the title 'De secunda expeditione'), in *Recueil des historiens des croisades: Historiens Grecs*, vol. 1 (Paris, 1881), p. 84; English translation in: *Deeds of John and Manuel Comnenus*, by John Kinnamos, trans. by C. M. Brand (New York, 1976), p. 70.

3. Guibert de Nogent, *Dei gesta per Francos et cinq autres textes*, ed. R. B. C. Huygens, Corpus Christianorum. Continuatio Mediaevalis, 127 A (Turnhout, 1996), Bk 1, part 1, lines 106–11, pp. 88–9.

4. *Peregrinationes tres: Saewulf, John of Würzburg, Theodoricus*, ed. R. B. C. Huygens, Corpus Christianorum. Continuatio Medievalis 139 (Turnhout, 1995), pp. 124–6.

5. *L'estoire de la guerre sainte par Ambroise*, ed. G. Paris (Paris, 1897), pp. 226–8, lines 8440–518; *The History of the Holy War: Ambroise's Estoire de la guerre sainte*, ed. M. Ailes and M. Barber, 2 vols (Woodbridge, 2003), vol. 1, lines 8424–98, vol. 2, pp. 145–6.

6. E. Martène and U. Durand, eds, *Thesaurus novus anecdotorum*, vol. 2 (Paris, 1717), col. 405, no. 379.

7. K. Skovgaard-Petersen, *A Journey to the Promised Land. Crusading Theology in the 'Historia de profectione Danorum in Hierosolymam' (c. 1200)* (Copenhagen, 2001).

8. N. Housley, *The Later Crusades, 1274–1580: From Lyons to Alcazar* (Oxford, 1992).

9. Hostiensis, *Summa aurea* (Basle, 1573), col. 905.

10. R. F. Cook and L. S. Crist, *Le second cycle de la croisade* (Geneva, 1972).

11. Torquato Tasso, *Gerusalemme liberata*, ed. Roberto Fedi (Rome and Salerno, 1993).

12. J. Bongars, ed., *Gesta Dei per Francos sive orientalium expeditionum et regni Francorum Hierosolymitani historia* (Hanover, 1611).

13. L. Maimbourg (le P.), *Histoire des croisades pour la délivrance de la Terre Sainte* (Paris, 1675–76, many reprints).

14. G. Constable, 'The Historiography of the Crusades', in *The Crusades from the Perspective of Byzantium and the Muslim World*, ed. A. Laiou and R. Mottahedeh (Dumbarton Oaks, 2001), pp. 1–22, esp. pp. 7–8.

15. Voltaire, *Histoire des croisades par M. Arouet de Voltaire* (Berlin, 1751), republished to follow *Micromegas* (London, 1752), returned to in *Essai sur les moeurs et l'esprit des nations*, first published under the title *Histoire universelle depuis Charlemagne jusqu'à Charles-Quint*, 2 vols (Colmar, 1754), chs 53–8.

16. J. Richard, 'Jean-Baptiste Mailly et l'*Esprit des croisades*', *Mémoires de l'Académie des sciences, arts et belles-lettres de Dijon*, 136 (1997–98), 349–59.

17. Mme Cottin (Sophie Ristaud), *Mathilde, ou mémoires tirés de l'histoire des croisades* (Paris, revolutionary era: year 13/1805), republished many times.

18. J. Richard, 'De Jean-Baptiste Mailly à Joseph-François Michaud: un moment de l'histoire des croisades (1772–1841)', *Crusades*, 1 (2002), 1–12.

19. M. G. Dickson, 'Reinventing the Crusades. The 1806 Prize Competition of the Institut de France', paper read to the 33rd conference of the Society for the Study of French History, University of Edinburgh, March 1999.

20. J. F. Michaud, *Histoire des croisades*, 4th edn (Paris, 1829), vol. 5.

21. C. Constans and P. Lamarque, *Les salles des croisades au château de Versailles* (Versailles and Dossard, 2002).

22. R. A. de Vertot, *Histoire des chevaliers hospitaliers de Saint-Jean de Jérusalem*, 4 vols (Paris, 1726).

23. J. Richard, 'L'histoire des croisades dans la galerie de Versailles', in *Les salles des croisades*, ed. Constans and Lamarque, pp. 7–22; cf. P. Roger, *La noblesse*

de l'ancienne France aux croisades (Paris, 1845) – showing the trust that was placed in these documents.

24. R-H. Bautier, 'La collection de chartes de croisades dite "Collection Courtois"', *Académie des Inscriptions et Belles-Lettres. Comptes rendus des Séances* (1956), pp. 382–86; R-H. Bautier, 'Forgeries et falsifications de documents par une officine généalogique au milieu du XIX siècle', *Bibliothèque de l'Ecole des Chartes*, 132 (1974), 75–93; D. Abulafia, 'Invented Italians in the Courtois Collection', *Crusade and Settlement*, ed. P. W. Edbury (Cardiff, 1985), pp. 135–43. An earlier creation was a 'Duke of Teck' who had supposedly taken part in the crusades: A. V. Murray, 'Walther, Duke of Teck. The Invention of a German Hero of the First Crusade', *Medieval Prosopography*, 13 (1998), 35–54.

25. H. de Boulainvilliers, *Essais sur la noblesse en France* (Amsterdam, 1732); M. de Choiseul-Daillecourt, *De l'influence des croisades sur l'état des peuples de l'Europe* (Paris, 1809).

26. A. Beugnot, 'Rapport sur la publication du *Recueil des historiens des croisades*', *Recueil des Historiens des Croisades, Historiens Occidentaux*, vol. 1 (Paris, 1844), pp. 9–11.

27. *Bibliothèque de l'École des Chartes*, 1st series 3 (1841–42), 409–13.

28. L. de Mas Latrie, *L'île de Chypre: sa situation présente, ses souvenirs du Moyen Age* (Paris, 1879). Cf. H. Wallon, 'Notice sur la vie et les travaux du comte J-M-J-L. de Mas-Latrie', *Institut de France. Académie des Inscriptions. Séance publique du 17 novembre 1899*, reprinted in *Bibliothèque de l'École des Chartes*, 60 (1899), 617–39.

29. Richard, 'De J. B. Mailly à J. F. Michaud', 10.

30. A. Knobler, 'Saint Louis and French Political Culture', *Studies in Medievalism in Europe*, 2.8, ed. L. Workmans and K. Verdurin (Cambridge, 1996), pp. 156–76; Y. Potin, 'Saint Louis l'Africain', *Afrique et histoire*, 1 (2003), 23–74, esp. 54–67.

31. On this scholarly quarrel prompted by a collection of charters from the Le Mans region, see Abbé A. Angot, *Les croisés de Mayenne en 1158. Étude critique* (Le Mans, 1896); J. Laurain, *Un dernier mot sur la croisade de 1158 et le chartrier de Goué* (Laval, 1916).

32. After *Ivanhoe* (1819), which recounted the crusader's return, Walter Scott wrote two novels set during Richard's crusade which make up his 'Tales of the Crusades': *Richard in Palestine, or the Talisman* and *The Betrothed* (1825).

33. The most important of these editions appeared in the *Fonti per la storia d'Italia* (Rome, 1887–) and in the *Regesta chartarum Italiae* (Rome, 1907–).

34. F. Wilken, *Geschichte der Kreuzzüge*, 7 vols in 8 (Leipzig, 1807–32).

35. H. C. L. von Sybel, *Geschichte der ersten Kreuzzuges* (Düsseldorf and Bonn, 1841). This German scholarship would later open up a new road of research with Carl Erdmann's *Die Entstehung des Kreuzzugsgedanken*, 'the origin of the idea of crusade' (Stuttgart, 1935); translated by M. W. Baldwin and W. Goffart as *The Origin of the Idea of Crusade* (Princeton, 1977).

36. F. W. Wentzlaff-Eggebert, *Kreuzzugsdichtung des Mittelalters* (Berlin, 1860).

37. P. Riant, 'Note sur la Société de l'Orient Latin', Paris, Bibliothèque Sainte-Geneviève, MS 3663, fol. 173f.

38. A. Dupront, *Le mythe de la croisade*, ed. P. Nora, 4 vols (Paris, 1997), vol. 1, pp. 520–40.

39. Ibid., pp. 539–40; Carole Hillenbrand, *The Crusades: Islamic Perspectives* (Edinburgh, 1999), p. 593; J. Riley-Smith, 'Islam and the Crusades in History

and Imagination, 8 November 1898–11 September 2001', *Crusades*, 2 (2003), 151–2.

40. On this see Elizabeth Siberry, 'Images of the Crusades in the Nineteenth and Twentieth Centuries', in *The Oxford Illustrated History of the Crusades*, ed. J. Riley-Smith (Oxford, 1995), pp. 383–4. See also Vivien Gilbert, *The Romance of the Last Crusade: With Allenby to Jerusalem* (New York and London, 1923).

41. A. M. Barrès, *Une Enquête aux pays du Levant*, 2 vols (Paris, 1923); L. Madelin, *L'expansion française de la Syrie au Rhin* (Paris, 1918).

42. C. Enlart, *Le monuments des croisés dans le royaume de Jérusalem*, 2 vols and 2 vols of pictures (Paris, 1925–27); P. Deschamps, *Les châteaux des Croisés en Terre Sainte*, 3 vols and 3 vols of pictures (Paris, 1934–73).

43. R. Grousset, *Le réveil de l'Asie. L'impérialisme britannique et la révolte des peuples* (Paris, 1924); R. Grousset, *Histoire des croisades et du royaume franc de Jérusalem*, 3 vols (Paris, 1934–36); R. Grousset, *L'Empire du Levant. Histoire de la question d'Orient* (Paris, 1946); Dupront, *Le mythe de la croisade*, p. 535, writes of 'the confrontation of two worlds'.

44. J. Longnon, *Les Français d'Outremer au Moyen Age*, 2nd edn (Paris, 1929).

45. G. Dodu, *Histoire des institutions monarchiques dans le royaume de Jérusalem* (Paris, 1894). For another unfavourable view of the Franks' behaviour in the Holy Land, see H. Prutz, *Kulturgeschichte der Kreuzzüge* (Berlin, 1883).

46. Steven Runciman, *A History of the Crusades*, 3 vols (Cambridge, 1951–54), vol. 3, pp. 472, 480.

part III
images of the protagonists

10

the crusaders' perceptions
of their opponents

margaret jubb

introduction

We would not expect western Christian writers to paint a neutral picture of their opponents in holy war, but the caricatured and contemptuous denigration of the Muslim enemy that we find in early chronicles and in epic poetry still has the power to shock us. How could these writers have maintained and perpetuated the manifest fiction that the Muslims were pagan idolaters, when direct contact during the crusades would have exposed the falsehood of such a preconception? How could later writers have perpetuated the equally manifest, but in this case conspicuously (self-)flattering, fiction that Saladin had a noble French mother, had been dubbed a knight in western fashion, and had even covertly baptized himself on his deathbed? Evidently these were fictions in which both writers and their audiences colluded and which they wanted to believe, but why? In order to address this question, it is necessary to set the texts in their historical and literary contexts, and to examine the conditions of their production, reception and consumption. What was the prevailing political and ideological climate, and how was the crusader movement faring at the time? Was the writer a cleric or a layperson, was he based in the West or the East, and what can we determine about the nature of his intended audience and the purpose of the writing – instruction, propaganda, and/or entertainment?

For the purposes of this chapter, we will limit our discussion to the crusaders' perceptions of their Muslim enemies in the East. As the suggestions for further reading show, there is no shortage of scholarship on the subject, but the earlier studies tend to be more descriptive than analytical.[1] Thus they catalogue the typical features of the conventional portrayal of the enemy, and comment on the surprising extent to which this was at odds with reality, in terms of what was known at the time in the West about Islam and its adherents.[2] However, they tend not to address the more interesting question of the motivation behind the image-making. Modern critics, by contrast, have deconstructed not only the medieval Christian writers' representation of their opponents, but also their own scholarly predecessors' representation of the medieval world. Thus, for example, Blanks shows how certain Protestant scholars viewed the medieval Christian mindset through the unsympathetic lens of their own distaste for Catholicism.[3] In more general terms, postmodernism has led scholars to reject universalizing tendencies. They have thus replaced the erroneous idea that the crusaders' perceptions of their opponents were uniform and static, and predominantly negative, with more nuanced views.

ethnicity and culture

The identifying labels that Christian writers attach to the enemy as a group are at once revealing of their perceptions and mindset, and yet also potentially confusing for modern readers to interpret. They have their roots in cultural and religious history, rather than in ethnological reality. The ethnocultural term 'barbarians' (*barbarae nationes*), used quite frequently by chroniclers of the First Crusade, is a case in point. It has its origins in Antiquity, when it was used by the Greeks to designate 'others' alien to their urban civilization, but it is best understood in its medieval crusading context in opposition to the term with which it commonly co-occurs, namely, 'Latins'.[4] The barbarians are those who are distinct from the Latin (western) crusaders, most notably in language and customs.

It is significant that the medieval perception of ethnicity was predominantly cultural, rather than racial. The oft-quoted Regino of Prüm (d. 900 AD) declared that 'the various nations differ from one another in descent, customs, language and law'.[5] Robert Bartlett has argued convincingly that to a large extent in the Middle Ages, and particularly within Europe itself, ethnicity was a social construct, rather than a biological given.[6] The last three of Regino's four parameters of difference are socially determined and therefore malleable, susceptible to change over time. Even descent is not as transparently biological as a modern reader might assume. From the medieval Christian viewpoint, all humanity was ultimately descended from Adam and Eve and originally spoke the same language. People were only split into different races when, post-Babel, they began speaking different languages; racial diversity arose from linguistic diversity, not vice versa. Moreover, the genetic component of race was outweighed by the environmental influences of climate and geography, so that, for instance, dark skin colour was determined by exposure to the sun in hot, dry conditions, and was susceptible to change over generations in a different climate. Hahn notes the disconnection between 'dominant medieval racial discourses ... and the common assumption that colour constitutes the default category of difference',[7] hence the incompatibility of race studies in the modern sense with medievalism.

Nevertheless, the black/white dichotomy was used widely in medieval texts and images to convey meaning, but it was a meaning symbolic of religious and cultural difference, as much as of race. In the fantasy of some epics, bodily colour was linked to religion and the skin of converts changed from black to white upon baptism.[8] The widespread association of blackness with strangeness carried strongly negative connotations and was used to create monstrous others.[9] It was exploited particularly in popular narrative where there was a need for obvious visual cues to evoke a communal response, and where dehumanization ensured that the audience could never identify or sympathize with the monstrous 'other'. In the *Song of Roland*, for instance, the black skin colour and diabolical physiognomy of the enemy were the surface signs of their perfidious nature. They connoted evil in antithesis to the righteousness of the Christians, and left no doubt that the enemy would be the losers in the end. In a seminal article, Cohen has used the discourse of psychoanalysis and postcolonialism to explore further the question of race as it was presented in France and England in the Middle Ages.[10] He investigates why the conventional portrayal of the black, demonic Saracen was perpetuated in western literature long after the religious and territorial ambitions that originally motivated it were relevant. An episode from the fourteenth-century *Grandes Chroniques de France* in which the Saracen foot-soldiers don black horned masks, which make them look like devils, in order to frighten the Christians enables him to expose both the constructed nature of racial difference and the writer's tacit admission of its artificiality. Cohen argues that the fantasy rested on a structure of collective pleasure, in which writers and audiences were complicit, and which explained its perpetuation and its resistance to change.

It is all the more important to downplay the significance of race in the modern sense to the medieval mind, given the reliance of many modern readers of medieval texts on translations, which render the original Latin *'nationes'* and *'gentes'*, in very different ways in different contexts.

Bartlett gives an illuminating and cautionary analysis of the renderings of 'gens/gentes' in an English translation of William of Malmesbury.[11] These range from the neutral 'people', through 'nation', 'tribe', to the distinctly biological 'blood', 'stock' and 'family'. It is true that the chroniclers of the First Crusade did use some apparently ethnic terms, such as Assyrians, Persians, Parthians, Publicans, Azymites, as well as the more strictly factual Turks and Arabs, to describe the enemy. However, as Luchitskaja has shown, these predominantly archaic terms represent a conservative superimposition of ancient history and literary tradition on medieval reality.[12] They are used for their resonance as stereotypical categories and for their power to impress the reader with the fearsome multitude of the enemy, rather than for their documentary accuracy.

The overtones of the term 'Saracen', which is the generic designation of the Muslim enemy in chronicles and epics alike, are evidently more religious than they are racial. Indeed, by the beginning of the fourteenth century, the term had come to designate indiscriminately any active enemies of Christendom, including Saxons and Vikings. Originally, however, it referred specifically to the Muslims and its justification is to be found in biblical tradition. The Christians were descended from Isaac, the son of Abraham by Sarah, whereas the Muslims were descended from Ishmael, his son by Sarah's Egyptian maid, Hagar. By adopting the name 'Saracens', the descendants of Ishmael falsely claimed descent from Sarah. For Christian writers, the term Saracens designated membership of a separate religious community, rather than an ethnic grouping.

the distorted depiction of religious practices

It is significant that the term 'Muslims' is absent from medieval sources. Instead, the crusaders' opponents are variously described by the chroniclers as 'infidels', 'Gentiles', 'enemies of Christ/God', and above all, 'pagans'. William of Tyre (c. 1130–86), as we will see further below, is interesting because he does not use the term 'pagans', but he value-loads the descriptors, 'infidels' and 'enemies of God', by setting them in binary opposition to terms such as 'the faithful' and 'soldiers of Christ', which designate the crusaders themselves.[13] These semantic oppositions are revealing of a clerical mindset that viewed the world in Manichean terms as a battleground on which the forces of Evil were engaged in an apocalyptic struggle with the forces of Good under the command of Christ. From this perspective, the crusaders' actions were both justified and glorified, and they themselves were seen as analogous to the Old Testament army of the God of Israel, or to the apostles and martyrs engaged in the eradication of paganism. It followed that their opponents must be the enemies of God and the persecutors of His church. Even Saladin, who later became an adoptive hero for the Christians, was initially cast by western clerical writers in the mode of an Antichrist, bent on persecuting the Christians and obliterating the practice of their religion.[14]

In the epics and in many of the crusading chronicles, the opponents of the Christians are described as 'pagans', and they are endowed with the polytheistic and idolatrous traits of ancient paganism. There is a blatant discrepancy between the idea of Saracens venerating the idols of Apollo, Tervagant, Jupiter and Mahoumet, Mahon, or other garbled versions of Mohammed, and the reality of Islam as a monotheistic, aniconic religion. Beginning with Munro,[15] scholars have observed the deliberate nature of the misrepresentation, and its curious persistence, even in juxtaposition to more accurate information. For example, in the work of Arnold of Lübeck, the account of an envoy sent by Frederick Barbarossa to the court of Saladin is quoted in detail. It explains, among other things, the Muslim belief that God was the creator of all things and that Mohammed was his Prophet. Yet, despite the inclusion of this information, Arnold has Saladin swear 'by virtue of my god, Mohammed'.[16] Munro does not venture to comment on the possible reasons for this inconsistency, but other scholars have offered a variety of explanations. C. Meredith Jones suggested that 'a traditional type of "Saracen" was invented and reproduced endlessly', and that western representations of Islam derived more from literary sources than from actual contact with Muslims.[17] More contentiously, and betraying his distaste both for Catholicism and for the medieval Christian worldview which he associated with it, Jones castigated the wilful and malicious misrepresentations as the products of fanaticism.

Norman Daniel, whose pioneering survey, *Islam and the West*,[18] is still the best starting point for study of this field, was also shocked by the wild inaccuracy and patent hostility of what he found in the medieval texts – crude insults to the Prophet, gross caricatures of Muslim ritual, and scurrilous portrayals of Muslims as libidinous, gluttonous, savage, bloodthirsty and semi-human. Daniel was the main source for the short section of Edward Said's famous book, *Orientalism*, which deals with the medieval period. Said concludes that 'Islam became an image ... whose function was not so much to represent Islam in itself, as to represent it for the medieval Christian'.[19] Richard Southern famously observed that Islam was Christendom's greatest problem,[20] not only because it was a military threat, but also because it raised important questions about definition and understanding of the 'other', and of the self in relation to the 'other'. In the modern period, which is the main subject of Said's *Orientalism*, derisive western attitudes towards the Orient arise from a Eurocentric sense of cultural superiority, but it is important to remember that in the medieval period, Christendom approached Islamic civilization from a position of inferiority, which gave rise to ambivalent feelings of attraction and repulsion. Tolan has observed that the pagan enemy in the *Song of Antioch* present a deformed mirror image of the crusaders. Devoted to the devil rather than God, and granted indulgences by the caliph rather than the pope, they hope to buy or fight their way into heaven.[21] By casting the Muslim enemy as a negative mirror image of themselves, libidinous where they were restrained, and worshipping hollow idols instead of the true God, Christian writers were able to enhance their threatened self-image and bolster their own faith. Westerners, as Tolan reminds us, defined their superiority primarily in religious terms, although cultural and other concerns were inevitably implicated.[22]

The motivation behind the negative stereotypes of the enemy has given rise to much scholarly debate in recent decades. Daniel himself adopted a less judgmental attitude towards the medieval Christian viewpoint in his later book, *Heroes and Saracens: An Interpretation of the Chansons de Geste*.[23] Dismissing the idea advanced by Southern that popular ignorance allowed the perpetuation of the notion of the Saracens as idolaters,[24] he suggests rather that the audience were called on to suspend their disbelief. The misrepresentation of the Saracens was playful exaggeration, a caricature intended to amuse; it was not the product of fanaticism.[25] In a reversal of his earlier position, he concludes, 'The songs are not Crusade propaganda, as I once believed, but they are good propaganda for a life of daring and adventure.'[26] Most recent scholars have taken issue with this disconnection of the early epics from political and religious concerns. For example, though he agrees that the portrayal of the Saracens in the epic is consciously distorted, Trotter argues that it was not intended as pure entertainment, and that it did have 'a historical role which the Church generally, and the crusade propagandists more particularly, were well aware of'.[27] Admittedly, the early epics, such as the *Song of Roland*, portray fictionally elaborated campaigns against the Saracens in Spain, which predate the historical crusades to the Holy Land. Nevertheless, they are roughly contemporary with the earliest chronicles of the crusades, and they reflect similar attitudes towards the enemy. Most scholars would now agree that the literary fiction of the idolatrous Saracens was deliberately created and propagated for the purposes of ideological propaganda, and played an important part in the creation of the crusading ideal. As Tolan has observed, by affirming the religious alterity of Islam, and denying it its status as a rival monotheistic religion, Christian writers kept the boundaries clear between religious truth and error.[28]

Flori gives a particularly illuminating account of the origins and meaning of the West's caricatured portrayal of Islam, known in medieval texts as 'the law of the Saracens'.[29] He notes that all the chroniclers of the First Crusade, with the exception of Albert of Aix or Aachen, who wrote later, report the polytheism of the Muslims and their worship of idols, particularly Mohammed. Guibert de Nogent, who is more circumspect than most, attracts particular attention because of what he tells us about his sources and, more interestingly, about his attitudes towards them. He evidently found little written information about Mohammed, but a profusion of defamatory oral tales, which he has no scruples about repeating, however sceptical he may be about their veracity. He justifies the repetition of these calumnies by saying that it is safe to speak ill of one whose wickedness has always transcended the evil told of him.[30] Guibert does refute the notion that Mohammed was regarded as a god, but in general, as far as he is concerned, ideological truth is more important than objective factual truth. Flori concludes that the medieval image of Islam in the West reflects more the ideological projection that the West made of it than Islam itself.[31]

As regards the motivation behind this ideological projection, Flori considers in turn the various explanations of other scholars.[32] Popular ignorance of Islam would have allowed false images to take root, but, given access over time through the accounts of returning crusaders and pilgrims to more accurate information about Islam, it is not a complete explanation. Popular indifference is not a viable explanation either. Evidently the epic poets sought to captivate and entertain their public with their negative images of the Saracens. In so doing they were undoubtedly pandering to audience expectations and preferences, but the very recognition of these preferences belies the notion of public indifference towards Islam. Far from being indifferent to Islam, westerners were both fascinated and repelled by it; they wanted and needed to control and subjugate it through discourse. In elaborating their portrayal of the idolatrous and bloodthirsty Saracens, the poets drew not, as has sometimes been suggested, on malicious deformation of reported fact, but rather on what Flori terms 'invention',[33] which we might expand as imagination fed by an amalgam of folklore, reading of the ancients, the Bible and what Tolan has called the 'technicolour horror stories'[34] of Christians martyred at the hands of pagan rulers. The role of 'invention' is particularly apparent in the names that the epic poets give to the

Saracen foe; they are drawn from biblical tradition, Graeco-Roman history, legend and fantasy.[35] The use of a well-known name like 'Judas' imparted instant disreputability and hostility to the true faith, whilst a large group of invented names beginning with 'Mal-' stressed the falseness of the enemy's own religion.

Some critics have proposed a psychoanalytical explanation for the denigration of the Saracens. Adducing Freudian theory, Brault argues convincingly that the Christians' fears were caused as much by something inside themselves as by the more obvious external threat posed by the military and cultural power of Islam.[36] Perhaps the Christians were unconsciously projecting their own vices, magnified, onto the enemy, and attempting in the process to exorcize their own feelings of guilt about their veneration of the relics and statues of saints. It is certainly the case that the medieval western image of Islam often has more in common with contemporary western Christianity than with Islam itself. The art historian, Camille, has observed that 'one way in which propaganda functions is by naturalizing the other, dressing him in deviations of our own convention to form a travesty we can understand'.[37] Hence we find in western sources the invention of a Saracen counter-Trinity, composed of Mohammed, Tervagant and Apollo. By blackening the Saracen enemy with the charge of idol worship, the crusaders could justify their conduct towards them. In a further literary twist, when the unholy Trinity proves powerless, the Saracens are shown cursing and ironically breaking their own idols. Thus, Camille argues, western writers constructed a set of images for the imageless religion of Islam in order 'to simulate and stimulate its destruction'.[38]

The Christians' espousal of holy war obviously represented a major shift away from the early pacifism of the church. In order to effect this volte-face, and perform an act of collective self-justification, Flori argues that the West needed to establish the complete ideological demolition of their adversaries.[39] The early martyrs had died at the hands of idolatrous pagans, so the crusaders should earn their heavenly crown at the hands of no less idolatrous pagans. The stereotype of the idolatrous Saracen was propagated in the final analysis, because it fitted crusading ideology.

In a fascinating article, based on the insights of postcolonial and feminist theory, Kinoshita argues that the ideological dichotomy of the *Song of Roland* ('pagans are wrong and Christians are right') masks a crisis of identity among the Franks, and a fear of non-differentiation.[40] The apparent dualism of the epic is belied both by the evident parallelism which constructs the Saracens as mirror images of the Christians and by the possibility of the Saracens' conversion. She suggests that the women characters, Bramimonde and Aude, play a pivotal role in the construction and maintenance of slippery otherness.

Taking a broader perspective, and drawing on the insights of sociologists and anthropologists, Blanks has argued that stereotypes are cognitive devices for coming to terms with the alien; they simplify the multiplicity of experience and enable us to cope with it.[41] The negative stereotype of the Saracen enabled the crusaders to accommodate the complex mixture of their feelings towards their opponents – a compound of fear, hatred, curiosity, envy and even, sometimes, as we will see, respect. The need that the stereotype fulfilled explains the seemingly inexplicable fact that premodern perceptions of Muslims were very resistant to change, even when more accurate information about Islam was available. In a curious example of a clash between illumination and text, at the very point where the chronicler William of Tyre explains that the Saracens rejected the worship of idols, the illuminator of one of the French translations of his text shows the Saracens worshipping a naked idol in the temple in Jerusalem.[42] Chronicles later than those of the First Crusade generally portrayed Islam as a variant, heretical version of Christianity, rather than as pagan idolatry, yet the idolatrous stereotype lived on in liturgical drama and saints' lives until the sixteenth century, assuring Christian audiences of the truth of their own religion and the error of the other. Hahn has argued that all fantasies are culturally grounded. 'Their force and intelligibility rely upon pervasive, well-established connections that don't require, and frequently resist, conscious explanation.'[43] Postmodernism rejects the notion of universals, so we should not be surprised if recent scholarship does not offer an integrated explanation for the crusaders' negative stereotyping of their opponents. It has at least encouraged critics to approach the past from a variety of angles, thus enriching our understanding of the crusaders with the insights of postcolonialism, literary theory, psychoanalysis and anthropology. These arguments are of general interest to non-medievalists, for they show how denigration of the other, as with the Nazis and the Jews, can serve to defend one's own ideology.

more positive images of the enemy

Despite the persistence of the stereotypes discussed above, it must be emphasised that the crusaders' perceptions of their opponents were not uniformly negative. They modulated considerably over time and ran the full range from contempt to admiration. Even early texts, such as the *Song of Roland* and the *Gesta Francorum,* show a degree of admiration for the enemy. The *Gesta Francorum* is the account of an anonymous fighting man actively involved in the First Crusade, and as such it is revealing of the mentality and perceptions of the founders of the crusader states. Although he disapproves of any non-Christian religion, the author evidently respects the Turks as valiant opponents in battle. Direct observation of their opponents prompted other chroniclers to praise the military prowess and valour of the Muslims. To account for it, and no doubt to flatter themselves, they recalled the legendary common descent of the Turks and Franks from the ancient Trojans.[44] According to the author of the *Gesta Francorum*, the Turks and Franks alone were naturally born to be knights.[45] The inclusion in the *Roland* of worthy individual Saracens might be partly explained in literary terms. The enemy in general are presented as dehumanized monsters, so alien that the audience has no compunction about their slaughter, but they cannot, as Tolan has argued, be seen as completely other, for that would reflect ill on the Christians.[46] In order for the Christians to emerge well from the tale, they need to be engaged with some opponents who are their equals in valour.

At first it was just the fighting qualities of their opponents that attracted the Christians' attention, but soon they began to recognize and respect their moral virtues as well. In his study of epic poetry, Bancourt has observed that by the last quarter of the twelfth century, the portrait of the loyal Saracen had grown in popularity.[47] Some of the Saracens still fitted the negative stereotype: proud, cruel, cowardly and treacherous, but others, such as Aumont in the *Chanson d'Aspremont*, were the equals in loyalty, courtesy and generosity of the Christians, and observed a common chivalric code. This emerges clearly from the encounter between Olivier and Fierabras in the epic *Fierabras*. When the eponymous Fierabras accidentally kills Olivier's horse, he offers him his own horse in its place. Olivier refuses, so in order not to disadvantage him, Fierabras dismounts and fights on foot.[48] As I have argued elsewhere, 'it is tempting to seek historical parallels to explain this new climate of mutual respect … between supposed enemies'.[49] One such parallel may be found in an incident that occurred during the siege of Jaffa, when Richard the Lionheart's horse fell under him, and Saladin's brother, Saphadin, sent a groom with two horses as a gift to his enemy.[50] In place of the old vertical divide between Christians and Muslims, Bancourt observes the emergence of a horizontal divide in each camp distinguishing the noble elite, with their superior chivalric ethos which transcends political and religious differences, from the common herd with their blinkered adherence to traditional loyalties.[51] Perhaps the most striking example of this is the funeral elegy given to the enemy Cornumarant in the crusade epic, the *Song of Jerusalem*. Despite the fact that he has died fighting the cause of a rival faith, the Christians clearly recognise his exceptional virtues.

Increasingly, the attribution of moral virtues to the epic enemy was accompanied by the possibility of their conversion to Christianity. Poets frequently observe that if only a noble opponent were to be baptised, there would be no knight to equal him. The Saracen Balan in the *Chanson d'Aspremont* does indeed convert, and is persuaded to do so in part by the military prowess of the Franks, but also by the perceived superiority of their culture and religion. If, as is generally supposed, this epic was composed between the capture of Jerusalem by Saladin in 1187 and the launch of the Third Crusade, it might indeed have served as crusading, even of missionary, propaganda. The conversion of the pagan king Corbaran in the late thirteenth-century crusade epic, *La Chrétienté Corbaran* is modelled, as Tolan has shown,[52] on the conversion of Constantine and that of Clovis. A former persecutor of the Christians becomes their ardent defender, and the hope is raised that a simple solution will thus be found to the Saracen problem. It is perhaps a rather fantastic, if nonetheless comforting hope, born of pessimism in the face of the crisis threatening the crusader kingdom in the thirteenth century. Epic tradition, from the *Song of Roland* to the Crusade Cycle, is rich in examples of Saracen women converting to Christianity, adopting western ways and marrying Christian husbands. This no doubt exemplifies epic wish-fulfilment, as Cook has observed.[53] Its effect is to reflect glory onto Christian culture, and to offer the hope of an eventual triumph over Islam by intermarriage and assimilation, rather than by force of arms, a vision which would have been all the more appealing in the light of the crusaders' declining military fortunes after 1187.

saladin – an extended case study

Direct observation and consequent admiration of the virtues of individual Muslims confronted the crusaders with a problem to which, as Hamilton has argued, the only 'theologically correct solution was that of conversion'.[54] Though this was possible in the literary world of epic, in the real world many of the Muslims whom the Christians most admired showed no inclination towards conversion. How then did Christian writers deal with the problem, particularly acute in the case of Saladin, whose reputation for magnanimity and chivalry, notably during the Third Crusade, made such a strong impression on them?[55] Dante famously dealt with the problem in his *Divine Comedy* by assigning

Saladin to Limbo, where he figures alongside other good pagans who are spared from Hell.[56]

Initially, Christian reactions to Saladin's devastating success in uniting the forces of Islam, inflicting a crushing defeat on the Franks at Hattin, and capturing Jerusalem in October 1187, were strongly hostile.[57] We have seen above how some western clerical writers cast him in the mode of an Antichrist. The bulk of critical commentary on Saladin was written in the West, and the most venomous and lurid of all, an anonymous Latin poem, was ostensibly produced as a piece of crusading propaganda. The writer focused on Saladin's rise to power, which had, from the Christian viewpoint, been alarmingly and apparently unnaturally rapid. Some of the accusations levelled against him may have had a basis in popular rumour reported by Christians from the Latin Kingdom. It is even possible that the disdain in which the relatively lowly born Kurd was initially regarded by the Muslim ruling classes may have coloured Frankish perceptions of his background. At any rate, the poem stigmatizes him as an ignominious upstart and a treacherous usurper of power, who had gained preferment within the household of his master Nūr al-Dīn by becoming the secret lover of his wife. He had then supposedly won control of Egypt by committing a double murder, before returning to take control of Syria by disposing of Nūr al-Dīn himself and his heir.

Saladin is further vilified in the *Itinerarium Peregrinorum*. The original short version of this text, from which the material relating to Saladin's early years derives, has been dated to 1191–92,[58] and was probably written by an Englishman who had come from the West with the Third Crusade. He may have drawn on gossip current among the Franks in the East to elaborate his account of Saladin's early years. The detail differs from that found in the Latin poem, but similar points are made; Saladin was an upstart who had risen from very lowly origins to be ruler of dominions far and wide. The origins ascribed to him in the *Itinerarium*, however, are particularly unsavoury and demeaning. His first kingdom was located in brothels and his army in taverns, for he started out in life as a pimp and regulator of prostitutes.

The chronicle of William, Archbishop of Tyre (c. 1130–86), is particularly interesting, because it is the work of a writer who was born and grew up in Jerusalem, but who spent 20 years studying in the West before returning to the crusader kingdom. It would be fascinating to know what picture he painted of the Muslim world in his lost work about the deeds of eastern princes, but, as it is, we have only the surviving chronicle to study. He wrote it in order to analyse the reasons for the declining fortunes of the crusader states and to advocate ways in which the Christians, helped by those in the West, could save Jerusalem. William's perceptions of the Muslims in general have attracted considerable scholarly attention and debate. As we saw above, unlike many Christian writers, William does not refer to the Muslims as 'pagans'; he seems to have regarded them as believers of a different kind. He recognized the virtues and achievements of individuals, albeit only those who were in the upper echelons of Muslim society, and hence his peers. Nūr al-Dīn, for all that he is described on his death as the 'greatest persecutor of the Christian name and faith', yet earns recognition in a quasi-obituary as a 'just, shrewd and provident prince, and religious according to his people's traditions'.[59] Schwinges has somewhat controversially described William's overall attitudes to Muslims as 'tolerance', which he glosses in a recent article as 'informal tolerance combined with dogmatic intolerance'.[60] The application of the modern notion of tolerance to the medieval period is of course fraught with danger. Such a notion would have been alien to the medieval viewpoint; both Christians and Muslims claimed Jerusalem as their holy city and there could be no permanent stand-off between them. There was no doubt a certain amount of respect between individuals on opposite sides of the religious divide, and a fair amount of mutual forbearance born of political necessity, but that is a long way from tolerance.

In any case, William is significantly less positive in his assessment of Saladin than he had been with Nūr al-Dīn. Though he praises his intelligence and perspicacity, he sharply criticizes his tyranny and pride. His assessment of Saladin as an individual seems to have been coloured, understandably so, by the threat posed to the crusader kingdom at the time of writing. It is revealing to compare and contrast the more positive picture of Saladin that emerges from the Old French translation and continuations of William.[61] Not only does the French text omit entirely William's insistence on Saladin's flouting of feudal and natural justice and on the role of fortune in his unnatural rise to power, it also adds small details which serve to increase the prestige and interest attaching to Saladin as an individual (and by association to the Christians), and credits him with behaviour which accords with a mutually recognised noble, chivalric ethos. The *Eracles*, as the French text together with its complicated network of continuations became known, was arguably less a tool of instruction and propaganda and more a source of interesting and inspiring deeds of days gone by. It points the way forward to a time when Saladin would be treated in western literature no longer as the terrifying and very present threat that he was to William, but as the adoptive chivalrous hero of the West. From the late thirteenth century, stories about Saladin's knightly and courtly virtues began to be circulated quite separately from narratives of crusade history in Italian and Spanish collections of tales and exempla, where clearly there was no political or ideological agenda to glorify the crusaders by association with a noble enemy, or to mitigate the impact of their defeat.

In order to account for Saladin's exceptionally generous and courteous behaviour, which was historically attested, further elaborated by legend, and even acknowledged in some early texts which were othewise hostile to him, western writers had recourse to three principal fictions, the combined effect of which enabled them to erase his Muslim otherness, and to appropriate him as a hero in their own image. The first of these stories credited Saladin with noble French blood; he was supposedly descended on his mother's side from the counts of Ponthieu. The story survives independently as *La Fille du comte de Pontieu*, composed some time before 1250 in the West for Marie of Ponthieu, whose lineage it must have been intended to aggrandize by association with the by now illustrious Saladin. It was subsequently associated with the history of the Latin kingdom by its incorporation in the *Estoires d'Outremer et de la naissance Salehadin*,[62] the archetype of which probably dates from about 1250.

The second story, the *Ordene de chevalerie* (*Order of Chivalry*), recounts Saladin's knighting by Hugh of Tiberias. We should note that both the *Itinerarium* and the Pseudo-Ernoul[63] in the late twelfth century had briefly mentioned the knighting of Saladin, albeit at the hands of Humphrey of Toron, rather than Hugh of Tiberias. The *Ordene*, like the *Fille* story, originated in northern France some time before 1250. It was immensely popular, it survives in both verse and prose versions and was incorporated in one of the surviving manuscripts of the *Estoires d'Outremer*. These stories about Saladin's supposed Christian descent and dubbing as a knight have been seen by some as an attempt by western writers to put a good face on defeat, but Hamilton does not accept this view.[64] He argues that Saladin's descendants, the Ayyūbid sultans of Egypt, ruled Jerusalem until 1250 and crusading zeal was still strong at the time of composition; the political and ideological climate was therefore not conducive to the idealization of an enemy who was responsible for the loss of Jerusalem. Hamilton sees the stories as a way of accommodating a good Muslim in the thought-world of western Christendom.[65] For my own part, I would emphasize their primary function as entertainment, and argue that Saladin was being transformed through them into a literary construct, a hero in the western mould, rather than an historical figure.

Since knighthood was essentially a Christian institution, the question of whether a Muslim could actually become a knight is an interesting one which I have explored in greater detail elsewhere.[66] In the original verse version of the *Ordene de chevalerie*, Hugh is quite blunt in his initial refusal to instruct his captor, Saladin, in the making of knights. The stench of a dungheap cannot be disguised under a silk cloth, nor can the unholy stench of the unbeliever be cloaked with the mantle of knighthood. Though he showed no inclination towards baptism, Saladin was nevertheless instructed as a knight, and also dubbed, at least in the prose version of the *Ordene*. It is noticeable that the dubbing ritual is presented in a completely secular way. Tolan argues that 'medieval authors assimilated Saladin into the order of knighthood in the same way they assimilated the great warriors of antiquity'.[67] The order of knighthood was thus seen to be more universal than the Christian culture with which it was usually associated.

It was not long, however, before wishful thinking prompted western writers to present Saladin as inclining towards Christianity, and even visiting the West to find out about the Christian way of life at first hand.[68] There was also a separate literary tradition which presented him as a sage reflecting on the merits of the three religions, Judaism, Islam and Christianity. Perhaps the most interesting stories, however, are those in which he observes Christian practice at first hand and is ultimately deterred from conversion by certain features which he finds offensive. These include the offertory, which he criticizes because it is made to the church rather than to the poor, the undue reverence in which the pope, a mere mortal, is held, and the immoral behaviour of the clergy in general. The purpose of such criticism is not to undermine the Christian faith towards which Saladin is supposedly inclining, but rather to make him the vehicle of some pointed anticlerical and anti-papal satire. According to some western writers, Saladin did take the ultimate step of converting, albeit covertly, to Christianity. Both the anonymous *Récits d'un ménestrel de Reims* (composed c. 1260) and the fifteenth-century prose *Saladin* recount how Saladin performed a curious auto-baptism on his deathbed, a ritual in which it is significant that no priest plays a part. Though the universal claims of Christianity are thus advanced by Saladin's apparent conversion, an anti-clerical agenda is once again in evidence.

Saladin as literary construct became a model that Christian writers could use, not only to castigate vices, particularly clerical abuses, on their own side, but also to reflect and promote values which they held dear in their own society and time. For example, his portrayal in the fifteenth-century prose *Saladin* as bold fighter, chivalrous opponent, generous host, great traveller, and courtly lover, accords with and glorifies the values of the Burgundian court for whom the text was composed, even as it may also have served to promote the ducal policy of crusade against the Turk, by raising the possibility that if other Muslims like Saladin could be persuaded of the superiority of Christianity, further crusades were highly feasible.

the image of the enemy in later texts

In her study of late medieval Italian literature, Allaire suggests that the softening and humanizing of the Muslim enemy in general into 'noble Saracen' may have been partly the result of European literary constructions inspired by the positive model of Saladin.[69] She notes that although some of the negative conventions of medieval epic survive in the Italian texts, there is an increasing tendency for Saracens to be portrayed as courageous and chivalrous opponents, and for the emphasis to be placed on the deeds of individuals. In a contrasting study of humanist texts from fifteenth-century Italy, Bisaha studies the negative portrayal of the Turks as a group.[70] They are labelled 'barbarians' and stand in binary contrast to the civilization of the West. Yet the term 'barbarians', though it may seem to echo the terminology of the early crusading chronicles, is here used with very different, secular overtones. These new barbarians are not the religious enemy of old, but rather the enemies of learning and culture. Equated with the Goths who were blamed for the destruction of ancient Rome, they are framed in the language of classical rhetoric. This marks a significant departure from the language of religion, or the language of chivalry with which they had been described in earlier texts. Though they emerge generally in a negative light as violent and lustful, yet occasionally a more neutral, or even positive picture intervenes, prompted by admiration and respect for their military machine and enormous empire. Bisaha argues that the humanists' vision of the Turks is interesting for two reasons. Firstly, it provided an alternative secular discourse in which to frame the enemy, a cultural and political discourse that was to prove influential in the post-Reformation world. Secondly, it shows how the humanists, like other Europeans before and after them, constructed an image of the Turks as a point of contrast against which they could define themselves. Wickedness and barbarity stood in opposition to a vision of European virtue and enlightenment.

conclusion

Some scholars have argued that it was essentially through contact with Islam and through recognition of Islam as 'other' that Europe forged its own identity.[71] Certainly, the construction of the Saracen or Turkish 'other', whether exaggeratedly negative or positive, or more nuanced, is significant above all for what it tells us about the self-image and ideology of the Christians themselves in different times and places. As this chapter has shown, scholarship has produced a variety of perspectives on and interpretations of the crusaders' perceptions of their opponents. Inevitably, scholars' interpretations have been coloured by their own cultural perceptions and agendas, but provided we approach their work with due critical awareness, there is something to be gained from all the studies discussed, but particularly from the more recent ones. They have deepened our understanding of the development of and motivation behind a variety of medieval and early modern western images of the Muslim world. At the same time, they have also contributed to a broader debate about the ways in which cultures define themselves against outside groups depicted as 'enemies'.

notes

1. They include: D. C. Munro, 'The Western Attitude toward Islam during the Crusades', *Speculum*, 6 (1931), 329–43; W. W. Comfort, 'The Literary Role of the Saracens in the French Epic', *Publications of the Modern Language Association of America*, 55 (1940), 628–59; C. M. Jones, 'The Conventional Saracen of the Songs of Geste', *Speculum*, 17 (1942), 201–25.
2. See B. Hamilton, 'Knowing the Enemy: Western Understanding of Islam at the Time of the Crusades', *Journal of the Royal Asiatic Society of Great Britain and Ireland*, series 3, vol. 7 (1997), 373–87, for a discussion of how the crusades led in the long term to a deeper knowledge of Islam in the West.
3. D. R. Blanks, 'Western Views of Islam in the Premodern Period: A Brief History of Past Approaches', in *Western Views of Islam in Medieval and Early Modern Europe: Perception of Other*, ed. M. Frassetto and D.R. Blanks (London, 1999), p. 23.
4. S. Luchitskaja, 'Barbarae nationes: Les peoples musulmans dans les chroniques de la première croisade', in *Autour de la première croisade, Actes du Colloque de la Society for the Study of the Crusades and the Latin East, Clermont-Ferrand, 22–25 juin, 1995*, ed. M. Balard (Paris, 1996), p. 100.
5. Regino of Prüm, *Epistula ad Hathonem archiepiscopum missa*, ed. F. Kurze, *Regionis Abbatis Prumiensis Chronicon*, Monumenta Germaniae historica, Scriptores rerum Germanicarum in usum scholarum separatim editi (Hanover, 1890), xix–xx.
6. R. Bartlett, 'Medieval and Modern Concepts of Race and Ethnicity', *Journal of Medieval and Early Modern Studies*, 31/1 (2001), 39–56.
7. T. Hahn, 'The Difference the Middle Ages Makes: Color and Race before the Modern World', *Journal of Medieval and Early Modern Studies*, 31/1 (2001), 8–9.

8. See J. J. Cohen, 'On Saracen Enjoyment: Some Fantasies of Race in Late Medieval France and England', *Journal of Medieval and Early Modern Studies*, 31/1 (2001), 121; J. B. Friedman, *The Monstrous Races in Medieval Art and Thought* (Cambridge, Mass., and London, 1981), p. 65; B. White, 'Saracens and Crusaders: From Fact to Allegory', in *Medieval Literature and Civilization. Studies in Memory of G.N. Garmonsway*, ed. D. A. Pearsall and R. A. Waldron (London, 1969), p. 186.

9. Hahn, 'The Difference the Middle Ages Makes', 12.

10. Cohen, 'On Saracen Enjoyment', 113–46.

11. R. Bartlett, 'Medieval and Modern Concepts of Race and Ethnicity', *Journal of Medieval and Early Modern Studies*, 31/1 (2001), 42–4.

12. S. Luchitskaja, 'Barbarae nationes', pp. 99–107.

13. S. Luchitskaja, 'L'image des musulmans dans les chroniques des croisades', *Le Moyen Age*, 105 (1999), 718–21.

14. See M. Jubb, *The Legend of Saladin in Western Literature and Historiography*, Studies in Comparative Literature, 34 (Lewiston, Queenston and Lampeter, 2000), p. 90; M. Camille, *The Gothic Idol: Ideology and Image-Making in Medieval Art* (Cambridge, 1989), pp. 138–9.

15. Munro, 'The Western Attitude Toward Islam During the Crusades'.

16. Ibid., 338, quoted in D. R. Blanks, 'Western Views of Islam in the Premodern Period', 22.

17. Jones, 'The Conventional Saracen of the Songs of Geste', 202–4.

18. N. Daniel, *Islam and the West: The Making of an Image* (Edinburgh, 1960).

19. E. W. Said, *Orientalism* (London, 1978), p. 60.

20. R. W. Southern, *Western Views of Islam in the Middle Ages* (Cambridge, Mass., 1962), p. 3.

21. J. V. Tolan, *Saracens: Islam in the Medieval European Imagination* (New York, 2002), p. 122.

22. Tolan, *Saracens*, p. xvii.

23. N. Daniel, *Heroes and Saracens: An Interpretation of the Chansons de Geste* (Edinburgh, 1984).

24. Southern, *Western Views of Islam in the Middle Ages*, p. 32.

25. Daniel, *Heroes and Saracens*, pp. 16–18.

26. Ibid., p. 267.

27. D. A. Trotter, *Medieval French Literature and the Crusades (1100–1300)* (Geneva, 1987), pp. 104–5. See also pp. 72–3.

28. Tolan, *Saracens*, p. 124.

29. J. Flori, 'La caricature de l'Islam dans l'Occident médiéval: Origine et signification de quelques stéréotypes concernant l'Islam', *Aevum*, 2 (1992), 245–56.

30. Guibert de Nogent, *Dei gesta per Francos et cinq autres textes*, ed. R. B. C. Huygens, Corpus Christianorum. Continuatio Mediaevalis 127A (Turnhout, 1996), Bk 1, lines 244–416, pp. 94–100, esp. lines 258–60, p. 94.

31. Flori, 'La caricature de l'Islam', 254.

32. Ibid., 254–6.

33. Ibid., 255.

34. Tolan, *Saracens*, p. 109.

35. G. Herman, 'Some Functions of Saracen Names in Old French Epic Poetry', *Romance Notes*, 2 (1969–70), 427–33.

36. G. J. Brault, 'Le Portrait des Sarrasins dans les chansons de geste, image projective?', in *Actes du Xe congrès de la Société Rencesvals*, 2 vols (Aix-en-Provence, 1987), vol. 1, pp. 301–11.
37. M. Camille, *The Gothic Idol: Ideology and Image-Making in Medieval Art* (Cambridge, 1989), p. 142.
38. Ibid., p. 151.
39. Flori, 'La caricature de l'Islam', 255–6.
40. S. Kinoshita, '"Pagans are Wrong and Christians are Right": Alterity, Gender and Nation in the *Chanson de Roland*', *Journal of Medieval and Early Modern Studies*, 31/1 (2001), 79–109.
41. Blanks, 'Western Views of Islam in the Premodern Period', pp. 38–41.
42. See Tolan, *Saracens*, p. 131; M. Camille, *The Gothic Idol*, pp. 136–7.
43. Hahn, 'The Difference the Middle Ages Makes', 25.
44. Guibert de Nogent, *Gesta Dei per Francos*, section 162, Bk 3, lines 641–51, pp. 158–9; Baudri, Archbishop of Dol, *Historia Jherosolimitana*, in *Recueil des historiens des croisades*, ed. Académie des Inscriptions et Belles-Lettres (Paris, 1841–1906), Historiens Occidentaux, vol. 4, pp. 1–111, at pp. 35–6; Petri Tudebodi seu Tudebovis, *Historia de Hiersosolymitane Itinere*, in ibid., vol. 3, pp. 1–111, at pp. 27–8.
45. Anonymous, *Gesta Francorum*, ed. R. Hill (Edinburgh, 1962), p. 21.
46. Tolan, *Saracens*, p. 126.
47. P. Bancourt, *Les Musulmans dans les chansons de geste du cycle du roi*, 2 vols (Aix-en-Provence, 1982).
48. *Fierabras*, published by A. Kroeber and G. Servois, Anciens poètes de la France, 5 (Paris, 1860), lines 1135–9.
49. M. Jubb, 'Enemies in the Holy War, but Brothers in Chivalry: The Crusaders' View of their Saracen Opponents', in *Aspects de l'épopée romane: Mentalités, Idéologies, Intertextualités, Actes du 13e congrès de la Société Rencesvals, Groningen 22–27 août, 1994*, ed. H. van Dijk and W. Noomen (Groningen, 1995), pp. 251–9 (p. 254).
50. S. Runciman, *A History of the Crusades*, 3 vols (Harmondsworth, 1978), vol. 3, p. 72.
51. Bancourt, *Les Musulmans dans les chansons de geste*, vol. 1, p. 324.
52. J. Tolan, 'Le baptême du roi "païen" dans les épopées de la croisade', in *Revue de l'Histoire des Religions*, 217 (2000), 707–31.
53. R. F. Cook, 'Crusade Propaganda in the Epic Cycles of the Crusade', in *Journeys Toward God: Pilgrimage and Crusade*, ed. B. N. Sargent-Baur (Kalamazoo, 1992), pp. 157–75 (p. 162).
54. Hamilton, 'Knowing the Enemy', 380.
55. For a fuller discussion see Jubb, *The Legend of Saladin in Western Literature and Historiography*; J. Tolan, 'Mirror of Chivalry: Salah Al-Din in the Medieval European Imagination', in *Images of the Other: Europe and the Muslim world before 1700*, ed. D. R. Blanks, Cairo Papers in Social Science, 19/2 (Summer 1996), pp. 7–38.
56. Dante, *Divine Comedy, Inferno*, IV, 129.
57. See Jubb, *The Legend of Saladin*, ch. 1, 'Hostile Accounts of Saladin's Rise to Power', pp. 5–18.
58. H. Nicholson, trans., *The Chronicle of the Third Crusade: The Itinerarium Peregrinorum et Gesta Regis Ricardi* (Aldershot, 1997), p. 10.

59. *Willelmi Tyrensis Archiepiscopi Chronicon*, ed. R. B. C. Huygens, Corpus Christianorum Continuatio Mediaevalis, 63, 63A (Turnhout, 1986), Bk 20, ch. 31, lines 2–4, p. 956.

60. R. C. Schwinges, *Kreuzzugsideologie und Toleranz: Studien zu Wilhelm von Tyrus*, (Stuttgart, 1977) and 'William of Tyre, the Muslim Enemy and the Problem of Tolerance', in *Tolerance and Intolerance: Social Conflict in the Age of the Crusades*, ed. J. Powell and M. Gervers (Syracuse, 2001), pp. 124–32, here p. 131.

61. See M. Jubb, 'Saladin vu par Guillaume de Tyr et par l'*Eracles*: changement de perspectives', in *Autour de la première croisade*, ed. Balard, pp. 443–51; Jubb, *The Legend of Saladin*, ch. 2, 'The Emergence of a More Positive View', pp. 19–32.

62. M. A. Jubb, *A Critical Edition of the 'Estoires d'Outremer'* (London, 1990).

63. See M. R. Morgan, *The Chronicle of Ernoul and the Continuations of William of Tyre* (Oxford, 1973).

64. Hamilton, 'Knowing the Enemy', 384.

65. Ibid., 387.

66. Jubb, 'Enemies in the Holy War, but Brothers in Chivalry', pp. 251–9.

67. Tolan, 'Mirror of Chivalry', 32.

68. See Jubb, *The Legend of Saladin*, pp. 90–111.

69. G. Allaire, 'Noble Saracen or Muslim Enemy? The Changing Image of the Saracen in Late Medieval Italian literature', in *Western Views of Islam*, ed. Frassetto and Blanks, p. 181.

70. N. Bisaha, 'New Barbarian or Worthy Adversary? Humanist Constructs of the Ottoman Turks in Fifteenth-Century Italy', in *Western Views of Islam*, ed. Frassetto and Blanks, pp. 185–205.

71. For an alternative argument that European identity was formed in the Middle Ages through the internal expansion of language and religion within an enlarged Europe, see R. Bartlett, *The Making of Europe: Conquest, Colonization and Cultural Change, 950–1350* (Oxford, 1993).

11
byzantine and modern greek perceptions of the crusades

eleni sakellariou

Imperial ideology had a great impact on the perception of the crusading movement by the Byzantines. Political theory in Byzantium had a strong theological dimension: God wished Christ's believers to live in one state, ruled by the Roman (Byzantine) emperor. The spiritual significance that was attached to the emperor, the empire and its capital city, had a decisive influence on Byzantine foreign policy. Its principal concerns were twofold: the security of the empire and its capital; and recognition of the emperor's claim to be the supreme overlord of the Christian world and the empire's claim to be the unique state endorsed by God. This imperial ideology was consolidated in the late tenth and early eleventh century, when the Byzantine state reached the peak of its territorial expansion and material wealth.[1]

The second half of the eleventh century was a period of political and financial crisis in Byzantium, while new enemies appeared at its frontiers. The situation was grave, but perhaps not unparalleled in its long history. For the defence of the empire, the emperors hoped to recruit mercenary soldiers. In doing so, the Byzantines now turned to the Christian West on an unprecedented scale. However, blinded by the legacy of their great past, they failed to comprehend the increase in papal authority in the West, and that this could lead to a clash between the two claimants to universal spiritual leadership within Christendom.[2]

the first crusade

In the second half of the eleventh century, when the Normans emerged as a formidable power in Italy, popular opinion in Byzantium became fearful.

245

These fears were confirmed by the Norman invasion of 1081, which had Pope Gregory VII's moral support. It was seen by the Byzantines as proof of the enmity of the Roman Church against that of Constantinople and of the West against their state. By the end of the century prophecies were circulating in Byzantium that the empire would be destroyed by the Latins.[3] However, the emperor who set out to deal with the Norman attack, Alexios I Komnenos, apparently did not refrain from recruiting Guiscard's men into his own service after the collapse of his enemy's final offensive in 1085.[4] Indeed Alexios I recruited mercenaries from as far afield as England and Flanders. According to the *Alexiad*, already in 1090/91, pressed by simultaneous attacks on his eastern and northern frontiers, Alexios summoned mercenaries 'from all quarters', including Rome. Since September 1089 there had been a rapprochement between the emperor and the pope. Urban II lifted Gregory VII's ban of excommunication against Alexios; Alexios responded by holding a synod in Constantinople to consider ways of restoring union between the eastern and western Churches.[5]

In the spring of 1095 a Byzantine embassy met the pope at the council of Piacenza. The embassy is not mentioned by any contemporary Byzantine source. Whether this was a deliberate attempt to hide Alexios's role in the origin of the First Crusade or a consequence of the fact that Byzantine historians usually showed little interest in events taking place outside Byzantium, we have to rely on western chronicles for the content of the embassy. The emperor presented the situation in the East as critical and begged help from his fellow Christians against the empire's infidel enemies. The appeal to Christian duty made a strong argument. It is also proof of Alexios's readiness to use phraseology that would appeal to the Latins. However, what Urban preached at Clermont in November 1095 was not the despatch of mercenaries under the emperor's command, but an armed penitential pilgrimage that would confirm his own claim to supreme authority in the Christian world, following the development of papal ideology in the eleventh century. Alexios could not have requested this at Piacenza. After all, by 1095 the crisis in Byzantium had been defused. What Alexios sought in the West was manpower, in the form of mercenary soldiers, to help him repel the Turks from Asia Minor.[6]

In 1096 Alexios I was faced with an unexpected situation. The crusader armies that arrived at Constantinople were very large and had their own leaders, causing great anxiety to the Byzantines. The leader of one of these armies was no other than Bohemond, the son of the Norman Robert Guiscard who, only a few years before, had invaded Byzantium. In the eleventh century many in Byzantium acknowledged the military prowess of the Latins but were fearful of them, because they perceived them as impetuous, irresolute, greedy for material goods, and treacherous: all features traditionally attached to the 'barbarians' by Byzantine authors. The principal Byzantine historian of the Crusade and daughter of Alexios I, Anna Komnene, stated that this was also the opinion of her father and his advisers when they heard of the arrival of the crusaders, which, the historian would have us believe, came as a great surprise to them.[7]

The religious enthusiasm of the crusaders remained incomprehensible to the Byzantines, whose concepts of war were very different from those developed by the reformed papacy in the eleventh century. War could be neither good nor holy; it was evil and was justified only when it was about the defence of the empire and its faith. Peace was always to be preferred. Public opinion in Byzantium was shocked at the sight of members of the Roman clergy leading military campaigns. Therefore, the declared aim of the Crusade, the liberation of the Holy Sepulchre, was regarded with scepticism by the Byzantines, especially as far as the leaders of the expedition were concerned. Anna Komnene conceded a religious motive only to the simple crusaders. By contrast, both her father and his advisers believed that their leaders intended to seize lordships for themselves and even, if possible, take possession of Constantinople. As for the people of Byzantium, they often took the crusaders to be 'no pilgrims but plunderers who had come to lay waste the land and threaten their lives'.[8]

The fears of the Byzantines were not entirely unjustified. By their sheer size the crusader armies posed problems regarding the regular supply of provisions, billeting and the maintenance of discipline. If they decided to turn against the empire, they could be a serious threat.[9] However, the crusade was also regarded in Byzantium as an opportunity. If they were properly organized, the crusaders could be used to strike a blow at the Seljuks in Asia Minor.[10] Alexios's foremost concern was the safety of his state. He resorted to methods that had been used by his predecessors when troops of foreign allies and mercenaries marched through Byzantine territory. When the Crusader leaders did not abide by his demands, Alexios did not refrain from using force against them; but when they accepted them, he showered them with gifts and honours to win their allegiance.[11]

Upon arrival at Constantinople, each of the leaders was asked to take an oath. The administration of oaths of good faith, loyalty or submission to the leaders of foreign troops was a traditional Byzantine practice. In addition, from the eleventh century onwards there was a general tendency to resort to oaths as a means of regulating relationships in the higher echelons of Byzantine society. However, the oath of the crusader leaders was special: the leaders became Alexios's vassals and the oaths seem to have involved bilateral agreements. The Latin sources insist that sworn pledges were made by both parties, the emperor as well as the crusade leaders. Alexios offered the leaders counsel, guidance and reinforcements, without which their expedition would have little hope of success. In return, the western leaders were expected not only to do nothing that might harm the emperor and to offer him service in time of war, but also to hand over to him all territory that they might conquer during their campaign and which had formerly been Byzantine. This has been interpreted to mean at least territory that had been Byzantine until the 1080s (which would include northern Syria), if not the whole of Syria and Palestine. If this is so, it is tempting to interpret the foreign policy of the Komnenoi as acquisitive rather than defensive.

As in the case of Alexios's appeal to the pope for assistance in 1095, the emperor adapted his diplomatic methods to western custom. However, although now the crusader leaders were the vassals of the emperor, to him they were no more than mercenaries who were expected to recover lost territory for Byzantium. This does not necessarily mean that Alexios intended to ignore his duties towards the crusaders, although it is difficult not to blame him temporizing in 1098–99. As long as the empire was not in danger, the Byzantines, or at least their emperor, probably had no desire to see the crusade fail. When the expedition came to an end, Alexios could claim that his policy towards the crusaders was at least partially successful. Byzantium had recovered a considerable portion of Asia Minor. However, the breach of the agreements by both parties led to the creation of the four crusader states. The loss of Antioch particularly disturbed the emperor, because possession of this most important city in northern Syria, which had great spiritual significance and had been lost to the Turks only in 1084, would consolidate his recent conquests in Asia Minor and Cilicia. The creation of the Latin principality of Antioch may explain why shortly after 1100 Byzantine policy towards the crusaders changed in more than one way.[12]

from the end of the first crusade to the first fall of constantinople

Alexios decided to resort to military force against Bohemond, who had kept Antioch. This was a turning point in the relations between Byzantium and the crusaders. Up until then there were misunderstandings and differences in attitude, but relations between the two parties, with the exception of a few skirmishes, remained essentially peaceful. After c. 1100 a period of military confrontation between Byzantium and the crusader states was inaugurated, although the object of such confrontation was almost exclusively Antioch, not the other crusader states. Alexios's son and successor, John II, organized two campaigns to northern Syria, in 1137–38 and in 1142–43. The aim of his Syrian campaigns was the establishment of direct Byzantine control in northern Syria.[13] But even with respect to the issue of Antioch John had to adopt a conciliatory stance in the end. He clearly had the military advantage, but the real outcome of his Syrian campaigns did not go beyond recognition of the emperor's overlordship by the prince of Antioch, who retained his principality.

John II acquiesced in this modest outcome of his policy of force not so much because the emperor and his advisers had limited their ambition to the acknowledgement of the supremacy of imperial authority and of the emperor's role as protector of the Christian people, but because they seem to have realized that their policy towards the crusader states could have serious repercussions on their overall relations with the West. A war waged by Byzantium against any of the crusader states could lead to an upsurge of anti-Byzantine propaganda in the West, the consequences of which could be grave.[14] It is not coincidental that shortly after John II's first Syrian campaign, in March 1138, Pope Innocent II wrote a letter in which he warned the faithful against the emperor, who was trying to occupy Antioch. In the pope's view, John had no rights of possession in northern Syria because he was schismatic. This argument was to be frequently used against Byzantium in the thirteenth century, and then as in the late 1130s the Byzantine response was to open negotiations for Church union.[15]

The loss of Edessa to the Muslims triggered the Second Crusade; the kings of Germany and France, Conrad III and Louis VII, took the cross. In Byzantium, John II's successor, Manuel I, was not pleased with the course of events. He had an alliance with Conrad, the aim of which was to keep Roger II of Sicily at bay; if Conrad left Europe on a crusade, this would no longer be possible. In addition, although Louis VII disagreed with Roger's anti-Byzantine plans, he was Roger's ally, and this could be viewed only with suspicion in Constantinople. The fact that in February 1147 the French and the Germans took the common decision to march through the Balkans to Asia Minor was interpreted in Byzantium as a sign that Conrad might have changed sides. Finally, a successful crusade would strengthen the crusader states and so weaken the Byzantine position in Syria, while the passage of any army of this size through any country was bound to cause serious problems. The arrival of the crusade forced Manuel to stay in Constantinople. Roger II of Sicily seized this opportunity to unleash yet another attack on Greece. The Byzantines and their emperor had many reasons to be very negative towards the Second Crusade, more so than Alexios.[16]

How the Byzantines perceived the Second Crusade and those who participated in it is clearly stated by the historian and secretary of Manuel I, John Kinnamos. The expedition to Palestine and the war against the Turks was a pretext concealing their real aim, the conquest of Byzantine territory. The crusaders, especially the Germans, were 'barbarians'. They were proud, boastful, impetuous, insolent, presumptuous, supercilious. They were innumerable, their physique was large, they were heavily armoured, but their cavalry was not swift. On the battlefield they relied on their numbers, but the Byzantines could defeat them although their army was smaller, because they were superior in 'military science'. When defeated, they, like all barbarians, became downcast and immoderately humbled. Kinnamos seems convinced that the crusaders were responsible for all the misunderstandings, whereas the position of the Byzantine authorities towards them was justified at all points.[17] In general, Niketas Choniates, who wrote a few years later, agrees with Kinnamos's description of the Latins as 'barbarians', although he relies less on their character for the construction of his narrative, while he is much more objective in the evaluation of events. Thus he acknowledges that the Byzantines were deceiving the crusaders when they sold them provisions, and he even implies that Manuel incited the Seljuks to attack them in Asia Minor.[18] Two poems written by 'Manganeios Prodromos' for his patrons in the imperial administration and performed within weeks of the passage of the German crusaders, adopt a far more hostile stance towards the crusaders than the two historians. Conrad and the crusaders had planned to capture Constantinople and its territories, and were boorish, bestial, greedy, deceitful, arrogant and aggressive; but when they were defeated, they were reduced to trembling fear. The poet systematically draws on pejorative animal imagery to describe them and their leader. The two poems are a snapshot of a reaction of intolerance and suspicion to the Second Crusade.[19] Thus the traditional Byzantine stereotype of the Latins as 'barbarians' but powerful warriors, which had prevailed at the time of the First Crusade and even before, was not abandoned, although one can now also detect a rediscovered confidence of the Byzantines in their state and ruler, clearly a result of the good government of the first three Komnenoi.

The Second Crusade was a failure, and many in the West blamed Byzantium for it. Byzantine esteem in the West, except in Germany, reached its lowest point. Although, some 50 years before, the First Crusade aimed at helping Byzantium against the Turks, now plans for a crusading expedition against Byzantium were openly mooted. Imperial ideology and political theory in Byzantium, enhanced by the Komnenian programme of recovery of those territories on which the Byzantines could lay a claim, could not but clash with the increasing confidence and ambitions of western Europeans, their territorial expansion in the Orient, and the claims of the Roman Church there.

Although in dealing with the Second Crusade Manuel did not diverge from the policy of his predecessors, in the 1150s a dramatic change in Byzantium's policy towards the Latins occurred. Manuel abandoned the traditional entente with Germany, and he concluded a treaty with his arch-enemies, the Normans of Sicily, who, like the Byzantines and the pope, felt threatened by the new German emperor, Frederick I. This reorientation in the West had its counterpart in the Levant. In 1158 Manuel could have humiliated Reynald of Antioch and annexed his principality to his empire. Instead the emperor chose to limit his demands to an oath of fealty on the part of Reynald and to the restitution of an Orthodox patriarch at the Church of Antioch, but he did not press the old demands for the handing over of the city itself. Clearly what Byzantium sought now in Syria was recognition of suzerainty, not direct government. Manuel may not have wished to continue his predecessors' policy of aggression towards the crusader states because he did not want to disturb his understanding with Sicily, France and the pope against Frederick I. This policy cost Manuel little. Between the late 1150s and the early 1170s, as there was little or no prospect of help reaching them from the West, the leaders of the crusader states sought an alternative source of assistance in their struggle for survival against the mounting Muslim threat. This source was Byzantium, whose support now appeared as inevitable. By offering this aid Manuel secured a great deal of influence in Syria and a good press in the West.[20]

Manuel's new and agile foreign policy is also documented in the sector of ecclesiastical relations. Manuel corresponded with the pope, while in 1166 a Church council was celebrated in Constantinople to discuss the differences between Constantinople and Rome. Thanks to his campaigns against the Muslims and his Church policy, Manuel could present himself as the protector of the Christians and of the crusader states. This was in harmony with one of the main concerns of Byzantine imperial ideology, but it was also politically expedient in the arena of the complex relations of Byzantium with the West since it improved the emperor's reputation there. Perhaps the culmination of this new policy was the Byzantine emperor's initiative to organize a crusade against the Muslims in 1175–76.[21]

Yet although Manuel was rather more open to the West and its customs than his ancestors,[22] his description as a 'Latinophile' should not be exaggerated. Above all, Manuel was a Byzantine emperor and his priority was to serve his state's interests; he had simply realized that it was in Byzantium's interest to be on good terms with the West and with the Latins of the Levant. Before and during Alexios's reign, many western mercenaries were among the military commanders of the Byzantine army. Under John II, and especially Manuel I, this changed. Although the number of Latins in Byzantium did not decrease under Manuel, westerners in the Byzantine army lost rather than gained in status.[23] It was Manuel who expelled the Venetians from Constantinople in 1171. In addition, for many of his contemporaries, perception of the Latins remained unchanged. In the oration by Eustathios, Metropolitan of Thessalonike, for Agnes of France, who was betrothed to Manuel's son in 1179, despite a new understanding of the complex web of alliances between Byzantium and the principal European states of the late twelfth century, we find the traditional Byzantine stereotype of the Latins as 'barbarians'. Here as elsewhere Eustathios uses imagery of beasts when he refers to the French, which is reminiscent of the poems of 'Manganeios Prodromos'.[24]

The disruption of Manuel's friendly policy towards the West and the deep political crisis in Byzantium in the last two decades of the twelfth century had grave consequences for Byzantium. Western plans for an attack against Byzantium multiplied in the closing years of the twelfth century, and this increased the fear and suspicion of the Byzantines towards the Latins and the crusades. Relations between the Byzantines and the Latins deteriorated in 1182–83, when Andronikos I Komnenos became emperor. The Third Crusade was called in October 1187, as an immediate reaction to the catastrophic defeat of the Latins at Hattin. Emperor Frederick I took the land route to the Holy Land in May 1189.[25]

Rising tensions between Byzantium and the West in the late twelfth century are reflected in contemporary accounts of the Third Crusade. Although the exact content of the agreement that Isaac II made with Saladin continues to be an issue of debate, the general impression remains that the Byzantines nourished strong anti-Latin feelings.[26] There was one group of Latins that was certainly the cause of deep antipathy. They were the citizens of the Italian maritime republics, who had gradually secured a very privileged position in the commercial sector of the Byzantine economy after 1082, when Alexios I ceded the first important commercial privilege to the Venetians, in return for their assistance in his struggle against the Normans. This resentment was probably behind Manuel I's decision to expel the Venetians from the capital in 1171, and certainly caused the massacre of the Genoese and the Pisans in Constantinople in 1182. However, although Kinnamos seems to have shared the dislike of the Byzantines towards the Italian merchants, Eustathios of Thessalonike condemned the massacre of the Italians and singled out this event as the cause of the Norman invasion of 1185.[27] That the emperors and their advisers in Byzantium grew increasingly suspicious of the West and of the crusades as the twelfth century drew to an end, after four Norman attacks and the airing of many crusading plans against Constantinople, is as beyond doubt as it is understandable. At the same time the fear and the hostility of the population of the regions through which the crusading armies marched on their way to Palestine must have also been increasing. Thus in 1189 Isaac II was suspicious of Frederick I, known in Byzantium as an enemy since 1147, and an ally of the Normans, the Serbs and the Seljuks at the eve of the crusade. It was widely believed in Constantinople that the real motive behind Frederick's campaign was an attack on the empire.[28] Isaac set about to deal with the problem using the same methods as his predecessors. Frederick found the passes from Bulgaria to the empire blocked, while the local population fled before the army, taking all provisions with them. But Isaac had not realized that he ruled at a time during which Byzantium was rapidly submerging into a deep political, institutional and financial crisis, while his adversary was one of the most powerful leaders of Europe. The high-handedness with which the Byzantine envoys and Isaac himself treated the Germans outraged Frederick, and when a Byzantine contingent clashed with the German army outside Philippopolis the superiority of the Germans and the weakness of the Byzantines became obvious.[29] The traditional ways of dealing with the crusades were no longer efficient.

In this atmosphere of mounting suspicion between East and West, the way in which Niketas Choniates, who wrote or revised his *History* shortly after 1204, perceived the Third Crusade is of great importance. Choniates did not spare negative adjectives to describe the Latins. In the context of the sack of Thessalonike by the Normans, Choniates emphatically contrasted the Latins and Byzantines. He wrote that the two people were diametrically opposed, and this inevitably caused hatred between them.[30] However, Choniates's judgement of the Latins was not universally negative. The historian was often even-handed in his evaluation of the Latins and of the crusading movement. His critical approach to some of Manuel's policies during the Second Crusade has already been mentioned. This criticism became more outspoken in his account of the Third Crusade. Choniates is very negative about Isaac's inconsistent, haphazard and ultimately inefficient policy towards Frederick I.[31] By contrast Choniates paints a panegyrical portrait of Frederick I. He was of noble origin, wise, invincible on the battlefield, sincere in his desire to fight for the Christians in Palestine. Choniates praised many other Latins, among them a hero of the Third Crusade, Conrad of Montferrat. It has been reasonably argued that Choniates, who wrote shortly after the fall of Constantinople to the Latins, presented many of the Latin leaders in this positive manner because he disagreed with the policies of Isaac II and his son, and because by that time he had come to the conclusion that Byzantine diplomacy towards the West had failed and led to the disaster of 1204.[32] The Third Crusade brought on the deterioration of relations between Byzantines and Latins, but perhaps the situation was not yet irreversible.

The events that led to the diversion of the Fourth Crusade against Constantinople are too well known to be repeated here. An enormous amount of ink has been expended by scholars in their effort to understand the causes of the diversion.[33] The prevailing historiographical traditions are the 'chance' and the 'intrigue' theories. The first accepts the account of Geoffrey of Villehardouin, according to whom the diversion to Constantinople was not planned in advance, but the decisive factor that led to it was accident.[34] The supporters of the 'intrigue' theory seek the culprit elsewhere: in the commercial interests of the Venetians, in the person of the German imperial claimant, Philip of Swabia, of Boniface of Montferrat, of Innocent III himself.[35]

In the last years of the nineteenth century, Walter Norden propounded a 'modified chance theory'. Norden placed the Fourth Crusade in the general framework of Western-Byzantine relations, not just that of the interaction between the empire and Venice. No one could have conspired in advance to divert the crusade, but there were underlying reasons that predisposed the Venetians and the crusaders to take advantage of the situation.[36] Norden's thesis is still very influential. Following his tradition, Sibyll Kindlimann placed the Fourth Crusade within a framework of long-term causes and isolated as one such cause the rise of the feeling in the West that Byzantium was an obstacle to the crusading movement unworthy to survive. From the Byzantine point of view, Charles Brand interpreted the Fourth Crusade as the consequence of the failure of Byzantine foreign policy. Jonathan Harris's recent book is a more wide-ranging and refined version of the same argument. The revised edition of *The Fourth Crusade* by Donald Queller and Thomas Madden belongs to the tradition of Norden's work.[37]

There are many other Byzantine historians who dismiss the idea that an event so important as the capture of Constantinople by the Latins in 1204 can be explained away as an accident. They seek an answer to the problem of Byzantium's collapse in the face of the Latin attack by examining not only the interaction between East and West, but also conditions in the empire itself on the eve of the crusade. In the last decades of the twelfth century the authority of the emperor in Constantinople was contested by holders of local power in the provinces, who were slowly slipping out of the control of the capital. Decentralized power was the outcome of the financial, administrative, social and political changes which occurred in Byzantium in the course of the eleventh century, as well as of the policy of compromise with local interests that the Komnenoi adopted when they came to power. An important effect of this was that an increasing amount of wealth was staying in the provinces and no longer made its way to the imperial treasury. This internal decomposition undermined the financial basis of the Byzantine state, and became apparent in the high number of rebellions against imperial authority.[38]

The principal source for the reaction of the inhabitants of Constantinople to the Fourth Crusade is the *History* of Niketas Choniates. Choniates was convinced that the Venetians, in the person of their doge, Enrico Dandolo, were responsible for the diversion of the crusade to Constantinople. Dandolo had not forgiven the Byzantines for the seizure of Venetian merchants and goods in 1171, and he grasped at the opportunity to turn the crusade away from the Levant and against the empire.[39] However, despite Choniates's dislike of the Venetians, he has little good to say of the Byzantine emperors. Alexios III was gracious and approachable, but he was also cowardly and incompetent. He had betrayed the hopes amidst which he had come to the throne. Alexios IV was immature and inexperienced, and was foolish and fatally irresponsible in relying so heavily on his Latin friends. Many of Choniates's co-citizens must have shared the same feelings. When Alexios IV appeared before the walls of Constantinople to claim the throne back from his uncle, the people of Constantinople initially remained faithful to emperor Alexios III; they were prejudiced against the nephew, because he was relying on paid Latin troops and had promised to accept Church union and the primacy of Rome.[40] With the capture and sack of Constantinople, the worst suspicions of the Byzantines materialised; the real aim of the crusades was not the salvation of Jerusalem, but the destruction of Byzantium. Relations with the West were damaged beyond repair.

Byzantine political theory dictated that the Byzantine Empire was an institution divinely ordained and capable of infinite survival and expansion. The most visible symbol of this continuity was the city of Constantinople itself. This ideology found justification in reality in the tenth and early eleventh centuries, when Byzantium prospered. The third quarter of the eleventh and the last decades of the twelfth centuries were periods of acute crisis in Byzantium, but intellectuals could still reiterate that the Byzantines had survived worse emergencies in the past and that as long as Constantinople remained in their hands the situation was not irreversible. The tragedy was that with few exceptions the Byzantines failed to wake up to the fact that western Europe was radically transformed in the course of the twelfth century. The traditional Byzantine perception of the westerners, which had been consolidated before the First Crusade and did not change thereafter, was one of an uncouth, arrogant, belligerent and greedy lot, all features attributed by the Byzantines to many other 'barbarian' people, not just the Latins. But as, in the course of the twelfth century, signs of the transformation of Europe became perceptible in Byzantium, in the ideology of the reformed papacy and the crusading movement, in the aggression of lay powers, such as the Normans and the German Empire, and in the occupation of a dominant position at the markets of the East by the Italian merchants, the tolerance of the Byzantines, who had imbibed an ideology of superiority, was severely tried, while it is not impossible that many in the West believed that Byzantium stood in the way of the development of western interests. In Byzantium the uneasy feeling developed that the threat to their existence now came not from their traditional enemies, the Bulgarians and the Turks, but from western Europe; the conviction, in all Byzantine accounts, that the real aim of the crusades was to cause harm to the empire seems to verify this argument.[41]

However, the Byzantines do not seem to have been prepared for the shock of 1204. Though many times besieged, Constantinople had never fallen to its enemies until the soldiers of the Fourth Crusade broke in. The fall of Constantinople to the Latins must have been a most shattering break with the past. This perhaps explains why, on the morning of 13 April 1204, when the Latins awoke from their fearful sleep within the walls of the capital, they were faced not with a Byzantine counter-attack, but by a delegation who seemed prepared to greet a new, if Latin, emperor and deliver the city into his hands. The empire could never be vanquished, it could only change emperor; the capital could resist a pretender but was loyal to the victor.[42]

from the first to the second fall
of constantinople: 1204–1453

In the aftermath of the Fourth Crusade, the Byzantine empire was dismembered by the crusade leaders, and a number of Latin states were created in former Byzantine territory. It soon became obvious that the Byzantines were determined to resist, to cling to their religion and ideology and to reject that of western Europe. In 1261 Constantinople was recovered, and the empire restored. If recovery created hopes that the old unity and prosperity of the empire would be reinstated, the mistrust and dislike of the Latins, which had prevailed before 1204, was now slowly transformed into open hatred. The efforts of the Latin titular emperors of Constantinople to recover their short-lived empire, often with the support of the papacy, consolidated the conviction of the Byzantines that the West desired the annihilation of their state. The gulf between Byzantines and Latins became ever deeper, and as Byzantine territory was now reduced to its purely Greek-speaking provinces, the desire of the Byzantines to stress that they were very different from the Latins may explain why some intellectuals started to describe the inhabitants of the empire both as 'Hellenes' and as 'Romans'. Innocent III saw the establishment of the Latin Empire as an opportunity to unite the eastern Church under Rome, by force if necessary, and his maladroit efforts to oblige the Byzantine clergy to submit strengthened the resolve of most of its members to defend their traditional faith. Thus the anti-Latin sentiment and the desire to remain loyal to the traditional principles and faith were further fostered by the eastern Church.[43]

The union of the Churches was a cause always dear to the Roman Church. Since the time of Alexios I and possibly even earlier, Byzantine emperors had used union negotiations as a means to improve temporarily their relations with the papacy. From the thirteenth century onwards, the Byzantine rulers offered Church union to the papacy with increasing frequency, in return for political advantages, usually the withdrawal of papal support to the anti-Byzantine plans of western European princes. These politically expedient efforts, however, failed, because they met with the violent reaction of the clergy and the people of Byzantium, to whom the defence of orthodoxy was more important than any political advantage.[44]

The most dramatic instance was the effort of emperor Michael VIII to achieve union in 1274. Michael VIII knew that the recovery of Constantinople by the Byzantines in 1261 gave the West an incentive to attack Byzantium. One of the principal concerns of the papacy remained the liberation of the Holy Land, a prerequisite for which was the union of the western and eastern Churches. If union could not be achieved by peaceful means, the papacy envisaged the possibility of a military campaign against the 'schismatic' Byzantines. This explains Michael VIII's consistent efforts to successfully conclude union negotiations. His aim was to secure the papacy's friendship and to neutralise the territorial claims of the Latin emperor and his supporters.[45]

Soon after the recovery of Constantinople, Michael VIII opened negotiations with the papacy.[46] However, between 1267 and 1282 Michael VIII was faced with the very real danger of an attack from the West. The new King of Sicily and the pope's champion in Italy, Charles I of Anjou, was planning a campaign against Byzantium, with the aim of restoring the Latin Empire and consolidating his own dominion east of the Adriatic. Charles sought to obtain the status of a crusade for his expedition, presenting the recovery of Byzantium as the *sine qua non* for that of the Holy Land. Michael VIII realized that the only way to avert the danger was to come to terms with the papacy. His negotiations led to a union of the Churches, which was celebrated at the Council of Lyons on 6 July 1274. Pope Gregory X's crusading plan could now proceed. In 1275 Michael VIII declared that he was willing to allow the crusader armies free passage through his territories, and to take an active part in the crusade. Charles I could not possibly attack an ally of the papacy.

Michael was motivated in his support of the union by the necessity of restraining Charles from his plan of conquest. His effort was successful for some time, but it was perceived in an entirely different way by the Byzantine world. The Byzantines were convinced that Charles I aimed at the conquest of Constantinople and at the creation of a Mediterranean empire for himself.[47] Michael VIII tried to convince them of the great political advantages that the union would bring, but the Byzantine clergy openly condemned the idea of union with Rome, while the people, and even members of the imperial family, turned against the emperor, who had to resort to violent measures of repression in order to impose the union.[48]

The Sicilian Vespers and the loss of Sicily in 1282 forced Charles I and his successors to put aside their plans for expansion in the eastern Mediterranean. Michael VIII's successor, Andronikos II, seeing that a western attack on Byzantium was no longer likely, repudiated the union of the Churches as soon as he came to the throne and proclaimed the restoration of Orthodoxy, thus bringing religious peace to his empire.[49]

In the 1320s, a significant change in the attitude of both the papacy and the Byzantines to the crusades occurred. The attention of the papacy and of those who advocated a new crusade now shifted from Byzantium to Egypt, and to Lesser Armenia in Cilicia and Cyprus, two Christian kingdoms in the Levant, which urgently needed to be rescued from the Muslims. At the same time, Andronikos II inaugurated an active western foreign policy. In 1324–27, he reopened the negotiations for the union of the Churches, which he had interrupted in 1282. He hoped to court the friendship of the pope, the king of France, and the Angevins. In the last few years of his reign, his attitude towards the Byzantine Church and towards the West underwent a complete reversal. This does not mean that the old Byzantine hatred for the Latins had eased. What urged many in Europe, especially the Venetians, and the Byzantines to change their policy was the fact that the Turks now emerged as the common enemy in the Aegean. Venice decided to seek allies to help her fight them. One of the allies could be the emperor of Byzantium.[50]

The West abandoned its claims on Constantinople, and decided to help Byzantium against the Turks. Such aid, however, remained conditional upon the acceptance of Church union by Byzantium on the terms of the papacy. The Church of Constantinople was expected to recognize the primacy of the Roman Church. Between 1334 and 1369 the Byzantines conducted union negotiations with the popes almost without interruption, hoping to secure assistance from the West against their enemies.[51] The representatives of the Roman Church demanded that union should precede military aid from the West. The emperors insisted that they could not convince their subjects of the necessity of union if the political advantages of it, in other words military support in the struggle against the Turks, did not become apparent to them. In 1339 Andronikos III's envoy, the monk Barlaam of Calabria, put this clearly to Pope Benedict XII: 'It is not so much difference in dogma that alienates the hearts of the Greeks from you, as the hatred that has entered their souls against the Latins, because of the many great evils that [...] the Greeks have suffered at the hands of the Latins [...] Until this hatred has been removed from them, there cannot be union [...] until you have done them some very great benefit [... no one] will dare to breathe a word to them about union.'[52] Although negotiations remained inconclusive, a number of small crusading expeditions against the Turks were organized in these years. To some of them the Byzantine emperor was invited to participate. But as, by 1368, the Turks had completed the conquest of Thrace with the exception of Constantinople and a small area around it, emperor John V Palaiologos took the desperate measure of travelling to Italy and professing his faith to the Roman Church. John V's conversion was a purely personal matter and no one could claim that it had led to any sort of Church union.

The union of the two Churches was finally accomplished at the Church council which started at Ferrara in 1438 and continued in Florence in 1439. The popes had managed to press their point, that military aid against the Turks could not be forthcoming unless the reunion of the Churches was first achieved. Although the union caused upheaval and bitterness in Orthodox Byzantium, Pope Eugenius IV kept his promise. By 1444 all was ready for a crusading expedition against the Ottomans. As opposed to the crusade of Nikopolis a few years earlier, the aim of this campaign was the relief of Constantinople itself. Unfortunately for the Christians, the crusade ended in disaster at the battle of Varna on 10 November 1444. Western Europe and the crusading movement could do nothing to save Constantinople from its fall to the Ottomans in 1453.

What stands out in the interaction between the Byzantines, the papacy and the representatives of the crusading movement from the thirteenth to the fifteenth century is the violently negative reaction of many among the Byzantine clergy and population against the Latins. The most apparent expression of this antipathy was their rejection of Church union on the terms of the papacy. This stern resistance to the acceptance of union, when the political advantages deriving from it were so obvious, has puzzled many historians. On a number of accounts the turning point was the Fourth Crusade. The devastation of Constantinople and the dismemberment of the empire transformed the old feeling of superiority, suspicion and dislike of the Byzantines towards the Latins into open hatred. Not only did the Byzantines not forget the acts of violence committed in their capital; even after the restoration of Byzantium in 1261 they were witness to the fact that their empire had never recovered from the blow of its partition among the westerners, exactly at the moment when all its forces were needed for the defence against the Turks. The economic success of the Italians in the cities of Byzantium and in the Eastern Mediterranean must have deepened their rancour. To all this was added the insistence of Rome to accept union only if the Byzantine Church professed submission to it. To many in Byzantium this was tantamount to abandoning the old imperial ideology, according to which the supreme protector of the Christian world was the emperor, while the Church of Constantinople defended the true faith. This ideology remained unshaken to the very end, despite the territorial reduction of Byzantium to no more than its capital. No wonder, then, that when one of the imperial legates returned from Lyons in 1274, he was faced with the accusation that he had become a Frank. No wonder, also, that in the aftermath of the Council of Florence and on the eve of the fall of Constantinople to the Ottomans, the anti-unionist party was so strong and so vociferous in the city, that the axiom 'better the turban than the tiara' encapsulated the preference of the Byzantines for Turkish rule to domination by the West.

However, to present the attitude of the Byzantines towards the Latins after 1204 exclusively in terms of an obsessive hatred is perhaps an exaggeration. From 1263 to the very last years of its existence, the rulers of Byzantium and their advisers, with an interval in the first part of the reign of Andronikos II, were convinced of the political advantages that would result from a compromise with the papacy and the West and thus pursued union negotiations. Their supporters among the Byzantine clergy and ruling elite were few. Some of them, however, among them Demetrios Kydones and Theodore Metochites in the fourteenth century, and Bessarion, Bishop of Nicaea, and Isidoros, Bishop of Kiev, in the fifteenth, went so far as not only to re-evaluate the Byzantine imperial myth, but also to admit with admiration that the Latins had much to offer on the intellectual plane. Finally, for many supporters of the anti-unionist party, some considerations that had nothing to do with theology and ideology were, perhaps, of overriding importance. Faced with the imminent reality of Ottoman occupation, they must have contemplated what that meant. The condition of the Orthodox Greeks who were already the sultan's subjects was not so deplorable after all. They were now considered infidels and hence inferior to his Muslim subjects, but the early Ottoman state was more tolerant in religious matters than the Latin regimes that had been established in the Romania after 1204. At the same time, in the economic and commercial sector the Christians had complete freedom of action, and many of them had obtained high-ranking positions in the administration and the army. In addition it was well known that those cities that surrendered to the Ottomans were spared the plundering and destruction to which those that were conquered after resistance were subjected. The Byzantine historians Laonikos Chalkokondyles and Kritoboulos of Imbros, writing just after 1453, seem to have accepted the fact that the Byzantine world had now been committed to the care of an emperor who was not a Christian, and that the tradition of the Christian empire was now continued by the Ottoman one.[53]

modern greek perceptions of the crusades

Modern Greek scholars have often interpreted the crusades in quite a different fashion from their Western counterparts. Konstantinos

Paparregopoulos is considered by many the father of modern Greek historiography. In his monumental *History of the Greek Nation*, which appeared in the second half of the nineteenth century, he put forward an interpretation of Greek history that linked the ancient, medieval and modern periods in a single continuum. This approach had the merit that it reconciled many intellectuals of the time with their medieval, Byzantine past. The idea of the unity and the continuity of a race may sound to many today as a national myth of questionable validity. But Paparregopoulos was writing at a time when the ideology of the nation state was becoming predominant, and at least, as Donald Nicol has put it, his myth was 'ably and often poetically expressed'. Paparregopoulos, like many intellectuals of his time, was disappointed by the fact that the war of liberation against the Turks had led to the creation of a severely truncated version of the independent state that previous generations had dreamed of. This embittered many modern Greeks towards the European powers, which had mediated with the Ottoman government for the concession of independence to Greece in 1831.

This ideological baggage is reflected in the historian's approach to the crusades. The hostility of the papacy and of the westerners against Byzantium even before the crusades is taken for granted. The author adopts the interpretation of the crusades given by Byzantine historians, especially Anna Komnene and Niketas Choniates. The westerners were brave and loyal warriors, but they were also greedy, violent and treacherous. Alexios I was taken by surprise when the first crusaders arrived at the Byzantine frontiers. He could not have possibly applied for help to the West. The Norman attack that coincided with the passage of the armies of the Second Crusade through Byzantium was the outcome of a conspiracy between Roger II and Conrad III. By the time of the Norman capture of Thessalonike and the Third Crusade, the gap between the Latins and Byzantines could no longer be bridged. The Fourth Crusade was diverted to Constantinople owing to a conspiracy by Enrico Dandolo, who had previously concluded a treaty with Egypt, and Innocent III. The fall of Constantinople to the crusaders and the need to resist to the Latin occupants led to the awakening of the Greek 'nation'. Latin rule in Romania was oppressive, especially in ecclesiastical matters, and the frequent revolts of the Cretans against the Venetians were an early manifestation of a national war of liberation. Emperor Michael VIII committed a grave mistake when he accepted the union of Lyons in 1274; he need not have done this, since later events proved that he could have defeated Charles I by the exclusive virtue of his own forces. Union negotiations by all subsequent emperors were equally erroneous. In the early modern period the Europeans failed to support the Greeks in their struggle against the Turks.[54]

The influence of Paparregopoulos is evident in the historical work of some contemporary historians. According to them, the crusaders were already hostile to Byzantium on the eve of the first campaign. The impact of Alexios I's initiatives on the origins of the First Crusade is tacitly rejected. The information about an understanding between Manuel I and the Seljuks during the Second Crusade is dismissed as unfounded. The diversion of the Fourth Crusade was entirely the responsibility of the vengeful doge of Venice. Others have put the deep divide between Latins and Greeks in cultural, religious, political and economic matters in the centre of their interpretation of the relationship between East and West and of the crusades, and they have insisted that the rulers of the Latin states which were created in Greece after the Fourth Crusade oppressed the local population. In recent decades, however, in the wake of Greece's economic recovery and integration in a community of western European countries, this approach has been gradually replaced by a far more sophisticated and informed understanding of the interaction between Byzantium and the crusades, and between East and West in the Middle Ages and the early modern period. Witness to this is the ninth volume of another *History of the Greek Nation*, a collective work that appeared in the 1980s. The title is a direct reference to the tradition of Paparregopoulos, but the authors of the ninth volume, which is dedicated to the middle and late Byzantine period, give a balanced, accurate and original account of the crusades.[55]

notes

1. Constantine Porphyrogenitos, *De administrando imperio*, ed. G. Moravcsik, trans. R. J. H. Jenkins (Washington, DC, 1967); D. Obolensky, *The Byzantine Commonwealth. Eastern Europe, 500–1453* (London, 1971); H. Ahrweiler, *L'idéologie politique de l'empire byzantin* (Paris, 1975); J. Harris, *Byzantium and the Crusades* (London, 2003), pp. 12–23.
2. E. M. C. Van Houts, 'Normandy and Byzantium in the Eleventh Century', *Byzantion*, 55 (1985), 544–59; J. Shepard, 'The Uses of the Franks in Eleventh-Century Byzantium', *Anglo-Norman Studies*, 15 (1993), 287–90, 302–5; Harris, *Byzantium and the Crusades*, pp. 35–8, 41–6.
3. Ahrweiler, *Idéologie*, ch. 5.1; H. E. J. Cowdrey, 'The Gregorian Papacy, Byzantium, and the First Crusade', *Byzantinische Forschungen*, 13 (1988), 156–7; J. Shepard, 'Aspects of Byzantine Attitudes and Policy Towards the West in the Tenth and Eleventh Centuries', *Byzantinische Forschungen*, 13 (1988), 96–7, 101–2; Shepard, 'Uses of the Franks', 277.
4. *The Alexiad of Anna Comnena*, trans. E. R. A. Sewter (Harmondsworth, 1969), p. 173; Shepard, 'Uses of the Franks', 303.

5. *Alexiad*, pp. 252, 256; Ekkehard of Aura, in: *Frutolfs und Ekkehards Chroniken und die Anonyme Kaiserchronik*, ed. F. J. Schmale and I. Schmale-Ott (Darmstadt, 1972), p. 136; Frutolf, in *Frutolfs und Ekkehards Chroniken*, p. 106; Shepard, 'Aspects of Byzantine Attitudes', 102–7; M. de Waha, 'La lettre d'Alexis I Comnène à Robert I le Frison', *Byzantion*, 47 (1977), 113–25; W. Holtzmann, 'Die Unionsverhandlungen zwischen Kaiser Alexios I. und Papst Urban II. im Jahre 1089', *Byzantinische Zeitschrift*, 28 (1928), 38–67; S. Runciman, *A History of the Crusades*, vol. 1 (Harmondsworth, 1965), pp. 102–3; Harris, *Byzantium and the Crusades*, pp. 37, 47.

6. Ekkehard of Aura, p. 136; Bernold of St Blaise, in: *Bernoldi Chronicon*, Monumenta Germaniae Historica [hereafter cited as MGH], Scriptores, 5, ed. G. H. Pertz (Hanover, 1844), p. 462; for diverging interpretations of the embassy, see Shepard, 'Aspects of Byzantine Attitudes', 109–15; Harris, *Byzantium and the Crusades*, pp. 47–51; Runciman, *Crusades*, vol. 1, pp. 104–5.

7. *Alexiad*, pp. 301, 308; Shepard, 'Aspects of Byzantine Attitudes', 96–7, 101–3, 115–16; R. J. Lilie, *Byzantium and the Crusader States 1096–1204*, trans. J. C. Morris and J. E. Riding (Oxford, 1988), pp. 1–3; Harris, *Byzantium and the Crusades*, pp. 53–5.

8. *Alexiad*, pp. 311, 313, 319–20; *Gesta Francorum et aliorum Hierosolimitanorum*, ed. R. Hill (Edinburgh, 1962), p. 8; Raymond d'Aguilers, *Historia Francorum qui Ceperunt Iherusalem*, trans. J. H. Hill and L. H. Hill (Philadelphia, 1968), p. 21; J. Chrysostomides, 'Byzantine Concepts of War and Peace', in *War, Peace and World Orders in European History*, ed. A. V. Hartmann and B. Heuser (London and New York, 2001), pp. 91–101; G. T. Dennis, 'Defenders of the Christian People: Holy War in Byzantium', in *The Crusades from the Perspective of Byzantium and the Muslim World*, ed. A. E. Laiou and R. P. Mottahedeh (Washington, DC, 2001), pp. 31–9; Lilie, *Byzantium and the Crusader States*, pp. 5–6, 51–3; Harris, *Byzantium and the Crusades*, pp. 56, 60, 102.

9. Fulcher of Chartres, *The First Crusade. The Chronicle of Fulcher of Chartres and Other Source Materials*, ed. E. Peters, 2nd edn (Philadelphia, 1998), p. 62.

10. *Alexiad*, p. 439; Lilie, *Byzantium and the Crusader States*, p. 6; Harris, *Byzantium and the Crusades*, p. 56.

11. Runciman, *Crusades*, vol. 1, pp. 127–33, 142–71; J. Shepard, 'When Greek Meets Greek: Alexius Comnenus and Bohemond in 1097–98', *Byzantine and Modern Greek Studies*, 12 (1988), 186–8, 201–5, 207–8, 214–15; Lilie, *Byzantium and the Crusader States*, pp. 3–15; Harris, *Byzantium and the Crusades*, 57–9.

12. *Alexiad*, pp. 89, 315, 323, 424–5; Fulcher of Chartres, p. 62; *Gesta Francorum*, p. 12; *Epistulae et chartae ad historiam primi belli sacri spectantes: Die Kreuzzugsbriefe aus den Jahren 1088–1100*, ed. H. Hagenmeyer (Innsbruck, 1901), pp. 138, 154; Raymond d'Aguilers, *Historium Francorum*, pp. 18–19; Albert of Aachen, *Alberti Aquensis Historia Hierosolymitana*, in *Recueil des historiens des croisades*, ed. Académie des Inscriptions et Belles-Lettres (Paris, 1841–1906), Historiens Occidentaux, vol. 4, p. 305; William of Tyre, *A History of the Deeds Done Beyond the Sea*, trans. E. A. Babcock and A. C. Krey, vol. 1 (New York, 1943), pp. 326–8; J. L. La Monte, 'To What Extent Was the Byzantine Empire the Suzerain of the Latin Crusading States?', *Byzantion*, 7 (1932), 253–64; Lilie, *Byzantium and the Crusader States*, pp. 6–9, 18–27, 53–68; Shepard, 'When Greek Meets Greek', 204, 214–15, 227–41; Shepard, '"Father" or "Scorpion"? Style and Substance in Alexios's Diplomacy', in *Alexios I Komnenos*, ed. M. Mullett and D. Smythe

(Belfast, 1996), pp. 105–13; Harris, *Byzantium and the Crusades*, pp. 23–5, 28, 58, 74–80; Ahrweiler, *L'idéologie*, chs 3.2, 4.3.

13. William of Tyre, *History of the Deeds*, vol. 2, pp. 83–5, 92–102, 123–30; John Kinnamos, *Deeds of John and Manuel Comnenus*, trans. C. M. Brand (New York, 1976), pp. 22–31; N. Choniates, *O City of Byzantium, Annals of Niketas Choniates*, trans. H. Magoulias (Detroit, 1984), pp. 17–24, 30–1, esp. p. 22; *Michel Italikos, lettres et discours*, ed. P. Gautier (Paris, 1972), pp. 239–70. Lilie, *Byzantium and the Crusader States*, pp. 68–70, 112, 138–9.

14. John II's Syrian policy as an effort to have imperial supremacy acknowledged in Harris, *Byzantium and the Crusades*, pp. 80–92; as an effort to establish territorial control over Antioch, restrained by concerns about its impact on relations with the West, Lilie, *Byzantium and the Crusader States*, pp. 99, 109–41. For an early upsurge of anti-Byzantine propaganda in the West, see J. G. Rowe, 'Paschal II, Bohemund of Antioch and the Byzantine Empire', *Bulletin of the John Rylands Library*, 49 (1966–67), 165–202.

15. For the union negotiations of 1139–41 there is an earlier dating in 1124–26: Lilie, *Byzantium and the Crusader States*, pp. 92–3, 97–8 n. 5, 131–2; Harris, *Byzantium and the Crusades*, pp. 88–91.

16. For relations during the crusade, see Kinnamos, *Deeds*, pp. 58–72; Choniates, *Annals*, pp. 35–42; Odo of Deuil, *De Profectione Ludovici VII in Orientem*, ed. V. G. Berry (New York, 1948), pp. 24–9, 40–5, 47–9, 54–61, 66–73, 76–9, 83, 109–13; *Recueil des Historiens des Gaules et de la France*, ed. L. Delisle, vol. 15 (Paris, 1878), p. 440, vol. 16 pp. 9–10 (letters of Manuel to Louis VII); H. E. Mayer, *The Crusades*, trans. J. Gillingham, 2nd edn (Oxford, 1988), pp. 93–106; Lilie, *Byzantium and the Crusader States*, pp. 145–63; P. Magdalino, *The Empire of Manuel I Komnenos, 1143–1180* (Cambridge, 1993), pp. 46–61; Harris, *Byzantium and the Crusades*, 94–101; J. P. Niederkorn, 'Die Bündnisverhandlungen König Konrads III. mit Johannes II. Komnenos', *Jahrbuch der österreichischen Byzantinistik*, 51 (2001),189–98.

17. Kinnamos, *Deeds*, pp. 58, 60, 61–5, 67–8.

18. Choniates, *Annals*, pp. 16, 22, 38–9; A. Kazhdan, 'Latins and Franks in Byzantium: Perception and Reality from the Eleventh to the Twelfth Century', in *The Crusades from the Perspective of Byzantium*, ed. Laiou and Mottahedeh, pp. 87–9.

19. E. Jeffreys and M. Jeffreys, 'The "Wild Beast from the West": Immediate Literary Reaction in Byzantium to the Second Crusade', in *The Crusades from the Perspective of Byzantium*, ed. Laiou and Mottahedeh, pp. 100–16. The anti-Byzantine bias that permeates the chronicle of Odo of Deuil, Louis VII's chaplain, offers a further glimpse into Byzantine attitudes towards the expedition.

20. Lilie, *Byzantium and the Crusader States*, pp. 179–81, 188–93, 204–11, 220–1; J. Phillips, *Defenders of the Holy Land. Relations Between the Latin East and the West, 1119–1187* (Oxford, 1996), pp. 100–26, 132–8, 158–9, 211–13.

21. A. Dondaine, 'Hugues Ethérien et le concile de Constantinople de 1166', *Historisches Jahrbuch*, 77 (1958), 473–83; J. Darrouzès, 'Les documents byzantins du XIIe siècle sur la primauté romaine', *Revue des Études Byzantines*, 23 (1965), 69–82; Lilie, *Byzantium and the Crusader States*, pp. 163–221; Magdalino, *Manuel I*, pp. 53–76, 83–108; Harris, *Byzantium and the Crusades*, pp. 101–10.

22. See L. Jones and H. Maguire, 'A Description of the Jousts of Manuel I Komnenos', *Byzantine and Modern Greek Studies*, 26 (2002), 104–48.

23. Kazhdan, 'Latins and Franks in Byzantium', pp. 94–7.

24. A. F. Stone, 'The Oration by Eustathios of Thessaloniki for Agnes of France: A Snapshot of Political Tension between Byzantium and the West', *Byzantion*, 73 (2003), 112–26.

25. Choniates, *Annals*, pp. 220–8; Ansbert, 'Historia de expeditione Friderici imperatoris', in *Quellen zur Geschichte des Kreuzzugs Kaiser Friedrichs I*, ed. A. Chroust, MGH, Scriptores Rerum Germanicarum nova series, vol. 5 (Berlin, 1928), pp. 26–72; 'Historia Peregrinorum', in ibid., pp. 131–53; *Chronicle of the Third Crusade*, trans. H. Nicholson (Aldershot, 1997), pp. 56–8; Runciman, *Crusades*, vol. 3, pp. 12–15; Mayer, *Crusades*, pp. 137–51.

26. For diverging opinions about the alliance between Isaac II and Saladin, see C. M. Brand, 'The Byzantines and Saladin, 1185–1192: Opponents of the Third Crusade', *Speculum*, 37 (1962), 167–81; Lilie, *Byzantium and the Crusader States*, pp. 230–42; Harris, *Byzantium and the Crusades*, pp. 128–36.

27. Kinnamos, *Deeds*, pp. 210–14 (with reference to the expulsion of 1171); Eustathios of Thessaloniki, *The Capture of Thessaloniki*, ed. and trans. J. R. Melville Rose (Canberra, 1988), pp. 32–7; see also Choniates, *Annals*, pp. 140–1.

28. Choniates, *Annals*, p. 222; Ansbert, 'Historia', pp. 15–16.

29. Choniates, *Annals*, pp. 221–2; Ansbert, 'Historia', pp. 49–50; Magnus of Reichersberg, *Chronicon*, MGH, Scriptores, vol. 17, ed. W. Wattenbach (Hanover, 1861), p. 509.

30. Choniates, pp. 166–7.

31. Ibid., pp. 222–3, 224–6; also pp. 233, 240.

32. Ibid., pp. 210, 228–9; C. Asdracha, 'L'image de l'homme occidental à Byzance: le témoignage de Kinnamos et de Choniatès', *Byzantinoslavica*, 44 (1983), 31–41; Kazhdan, 'Latins and Franks in Byzantium', pp. 88–9; Lilie, *Byzantium and the Crusader States*, pp. 280–4; S. Rakova, 'Eastern and Western Man in Nicetas Choniates', *Études Balkaniques*, 29.4 (1993), 55–63; O. J. Schmitt, 'Das Normannenbild im Geschichtswerk des Niketas Choniates', *JÖB*, 47 (1997), 157–77; J. Harris, 'Distortion, Divine Providence and Genre in Nicetas Choniates's Account of the Collapse of Byzantium 1180–1204', *Journal of Medieval History*, 26 (2000), 19–31.

33. D. E. Queller and S. J. Stratton, 'A Century of Controversy on the Fourth Crusade', *Studies in Medieval and Renaissance History*, 6 (1969), 233–77; C. M. Brand, 'The Fourth Crusade: Some Recent Interpretations', *Mediaevalia et Humanistica*, 12 (1984), 33–45; Mayer, *Crusades*, pp. 201–3; D. E. Queller and T. F. Madden, *The Fourth Crusade. The Conquest of Constantinople*, 2nd edn (Philadelphia, 1997), pp. 299–313, 318–24.

34. Geoffrey of Villehardouin, *La conquête de Constantinople*, ed. and trans. E. Faral, 2 vols, 2nd edn (Paris, 1961).

35. Venetian responsibility in Choniates, *Annals*, p. 295; Runciman, *Crusades*, vol. 3, pp. 107–31; D. M. Nicol, *Byzantium and Venice. A Study in Diplomatic and Cultural Relations* (Cambridge, 1988), pp. 124–47.

36. W. Norden, *Der vierte Kreuzzug in Rahmen der Beziehungen des Abendlands zu Byzanz* (Berlin, 1898).

37. S. Kindlimann, *Die Eroberung von Konstantinopel als politische Forderung des Westens im Hochmittelalter* (Zurich, 1969); C. M. Brand, *Byzantium Confronts the West 1180–1204* (Cambridge, Mass., 1968); Queller and Madden, *The Fourth Crusade*; Harris, *Byzantium and the Crusades*.

38. A. Harvey, *Economic Expansion in the Byzantine Empire 900–1200* (Cambridge, 1989); N. Oikonomides, *Fiscalité et exemption fiscale à Byzance (IXe–XIe s.)* (Athens, 1996); N. Oikonomides, 'La décomposition de l'empire byzantin à la veille de 1204 et les origines de l'empire de Nicée: à propos de la *Partitio Romaniae*', in *XVe Congrès international d'études byzantines. Rapports et corapports*, vol. 1.1 (Athens, 1976), 3–28; J. C. Cheynet, *Pouvoir et contestation à Byzance (963–1210)* (Paris, 1990); M. Angold, 'The Road to 1204: The Byzantine Background to the Fourth Crusade', *Journal of Medieval History*, 25 (1999), 257–78.

39. Choniates, *Annals*, pp. 295–6; Queller and Madden, *The Fourth Crusade*, pp. 83–4.

40. Choniates, *Annals*, pp. 261–6, 295–6, 298–302; Queller and Madden, *The Fourth Crusade*, pp. 105, 111, 140–1; Villehardouin, *La conquête*, vol. 1, pp. 189–93.

41. D. M. Nicol, *The Last Centuries of Byzantium 1261–1453*, 2nd edn (Cambridge, 1993), pp. 1–8.

42. Choniates, *Annals*, p. 314; *Devastatio Constantinopolitana*, in *Chroniques Gréco-Romanes inédites ou peu connues*, ed. C. Hopf (Berlin, 1873), p. 92; Villehardouin, *La conquête*, vol. 2, p. 51; Queller and Madden, *The Fourth Crusade*, pp. 191–2.

43. Nicol, *Last Centuries*, pp. 16–18; Harris, *Byzantium and the Crusades*, pp. 163–71; see also L. Maurommates, 'Ρωμαϊκή ταυτότητα, Ελληνική Ταυτότητα (ΙΓ'-ΙΕ' αι.)' ('Roman Identity, Greek Identity (13th–15th Centuries)'), *Symmeikta*, 7 (1987), 186–7.

44. Nicol, *Last Centuries*, pp. 26–7.

45. A. E. Laiou, *Constantinople and the Latins. The Foreign Policy of Andronicus II 1282–1328* (Cambridge, Mass., 1972), pp. 2–3, 43–4, 202, 252; S. Schein, *Fideles Crucis. The Papacy, the West, and the Recovery of the Holy Land 1274–1314* (Oxford, 1991), pp. 42–3; P. Lock, 'The Latin Emperors as Heirs to Byzantium', in *New Constantines*, ed. P. Magdalino (Aldershot, 1994), p. 301.

46. *Les Registres de Clément IV*, ed. E. Jordan, vol. 1 (Paris, 1893), pp. 404, 406; *Acta Urbani IV, Clementis IV, Gregorii X (1261–1276)*, ed. A. Tautu (Rome, 1953), pp. 71–3; S. Borsari, 'La politica bizantina di Carlo I d'Angiò dal 1266 al 1271', *Archivio Storico per le Province Napoletane*, 35 (1956), 327–8; D. J. Geanakoplos, *Emperor Michael VIII Palaeologus and the West 1258–1282. A Study in Byzantine-Latin Relations* (Cambridge, Mass., 1959), pp. 204–5.

47. George Pachymérès, *Relations Historiques*, ed. A. Failler, Corpus Fontium Historiae Byzantinae, 2 vols (Paris, 1984), v, 8–12, 18–19, 23; vi, 24, 32; vol. 2, pp. 461–83, 495–501, 511–13, 611–21; Nikephoros Gregoras, *Byzantina Historia*, ed. L. Schopen, Corpus Scriptorum Historiae Byzantinae, 3 vols (Bonn, 1829–55), v, 6: vol. 1, p. 146; M. Sanudo Torsello, *Istoria del Regno di Romania*, in *Chroniques*, ed. Hopf, pp. 129–31.

48. For the relations of Michael VIII with the papacy and the West, see Geanakoplos, *Emperor Michael VIII*. For the Council of Lyons, see *Sacrorum conciliorum nova et amplissima collectio*, ed. J. D. Mansi, vol. 24 (Venice, 1780),

cols 61–8; C. Héfelé, *Histoire des Conciles*, ed. H. Leclercq, vol. 6.1 (Paris, 1914), pp. 173–8; V. Laurent and J. Darrouzès, *Dossier grec de l'Union de Lyons* (Paris, 1976); Schein, *Fideles Crucis*, pp. 58–62; Nicol, *Last Centuries*, pp. 78–9.

49. Laiou, *Constantinople and the Latins*, pp. 17–22, 32–3.

50. Ibid., pp. 195–7, 249, 288, 298–329; Schein, *Fideles Crucis*, pp. 206–11; N. Housley, *The Later Crusades, 1274–1580. From Lyons to Alcazar* (Oxford, 1992), pp. 29–31.

51. K. M. Setton, *The Papacy and the Levant (1204–1571)*, vol. 1 (Philadelphia, 1976), pp. 163–223, 285–404; vol. 2 (Philadelphia, 1978), pp. 54–107; Housley, *The Later Crusades*, pp. 49–150; Nicol, *Last Centuries*, pp. 172–368.

52. Cited in T. M. Kolbaba, 'Byzantine Perceptions of Latin Religious "Errors": Themes and Changes from 850 to 1350', in *The Crusades from the Perspective of Byzantium*, ed. Laiou and Mottahedeh, p. 117.

53. D. M. Nicol, 'The Byzantine View of Western Europe', *Greek, Roman and Byzantine Studies*, 8 (1967), 331–9; G. Dagron, 'Orthodoxie byzantine et culture hellénique autour de 1453', *Mélanges de l'École Française de Rome, Moyen Age*, 113 (2001), 767–91; J. Gill, 'The Divine East-Roman Empire', in *Greece: The Legacy. Essays on the History of Greece, Ancient, Byzantiune, and Modern*, ed. J. A. Koumoulides (Maryland, 1998), pp. 69–70; E. Zachariadou, 'Η εττέκταση των Οθωμανών στην Ευρώπη ώς την άλωση της Κωνσταντινουπόλεως (1354–1453)' ('The Ottoman Expansion in Europe to the Fall of Constantinople (1354–1435)'), in *Ιστορία του Ελληνικού Έθνους (History of the Greek Nation)*, vol. 9 (Athens, 1980), pp. 207–9.

54. K. Paparregopoulos, *Ιστορία του Ελληνικού Έθνους (History of the Greek Nation)*, 2nd edn, vol. 4 (Athens, 1887), pp. 424–27, 448–506, 526–651; vol. 5 (Athens, 1887), pp. 42–377, 619–44. D. M. Nicol, 'Greece and Byzantium', in *Greece: The Legacy*, ed. Koumoulides, pp. 86–7.

55. Compare A. E. Vakalopoulos, *Ιστορία του Νέου Ελληνισμού* (A History of the Modern Greek Nation), vols 1, 3 (Thessaloniki, 1961, 1968); A. Christophilopoulou, *Βυζαντινή Ιστορία, Γ´, 1081–1204 (Byzantine History, volume 3, 1081–1204)* (Athens, 2001), pp. 10, 21, 52, 58–63, 129–30, 215–26, and B. G. Spiridonakis, *Grecs, Occidentaux et Turcs de 1054 à 1453* (Thessaloniki, 1990), pp. 69–138, to the chapters by A. E. Laiou, N. Oikonomides and E. Zachariadou in *Ιστορία του Ελληνικού Έθνους (History of the Greek Nation)*, vol. 9 (Athens, 1980); N. Oikonomides, 'Byzantium Between East and West (XIII–XV centuries)', *Byzantinische Forschungen*, 13 (1988), 319–32; *Όψεις της Ιστορίας του Βενετοκρατούμενου Ελληνισμού (Aspects of the History of Hellenism under Venetian Rule)*, ed. C. A. Maltezou (Athens, 1993). For a criticism of the traditional view of the Venetian colonies in Romania as entities consisting of fundamentally antagonistic 'ethnic' groups, see S. McKee, *Uncommon Dominion. Venetian Crete and the Myth of Ethnic Purity* (Philadelphia, 2000), pp. 168–77.

12
muslim reactions to the crusades

helen j. nicholson[1]

No event, certainly none before Napoleon's invasion of Egypt in 1798, has seared modern Islamic consciousness and unified the modern Arabic-Islamic world as have the crusades. Whereas some Arab scholars may debate the value of the Napoleonic incursions and their rippling effects of modernization and westernization, nearly all Arabs, regardless of religious affiliation, oppose the crusades and impugn their perceived expansionist politics and religious extremism. Even today, more than seven centuries after the last crusading remnants ignominiously left Acre, the words 'crusader', 'carriers of the Cross', 'Saladin', 'Hattin' and 'Jerusalem' still inflame emotions and stir anti-western sentiments.[2] Constantly evoked by politicians, journalists, preachers and scholars, these events and personalities resonate widely among Arab populations as they are invariably linked with contemporary problems of colonialism, Zionism, exploitation and the need for liberation.[3]

Was it always so? Did the crusades immediately give rise to such visceral reactions and lead toward military and ideological resistance? Did the Muslims immediately recognize the nature of the crusades? Were the various dynasties in the Levant – Seljuks, Zangids, Ayyūbids or Fatimids – always united in their opposition to the crusades and their antagonism to its policies?

These are questions that have been frequently asked by western students as they view the modern Arab/Muslim views of the crusades propagated in the media and by politicians, but they are so broad and complex that at the time of writing Arab/Muslim scholars have hardly begun to tackle them, and where they have done so (such as the study by Muhammad Sayyid Kilani published in 1985[4]), their work is not available in translation into English. The events of 11 September 2001 and the invasion of Iraq by US and UK forces in 2003 has increased pressure on Arab/Muslim scholars of the crusades to produce answers, but have also made objective analysis much more difficult. Partly as a result of this pressure, this chapter, unlike the others in this volume, has regrettably had to be compiled by the editor on the foundation of a contribution from other scholars. It therefore presents a far more superficial consideration of the material than the other chapters, being based mainly on secondary studies.

The subject is considered here through focusing primarily on two periods, medieval and modern. Regardless of restrictions of length and feasibility, a focus on these two periods in fact corresponds to the historiographic situation, for apart from the contemporary reactions elicited by the crusading movements, one must wait until the first decades of the twentieth century to find any detailed commentary and critique from the Islamic world of the events of the twelfth and thirteenth centuries. Furthermore, it is in these two periods that Muslim reactions to the crusades achieved depth and variation that encompassed poetry, architecture, titulature, as well as film and television in recent times. This chapter will selectively address some of these media.

Despite the importance of this subject and its pertinence to a deeper understanding between Islam and the West, it has only relatively recently been studied by scholars of the crusades. With the exception of some early works by the French medievalist Claude Cahen and the excellent compendium *Arab Historians of the Crusades* by Francesco Gabrieli, one could say that the study of the 'counter-crusade' (as the Muslim reaction to the crusades is commonly termed) is only one generation old.[5] Possibly the first book entirely dedicated to this subject was the ground-breaking *L'Islam et la Croisade* (1968) by the Israeli scholar Emanuel Sivan, the culmination of a series of articles that discussed the origins of the reaction against the crusades and the sanctification of Jerusalem in the twelfth and thirteenth centuries.[6]

Undoubtedly the most influential book to appear on the subject is the recent study by Carole Hillenbrand, *The Crusades: Islamic Perspectives* (Edinburgh and New York, 1999), a comprehensive assessment of the Muslim reaction to the crusades. This excellent study, which is certainly ground-breaking and invaluable to scholars, does suffer from the drawback that the author is a specialist in Arabic and Islamic studies rather than a historian of the crusades and is not fully conversant with the problems and debates attendant on the western crusade sources. In addition, although its value and readability is greatly enhanced by its numerous illustrations, Hillenbrand's book does not fully exploit the visual or architectural aspects of the counter-crusade. The impressive array of photographs and line drawings are rarely discussed in the text but rather serve an illustrative or contextual purpose. For fuller consideration of the visual evidence we must turn to the works of specialists such as Yasser Tabbaa.[7]

medieval views

early reactions

Recent scholarship, beginning with Sivan, has tended to minimize the Muslim opposition to the crusades, describing it variously in terms of confusion, ineptitude, or at least delayed reaction. Pointing to the initial tendency among Muslim writers to confound crusaders with Byzantines, to the prevailing political confusion among Muslim dynasts around the turn of the twelfth century, and to the lack of any coherent military opposition to the First Crusade, Sivan and others have concluded that it took Muslims a little more than one generation to realize fully the nature of the crusades and to provide an adequate opposition.[8] This is generally true, but it fails to take into account several rather prescient reactions to the crusades, on the dynastic, populist, and literary levels. It also tends to minimize the dynastic and theological divisions within the Islamic world, particularly the irreparable rift between the Fatimids and the Seljuks and their various successors.

Interestingly, it seems likely that it was the Fatimids, who are often criticized for their equivocal position with respect to the crusades, who actually took the first concrete steps against the crusades by pre-emptively taking Jerusalem in 1097, even though they were simultaneously wresting it from the control of the Sunni Artuqids. According to the Aleppine historian al-'Azimi, writing in around 1160, the Fatimids had been warned as early as the year 489/1095–96 by the Byzantine emperor about the impending First Crusade.[9] Alternatively, the Fatimids may have been simply trying to recover Jerusalem from the hands of the Sunni Artuqids and restore it to its original dominion. Their aggressive and decisive action is only to be contrasted with the impotence of the Abbasid Caliphate, who, in fact, had to be shaken into awareness by eyewitnesses of the crusader onslaught and Frankish atrocities. In 1099 a delegation of patricians from Aleppo went to Baghdad where they expressed their anguish to the Abbasid caliph and the Seljuk sultan, resorting to the symbolically destructive acts of breaking two *minbars* (pulpits) in the main mosques of Baghdad.[10] The Muslim art historian Yasser Tabbaa explains their action:

The act of breaking the *minbars* of the Sultan's and Caliph's mosque during the Friday sermon must have had the symbolic connotation that the Sultan and the Caliph, by failing to defend Islamic lands against the infidels, no longer deserved to be honored every Friday on the *minbars* of Baghdad. Breaking their *minbars* was tantamount to challenging their political authority over the lands of Islam.[11]

Whereas it is generally true that the ideological apparatus of the counter-crusade took another generation to form, one writer, 'Ali ibn Tahir al-Sulami in his *Kitab al-Jihad* (*Book of Holy War*) produced an important treatise concerning the legal requirements of fighting non-Muslim invaders.[12] Although apparently unique for its time and not widely circulated, this treatise certainly problematizes the common assertion that 'The Muslim response to the coming of the crusades was initially one of apathy, compromise and preoccupation with internal problems.'[13]

Curiously, when a coherent and specific Muslim reaction to the crusades did indeed begin to take shape, it was spearheaded by the urban notables, not the non-Arab rulers. Sivan has long pointed to the rather populist actions of his so-called pietistic party, led by the Shi'ite judge Ibn al-Khashshab, in agitating against the crusaders and in putting pressure on the Christian population of Aleppo. Ibn al-Khashshab's constant pleas for closing ranks against an enemy whose atrocities near Aleppo went far beyond the acceptable norms of warfare, may have actually impelled the initially reluctant Turkish mercenaries to fight the crusaders. Just as important, the Shi'ite judge is known to have led a mob in 1124 that forcibly took four churches, including the ancient church of St Helena near the Great Mosque, and converted them into mosques. This conversion most likely did not at first involve any more than the destruction of the altar, removal of crosses and icons, and the addition of a *mihrab*. But a few decades later under Nūr al-Dīn both were converted into *madrasas* (religious colleges), successively renamed the madrasa al-Hallawiyya of 1148 and the madrasa al-Muqaddamiyyya of 1163.

The secondary conversion of these mosques to madrasas is also significant, for it marks the increasing dominance of Sunnism and the marginalization of Shi'ism. What had begun as a pietistic Islamic reaction to the atrocities of the crusades had been turned by Nūr al-Dīn and his successors into a political weapon against the previously dominant Shi'ite community in Aleppo and elsewhere.

Jihād

Another example of Nūr al-Dīn's use of religious propaganda is the *minbar* that he commissioned to be placed in the Aqsa mosque when he had conquered Jerusalem.[14] In 1986 Yasser Tabbaa published a study of Nūr al-Dīn's 'monuments with a message', in which he situated this *minbar* within Nūr al-Dīn's military and diplomatic policies.[15] Nūr al-Dīn commissioned the *minbar* in around 1168, when he had Egypt under his control and had reasonable expectations of capturing Jerusalem. An inscription extended around the four sides of the *minbar*, describing Nūr al-Dīn as 'the defender against the enemies of [God's] faith, the pillar of Islam and the Muslims, the helper of the oppressed against the oppressors' and asking God to give Nūr al-Dīn glorious victories and expand his territories: 'grant him conquest at his own hands and delight his eyes with victory and closeness to him'. Tabbaa argued that this inscription referred to Nūr al-Dīn's intended attack on Jerusalem, and gave 'a moral and religious tone to Nūr al-Dīn's plea for conquest, for he hopes that this conquest will bring him closer to God'.[16]

Nūr al-Dīn's use of the concept of *jihād* to promote his own position as ruler and unite his Muslim subjects against the crusader conquerors has received particular attention from scholars, but he was not the first Islamic ruler to promote *jihād* for this purpose. The *jihād* is a struggle in God's name against the spiritual forces of evil or the physical enemies of Islam, although the former is more important. The first battles that the Muslims fought against the crusaders in the Middle East during the First Crusade were not fought as *jihād*, and in his book *L'Islam et la Croisade*, Emmanuel Sivan argued that it was not until the time of Zengi of Mosul (d. 539/1144) that *jihad* became an important weapon against the crusaders.[17] Since Sivan published his work scholars have investigated this theme further and showed that while the concept was employed earlier, it was not until after the crusader conquest of Jerusalem in 1099 that the first work was produced on the subject, in around 1105, when 'Ali ibn Tahir al-Sulami produced his *Kitab al-Jihad*, in which he called on Muslims to reform their spiritual lives so that they could unite against the crusaders.[18] Hillenbrand, tracing the development of the use of the concept of *jihād* against the crusaders, has noted a number of examples of its use by writers in Aleppo in the following decades. In particular, she noted that the funerary inscription of Balak, nephew of the Artuqid military leader Il-ghazi, describes Balak as 'sword of those who fight the Holy War, leader of the armies of the Muslims, vanquisher of the infidels and polytheists' (that is, the Christians, who venerate God as a Trinity) and 'martyr', words which certainly indicate that whoever composed the inscription conceived Balak's achievements in terms of *jihād* similar to that which would later be promoted by Zengi of Mosul and Nūr al-Dīn.[19]

Nevertheless, scholars generally agree with Sivan that it was during the rule of Zengi of Mosul that Muslim writers began systematically to present the war against the crusaders as *jihād*, rather than as a simple conflict over land, and that his son Nūr al-Dīn went further, depicting his own war against the crusaders in the Middle East as a *jihād*.[20] Arguably he used the concept of *jihād* as propaganda to unite his subjects behind him and establish himself as a legitimate ruler and overlord. Not only did Nūr al-Dīn's reign see the production of monuments, as considered above, but also poetry promoting *jihād*.[21] The city of Jerusalem itself became a focus for *jihād*, although scholars have not agreed when this occurred: Sivan argued that it began to become important towards the end of Zengi's reign, but Hadia Dajani Shakeel, in an article published in 1986, saw the focus on Jerusalem as the result of 'a long and well-orchestrated ideological campaign in response to the loss of Palestine to the crusaders', which became more intense during the rules of Nūr al-Dīn and Saladin.[22]

The most consistent visual and textual manifestation of the counter-crusade was in titulature. Ibn Jubayr, the famous Andalusian traveller, had some rather scathing remarks about regnal titles among the Turkish and Turkoman dynasties of the Levant: 'all these rulers embellish themselves with titles connected with religion [Din]', stating that the pettier was the dynast the more inflated his titles were likely to be.[23] Although Ibn Jubayr's assessment is right on the mark, there is little question that the augmented titles of the twelfth century mirrored the prevailing state of anti-crusader warfare and gradually reflected the triumph of Sunnism against Shi'ism. Yasser Tabbaa, in his article of 1986, discussed this significant development in titulature within the context of the accompanying monuments and the circumstances of their creation, proposing that this transformation began under Zengi and reached its peak under Nūr al-Dīn.[24]

The concept of *jihād* continued to be an important ideological weapon against the crusaders throughout the existence of the so-called crusader states in the Middle East, but was also used against the pagan Mongols (arguably a much greater threat to Islam than the Christians of western Europe) and heretics within Islam.[25] The concept was later used by the Ottoman sultans. Colin Imber has noted that Ottoman rulers may have adopted the title of *ghazi*, 'holy warrior', as early as the fourteenth century, and depicted themselves as fighting God's wars. Certainly by the late fifteenth century the Ottoman sultans regarded themselves as the 'pre-eminent *ghazis*', not only in their territorial wars against Christians, but also against their Muslim opponents, particularly (in the sixteenth and seventeenth centuries) the Shi'ite Safavids of Iran, whom the Sunni Ottomans depicted as heretics; war against heretics was even more important than fighting the infidel Christians.[26] Robert Irwin, however, has argued that by the early seventeenth century some Ottoman officials no longer regarded the sultan's chief duty as to wage *jihād* but to keep justice and ensure his subjects' well-being.[27]

other crusading fronts

The Levant was not the only area of Christian-Islamic contact. In Sicily in the eleventh century, in the Iberian Peninsula from the eleventh to the fifteenth centuries, and from the fourteenth century onwards in the Balkans, wars were fought both over territory and religious ideology. The Ottomans' use of the concept of *jihād* to justify their wars of expansion has already been noted. In Sicily, the Islamic rulers were defeated by Norman invaders before the era of the crusades 'proper' had begun. Sicily already had a mixed religious population, being ruled by Muslims but with many Greek Christians, as the island had formerly been under Byzantine government. The surviving Islamic sources on the western Christian conquest of Sicily were written over a century after events, and blamed the Muslim defeat on a Muslim rebel, one Ibn Timnah, who had called on the Norman leader Count Roger of Calabria to assist him against Emir Ibn al-Hawwas. But Graham Loud has pointed out that Muslim authority in Sicily was already divided between three rival emirs, and that the Normans had already decided to attack Sicily before Ibn Timnah requested aid.[28] Having conquered the island, the Normans adopted a policy of religious tolerance, but their Muslim subjects were discontented under infidel rule and there were a number of rebellions. Those who could emigrated to North Africa or Muslim Spain.[29]

In Spain, from the eleventh century onwards Christian rulers and their subjects slowly won control of territory. Taking advantage of political divisions and rivalry between the Muslim states,[30] they gradually pushed the Christian/Islamic frontier towards the south. The Christian rulers allowed the Muslims of the territories that they took over to continue practising their faith, although in the fourteenth and fifteenth centuries their rights were reduced.[31] The Muslims of the Iberian Peninsula appealed to the Muslims of North Africa for aid against the enemies of their faith. A poem of 1267 appeals to religious ties of brotherhood, lamenting 'over dwellings emptied of Islam that were first vacated and are now inhabited by unbelief'; 'what means this severing of the bonds of Islam on your behalf, when you, O worshipers of God, are [our] brethren?' and also raises the emotive spectacle of mothers separated from their children, young women taken prisoners 'led off to abomination by a barbarian'; 'the heart melts with sorrow at such, if there is any Islam or belief in that heart!'[32]

When Granada came under siege from the forces of Castile-Aragon in 1492, the inhabitants appealed to their co-religionists in North Africa for aid, but when none came the emir, Muhammad ibn 'Alī (known to the Christians as Boabdil) agreed to allow the leading citizens to negotiate for peace. Rumour then spread that the emir and his generals had already agreed to surrender and had been keeping the common people in the dark over their intentions.[33] In the early sixteenth century a Muslim of Granada wrote to the Ottoman sultan Bayezid II asking for aid. He lauded the sultan as a leader of Islam who had received God's blessings, and depicted the Muslims of al-Andalus (Muslim Spain) as his subjects, albeit distant, to whom the sultan had obligations as his co-religionists. He appealed for aid on the basis that the Muslims of al-Andalus had fought the Holy War against the Christians faithfully, and withstood them for a long time, finally overcome by sheer weight of numbers. The promises made to them when they surrendered have now been broken and they have been forced to convert to Christianity: 'alas for the exchanging of Mohammad's religion for that of the Christian dogs, the worst of enemies!'; 'alas for those mosques that have been walled up to become dung heaps for the infidel after having enjoyed ritual purity!'[34]

As in the Levant, therefore, the Muslims of Spain regarded the war against the Christians as a holy war, fought in the name of true religion against the filth of false religion. In this conflict, they regarded themselves as being united with other Muslims elsewhere in the Muslim world, to whom they appealed for aid in times of need. However, unlike the Muslims of the Levant, they were eventually defeated in their struggle.

positive interchange

It is undeniable that medieval Muslim chronicles describing the crusaders in the Levant presented an image of unremitting hatred and contempt for their opponents. In so doing they were writing within a traditional discourse based partly on classical writing and partly on the fact that in their view all those outside the House of Islam were infidels with whom Islam was technically at war. In fact, by the late eleventh century, Christianity was acknowledged to be a revealed religion, but none the less inferior to Islam. The Christians of western Europe were regarded as barbarians.[35] Muslim historical writers associated them with pollution, darkness and demons: 'Imād al-Dīn al-Isfahānī, Saladin's secretary, described the Hospitallers, warriors of the Christian military religious order, as launching an attack in 'a night fertile in terrors, dark, obscure, shadowy, pitch-black, deep, cold, making one shiver, all light gone, a night abundant in rain which fell in torrents – impenetrable cloud, black everywhere, with an icy wind'; appropriate conditions for the associates of darkness. In similar vein, he described the Templars' castle of Baghras in the Amanus March as a haunt of wild beasts such as hyenas and wolves.[36] His colleague Bahā' al-Dīn ibn Shaddād referred to the western Christians' forces at Hattin on 4 July 1187 as 'the forces of unbelief and impiety'.[37] Abu'l-Fidā', writing over a century later and describing the capture of the Hospitallers' castle of Marqab in 1285, called this event 'a memorable day in which ... the sign of the night was effaced by the sign of the day'.[38] These depictions were remarkably similar to western Christian chroniclers' depictions of Muslims, which have been discussed above by Margaret Jubb.

However, just as Christian epic writing depicted the Muslims as doughty warriors who should be admired, so some Muslim 'popular' literature held more positive views of crusaders. Although, as Hillenbrand has pointed out, 'such popular literature is a ... largely untapped source', an article by the Hungarian scholar Tivadar Palágyi, published in 2003, has shown that at least in some Turkish *destâns* (religious epic prose/poetry), Christian warriors could be depicted as loyal to their faith, noble in suffering and admirable in battle. Nevertheless, like the Christian epic depictions of Muslim warriors discussed by Jubb, in these works the Christian warrior is doomed to Hell when he dies.[39]

Some modern scholars have pointed to instances of good relations and cultural interchange between crusaders and Muslims in the Levant.[40] Robert Irwin has drawn attention to the passages in the work of the twelfth-century 'Arab-Syrian gentleman and warrior' (as his editor Philip Hitti termed him) Usama ibn Munqidh, who produced 'a remarkably balanced account of the customs of the Franks', in which 'he is at pains to point to both positive and negative aspects'. 'On the one hand, some Franks who have newly arrived in the Holy Land behave like barbarous bullies; on the other, there are Franks who are Usamah's friends and who have a real understanding of Islam.'[41]

Bernard Lewis, in his seminal work *The Muslim Discovery of Europe* (1982), also drew attention to Usama's attitude, but added that because memoirs are a very rare form of literature in Islam, it is difficult to find similar sentiments expressed by other Islamic writers. He found a few other examples of writers recording personal impressions based on contact with European Christians, most notably the twelfth-century traveller Ibn Jubayr, who has already been mentioned above. While he was very critical of the European Christians in some respects and repeated the usual descriptions of them as filthy and impious, Ibn Jubayr did note that the Franks treated their Muslim peasant farmers humanely, and that such peasants were better off than those who were under Muslim rule.[42] Probably he intended to send a moral message to his readers, to shame landowners into changing their ways; he certainly worried that the contrast in practice would lead Muslim peasants to defect to Frankish rulership.

Yet Lewis noted that such descriptions are very rare in Islamic writing of the crusade period. In general, he argued, medieval Muslims knew very little of European Christians and of the West and for the most part they were not interested.[43]

Nevertheless, it would be misleading to depict Christians and Muslims as being unremitting enemies at all times throughout the period of the crusades. Recent studies have drawn attention to the fact that in Syria and in the Iberian Peninsula Christians and Muslims kept the same holy days and shared devotion to certain saints, even worshipping at the same shrines.[44] Alliances between Christians and Muslims against a mutual enemy were not uncommon.[45] In particular, during the period 1239–44 in the Levant, the rival Ayyūbid rulers of Damascus, Egypt and Kerak allied with different interests within the Frankish territories.[46] It was not unusual for Muslim rulers to employ Christian mercenaries or officials.[47] As discussed by Maria Georgopoulou earlier in this volume, there was considerable cultural interchange in the field of art, where the Franks who settled in the Levant adopted Islamic styles, while typically Frankish Christian designs could appear in Islamic art.[48] Nevertheless, the two religions remained essentially irreconcilable. The ideology of each faith made full and lasting compromise not only unachievable but – in the eyes of religious and political leaders – undesirable.

summary: medieval views

The Muslim reaction to the crusades in medieval times was, therefore, complex. It comprised not only a military reaction to invasion, but also prompted religious reform, including action against other religious groups within Islam, the production of monuments and poetry and the use of religious titles by political leaders to stress their role as defenders of the Islamic faith. It also comprised the adoption of Frankish art styles while to some degree the crusaders aroused Muslims' admiration for their courage and devotion to their (false) faith. It must be said, however, that the impact of the crusades on the Muslim world was relatively small when compared (for example) to the impact of the Mongol invasions of the thirteenth century, or the internal disputes between different religious groups within Islam.

modern views

It is a commonplace of modern crusading historiography that until the nineteenth century the Islamic world had very little interest in the West.[49] Otherwise, only in the 1820s did the first translations of western books began to appear in Egypt, while in other Muslim countries interest in western culture and history came much later.[50] It was not until western imperialism began to make its presence felt in the Islamic world that Muslim writers began to take any great interest in the history of the crusades, which in their view had formed a comparatively unimportant part of Muslim history. As Jean Richard has shown in his chapter, above, western European nations of the nineteenth century were becoming increasingly aware of their crusading past. From the French occupation of Algeria in 1830 (compared to King Louis IX's siege of Tunis in 1270) onwards, western Europeans referred to the medieval crusades in justifying their interventions in the Muslim world.[51] In this respect, the modern Muslim view of the crusades is the result of modern western intervention in the Middle East, rather than the inheritance of the Middle Ages.

As Hillenbrand has observed, even the modern Arab terms for the crusades, *al-hurub al-Salibiyya* and *harb al-salib*, the 'cross wars' and the 'war of the cross', did not appear in Arab writing until the late nineteenth century, and were introduced 'after Christian Arab writers began to translate the history of the crusades from European sources'.[52] The first Arabic history of the crusades, published in 1865, was a translation from a history in French; the first Muslim Arab work on the crusades was not published until 1899. The author, the Egyptian scholar Sayyid 'Ali al-Harari, drew his reader's attention to parallels between the medieval crusades and the modern western attempts to gain control of Muslim territories in the Levant.[53] He was echoing the views of the Ottoman sultan Abdulhamid II (1876–1909), who had frequently stated that the European states were waging a crusade against the Ottoman Empire. These views were also taken up and repeated by the Islamic press.[54]

European conquests in Syria and Palestine during the First World War, with the collapse of the Ottoman Empire, British and French occupation of territory and the conquest of Jerusalem, were depicted by some Muslim writers as a continuation of the medieval crusades.[55] In this they were mirroring western views of these campaigns.[56] This image of the crusades was utilized by these Muslim writers as a focus for their opposition to western policies and western political expansion into the Levant. The focus was strengthened by the development of the figure of Saladin into a new hero of Islam. Until the end of the nineteenth century, although Saladin was greatly admired in western Europe (as Margaret Jubb's study has shown, above), the Muslim world had not taken a great interest in him: Nūr al-Dīn and Baibars were far more important in Islamic historiography.[57] However, prompted by western interest in Saladin, Muslims who were opposed to western influence in the Levant and particularly in Palestine now adopted Saladin as their inspiration. In the words of Hillenbrand: 'Saladin's victory over the Crusaders at Hattin became a central theme in the Palestinians' political struggle against the Zionists'.[58]

Sivan pointed out that an older generation of Muslim historians traced the struggle between Islam and Christianity back to the Arab conquests of the seventh century. This belief was inherent in the work of Mohammad 'Abd Allah 'Inān, published in Cairo in 1932 and republished many times until 1962, including an English edition published in Pakistan: *Decisive Moments in the History of Islam*. Michael Brett has situated this work within the Islamic reformist tradition, where the crusades were regarded as 'a mere episode' in an Islamic-Christian conflict which began in the seventh century and is still in progress. Yet by the end of the 1930s other scholarly writers were primarily blaming the crusades for the historical conflict between the two religious groups.[59] This religious interpretation of history appears alien to modern western Europeans who are accustomed to see divisions between peoples in terms of nationality rather than religion.

since 1945

Since the Second World War, and especially since the establishment of the state of Israel in 1948, this modern Muslim interpretation of the crusades has become more widely disseminated and accepted. Modern western intervention in the Middle East is explained in terms of the West's desire to reverse the defeat of 1291 and 'win' the crusades. As in the late nineteenth and early twentieth centuries, this view finds some justification in western depictions of western intervention in the Muslim world.[60] According to this interpretation, the crusades are still in progress, and so it is the duty of pious Muslims to fight. Hillenbrand has drawn attention in particular to the work of Sayyid Qutb, an Egyptian fundamentalist who was the leading spokesperson for the 'Muslim Brothers' movement after 1954; he regarded the crusades as a key stage in what he regarded as the continual struggle between Islam and the polytheists.[61]

But it was not only religious extremists in the Muslim world who depicted the crusades as a precursor of modern western political and territorial ambitions in the Levant. Sivan pointed out that the historian Sa'id Ashur, in his two-volume *History of the Crusades*, published in 1963, commented on the parallels between the situation in the Levant in the medieval period and in his own time.[62] In 1984 there appeared a translation of a history of the crusades by the writer Amin Maalouf, based firmly on the Arab sources for the crusades, which had been originally published in French in 1983. Maalouf concluded with the assertion that 'there can be no doubt that the schism between these two worlds dates from the crusades'.[63] As we have seen, this is untrue, but is now generally believed in the Muslim world.

The crusades are also blamed for the decline of the Arab people. Michael Brett has noted that in 1953 Muhammad al'Arūsī al-Matwī, a Tunisian historian, published a textbook for students entitled *The Crusades to East and West*. Republished in 1982, it follows the Islamic reformist tradition, but deals only with the crusades and does not even discuss the impact of the Mongol invasions in the same period. The author concluded that the crusades were responsible for the decline of the Arab people and the fact that they fell under Turkish rule. Amin Maalouf also blamed the crusades for speeding up the process of Turkish domination. He, and others, are puzzled how it is that the crusaders 'lost' the crusades, and yet 'won' the peace, in that western European culture is now dominant in the world.[64]

Like the Baltic peoples whose views of the crusades were discussed by Sven Ekdahl earlier in this book, the Muslims of the Levant regard themselves as victims of crusader violence, but arguably the Christian peoples of the Levant were just as much victims. Their views of the crusades are more elusive, although some studies have been made.[65] The Levantine Christians did not necessarily support their co-religionists from western Europe: in Egypt during the twelfth and thirteenth centuries, the Christian Copts gave political support to their Muslim rulers and opposed the crusaders.[66] In the film *Saladin (al-Nasir Salah al-Din)*, made in Egypt in 1963 and directed by Youssef Chahine, this unity of Arabs, both Muslim and Christian, is constantly stressed. Saladin is depicted as the natural leader of all Arabs, whatever their faith. Following the contemporary depictions of the Third crusade by 'Imād al-Dīn al-Isfahānī and Bahā' al-Dīn ibn Shaddād, the crusaders here include warrior women;[67] Louise de Lusignan, a fictional figure, describes herself as a commander of the

Hospitallers and leads them in battle. She eventually marries Isa, one of Saladin's faithful commanders, who is an Arab Christian. The crusaders are depicted as unscrupulous and untrustworthy barbarians, although they are valiant warriors; alone among the crusaders, King Richard of England is a chivalrous knight, although not so wise as Saladin. On Christmas Eve, we see the native Christians of Jerusalem celebrating their holy rites while the *muezzin* calls to the Muslims; encamped in the mud and snow outside the holy city, the crusaders hear the singing of hymns and – with the audience – wonder why they are fighting the crusade, when Christian and Muslim can so plainly live in peace together. The primary intended audience of the film was clearly the Christians and Muslims of Egypt, who are urged to remember their Arab unity rather than their religious differences, but the film offers hope of a peaceful future to the whole world.[68]

Such reconciliatory attitudes have, however, been overshadowed by the continued political tensions in the Middle East, not only between Israel and its neighbours, but also between the oil-producing countries and the West. While oil remains the major source of energy for the West, and the Middle Eastern Arab states the major suppliers, the perceived necessity of ensuring the West's supply of oil has led to continued Western intervention in the Middle East, arousing increasingly vehement resentment within that area. As the crusaders occupied the holy city of Jerusalem, so the US has set up military bases in Saudi Arabia, the country sanctified by the cities of Mecca and Medina.[69] Some writers have drawn parallels between the modern state of Israel and the 'crusader' kingdom of Jerusalem.[70]

The deep politicization of Arabic studies of the crusades impacts even otherwise scholarly publications such as Fayid Hammad Muhammad 'Ashur, *Al-Jihad al-Islami dida al-salibiyyin wa'l-maghul fi al-asr al-mamluki* (Tripoli, Lebanon, 1995). Despite its detailed historical discussions of subjects little known by the Arabic reader, the book often reads as a diatribe against contemporary Arab and Muslim governments whose feeble responses to Israel and the West pales in comparison with the *jihād* of the Mamluks.

today

Even as the present chapter was being composed, Syrian television was showing a programme that juxtaposes contemporary depictions of the battles of the crusades with the Israeli takeover of Jerusalem in 1967, while reports by al-Qaeda have normalized the equating of Christians or Westerners with the historical crusaders. On the other hand, at least one Arab writer writing in Arabic has produced a highly nuanced, even self-critical study of the Muslim reactions towards the crusade: this is Muhammad Sayyid Kilani, *Al-Hurul al-Salibiyyya wa-atharuha fi'l-adab al-Arabi fi Musr wa'l-Sham* (London, 1985).

The deep politicization of Arabic studies of the crusades has resulted in relatively few scholars working within the Muslim world specializing in the study of the crusades. Nevertheless, some historians have produced valuable scholarly work. Apart from those mentioned above, Professor Mahmoud Said Omran of the University of Alexandria has published a history of the crusades in Arabic and a study of the Mongols, Europeans, crusaders and Jerusalem,[71] and in English a study of truces between Muslims and crusaders,[72] while also publishing on closely related topics such as the Byzantine Empire and the Ayyūbids.[73] The Egyptian historian Dr Hussein M. Attiya has published both in Arabic and English on the crusades.[74] The most prolific scholar is Suhayl Zakkār, who as Michael Brett has noted was a student of Bernard Lewis. Zakkār has published many scholarly works relating to the crusades, assembling the Arabic sources for the study of the crusades. According to Brett, his concern has been in particular to explain why the world of Islam initially failed to repulse the crusaders, but later succeeded. Although this is a question that has attracted great attention from modern western scholars, Brett notes that Zakkār does not use their work. Nevertheless, his conclusion has been the same: the crusaders' early success was due to Arab disunity, and their later failure to Arab unity.[75]

Another modern focus of research is the subject of *jihād* and what it meant to the Muslims who opposed the crusaders. Brett has drawn attention to a recent English-language volume, *The Jihād and its Times*, in which Muslim scholars have debated this problem. One of the editors of this volume, Hadia Dajani Shakeel, has argued that the Muslims who opposed the crusaders did acknowledge the crusade as something new, and formulated their reponse in terms of *jihād*. She uses the recent work of western scholars as well as her own careful reading of the Arabic sources. At the same time, her work is stimulated by current concerns and issues, focusing on Palestine and the centrality of Jerusalem.[76]

Recent years have also seen some academic conferences on the crusades being organized by academics in predominantly Muslim countries, sometimes incorporating scholars from both the Muslim world and the West.[77] It is to be hoped that such meetings will encourage the exchange of interpretations and encourage the expansion of scholarly study of the crusades in the Muslim world, although in the present political climate this hope may seem unlikely to be fulfilled. The modern Muslim interpretation of the crusades has become not only a symptom of tensions between the Muslim world and the West but also, by a circular process, a cause of that tension. Yet, ironically, the modern West could be blamed for this situation, for exploiting the crusading conflicts of the Middle Ages to justify its own interventions in the Middle East in the nineteenth and twentieth centuries.

notes

1. I am indebted to Dr Yasser Tabbaa and Prof. Peter Edbury for their assistance in the compilation of this chapter. They bear no responsibility for the final product.
2. See, for example, K. Armstrong, *Holy War: The Crusades and Their Impact on Today's World* (New York, 2001), juxtaposing historical events against the recent and contemporary situation in Israel: see especially pp. vii-ix, the preface to the new edition, and pp. 531–39. See also the briefer discussion of this phenomenon in scholarly literature by C. Hillenbrand, *The Crusades: Islamic Perspectives* (Edinburgh and New York, 1999), especially pp. 4–5 and 589–616.
3. See, for example, the material cited by Hillenbrand, *The Crusades*, pp. 605, 616 n. 50; J. Riley-Smith, 'Islam and the Crusades in History and Imagination, 8 November 1898–11 September 2001', *Crusades*, 2 (2003), 151–67.
4. M. S. Kilani, *Al-Hurub al-Salibiyya wa-athariuha fi'l-adab al-'Arabiyy fi Misr wa'l-Sham* (London, 1985).
5. The publications of Claude Cahen are listed by Hillenbrand, *The Crusades*, p. 623; F. Gabrieli, *Arab Historians of the Crusades*, trans. E. J. Costello (London, 1969); originally published in Italian in 1957. For the term 'counter-crusade' see Hillenbrand, *The Crusades*, p. 600.
6. E. Sivan, 'La genese de la contre Croisade: un traité Damasquin du début fu XIIe siècle', *Journal Asiatique*, 34 (1966), 197–224; E. Sivan, 'La caractere sacré de Jerusalem dans l'Islam au XIIe–XIIIe siècles', *Studia Islamica*, 27 (1967), 149–82. These studies culminate in the masterful *L'Islam et la Croisade: Idéologie et propagande dans la reaction musulmane aux Croisades* (Paris, 1968). Interestingly, the more recent book by M. S. Kilani, *Al-Hurub al-Salibiyya wa-athariuha fi'l-adab al-'Arabiyy fi Misr wa'l-Sham* (1985), discusses many of the same themes covered by Sivan, although the author does not seem to have been aware of Sivan's work.
7. Y. A. al-Tabba, 'The Architectural Patronage of Nur al-Din, 1146–74 (Syria, Iraq)', unpublished PhD thesis, New York University, 1982; Y. Tabbaa, *Constructions of Power and Piety in Medieval Aleppo* (Philadephia, 1997); Y. Tabbaa, *The Transformation of Islamic Art During the Sunni Revival* (Seattle, 2001).
8. Apart from Sivan's work, cited above, see Carole Hillenbrand, 'The First Crusade: The Muslim Perspective', in *The First Crusade: Origins and Impact*, ed. J. Phillips (Manchester, 1997), pp. 130–41.
9. Cited by Hillenbrand, *The Crusades*, p. 44.
10. Ibid., pp. 78–9.

11. Yasser Tabbaa, 'Monuments with a Message: Propagation of *jihād* under Nūr al-Dīn (1146–1174)', in *The Meeting of Two Worlds: Cultural Exchange between East and West During the Period of the Crusades*, ed. V. P. Goss and C. V. Bornstein (Kalamazoo, Mich., 1986), pp. 223–40, here p. 231: see also Hillenbrand, *The Crusades*, p. 79.

12. Emmanuel Sivan may have been the first to note the importance of this treatise in his 'La genese de la contre Croisade'. The treatise was also dicussed by H. Dajani-Shakeel, 'Al-Quds: Jerusalem in the Consciousness of the Counter-Crusader', in *The Meeting of Two Worlds*, ed. Goss and Bornstein, pp. 215–17. Cf. Hillenbrand, p. 21, who generally skips over this important treatise due to its inaccessibility.

13. Hillenbrand, *The Crusades*, p. 20.

14. Ibid., pp. 151–61.

15. Tabbaa, 'Monuments with a Message', pp. 232–3.

16. Ibid., p. 233.

17. E. Sivan, *L'Islam et la Croisade*, p. 44; cited by Hillenbrand, *The Crusades*, p. 103.

18. Hillenbrand, *The Crusades*, pp. 105–8.

19. Ibid., pp. 108–10; quotation from p. 110.

20. The historiography is summarized by Hillenbrand, *The Crusades*, pp. 117–67.

21. See, for example, R. Irwin, 'Usamah ibn Munqidh: An Arab-Syrian Gentleman at the Time of the Crusades Reconsidered', in *The Crusades and Their Sources: Essays Presented to Bernard Hamilton*, ed. J. France and W. G. Zajac (Aldershot, 1998), pp. 71–87, here pp. 84–5.

22. Dajani-Shakeel, 'Al-Quds', p. 205; Hillenbrand, *The Crusades*, p. 150.

23. Ibn Jubayr, English translation in *The Travels of Ibn Jubayr*, trans. R. J. C. Broadhurst (London, 1952; repr. New Delhi, 2001), pp. 250–1 ('The Month of Rabi' al-Awwal (580)').

24. Tabbaa, 'Monuments with a Message', pp. 223–40.

25. Hillenbrand, *The Crusades*, p. 243.

26. C. Imber, *The Ottoman Empire, 1300–1650: The Structure of Power* (Basingstoke and New York, 2002), pp. 120–1.

27. R. Irwin, 'Islam and the Crusades, 1096–1699', in *The Oxford Illustrated History of the Crusades*, ed. J. Riley-Smith (Oxford, 1995), pp. 217–59, here p. 258.

28. G. Loud, *The Age of Robert Guiscard: Southern Italy and the Norman Conquest* (Harlow, 2000), pp. 147–9.

29. Ibid., pp. 163, 170–3.

30. See, for example, the dilemma of 'Abd Allah ibn Buluggīn, caught between the Christian king Alfonso VI of Castile and al-Mu'tamid, Muslim ruler of Seville, translated by A. T. Tibi in *Medieval Iberia: Readings from Christian, Muslim and Jewish Sources*, ed. O. R. Constable (Philadelphia, 1997), pp. 103–7.

31. J. N. Hillgarth, *The Spanish Kingdoms, 1250–1516*, vol. 1: *1250–1410: Precarious Balance* (Oxford, 1976), pp. 178–90.

32. Abū al-Baqā' al-Rundī, 'Lament for the Fall of Seville (1267)', trans. J. T. Monroe, in *Medieval Iberia*, ed. Constable, pp. 220–2.

33. 'Nubdhat al-'Asr', trans. L. P. Harvey, in *Medieval Iberia*, ed. Constable, pp. 350–1.

34. 'Morisco appeal to the Ottoman sultan': verses to Bayazid II (ca. 1502), trans. J. T. Monroe, in *Medieval Iberia*, ed. Constable, pp. 364–70.

35. B. Lewis, *The Muslim Discovery of Europe* (New York, 1982), pp. 60–9. On the tradition of Muslim historical writing more broadly see C. F. Robinson, *Islamic Historiography* (Cambridge, 2003).

36. 'Imād al-Dīn al-Isfahānī, *Conquête de la Syrie et de la Palestine par Saladin (al-Fath al-qussî fî l-fath al-qudsî,* trans. Henri Massé (Paris, 1972), pp. 81–2, 142; English translation by H. J. Nicholson.

37. Bahā' al-Dīn ibn Shaddād, *The Rare and Excellent History of Saladin, or al-Nawādir al-Sutāniyya wa'l Mahāsin al-Yūsufiyya,* trans. D. S. Richards (Aldershot, 2001), p. 74.

38. *The Memoirs of a Syrian Prince: Abu'l-Fidā', Sultan of Hamāh (672–732/1273–1331),* trans. P. M. Holt (Wiesbaden, 1983), p. 12.

39. T. Palágyi, 'Regards croisés sur l'épopée française et le *destân* turc', *Crusades,* 2 (2003), 41–54; Hillenbrand, *The Crusades,* p. 273. M. C. Lyons, 'The Land of War: Europe in the Arab Hero Cycles', in *The Crusades from the Perspective of Byzantium and the Muslim World,* ed. A. E. Laiou and R. P. Mottahedeh (Washington, DC, 2001), pp. 41–51, considers that the works of the 'hero cycles' tell us little about Islamic views of crusaders but more about divisions and conflicts within Islam.

40. See in general the articles in *The Meeting of Two Worlds,* ed. Goss and Bornstein.

41. *An Arab-Syrian Gentleman and Warrior in the Period of the Crusades: Memoirs of Usāmah ibn-Munqidh,* trans. P. K. Hitti (New York, 1929; repr. Princeton, 1987), pp. 161–70; Irwin, 'Islam and the Crusades', pp. 233–5: quotation from p. 234; see also his 'Usamah ibn Munqidh', in *The Crusades and Their Sources,* ed. France and Zajac.

42. Lewis, *Muslim Discovery,* pp. 96–8.

43. Ibid., pp. 89–151, esp. p. 98.

44. A. MacKay, 'Religion, Culture and Ideology on the Late Medieval Castilian-Granadan Frontier', in *Medieval Frontier Societies,* ed. R. Bartlett and A. MacKay (Oxford, 1992), pp. 217–43, here pp. 225–6; B. Z. Kedar, 'Convergences of Oriental Christian, Muslim and Frankish Worshippers: The Case of Saydnaya and the Knights Templar', in *The Crusades and the Military Orders: Expanding the Frontiers of Medieval Latin Christianity,* ed. Z. Hunyadi and J. Laszlovszky (Budapest, 2001), pp. 89–100; B. Hamilton, 'Our Lady of Saidnaiya: An Orthodox Shrine Revered by Muslims and Knights Templar at the Time of the Crusades', in *The Holy Land, Holy Lands, and Christian History,* ed. R. N. Swanson, *Studies in Church History,* 36 (2000), 207–15. On this see also Chapter 7, this volume, by Nora Berend.

45. For example, H. E. Mayer, *The Crusades,* trans. J. Gillingham, 2nd edn (Oxford, 1988), p. 285; Hillgarth, *The Spanish Kingdoms,* vol. 1, p. 324; A. Luttrell, 'The Hospitallers of Rhodes Confront the Turks: 1306–1421', in *Christians, Jews and Other Worlds: Patterns of Conflict and Accommodation,* ed. P. F. Gallagher (Lanham, 1988), pp. 80–116, here pp. 84, 85, 89, 92, 99–102, 105–6; reprinted in A. Luttrell, *The Hospitallers of Rhodes and their Mediterranean World* (Aldershot, 1992), ch. 2; N. Housley, *The Later Crusades: From Lyons to Alcazar, 1274–1580* (Oxford, 1992), pp. 112–15, 228–9.

46. For a careful analysis of these alliances see P. Jackson, 'The Crusades of 1239–41 and their Aftermath', *Bulletin of the School of Oriental and African Studies,* 50 (1987), 32–60.

47. For example, see A. Mackay, *Spain in the Middle Ages: From Frontier to Empire, 1000–1500* (Basingstoke, 1977), pp. 18–20; *Papsttum und Untergang des Templerordens*, ed. H. Finke, 2 vols (Münster, 1907), vol. 2, pp. 226–7, no. 121.

48. See in particular her discussion of the two gilt enamelled glass beakers now at the Walters Art Gallery in Baltimore, Chapter 4, this volume p. 98–9.

49. In a paper presented at a conference at Teruel in 2001, Michael Brett noted the publication by Suhayl Zakkār of a short sixteenth-century 'Description and Explanation of the Attack of the Accused Franks upon the Homes of the Muslims', but this is an exception: M. Brett, 'Islamic Historiography of the Crusades, 1951–2001', paper presented at 'Terceras Jornadas Internacionales: Medio siglo de estudios sobre las Cruzadas y las Órdinas Militares, 1951–2001. A Tribute to Sir Steven Runciman', Universitad de Zaragoza y Ayuntamiento de Teruel, Teruel (Aragon) Spain, organized by Professor Luis García-Guijarro Ramos, 19–25 July 2001. The conference proceedings are forthcoming. I am very grateful to Dr Brett for permission to cite his unpublished paper.

50. Lewis, *Muslim Discovery of Europe*, p. 170.

51. Riley-Smith, 'Islam and the Crusades', 151–8.

52. Hillenbrand, *The Crusades*, pp. 591–2; see also Riley-Smith, 'Islam and the Crusades', 161.

53. Hillenbrand, *The Crusades*, p. 592; Riley-Smith, 'Islam and the Crusades', 160.

54. Hillenbrand, *The Crusades*, p. 593; Riley-Smith, 'Islam and the Crusades', 160.

55. Hillenbrand, *The Crusades*, pp. 594–5; Riley-Smith, 'Islam and the Crusades', 163.

56. Riley-Smith, 'Islam and the Crusades', 157–8; E. Siberry, 'Images of the Crusades in the Nineteenth and Twentieth Centuries', in *Oxford Illustrated History of the Crusades*, ed. Riley-Smith, pp. 365–85, here pp. 381–4; V. Gilbert, *The Romance of the Last Crusade: With Allenby to Jerusalem* (New York and London, 1923).

57. Hillenbrand, *The Crusades*, pp. 592–4; Riley-Smith, 'Islam and the Crusades', 151–5, 162.

58. Hillenbrand, *The Crusades*, p. 594.

59. Brett, 'Islamic Historiography'; Riley-Smith, 'Islam and the Crusades', 163.

60. In the 1950s, as a journalist in Algiers, Peter Partner was 'told by a group of French generals that they regarded their mission in North Africa as an authentic part of the crusades': P. Partner, 'Holy War, Crusade and *jihād*: An Attempt to Define some Problems', in *Autour de la première croisade: Actes du Colloque de la Society for the Study of the Crusades and the Latin East (Clermont-Ferrand, 22–25 juin 1995)*, ed. M. Balard (Paris, 1996), pp. 333–43, here p. 342; for more recent uses of the concept of the crusade in western propaganda see D. Gutwein and S. Schein, 'Just War, Crusade and *Jihad*; Conflicting Propaganda Strategies during the Gulf Crisis (1990–1991)', *Revue Belge de Philologie et d'Histoire*, 80 (2002), 385–400.

61. Hillenbrand, *The Crusades*, pp. 600–2; for another example see Partner, 'Holy War, Crusade and *jihād*', here p. 342.

62. Riley-Smith, 'Islam and the Crusades', 163.

63. A. Maalouf, *The Crusades Through Arab Eyes*, trans. J. Rothschild (London, 1984), p. 266; discussed by Riley-Smith, 'Islam and the Crusades', 160.

64. Brett, 'Islamic Historiography'.

65. *The Cilician Kingdom of Armenia*, ed. T. S. R. Boase (Edinburgh, 1978); B. Hamilton, *The Latin Church in the Crusader States: The Secular Church* (London, 1980), pp. 188–211; R. W. Thomson, 'The Crusaders Through Armenian Eyes', in *The Crusades from the Perspective of Byzantium and the Muslim World*, ed. A. E. Laiou and R. P. Mottahedeh (Washington, DC, 2001), pp. 71–82.

66. See, for example, C. Cannuyer, *Coptic Egypt: Christians of the Nile* (London, 2001), pp. 70–81.

67. For a discussion of this depiction of the crusaders see H. Nicholson, 'Women on the Third Crusade', *Journal of Medieval History*, 23 (1997), 335–49.

68. A dubbed version of the film was shown at the International Medieval Congress at Leeds University, England, in July 2004, and introduced by Ulrich Müller. This description is based on my own viewing of the film and on Ulrich Müller's introduction.

69. This interpretation is discussed by Riley-Smith, 'Islam and the Crusades', 164–6.

70. Discussed by Hillenbrand, *The Crusades*, pp. 605–9.

71. M. S. Omran, 'A History of the Crusades' (in Arabic) (Alexandria, 1995), 395pp., publication announced in the *Bulletin of the Society for the Study of the Crusades and the Latin East*, no. 15 (1995); M. S. Omran, 'The Mongols, Europeans, Crusaders and Jerusalem' (in Arabic) (Alexandria, 2003), 473pp.; publication announced in the *Bulletin of the Society for the Study of the Crusades and the Latin East*, no. 23 (2003).

72. M. S. Omran, 'Truces Between Moslems and Crusaders (1174–1217 A.D.)', in *Autour de la première croisade*, ed. Balard, pp. 423–41.

73. Publications in Arabic announced in the *Bulletin of the Society for the Study of the Crusades and the Latin East* include a study of the Mongols and Europe (Alexandria, 1996), 292pp.; a study of the History of Egypt during the Byzantine dynasty (Alexandria, 1996), 223pp.; a study produced with G. Dabboura on the Citadel of Damascus: A Thirteenth-Century Fortress of the Ayyubid Sultan al-'Adil (Damascus, 1997), 85pp.; a study of the Byzantine Empire and its Civilisation (Beirut in Lebanon, 2002), 379pp.

74. H. M. Attiya, 'Knowledge of Arabic in the Crusader States in the Twelfth and Thirteenth Centuries', *Journal of Medieval History*, 25 (1999), 203–13; H. M. Attiya, an Arab translation of J. H. Hill and L. Hill, eds, Peter Tudebode's *Historia de Hierosolymitano Itinere* (Alexandria, 1999).

75. Brett, 'Islamic Historiography'.

76. Ibid. citing H. Dajani-Shakeel, 'A Reassessment of some Medieval and Modern Perceptions of the Counter-Crusade', in *The Jihād and its Times*, ed. H. Dajani-Shakeel and R. A. Messier (Ann Arbor, 1991), pp. 41–70; Dajani-Shakeel, 'Al-Quds'.

77. For example, the 'International Conference on Crusade' organized by the Turkish Historical Society in Istanbul, 23–25 July 1997. The proceedings were published as: *Uluslararası Haçlı Seferlerli Sempozyumu, 23–25 Haziran 1997. Istanbul.* (AKDTYK Türk Tarih Kumuru yayınları, XXVI. Dizi.Sa. 8) (Ankara, 1999).

further reading

introduction: definition and scope

T. S. R. Boase, 'Recent Developments in Crusading Historiography', *History*, 22 (1937), 110–25

J. Brundage, 'Recent Crusade Historiography: Some Observations and Suggestions', *Catholic Historical Review*, 49 (1964), 493–507

G. Constable, 'The Historiography of the Crusades', in *The Crusades from the Perspective of Byzantium and the Muslim World*, ed. A. E. Laiou and R. P. Mottahedeh (Washington, DC, 2001), pp. 1–22

R. Irwin, 'Orientalism and the Early Development of Crusader Studies', in *The Experience of Crusading*, vol. 2, *Defining the Crusader Kingdom*, ed. P. Edbury and J. Phillips (Cambridge, 2003), pp. 214–30

J. La Monte, 'Some Problems in Crusading Historiography', *Speculum*, 15 (1939), 57–75

J. Riley-Smith, *The First Crusade and the Idea of Crusading* (London, 1986)

J. Riley-Smith, 'Erdmann and the Historiography of the Crusades, 1935–95', in *La primera cruzada novecientos años después: el Concilio de Clermont y los orígenes del movimiento cruzado*, ed. L. García-Guijarro Ramos (Madrid, 1997), pp. 17–32

J. Riley-Smith, *What were the Crusades?* 3rd edn (Basingstoke, 2002)

C. Tyerman, *The Invention of the Crusades* (Basingstoke, 1998)

chapter 1: ideology and motivation in the first crusade

P. Alphandéry and A. Dupront, *La chrétienté et l'idée de croisade*, 2 vols (Paris, 1954; réédition, 1995)

M. Bull, *Knightly Piety and the Lay Response to the First Crusade: The Limousin and Gascony (c. 970–c. 1130)* (Oxford, 1993)

P. J. Cole, *The Preaching of the Crusades to the Holy Land, 1095–1270* (Cambridge, Mass., 1991)

J. Flori, *Croisade et chevalerie, XIe–XIIe siècles* (Paris and Brussels, 1998)

J. Flori, *Pierre l'ermite et la première croisade* (Paris, 1999)

J. Flori, *La guerre sainte. La formation de l'idée de croisade dans l'Occident chrétien* (Paris, 2001)

C. T. Maier, *Crusade Propaganda and Ideology. Model Sermons for the Preaching of the Cross* (Cambridge, 2000)

H. E. Mayer, *The Crusades*, trans. J. Gillingham, 2nd edn (Oxford, 1988)

J. Richard, *L'esprit de la croisade* (Paris, 1969, repr. 2000)

J. Riley-Smith, *The First Crusade and the Idea of Crusading* (London, 1986)

J. Riley-Smith, *The First Crusaders, 1095–1131* (Cambridge, 1997)

P. Rousset, *Les origines et les caractères de la première croisade* (Neuchâtel, 1945)

P. Rousset, *Histoire d'une idéologie: la croisade* (Lausanne, 1983)

K. M. Setton, *A History of the Crusades*, vol. 1: *The First Hundred Years*, ed. M. W. Baldwin (Philadephia, 1955); vol. 6: *The Impact of the Crusades on Europe*, ed. H. W. Hazard and P. Zacour (Madison, 1989)

J. V. Tolan, *Saracens: Islam in the Medieval European Imagination* (New York, 2002)

chapter 2: crusading and canon law

J. A. Brundage, *The Crusades, Holy War and Canon Law* (Aldershot, 1991)

B. Z. Kedar, J. Riley-Smith and R. Hiestand, eds, *Montjoie: Studies in Crusade History in Honour of Hans Eberhard Mayer* (Aldershot, 1997)

H. E. J. Cowdrey, *Popes, Monks and Crusaders* (London, 1984)

H. E. Mayer, *The Crusades*, trans. J. Gillingham, 2nd edn (Oxford, 1988)

T. Meron, *Henry's Wars and Shakespeare's Laws: Perspectives on the Law of War in the Later Middle Ages* (Oxford, 1993)

T. P. Murphy, ed., *The Holy War* (Columbus, Ohio, 1976)

E. Siberry, *Criticism of Crusading, 1095–1274* (Oxford, 1983)

J. Sumption, *Pilgrimage: An Image of Medieval Religion* (London, 1975)

P. Moffitt Watts, 'Prophecy and Discovery: On the Spiritual Origins of Christopher Columbus's "Enterprise of the Indies"', *American Historical Review*, 90 (1985), 73–102

chapter 3: crusading warfare

M. Barber, 'The Albigensian Crusades: Wars Like Any Other?' in *Dei Gesta per Francos: Crusade Studies in Honour of Jean Richard*, ed. M. Balard, B. Z. Kedar and J. Riley-Smith (Aldershot, 2001), pp. 45–55

P. W. Edbury, 'Warfare in the Latin East', in *Medieval Warfare. A History*, ed. M. Keen (Oxford, 1999), pp. 89–112

R. Ellenblum, *Frankish Rural settlement in the Latin Kingdom of Jerusalem* (Cambridge, 1998)

J. France, *Victory in the East. A Military History of the First Crusade* (Cambridge, 1994)

J. France, *Western Warfare in the Age of the Crusades 1000–1300* (London, 1999)

Y. Harari, 'The Military Role of the Frankish Turcopoles', *Mediterranean History Review*, 12 (1997), 75–116

C. Hillenbrand, *The Crusades. Islamic Perspectives* (Edinburgh, 1999)

N. Housley, *Religious Warfare in Europe, 1400–1536* (Oxford, 2002)

B. Z. Kedar, 'The Battle of Hattin Revisited', in *The Horns of Hattin*, ed. B. Z. Kedar (Jerusalem, 1992), pp. 190–207

H. Kennedy, *Crusader Castles* (Cambridge, 1994)

C. Marshall, *Warfare in the Latin East 1192–1291* (Cambridge, 1992)

J. H. Pryor, *Geography, Technology and War. Studies in the Maritime History of the Mediterranean 649–1571* (Cambridge, 1992)

J. Riley-Smith, *Atlas of the Crusades* (London, 1991)

J. Riley-Smith, ed., *The Oxford Illustrated History of the Crusades* (Oxford, 1995)

R. Rogers, *Latin Siege Warfare in the Twelfth Century* (Oxford, 1992)

R. C. Smail, *Crusading Warfare, 1097–1193*, 2nd edn, ed. C. Marshall (Cambridge, 1995)

chapter 4: the material culture of the crusades

A. J. Boas, *Crusader Archaeology: The Material Culture of the Latin East* (London and New York, 1999)

C. V. Bornstein and P. Parsons Soucek, *The Meeting of Two Worlds: The Crusades and the Mediterranean Context* (Ann Arbor, 1981)

H. Buchthal, *Miniature Painting in the Latin Kingdom of Jerusalem* (Oxford, 1957)

R. Ellenblum, *Frankish Rural Settlement in the Latin Kingdom of Jerusalem* (Cambridge, 1998)

C. Enlart, *Gothic Art and the Renaissance in Cyprus* (London, 1987)

J. Folda, *Crusader Manuscript Illumination at Saint-Jean d'Acre, 1275–1291* (Princeton, 1976)

J. Folda, ed., *Crusader Art in the Twelfth Century* (Oxford, 1982)

J. Folda, *The Art of the Crusaders in the Holy Land, 1098–1187* (Cambridge and New York, 1995)

M. Georgopoulou, 'Orientalism and Crusader Art: Constructing a New Canon', *Medieval Encounters*, 5, no. 3 (1999), 288–321

S. Gerstel, 'Art and Identity in the Medieval Morea', in *The Crusades from the Perspective of Byzantium and the Muslim World*, ed. A. E. Laiou and R. P. Mottahedeh (Washington, DC, 2001), pp. 263–302

V. P. Goss and C. V. Bornstein, eds, *The Meeting of Two Worlds: Cultural Exchange between East and West during the Period of the Crusades* (Kalamazoo, Mich., 1986)

H. W. Hazard, ed., *The Art and Architecture of the Crusader States*, vol. 4 of *The History of the Crusades*, ed. K. M. Setton (Madison, 1977)

L.-A. Hunt, 'Art and Colonialism: The Mosaics of the Church of the Nativity in Bethlehem (1169) and the Problem of "Crusader" Art', *Dumbarton Oaks Papers*, 45 (1991), 69–85

Z. Jacoby, 'The Workshop of the Temple Area in Jerusalem in the Twelfth Century: Its Origin, Evolution, and Impact', *Zeitschrift für Kunstgeschichte*, 45 (1982)

B. Kühnel, *Crusader Art of the Twelfth Century: A Geographical, an Historical, or an Art Historical Notion?* (Berlin, 1994)

D. Pringle, *The Churches of the Crusader Kingdom of Jerusalem: A Corpus* (Cambridge, 1993)

D. Pringle, *Secular Buildings in the Crusader Kingdom of Jerusalem : An Archaeological Gazetteer* (Cambridge, 1997)

S. Rozenberg, ed., *Knights of the Holy Land: The Crusader Kingdom of Jerusalem.* (Jerusalem, 1999)

D. H. Weiss, *Art and Crusade in the Age of Saint Louis* (Cambridge, 1998)

K. Weitzmann, 'Icon Painting in the Crusader Kingdom', *Dumbarton Oaks Papers*, 20 (1966), 51–83. Reprinted in K. Weitzmann, *Studies in the Arts at Sinai* (Princeton, 1982), 325–57

K. Weitzmann, 'Crusader Icons and Maniera Greca,' in *Byzanz und der Westen* (1984), 143–70

A. Weyl Carr, 'Art in the Court of the Lusignan in Cyprus', in *Cyprus and the Crusades*, ed. N. Coureas and J. Riley-Smith (Nicosia, 1995), pp. 239–74

B. Zeitler, '"Sinful Sons, Falsifiers of the Christian Faith": The Depiction of Muslims in a "Crusader" Manuscript', *Mediterranean Historical Review*, 12 (1997), 25–50

chapter 5: prosopography

J. Longnon, *Les Compagnons de Villehardouin: Recherches sur les croisés de la Quatrième Croisade* (Geneva, 1978)

A. V. Murray, 'The Prosopography and Onomastics of the Franks in the Kingdom of Jerusalem, 1099–1187', in *Onomastique et parenté dans l'Occident médiéval*, ed. K. S. B. Keats-Rohan and Christian Settipani (Oxford, 2000), pp. 283–94

A. V. Murray, *The Crusader Kingdom of Jerusalem: A Dynastic History, 1099–1125* (Oxford, 2000)

W. Paravicini, *Die Preußenreisen des europäischen Adels*, 2 vols to date (Sigmaringen, 1989-)

J. Powell, *Anatomy of a Crusade, 1213–1221* (Philadelphia, 1986)

J. Riley-Smith, *The First Crusaders, 1095–1131* (Cambridge, 1997)

I. Shagrir, *Naming Patterns in the Latin Kingdom of Jerusalem* (Oxford, 2003)

chapter 6: gender theory

J. M. Bennett, 'Feminism and History', *Gender and History*, 1 (1989), 251–72

J. M. Bennett, 'Medievalism and Feminism', *Speculum*, 68 (1993), pp. 309–31

R. Bridenthal, S. Mosher Stuard and M. E. Wiesner, eds, *Becoming Visible: Women in European History*, 3rd edn (Boston, 1998)

V. L. Bullough and J. A. Brundage, eds, *Handbook of Medieval Sexuality* (New York, 1996)

S. B. Edgington and S. Lambert, eds, *Gendering the Crusades* (Cardiff, 2002)

B. Fay, P. Pomper and R. T. Vann, eds, *History and Theory: Contemporary Readings* (Malden, Mass., 1998)

W. L. Guerin, E. Labor, L. Morgan, J. C. Reesman and J. R. Willingham, eds, *A Handbook of Critical Approaches to Literature* (New York, 1998)

D. O. Helly and S. M. Reverby, eds, *Gendered Domains: Rethinking Public and Private in Women's History* (Ithaca, 1992)

A. Jagose, *Queer Theory: An Introduction* (New York, 1996)

D. Kandiyoti, 'Bargaining with Patriarchy', *Gender and Society*, 2 (1988), 274–90

C. Maier, 'The Roles of Women in the Crusade Movement: A Survey', *Journal of Medieval History*, 30 (2004), 61–82

A. Molho and G. S. Wood, eds, *Imagined Histories: American Historians Interpret the Past* (Princeton, 1998)

N. Partner, ed., *Studying Medieval Women: Sex, Gender, Feminism* (Cambridge, Mass., 1993)

K. Offen, R. Roach Pierson and J. Rendall, eds, *Writing Women's History: International Perspectives* (Bloomington, 1991)

J. Wallach Scott, *Gender and the Politics of History* (New York, 1988)

J. Wallach Scott, ed., *Feminism & History* (Oxford, 1996)

A.-L. Shapiro, 'History and Feminist Theory, or Talking Back to the Beadle', *History and Theory*, 31 (1992), 1–14

S. Mosher Stuard, 'The Chase after Theory: Considering Medieval Women', *Gender and History*, 4 (1992), 135–46

R. Putnam Tong, *Feminist Thought: A More Comprehensive Introduction* (Boulder, 1998)

M. E. Wiesner-Hanks, *Gender in History* (Oxford, 2001)

I. M. Young, 'Gender as Seriality: Thinking about Women as a Social Collective', *Signs: Journal of Women in Culture and Society*, 19 (1994), 713–38

chapter 7: frontiers

D. Abulafia and N. Berend, eds, *Medieval Frontiers: Concepts and Practices* (Aldershot, 2002)

C. de Ayala Martínez, P. Buresi and P. Josserand, eds, *Identidad y representación de la frontera en la España medieval (siglos XI–XIV)* (Madrid, 2001)

R. Bartlett and A. MacKay, eds, *Medieval Frontier Societies* (Oxford, 1989; 2nd edn 1996)

N. Berend, 'Medievalists on the Frontier', in her *At the Gate of Christendom: Jews, Muslims and 'Pagans' in Medieval Hungary, c. 1000–c.1300* (Cambridge, 2001), pp. 6–17

C. J. Bishko, *Studies in Medieval Spanish Frontier History* (London, 1980)

R. I. Burns, *The Crusader Kingdom of Valencia: Reconstruction of a Thirteenth-Century Frontier*, 2 vols (Cambridge, Mass., 1967)

E. Christiansen, *The Northern Crusades: The Baltic and the Catholic Frontier 1100–1525*, 2nd edn (Harmondsworth, 1997)

R. Ellenblum, *Frankish Rural Settlement in the Latin Kingdom of Jerusalem* (Cambridge, 1998)

N. Housley, 'Frontier Societies and Crusading in the Late Middle Ages', in *Intercultural Contacts in the Medieval Mediterranean*, ed. B. Arbel (London, 1996), pp. 104–19

O. Lattimore, *Studies in Frontier History: Collected Papers 1928–1958* (London, 1962)

A. MacKay, *Spain in the Middle Ages: From Frontier to Empire 1000–1500* (London, 1977)

E. Manzano Moreno, *La organizacion fronteriza en Al-Andalus durante la epoca omeya: aspectos militares y sociales (756–976/138–366H.)* (Madrid, 1989)

E. Manzano Moreno, 'Christian-Muslim Frontier in Al-Andalus: Idea and Reality', *The Arab Influence in Medieval Europe*, ed. D. A. Agius and R. Hitchcock (Reading, 1994), pp. 83–99

A. V. Murray, ed., *Crusade and Conversion on the Baltic Frontier 1150–1500* (Aldershot, 2001)

D. Power and N. Standen, eds, *Frontiers in Question: Eurasian Borderlands 700–1700* (London, 1999)

P. Sénac, *La Frontière et les hommes (VIIIe–XIIe siècle). Le peuplement musulman au nord de l'Ebre et les débuts de la reconquête aragonaise* (Paris, 2000)

W. Urban, 'The Organization of the Defense of the Livonian Frontier in the Thirteenth Century', *Speculum*, 48 (1973), 525–32

J. L. Wieczynski, *The Russian Frontier: The Impact of Borderlands upon the Course of Early Russian History* (Charlottesville, 1976)

chapter 8: crusades and colonization in the baltic

G. Armstrong and I. N. Wood, eds, *Christianizing Peoples and Converting Individuals* (Turnhout, 2000)

R. Bartlett, *The Making of Europe: Conquest, Colonization and Cultural Change, 950–1350* (Oxford, 1993)

N. Blomkvist, ed., *Culture Clash or Compromise? The Europeanisation of the Baltic Sea Area, 1100–1400 AD*, Acta Visbyensia XI (Visby, 1998)

M. Burleigh, *Prussian Society and the German Order: An Aristocratic Corporation in Crisis, c. 1410–1466* (Cambridge, 1984)

E. Christiansen, *The Northern Crusades. The Baltic and the Catholic Frontier 1100–1525* (London, 1980; 2nd edn Harmondsworth, 1997)

S. Ekdahl, 'Horses and Crossbows: Two Important Warfare Advantages of the Teutonic Order in Prussia', in *The Military Orders*, vol. 2: *Welfare and Warfare*, ed. H. Nicholson (Aldershot, 1998), pp. 119–51, and at: <www.deremilitari. org/RESOURCES/ARTICLES/ekdahl.htm>

S. Ekdahl, 'The Strategic Organization of the Commanderies of the Teutonic Order in Prussia and Livonia', in *La Commanderie, institution des ordres militaires dans l'Occident médiéval*, ed. A. Luttrell and L. Pressouyre (Paris, 2002), pp. 219–42

R. Fletcher, *The Conversion of Europe. From Paganism to Christianity, 371–1386 AD* (London, 1997)

N. Housley, *The Later Crusades, 1274–1580. From Lyons to Alcazar* (Oxford, 1992)

Z. Kiaupa, J. Kiaupienė, A. Kuncevičius, *The History of Lithuania before 1795* (Vilnius, 2000)

Z. Kiaupa, A. Mäesalu, A. Pajur and G. Straube, *The History of the Baltic Countries*, 2nd edn (Tallinn, 2000)

N. S. Kollmann, 'The Principalities of Rus' in the Fourteenth Century', in *The New Cambridge Medieval History*, vol. 5, ed. D. Abulafia (Cambridge, 1999), pp. 764–94, 1051–8

C. S. Jensen, K. V. Jensen and J. H. Lind, 'Communicating Crusades and Crusading Communications in the Baltic Region', *Scandinavian Economic History Review*, 49.2 (2001), 5–25

A. V. Murray, ed., *Crusade and Conversion on the Baltic Frontier 1150–1500* (Aldershot, 2001)

S. C. Rowell, *Lithuania Ascending. A Pagan Empire within East-Central Europe, 1295–1345* (Cambridge, 1994)

W. Urban, *The Samogitian Crusade* (Chicago, 1989)

W. Urban, *The Baltic Crusade*, 2nd edn (Chicago, 1994)

W. Urban, *The Prussian Crusade*, 2nd edn (Chicago, 2000)

W. Urban, *The Teutonic Knights. A Military History* (London, 2003)

W. Urban, *The Livonian Crusade*, 2nd edn (Chicago, 2004)

chapter 9: national feeling and the legacy of the crusades

P. Alphandéry and A. Dupront, *La chrétienté et l'idée de croisade*, new edn with afterword by M. Balard (Paris, 1995). The afterword sets out a survey of research on the crusades

A. S. Atiya, *The Crusades: Historiography and Bibliography* (Bloomington and London, 1962)

L. Boehm, '*Gesta Dei per Francos* – oder *Gesta Francorum*? Die Kreuzzüge als historiographisches Problem', *Saeculum*, 8 (1957), 43–81

L. Boehm, 'Die Kreuzzüge in bibliographischer und historiographischer Sicht', *Historisches Jahrbuch*, 81 (1962), 223–37

G. Constable, 'The Historiography of the Crusades', in *The Crusades from the Perspective of Byzantium and the Muslim World*, ed. A. Laiou and R. P. Mottahedeh (Washington, DC, 2001)

J. Dakyns, *The Middle Ages in French Literature, 1851–1900* (Oxford, 1973)

A. Dupront, *Le mythe des croisades*, ed. P. Nora, 4 vols (Paris, 1997)

R. Ellenblum, *Crusader Castles and National Identities* (Cambridge, forthcoming)

J. Riley-Smith, 'The Crusading Movement and Historians', in *The Oxford Illustrated History of the Crusades*, ed. J. Riley-Smith (Oxford, 1995), pp. 1–12

J. Riley-Smith, 'Islam and the Crusades in History and Imagination, 8 November 1898–11 September 2001', *Crusades*, 2 (2003), 151–67

E. Siberry, 'Tales of the Opera: The Crusades', *Medieval History*, 3 (1993), 21–5

E. Siberry, 'Images of the Crusades in the Nineteenth and Twentieth Centuries', in *The Oxford Illustrated History of the Crusades*, ed. J. Riley-Smith (Oxford, 1995), pp. 365–85

E. Siberry, *The New Crusaders: Images of the Crusades in the Nineteenth and Early Twentieth Centuries* (Aldershot, 2000)

chapter 10: the crusaders' perceptions of their opponents

P. Bancourt, *Les Musulmans dans les chansons de geste du cycle du roi*, 2 vols (Aix-en-Provence, 1982)

M. Barber, 'How the West saw Medieval Islam', *History Today*, 47 (1997), 44–9

R. Bartlett, *The Making of Europe: Conquest, Colonization and Cultural Change 950–1350* (Oxford, 1993)

M. Bennett, 'First Crusaders' Images of Muslims: The Influence of Vernacular Poetry?' *Forum for Modern Language Studies*, 22 (1986), 101–22

D. R. Blanks, ed., *Images of the Other: Europe and the Muslim World before 1700* (Cairo, 1997)

M. Camille, *The Gothic Idol: Ideology and Image-Making in Medieval Art* (Cambridge, 1989)

J. J. Cohen, ed., *The Postcolonial Middle Ages* (New York, 2000)

M.-T. D'Alverny, *Connaissance de l'Islam dans l'Occident médiéval* (London, 1994)

N. Daniel, *Islam and the West: The Making of an Image* (Edinburgh, 1960)

N. Daniel, *Heroes and Saracens: An Interpretation of the Chansons de Geste* (Edinburgh, 1984)

P. W. Edbury, and J. G. Rowe, *William of Tyre: Historian of the Latin East* (Cambridge, 1988)

J. Flori, 'La caricature de l'Islam dans l'Occident médiéval: Origine et signification de quelques stéréotypes concernant l'Islam', *Aevum*, 2 (1992), 245–56

M. Frassetto and D. R. Blanks, eds, *Western Views of Islam in Medieval and Early Modern Europe: Perception of Other* (London, 1999)

M. Gervers and J. Powell, eds, *Tolerance and Intolerance: Social Conflict in the Age of the Crusades* (Syracuse, 2001)

T. Hahn, ed., *Race and Ethnicity in the Middle Ages*, Journal of Medieval and Early Modern Studies, 31.1 (2001)

B. Hamilton, 'Knowing the Enemy: Western Understanding of Islam at the Time of the Crusades', *Journal of the Royal Asiatic Society of Great Britain and Ireland*, series 3, vol. 7 (1997), 373–87

C. M. Jones, 'The Conventional Saracen of the Songs of Geste', *Speculum*, 17 (1942), 201–25

M. Jubb, *The Legend of Saladin in Western Literature and Historiography* (Lewiston, Queenston and Lampeter, 2000)

B. Z. Kedar, *Crusade and Mission: European Approaches to the Muslims* (Princeton, 1984)

S. Luchitskaja, 'Muslims in Christian Imagery of the Thirteenth Century: The Visual Code of Otherness', *Al-Masaq: Islam and the Medieval Mediterranean*, 12 (2000), 37–67

D. C. Munro, 'The Western Attitude towards Islam during the Crusades', *Speculum*, 6 (1931), 329–43

E. W. Said, *Orientalism* (London, 1978)

P. Sénac, *L'Image de l'Autre: histoire de l'Occident médiéval face à l'Islam* (Paris, 1983)

R. W. Southern, *Western Views of Islam in the Middle Ages* (Cambridge, Mass., 1962)

J. V. Tolan, ed., *Medieval Christian Perceptions of Islam: A Book of Essays* (New York, 1996)

J. V. Tolan, *Saracens: Islam in the Medieval European Imagination* (New York, 2002)

chapter 11: byzantine and modern greek perceptions of the crusades

M. Angold, *A Byzantine Government in Exile: Government and Society under the Laskarids of Nicaea, 1204–1261* (Oxford, 1975)

M. Angold, *The Byzantine Empire, 1025–1204: A Political History*, 2nd edn (Harlow, 1997)

B. Arbel, B. Hamilton and D. Jacoby, eds, *Latins and Greeks in the Eastern Mediterranean* (London, 1989)

D. J. Geanakoplos, *Byzantine East and Latin West. Two Worlds of Christendom in Middle Ages and Renaissance. Studies in Ecclesiastical and Cultural History* (Oxford, 1966)

J. Gill, *Byzantium and Papacy 1198–1400* (New Brunswick, 1979)

J. Koder, 'Latinoi – the Image of the Other According to Greek Sources', in *Bisanzio, Venezia e il mondo franco-greco (XIII–XV secolo)*, ed. C. Maltezou (Venice, 2002), 25–39.

P. Lock, *The Franks in the Aegean 1204–1500* (London, 1995)

P. Magdalino, *The Byzantine Background to the First Crusade* (Toronto, 1996)

D. M. Nicol, *Byzantium and Venice. A Study in Diplomatic and Cultural Relations* (Cambridge, 1988)

J. Phillips, *Defenders of the Holy Land. Relations between the Latin East and the West, 1119–1187* (Oxford, 1996)

D. Ricks and P. Magdalino, eds, *Byzantium and the Modern Greek Identity* (Aldershot, 1998)

S. Runciman, *The Sicilian Vespers. A History of the Mediterranean World in the Later Thirteenth Century* (Cambridge, 1958)

F. H. Russell, *The Just War in the Middle Ages* (Cambridge, 1975)

J. Shepard and S. Franklin, eds, *Byzantine Diplomacy. Papers from the 24th Spring Symposium of Byzantine Studies, Cambridge, March 1990* (Aldershot, 1992)

R. D. Thomas, 'Anna Comnena's Account of the First Crusade. History and Politics in the Reigns of the Emperors Alexius I and Manuel I Comnenus', *Byzantine and Modern Greek Studies*, 15 (1991), pp. 269–312

W. Treadgold, *A History of the Byzantine State and Society* (Stanford, 1997)

A. E. Vakalopoulos, *The Byzantine Period, 1204–1461* (New Brunswick, 1970)

A. E. Vakalopoulos, *The Greek Nation, 1453–1669* (New Brunswick, 1976)

chapter 12: muslim reactions to the crusades

H. Dajani-Shakeel and R. A. Messier, eds, *The Jihād and its Times* (Ann Arbor, 1991)

F. Gabrieli, *Arab Historians of the Crusades*, trans. E. J. Costello (New York, 1969)

V. P. Goss and C. V. Bornstein, eds, *The Meeting of Two Worlds: Cultural Exchange between East and West During the Period of the Crusades* (Kalamazoo, Mich., 1986)

C. Hillenbrand, *The Crusades: Islamic Perspectives* (Edinburgh, 1999)

R. Irwin, 'Islam and the Crusades, 1096–1699', in *The Oxford Illustrated History of the Crusades*, ed. J. Riley-Smith (Oxford, 1995), pp. 217–59

A. E. Laiou and R. P. Mottahedeh, eds, *The Crusades from the Perspective of Byzantium and the Muslim World* (Washington, DC, 2001)

B. Lewis, *The Muslim Discovery of Europe* (New York, 1982)

A. Maalouf, *The Crusades Through Arab Eyes*, trans. J. Rothchild (London, 1984)

J. Riley-Smith, 'Islam and the Crusades in History and Imagination, 8 November 1898–11 September 2001', *Crusades*, 2 (2003), 151–67

E. Sivan, *L'Islam et la Croisade: Idéologie et propagande dans la reaction musulmane aux Croisades* (Paris, 1968)

index